GO DOWN TO THE BEATEN

Tales of the Grand National

*Peter Morris leads Nephin Beg away from the
nineteenth fence in the 1972 Grand National.
Marooned on the fence is Buck Jones.*

GO DOWN
TO THE
BEATEN

Tales of the Grand National

CHRIS PITT

with a foreword by
BOB CHAMPION

RACING POST

First published in Great Britain in 2011 by
Racing Post Books
Axis House, Compton, Newbury, Berkshire, RG20 6NL

10 9 8 7 6 5 4 3 2 1

A catalogue record for this book is available from the British Library.

ISBN 978-1-905156-95-5

Designed by Soapbox, www.soapbox.co.uk

Printed and bound in Great Britain by the MPG Books Group

www.racingpost.com/shop

CONTENTS

FOREWORD
by Bob Champion

*Bob Champion wins the 1981
Grand National on Aldaniti.*

I AM ONE of a few very lucky people who know how it feels to ride the winner
of the Grand National. But I can also empathise with those who didn't.

My first ride in the National was on a horse called Country Wedding in 1971.
We were brought down at the very first fence, through no fault of our own, and
I still recall the sense of utter dejection at being out of the race before it had
begun. So when I read the stories of those such as Clive Cox and Luke Harvey
and other first fence casualties I know exactly how they felt.

But this book isn't just about those that played virtually no part in the race,
or whose ambition was just to get round. It also tells of those who came close
to winning the world's greatest steeplechase, some more than just once, like
George Slack and Chris Grant who both finished second three times.

A dozen other jockeys who were runners-up relive their stories here
and what I find particularly interesting is that, for those who still feel that
sense of despair about narrowly missing out on their life's ambition, there
are others who remain grateful for the experience. Just So's connections
celebrated for days afterwards because they'd 'had a chance that not many
people get'. Colin Magnier, second on Greasepaint, called it 'the best thrill of
all'; while Lorcan Wyer, second on Blue Charm, reckons it was 'the biggest
fucking kick ever'.

Chris Pitt has done a fantastic job in assembling such a wide variety of Grand
National tales from an equally wide range of jockeys, from the leading professionals to the most enthusiastic of amateurs. To have traced and spoken with

someone for every post-war National is an achievement in itself and many of their tales are quite extraordinary.

As Chris rightly comments at the beginning and the end of his introduction, for every winner's tale there are many more that go untold, and once those people have gone, their stories die with them. I'm delighted that someone has taken the trouble to 'Go Down to the Beaten' and obtain their special memories of our nation's most famous race, memories which would otherwise be lost forever.

Reading this unique book has taught me a lot about the race, even for those years when I rode in it, and I'll guarantee that even the most committed of Grand National experts will discover plenty they didn't know either.

INTRODUCTION

Go down to the beaten, who have come to the truth
That is deeper than sorrow and stronger than youth
John Masefield, 'Right Royal'

FOR EVERY GRAND NATIONAL winner's story, there are thirty-nine (it used to be more) that go untold. Here are some; the tales of people and horses who didn't win the Grand National. To hear them I really had to Go Down to the Beaten.

I've endeavoured to cover as wide a range of subjects as possible, from those who finished second three times, to those who only ever got one chance and didn't get beyond the first fence. Hence you will find the well-known, like Stan Mellor, John Francome and Peter Scudamore, alongside the largely forgotten, such as Sam McComb, Peter Cullis and Keith Barnfield. All have their stories to tell – and they are worth hearing, revealing hitherto unknown items of Grand National lore and, in some cases, contradicting widely-held beliefs.

When setting out to compile this book I imposed certain criteria, the most important of which was that all of the human subjects must still be alive, because I wanted to get their Grand National stories at first hand and not through reference books or biographies. This inevitably narrowed the choice in the early years but made the tracking down even more worthwhile. It also explains the unavoidable absence of such worthies as Tim Brookshaw, the Duke of Alburquerque and Lord Mildmay.

It was always my intention to choose one person for each year from the first post-war Grand National in 1946, except for the occasional chapter where it made sense to include two, or even three, people due to the link between them.

I have also tried to include as many as possible of the horses that ran in the Grand National year after year, whose names and performances stamped their indelible impression upon the race, even among the once a year punters; those such as Tudor Line, Freddie, Rondetto, Black Secret, Spanish Steps, The Pilgarlic, Rough And Tumble, Greasepaint and Durham Edition. All of them became synonymous with Aintree and with gallant failure but none was more heroic than three-time runner-up Wyndburgh, who, deservedly in my opinion, has a piece of his own.

It was tempting to include what were probably the two unluckiest losers of all, Devon Loch and Crisp. However, I decided not to ask either Dick Francis or Richard Pitman because their memories of those races had already been well documented. Furthermore, I'd discovered a different angle to Devon Loch's year and a hitherto untold story for Crisp's.

In addition to all the past and present jockeys, I'd particularly like to thank Brough Scott and Sean Magee for their support, without which this book may well not have seen the light of day; Grand National historian John Pinfold for his input in checking the chapters for accuracy; and my wife Mary for her extensive involvement and unstinting encouragement throughout what has been a ten-year project.

I am also very grateful to the following individuals who have provided information and photographs for inclusion in the book: Patricia Ancil, Anne Barnes, Lady Bridget Bengough, Ed Byrne, Jane Clarke, Gerry and Mark Cranham, Derek Gay, Les Hudson, Kathy Milligan, Bernard Parkin, Heather Pearn, Irene Renfree, George Selwyn, Andrew Smart, Bill Tallon and Matthew Webb.

Meeting so many of the people who were my heroes when I was a lad has been the most enjoyable part of undertaking this venture. Sadly, some have passed away since sharing their stories with me. I would therefore like to dedicate this collection of Grand National tales to the memories of Bill Balfe, Bill Denson, Glen Kelly, Derek Ancil, George Slack, Sir Piers Bengough, John Hudson, Clive Chapman, Jim Renfree and Roy Edwards.

And therein lies the reason for the book. Once they leave us, their stories die with them – some funny, some strange, some sad, some tragic – all stories that deserve to be told. I hope you enjoy reading them.

PROLOGUE

Wyndburgh – the National's three-time runner-up

Wyndburgh and a stirrup-less Tim Brookshaw finish second in the 1959 Grand National.

SIXTEEN HORSES HAVE finished second twice in the Grand National. Two of those, Cloister and Red Rum, also won it. Only two, Frigate and Wyndburgh, have been runner-up on three occasions.

Frigate, who was second in 1884, 1885 and 1888, finally triumphed in 1889. Wyndburgh, for all his gallant efforts, never did, and so remains the only horse in Grand National history to have been second three times without winning. Thus, in a book that relates stories of those who didn't win the great race, he fully merits his own chapter.

Wyndburgh's was a tale of humble origin. His story began at a market in the Scottish Borders town of Hawick just after the war when a local farmer, Major P.C.E. Wilkinson, bought a mare for his daughter Rhona to ride for £18. When Rhona went off to an agricultural college, it was decided to try and put the mare, named Swinnie, in foal. The chosen stallion was Maquis, a son of 1938 Derby winner Bois Roussel, who stood at nearby Midshiels Farm at a stud fee of a mere £25. The product of that mating, foaled in 1950, was an under-sized colt which they named Wyndburgh, after a hill located south of Hawick.

He was sent to Bobby Fairbairn's livery yard at St Boswells for breaking in and made his racecourse debut over hurdles, running six times during the 1954/55 season without once making the frame. It was decided not to put him back into training the next year but that Rhona would hunt him and ride him in ladies' point-to-points. They took part in two races and were placed both times.

By now Major Wilkinson had taken out a permit which allowed him to train horses belonging to himself and his immediate family. In the spring of 1956, ridden by leading northern amateur Danny Moralee, Wyndburgh finished second in a Kelso hunter chase and followed that by winning a novice chase at Cartmel's annual Whitsun meeting in the hands of Pat Morgan.

In September 1956 Wyndburgh won the three-mile Perthshire Challenge Cup, again ridden by Morgan. He continued to improve and won four more times that season, culminating, on 16 February 1957, in victory in the 4 mile 350 yards Tote Investors Cup at Newcastle, partnered on that occasion by Mick Batchelor as Morgan was unable to do the weight.

Although still only seven, his next start was that year's Grand National, where he was again ridden by Batchelor and ran a fine race for one so young to be second to Sundew, beaten eight lengths.

Batchelor rode Wyndburgh throughout the following season, during which he repeated his success in the Perthshire Challenge Cup and six weeks later won the Grand Sefton over part of the Grand National course. In February they returned to Newcastle to win the race they'd won the year before – by then known as the Eider Chase – a victory that ensured Wyndburgh went off as clear 6-1 favourite for the 1958 Grand National. Although within striking distance for much of the race, he could only finish fourth behind Mr What, Tiberetta and Green Drill.

Six weeks later Rhona Wilkinson married Ken Oliver, a former amateur rider who had won the 1950 Scottish Grand National on Sanvina. He lived at Hassendean Bank, five miles from Hawick, and when Wyndburgh reappeared at the start of the 1958/59 season his owner was now Mrs J.K.M. Oliver and he was trained under permit by her husband.

That campaign brought only one victory for Wyndburgh, when beating 1956 National hero E.S.B. in a long-distance chase at Warwick, yet he was still rated a live contender for the 1959 Grand National, in which Tim Brookshaw had the mount. But disaster struck on landing over Becher's second time round when Brookshaw's offside stirrup iron broke. Kicking the other foot free, he joined the leader Oxo and the pair raced alongside until Oxo gradually began to draw clear. Oxo had a lead of four or five lengths at the last fence but hit it hard and, slowly but surely, Wyndburgh and stirrup-less Brookshaw began to close the gap. Oxo's lead was down to three lengths at the Elbow and just a length and a half at the line. Wyndburgh had finished second again.

Ken Oliver had become a public trainer by the start of the 1959/60 campaign. Ridden by Fred Winter, Wyndburgh finished an unlucky second in the 1959 Grand Sefton but made amends the following month when winning the Christmas Cracker Chase over the smaller Mildmay fences. Oxo's rider, Michael Scudamore, rode Wyndburgh in the 1960 Grand National but the partnership hit the deck at Becher's first time.

Wyndburgh was Oliver's first winner of the 1960/61 season when winning the Melleray's Belle Challenge Cup at Ayr in October, ridden by Gerry Scott.

Becher's again proved his downfall in the Grand Sefton and, reunited with Brookshaw, he finished sixth behind Nicolaus Silver on ground that was far too fast for him in the 1961 National.

It was decided to let Wyndburgh have one more crack at the National in 1962, by which time he would be twelve. After running third in the Melleray's Belle Challenge Cup, Gerry Scott rode him in the Grand Sefton, where he finished only ninth, but he bounced back to form later that month when winning a 3½ mile chase at Haydock, again ridden by Scott.

Scott was on the injured list when the 1962 Grand National came around. The jockey chosen to ride Wyndburgh in his final bid for Grand National glory was Cumbrian farmer Tommy Barnes, whose son Maurice was destined to win it on Rubstic in 1979. He had never even been to Aintree before, let alone ridden there, so Oliver provided him with a ride, Brief Sparkle, in the Topham Trophy over the National fences on the first day of the meeting. They completed the course, albeit in arrears.

In total contrast to the previous year, the ground in 1962 was deep, conditions much more to Wyndburgh's liking. With two fences left to jump the race lay between four horses – Gay Navaree, Wyndburgh, Mr What and the improving Kilmore. There was little between this quartet at the last but Fred Winter and Kilmore quickly drew clear on the run-in to win by ten lengths from Wyndburgh, who was the same distance in front of Mr What in third.

Tommy Barnes is a shy man of few words, but speaking with him in 2010, he recalled that day 48 years earlier when Wyndburgh finished second in the Grand National for the third time.

'I only rode him three times, his last three races,' he told me. 'He was a very easy ride, a horse who went his own way. He was very careful, didn't stand off a mile and take a chance.'

Was there a moment when he thought he might win? 'No,' he replies. 'Kilmore was always going better than me.'

That was Wyndburgh's last race. He'd run at least five times for eight consecutive seasons. He'd had ten races over the big fences including six Grand Nationals; he'd won the Grand Sefton and finished second four times altogether. He deservedly enjoyed a long and happy retirement, living to the ripe old age of 31 before being put down in 1981.

1946

BILL BALFE

The man who rode Elsich

Bill Balfe, rider of Elsich.

ON THE GREAT Racecourse of Life, Elsich will forever be remembered as a 'did not finish', but at least his exploits instilled a degree of levity to those austere, ration-bound days following the Second World War.

Was he, as has often been claimed, the worst horse ever to run in the Grand National? It's hard to say. There were plenty of fully paid-up members of the Society for Hopeless Causes in the days when the race was open to all and sundry. In an effort to reduce the number of runners following the record field of 66 in 1929, new qualification rules were introduced two years later. They stipulated that horses must have been placed in a steeplechase of not less than three miles, or have won a race of £500 or over to be eligible to run. Elsich fluked his way through to the 1946 race by finishing a remote last of three, thanks to an unfashionable jockey named Bill Balfe.

Elsich was foaled in 1936, a bay gelding out of an unregistered mare by an unheard-of stallion called Services Rendered. He was born in obscurity, which is precisely where he belonged. However, his owner-trainer, Charles Edwards, had far grander aspirations. Edwards, a former rough rider, trained half a dozen equine nonentities of the humblest order at his Mount Seifton stables in Craven Arms, Shropshire. In 1890, aged 18, he had travelled to Canada where he bought 160 acres of land not far from Calgary for next to nothing, built himself a log cabin and settled there for four years.

Following the resumption of National Hunt racing in Britain at the start of 1945, Edwards lost no time in pitching Elsich in at the deep end. He made his first start in a two-mile handicap chase at Cheltenham on 17 February, carrying automatic top-weight of 12st 7lb. He fell, but Edwards evidently felt that the experience had done the horse no harm, for he turned him out again 90 minutes later in the three-mile Cirencester Chase. He fell a second time.

His third start was another Cheltenham handicap chase in which he was once more lumbered with top-weight. He pulled up. Surprisingly, Edwards then decided to run him in that year's Gold Cup. Frank Wren had the mount but didn't get far, as Elsich ran out at the second fence. Nor did he get beyond the second on his next start a fortnight later.

His 1945/46 campaign began with another fall at Cheltenham before crashing out at the first at Worcester. Back at Cheltenham, his rider baled out after jumping the second fence, self-preservation being his main concern. Elsich was declared to run there again the following day and it is here that Bill Balfe enters the story.

Bill was born in County Limerick on 24 March 1912. His father and grandfather had both been jockeys so it was natural that he should follow in their boots. His first ride in public, over hurdles at Limerick on St Patrick's Day 1931, resulted in a broken jaw and a broken wrist, which set the tone for his injury-riddled future. Another bad fall put him out of action for nine months, during which he travelled Europe with the Irish Bloodstock Agency. He then had a stint riding in Belgium prior to settling in Britain. He rode his first winner in Britain on Old Edinburgh in a Hexham selling chase on 28 April 1938.

Like so many, Bill lost a large chunk of his career due to the outbreak of war, when he became Bombardier W. Balfe of the 86th Field Regiment. After hostilities ended he endeavoured to resurrect his riding career but found the going tough.

He told the BBC's David Coleman when interviewed about Elsich at Aintree: 'I was just coming out of the army and spare rides were thin on the ground. I would have ridden anything. I first got on Elsich at Cheltenham. He'd run the day before but what I didn't know was that his jockey, Dick Matthews, had jumped off him on the flat after jumping two fences.

'I smelt a rat when Charlie Kelly, the trainer from Banbury, came up to me and said "I've got a ride for you. My son Glen is supposed to ride it but I don't want him to get hurt." When I got on him I found he was like a giraffe, long neck, nose up in the air, unbroken, no mouth. You just had to trust to luck that he saw his fences.'

For the first time in his life, Elsich got round safely, seventh of the nine finishers. Two weeks later, Bill rode him at Worcester, where he started the 50-1 outsider of three in a three-mile chase. Again they got round, albeit four fences behind the other pair. In so doing, Elsich had qualified for the Grand National.

Bill told Coleman: 'I broke three fences on the way round Worcester. Nat Dixon, who was riding for Keith Piggott at the time, was stood at the fence down by the stables and he told me that I'd smashed the take-off board of the ditch. Somebody let a mongrel dog loose when I jumped the last fence and he yapped at my knees all the way up to the winning post.

'Usually, after he'd hit a few and frightened himself, he used to jump a bit better. But when he did fall, he fell so fast that he did a sort of "Olga Korbut". Actually, he had two ways of falling. He either went up in the clouds, forgot to drop his undercarriage and did a "Fosbury Flop", or else he'd hit it at the roots and turn a somersault.'

Those familiar with the respective styles of Soviet gymnast Olga Korbut and 1968 Olympic high jump champion Dick Fosbury will relate to Bill's analogies.

On his next start at Cheltenham, Elsich once more completed the course, finishing last of five, although Bill did have to remount after falling. Next time he fell two out, but Bill got back on, only for the horse to fall again at the last. He remounted a second time to finish the race. Despite this catalogue of blunders, Edwards nominated the Cheltenham Gold Cup as his next start.

'In the Gold Cup we made the early running and then Tim Hyde passed me on Prince Regent as if I was riding a bicycle. Then at the water he went up in the clouds over it, forgot to drop his undercarriage as usual, and he lay there, winded.

'I had a ride in a later race, the Cathcart Challenge Cup, and I wanted the saddle but this feller wouldn't move. He wasn't even blinking. We got the saddle and bridle off and signalled for the knacker man and the vet, then lo and behold, he stood up and was off like a scalded cat up Cleeve Hill. He left me standing there with the saddle and bridle. That's the only time he ever went away and left me. I used to find him grazing beside me.'

He got as far as the seventh fence before falling at Ludlow on his next start, after which his trainer launched his most ambitious plan yet – a tilt at the 1946 Grand National.

During the intervening six years since the last Grand National in 1940, Aintree's racecourse had been hit by German bombs, firstly during the bombing of Merseyside in September and October 1940, and again during the Blitz of May 1941. The offices of Tophams Ltd in the centre of Liverpool were also destroyed, with the loss of much of the company's archive relating to the history of the racecourse.

In 1942 the racecourse had been occupied by the U.S. Army and used as a transport depot in the build up to D-Day. The last American troops vacated the racecourse on 21 February 1946, just six weeks before the Grand National was due to be run.

Edwards had some unusual theories about training racehorses. 'He was a great horseman in his own right,' recalled Bill. 'He wouldn't settle for second best and he didn't want any softies. When he was out in Calgary he used to do John Wayne-style round-ups. He had a big western saddle and when I sat in it I wasn't supposed to be dislodged. The idea was to school Elsich in it at home and if he fell or hit a fence badly and I didn't move, the guv'nor thought it would have a psychological effect on the horse, who'd think, "There's no point me hitting them if I can't get rid of this feller on top." It was a bit uncomfortable – I sang soprano for a couple of weeks.'

There was a bid to prevent him running in the Grand National and one bookmaker offered 250-1 about him completing the course. However, he was qualified to take part and Edwards was determined to run. So Elsich took his lousy chance – and fell at the first fence.

Said Bill: 'He went up about 6ft over the Melling Road but forgot to take off at the first fence. Turned base over apex. Three of us, Micky Gordon in Miss Paget's colours on Astrometer, Tommy Cullen on Yung Yat, and myself, we all fell there. Micky blamed me for bringing him down but I didn't. The photograph proves that Micky hit the floor first.'

The Pathé News film of the race shows Bill sitting alongside the fence as the remaining runners jumped it on the second circuit. Prince Regent, the heavily backed 3-1 favourite, led the way there, accompanied by a posse of loose horses.

Prince Regent headed the handful of survivors back into the straight, but by then his huge 12st 5lb burden was starting to take its toll. He had no answer when Lovely Cottage, ridden by Captain Bobby Petre of the Scots Guards, wearing John Morant's colours of pearl grey, grass green hooped sleeves and cap, swept past him and went on to win by four lengths. Second was 100-1 shot Jack Finlay, the mount of Bill Kidney, with Prince Regent labouring in third, beaten by the weight. Only six of the 36 who set out completed the course.

Elsich got as far as the third last on his next start at Cheltenham, then finished fourth of five at Hereford on Easter Monday. This effort marked the start of the most 'successful' period of his career, for he completed on eight of his next ten attempts. But despite finishing second (of two, beaten a distance) and third (a tailed off last of three) on successive days at Ludlow, then fourth (last again) at Woore Hunt, Bill was 'jocked off' and never rode him again.

A number of jockeys then had short-lived associations with this perennial no-hoper. His form – what there was of it – reached its nadir when he fell six times, ran out twice and pulled up once in his next eleven starts. Tommy Cross was the only man to get him round, finishing last at Cheltenham, then remounting twice to be last at Leicester.

Renfield Jenkins inherited the mount and rode Elsich for his last thirteen starts. Edwards was still convinced that his horse was better than his alphabet form figures suggested and made an audacious third bid for Cheltenham Gold Cup glory in 1947, but he only got as far as the third fence before his jockey pulled him up.

Elsich's next ten races brought three more falls and two 'pulled ups'. The end of the line came after he refused halfway round at Newport on 14 June 1947. The National Hunt Committee advised Edwards that they would not accept any more entries for the horse. It was an understandable decision, for he had fallen in 22 of his fifty races, and either pulled up, refused or ran out in another nine.

When Elsich disappeared from the scene the occupants of the weighing room heaved a collective sigh of relief. All except Bill Balfe, perhaps, who had succeeded in getting him round on eight of the twelve occasions he rode him.

Bill carried on riding moderate and dangerous horses round the gaffs. There were plenty of spills along the way, including a broken pelvis when brought down at Cheltenham in October 1947. He hung up his boots in the 1953/54 season and ended his working days as a fork-lift truck driver on the night-shift at British Leyland's Cowley plant.

He continued to enjoy going racing and meeting old friends. His association with Elsich brought him not only television interviews but also an invitation to a luncheon to celebrate 75 years of the Cheltenham Gold Cup in 1998.

Bill Balfe died in July 2000, aged 88, but his association with (possibly) the worst horse ever to run in the Grand National lives on. For he was the man who rode Elsich, the one other jockeys chose to avoid.

As for Lovely Cottage, the winner of that year's Grand National, he too had a long life, attaining the age of 27 before being put down in November 1964.

Date: Friday 5 April 1946 Going: Good Value to Winner: £8,805

Horse	Owner	Trainer	Age / weight	Jockey	SP
1 Lovely Cottage	Mr J Morant	T Rayson	9-10-8	Capt R Petre	25-1
2 Jack Finlay	Mr L S Elwell	Owner	7-10-2	W Kidney	100-1
3 Prince Regent	Mr J V Rank	T Dreaper	11-12-5	T Hyde	3-1fav
4 Housewarmer	Miss D Paget	W Nightingall	9-10-2	A Brabazon	100-1

Distances: 4 lengths, 3 lengths, 8 lengths. Time: 9 mins 38 1/5 secs. 34 ran

Winner trained at Headborne Worthy, Hampshire

1947

BILL DENSON
The 10,000-1 Spring Double

Shanakill and Bill Denson fall at the Canal Turn.

IT WAS THE worst winter in living memory, with heavy snow and freezing temperatures gripping the country for almost two months. The early part was fine but after Birmingham's two-day fixture ended on 21 January there was no more racing in Britain until Taunton on 15 March. Altogether 55 meetings were lost, making it the worst season since 1895/96. The National Hunt Meeting at Cheltenham was put back a week and subsequently abandoned. The main events were eventually held in April, a fortnight after the Grand National.

Ireland fared little better, with only one meeting being held during February. It featured the Leopardstown Chase, in which Cloncarrig narrowly beat Happy Home. Among the also-rans were Caughoo and Lough Conn, who were destined to play the leading roles at Liverpool the following month. Of the 57 runners that lined up for the National – the previous year's winner Lovely Cottage was a late non-runner through injury – they would be among the fittest.

When racing resumed it took place on heavy ground. Conditions were so testing at rain-soaked Aintree that, on the opening day of the meeting, all 16 runners in the Stanley Chase fell, with just two being remounted to finish the race.

In addition to the hock-deep going, Grand National day dawned with the course shrouded in a vale of fog. But the wretched conditions did not put off

23-year-old Bill Denson, who was eagerly anticipating his first ride in the race.

Born on the family farm in Cheshire, 'in the Wirral country, just outside Chester', on 22 November 1923, he was the youngest of six children, and the only boy. His mother died a month after he was born.

'Father was always hunting and racing and had some good point-to-pointers,' he recalled. 'My cousin, George Owen, won the Cheltenham Gold Cup on Brendan's Cottage and trained Russian Hero. My cousins on my mother's side were the Goswells, John and Gordon, who both rode jumping. There's a famous picture of Gordon falling from May King at Becher's in the 1930 Grand National.

'In 1937 – I left school when I was fourteen – I went to George Digby, who trained just outside Newmarket, at Exning. I was there until war broke out and racing was temporarily stopped.'

Rejected for armed service on medical grounds, having been born with a crooked foot, he joined Jack Colling's yard at Newmarket, riding out in the morning and working on Colling's farm in the afternoon. Then, when Gerry Wilson began training at Andoversford in 1944, George Owen arranged for Bill to go there. The following year Wilson sent out Brains Trust to win the Champion Hurdle.

'I looked after Brains Trust and I rode him at Cheltenham the first time he ran for us. Gerry said to me "Don't be in the first four, chap". I'd only had three or four rides then and I came down the hill to the last two hurdles running away.'

Not knowing what else to do, he sat still and finished seventh.

'That evening, Gerry said to me "You listen, my boy, before you learn to make one go, you want to learn to stop one." Fred Rimell rode him the next time he ran and he didn't get beat again that season, including the Champion Hurdle.'

Bill's first winner came on Tintern Abbey in a novice chase at Woore on 17 October 1946. The combination scored again at Wincanton the following week. Barely five months later he picked up a spare ride in the Grand National.

'It was a matter of being in the right place at the right time,' he recounted. 'I was getting changed next to Bryan Marshall at Birmingham when a chap I'd never seen before came into the weighing room and said to Bryan "I still haven't got a jockey for that horse in the National". Bryan turned towards me and said "This fellow'll give him a good ride", and that's how it came about.'

The trainer was Billy Smallwood and the horse was called Shanakill, owned by one of the Sainsbury's family, back in the days when they merely had corner shops.

'I'd never seen the horse before so I went up to Yorkshire to school him on the Wednesday before the race. Afterwards I was having breakfast with the trainer when his travelling head lad came in. They'd got a runner, Jockey Treble, in the "Lincoln" that day. Smallwood said, "I'm not going; the horse hasn't got much of a chance, but tell that silly boy [his apprentice rider] to jump off and keep straight. There's a lot of runners and I don't want him knocking everybody about."

'Later, one of his men gave me a lift to Mexborough station to catch the train to Liverpool, as Gerry's horses were coming up later that day. When I got off the train at Liverpool I asked the newspaper seller what had won the Lincoln. He said, "Jockey Treble, 100 to 1." The "silly boy" who rode him was Manny Mercer!' (Manny Mercer went on to become one of the leading jockeys of the 1950s. His big race successes included the 1954 Two Thousand Guineas on Darius and the following year's One Thousand Guineas on Happy Laughter. He also rode Wilwyn to win the inaugural running of the Washington DC International at Laurel Park in 1952. Mercer was killed instantly after being thrown from his mount Priddy Fair on the way to the start of the Red Deer Stakes at Ascot on 26 September 1959.)

With part of the straight mile waterlogged, that 1947 Lincolnshire Handicap was run on the round course, and Mercer had ridden him perfectly. After his shock victory Jockey Treble was sent to race in South Africa and never ran in Britain again.

Hopes of Smallwood bringing off the Spring Double with another 100-1 shot were slim. Shanakill, despite having won the two-mile Rank Cup Chase at Killarney eight months earlier when ridden by Bryan Marshall, was a genuine outsider, but it was a day Bill Denson will never forget.

'To be in the parade with 57 runners in front of those packed stands, and to canter back to the start, was absolutely incredible. I was half nervous, half excited. I can understand how those boys who rode in lots of Nationals had such wonderful experiences.

'Before I walked the course, I asked old Jack Moloney, who used to ride out for Gerry Wilson, whether the fences were really as big as people made out. He looked at me and said, "B'jaysus, Billy, they're huge."

'Landing over the first fence I remember thinking "Blimey! If that's the first, whatever's Becher's going to be like?"

'I jumped Becher's well, but then he caught the top of the Canal Turn and it turned him completely over. I show people the picture and tell them at least they can't say I fell off!'

The thick mist had contrived to ensure that little of the action out in the country would be seen from the stands. It was Caughoo and jockey Eddie Dempsey who emerged from it to score an unlikely 100-1 victory by 20 lengths from Lough Conn, with French-bred Kami third. The favourite, Prince Regent, again found his 12st 7lb burden too much and finished fourth.

The 'whoopee' of the bookmakers was about the only thing that enlivened a dismal day. They didn't mind the mud and drizzle because, following Jockey Treble's 100-1 Lincoln victory three days earlier, their satchels had now become even fuller. The Spring Double had come to 10,000-1. It was a repeat of the bookies' bonanza of 1929, when Elton and Gregalach had been the 100-1 winners of the Lincoln and Grand National. Only two punters had coupled Caughoo with Jockey Treble. They each won £8,899 10s on the Tote.

Not many people knew how to pronounce Caughoo's name. Mary McDowell, the auburn-haired sister of the triumphant owner, Dublin jeweller Jack McDowell, cleared up that point.

'You pronounce it 'Cawhoo', she informed the assembled reporters, going on to explain that the horse had twice won the Ulster National and had never fallen. He had been bought for £50 at Ballsbridge sales as a two-year-old and named after her father's estate in County Cavan. She added that the owner's brother, Herbert McDowell, who was a vet with stables located near Baldoyle racecourse, had trained him on the sands at Sutton, seven miles outside Dublin.

Caughoo ran in the next two Grand Nationals but failed to get round on either occasion. He died at Sutton in March 1964, aged 25.

As for Shanakill, he suffered no ill effects from his spectacular eighth fence tumble. Bill rode him again at Southwell the following week, finishing fourth after remounting.

Gerry Wilson saddled First Of The Dandies, ridden by Jimmy Brogan, to finish runner-up in the 1948 National, collared close home by Sheila's Cottage who got up to win by a length. Bill felt that had Eddie Reavey not taken the wrong course on Zahia approaching the last fence when upsides First of the Dandies, the result might have been different.

'Zahia's departure left First Of The Dandies on his own jumping the last. He was a big, lazy horse and he just dawdled. If he'd had something to race with or if Sheila's Cottage had got to him earlier...'

He didn't complete the sentence; he didn't need to. It's just another case of what might have been.

Bill returned to Liverpool that autumn and rode Loyal Knight in the Valentine Chase, leading the field over Becher's before fading to finish last of the seven finishers behind Ulster Monarch. His final victory came on Allen's Bridge, at Worcester on 20 September 1949. His career was ended by a fall in which he broke seven ribs, punctured a lung and suffered severe concussion.

'When I had to give up race riding I took the travelling head lad's job at Gerry's, until he packed up in 1956. Then I joined Tom Yates in a similar role at Letcombe Bassett for four years until 1960.

'A Cheltenham permit holder named Ernie Excell was looking for somebody to train his horses. He'd got a nice place at Woodmancote so I left Tom's and went there. I applied for a licence as a public trainer, got one and was there for ten years.'

He commenced training at the start of the 1961/62 National Hunt season and achieved his first winner with only his third runner, when Midanne scrambled home by a short head at Wincanton on 21 September 1961.

He admitted to landing 'one or two good touches', both on the Flat and over jumps, but said the highlight of his training career was saddling Princeful, an acquisition from Fred Rimell, to finish ninth in the 1968 Grand National. 'Three weeks before the race he ran at Worcester and finished third but he tweaked his back, so I didn't really get as much work as I'd have liked into him before Liver-pool,' he recalled. Sadly for all concerned, Princeful broke down irreparably next time out in the Worcester Royal Porcelain Chase.

When the stable's owner elected to sell the property, Bill handed in his licence and became head lad and assistant to Peter Bailey at Wantage. During his ten-year stint there the yard boasted a clutch of top chasers, including Canasta Lad, Prince Rock, Strombolus and Zeta's Son. Bill partnered Strombolus in all his work, until one day a young horse slipped up with him in the stable yard and smashed his hip.

When Bailey gave up training, Bill decided to 'find a little cottage in the Cotswolds and give somebody a hand with their point-to-pointers.' That's what he did – the aptly named 'Hill View' in the Gloucestershire village of Weston Sub-Edge, which became his home for more than 25 years until he died, aged 85, in September 2009.

Remarkably, he'd attended at least one day of the Cheltenham Festival for 62 consecutive years, and he had been in fine form when attending an Injured Jockeys Fund race day at Bangor-on-Dee less than a month before his death.

'I've thoroughly enjoyed my years in racing. I had a lot of fun,' he reflected. 'And at least it's something to say that I've had the pleasure of being there at Aintree, of riding in the biggest Grand National field since the war.'

Date: Saturday 29 March 1947 Going: Heavy Value to Winner: £10,007

Horse	Owner	Trainer	Age / weight	Jockey	SP
1 Caughoo	Mr J J McDowell	H McDowell	8-10-0	E Dempsey	100-1
2 Lough Conn	Mrs M Rowe	F Boland	11-10-1	D McCann	33-1
3 Kami	Sir A Gordon-Smith	T Masson	10-10-13	Mr J Hislop	33-1
4 Prince Regent	Mr J V Rank	T Dreaper	12-12-7	T Hyde	8-1fav

Distances: 20 lengths, 4 lengths, 6 lengths. Time: 10 mins 3 4/5 secs. 57 ran

Winner trained at Malahide, County Dublin, Ireland

1948

GLEN KELLY
Miss Paget's spare ride

Glen Kelly, fourth on Dorothy Paget's Happy Home.

GRAND NATIONALS MEANT a lot to Charlie Kelly, irrespective of their nationality. Back in 1905 he won the Irish Grand National on a five-year-old named Red Lad, the 6-4 favourite. The following year he rode that horse to finish second to Ascetic's Silver in the Grand National at Liverpool.

In 1910 he was runner-up in the Scottish Grand National on Greek Play. In 1914 he dead-heated for the Welsh version at Cardiff on Succubus, then won the deciding run-off against Dick Dunn, the mount of Spink Walkington. A run-off to decide the Welsh National – they did that sort of thing in those days!

Charlie was by then riding for Bob Gore at Findon. He subsequently moved to Danebury, near Stockbridge, where his second son, Glen, was born in 1916. By the early 1930s Charlie was training at Bicester, in Oxfordshire. His eldest son, Bill, also trained nearby at Oxford Lodge, and Glen was riding for both.

Christened Glenville but known to all as Glen, he was still two months short of his fifteenth birthday when riding his first winner on Huncoat, owned by his father, in a selling hurdle at Towcester on Easter Monday 1931. The Kelly family enjoyed plenty of success during that decade. Tetrastyle, owned by Charlie, trained by Bill and ridden by Glen, won the Three Mile Chase at Hawthorn Hill in 1933. At that year's Brocklesby Hunt fixture, they produced a mare called Rusty to win two chases on the same day.

They also had a useful gelding called Tuckmill, on whom Glen won an amateur riders' chase at Newton Abbot in 1936. He turned professional soon after and rode the horse to victory at Gatwick in January 1937. Charlie trained Tuckmill to win many races at long-lost courses such as Torquay, Totnes, Buckfastleigh and Bridgnorth.

Tuckmill also provided Glen with his first two rides in the Grand National. They were carried out by loose horses in a melee at the 21st fence in 1939 but completed the course the following year, albeit last of the seventeen finishers behind Lord Stalbridge's Bogskar.

During the war Glen served in the same Cavalry Regiment squadron as several other jockeys, including Ron Smyth, Bob Turnell and Dave Dick. By the time he emerged from the army he had lost the patronage of many of the owners he rode for previously. However, he did come in for the job as stable jockey to Lord Stalbridge.

It got off to a good start when Red Rower, the 1945 Cheltenham Gold Cup winner, scored at Windsor in February 1946, but there was a shock in store for Glen the following day.

'I wasn't supposed to be at Windsor that day,' he admitted. 'I was still in the army and I took unauthorised time off to go there. I thought I'd be alright but when the paper came out the next day, it had my photograph in it!'

Although Lord Stalbridge held the licence, it was his head lad Vernon Cross who did the training. They had three top-class chasers entered for the first post-war Grand National in 1946: Bogskar, Red Rower and the latter's half-brother Red April, on whom Glen had finished third to Prince Regent in the Gold Cup. It was decided to save Red April for the Becher Chase the day after the National, so Glen rode Red Rower. Alas, Red Rower's best days were behind him and he was pulled up, while Red April's participation in the Becher Chase ended with a fall at the water jump.

Glen rode George Beeby's Rearmament in the 1947 Grand National, remounting to complete the course after being brought down three out. He then came in for two spare rides in successive years, starting with Dorothy Paget's Happy Home in 1948.

'Fulke Walwyn rang up and asked me if I would ride him. He'd finished second to Cottage Rake in that year's Gold Cup with Martin Molony. Martin couldn't ride him in the Grand National because he was first jockey to Lord Bicester, so he rode Silver Fame instead.

'Happy Home gave me a super ride. He was always up there in the first three and I thought he was going to win four fences out, but he made a bad mistake there and very nearly fell and that was the end of his chance.'

Even so, Happy Home battled on to jump the last in third place, while in front of him, Zahia's jockey Eddie Reavey steered his mount the wrong side of the fence. This left Sheila's Cottage, trained by Neville Crump and ridden by Arthur Thompson, to get the better of a battle up the run-in with First Of The Dandies.

Sheila's Cottage became the first mare to win the race since Shannon Lass in 1902. Had Zahia not taken the wrong course, it is probable that the first two to finish would have both been mares.

Cromwell, despite his owner-rider Lord Mildmay's neck being slumped in his chest through severe cramp, a legacy of previous falls, rendering him little more than a helpless passenger, passed the tiring Happy Home in the closing stages to take third. Glen was delighted with fourth place and was hopeful of further rides for Happy Home's imperious owner. However, one telephone call changed all that.

'Miss Paget rang me a week after the race. I was riding out so my father's housekeeper took the message and asked me to ring her back. I was rubbing my hands thinking I was going to get a job riding for her. Instead, she gave me a ticking off for not replying to thank her for the present she'd sent. I replied that I'd acknowledged it via Fulke Walwyn. Bang – the phone went down, and that was the end of my association with Dorothy Paget.'

His second 'spare' came on Neville Crump's Wot No Sun in 1949, after stable jockey Arthur Thompson had elected to ride Astra.

'Neville engaged me to ride Wot No Sun at Cheltenham in the National Hunt Handicap Chase. I finished second on him. He didn't have too hard a race and I thought he was a certainty with only 10st 3lb in the Grand National. I got down to the weight with a struggle and we led the field out onto the second circuit. I was going super coming down to Becher's. Then a loose horse ran across me going into it and, suddenly, we were on the floor.'

By 1950 Glen was riding for the well-known owner James V Rank. He won that year's Grand Sefton Chase for him on Shagreen, trained in Ireland by Tom Dreaper, beating Freebooter, Finnure and Russian Hero. He also rode Shagreen in two Grand Nationals, going well when coming down at the 23rd fence in 1950 and falling at the fifth in 1951.

Rank had a number of trainers in England, including Frank Horris, formerly head lad to Fred Withington, who trained exclusively for Rank at historic Druid's Lodge, near Salisbury. Among Horris's string was Greenogue, who came within an inch of giving Glen his greatest victory in the 1951 Cheltenham Gold Cup. He was beaten a short head – or so the form book says – by Martin Molony on Silver Fame. However, there was no photo finish in those days and many disagreed with the judge's decision.

Glen was convinced he won it: 'I'm bloody sure I did. I had my whip in my right hand and Silver Fame came at me on my right, so I could see him quite clearly. But I didn't get the verdict and that was that.'

Soon after that Gold Cup defeat, he received a letter from Mr Rank: 'Dear Kelly, First of all I want to say I was sorry I was not the winner of the Gold Cup and that you did not get the decision. This was very sad indeed. Anyway, the horse ran a great race and I understand from one of my friends you gave him a great ride. I hope we shall have better luck another time.'

Better luck came that autumn when Glen rode Greenogue to victories in Hurst Park's Grand Sefton Trial and Liverpool's Becher Chase.

He had one more ride in the Grand National, falling at Valentine's first time round on Peter Cazalet's Another Delight in 1952. Weight problems led him to announce his retirement at the end of the following season, during which he had achieved a final big race success aboard Arctic Gold in the Cathcart Challenge Cup at Cheltenham. His last victory was on Lisagally for Gerald Balding on 23 May 1953, at Towcester, the place where he had ridden his very first winner 22 years earlier.

Unlike his father and brother, Glen declined the chance to become a trainer. He had already invested his money in a mixed arable and dairy farm and that was the life he chose to follow.

He lived on the outskirts of the Oxfordshire village of Kirtlington, where he died peacefully on 20 October 2002, aged 86.

When I had met him the previous year, he recalled not just his rides at Liverpool and Cheltenham but also the days of Brocklesby and Bungay, and of Bridgnorth, Torquay, Hawthorn Hill and Gatwick too. He told of the time when Charlie Kelly claimed a horse out of a seller at Totnes and Glen walked it all the way to Newton Abbot to run the next day.

His stories evoked memories of an era long gone, far removed from the agents-on-the-phone, entries-via-the-internet world of today. He was proud of the fact that, throughout his career, not once did he ring a trainer for a ride. They always rang him.

Date: Saturday 20 March 1948 Going: Good Value to Winner: £9,103 12s 6d

Horse	Owner	Trainer	Age / weight	Jockey	SP
1 Sheila's Cottage	Mr J Proctor	N F Crump	9-10-7	A P Thompson	50-1
2 First Of The Dandies	Maj D J Vaughan	G Wilson	11-10-4	J Brogan	25-1
3 Cromwell	Lord Mildmay	P Cazalet	7-10-11	Lord Mildmay	33-1
4 Happy Home	Miss D Paget	F Walwyn	9-11-10	G Kelly	33-1

Distances: 1 length, 6 lengths, 6 lengths. Time: 9 mins 25 2/5 secs. 43 ran

Winner trained at Middleham, Yorkshire

1949

DEREK ANCIL
Batchelor's report

Derek Ancil and Perfect Night (left) are brought down by the fallen Magnetic Fin.

THIS WAS MORE than just another Grand National article. Written by Denzil Batchelor in 1949 for the *Picture Post*, it described not only a horse race but also a race of people, and a portrait of a changing lifestyle. The *Picture Post* ceased publication eight years later but the matchless prose of Batchelor's report lives on.

Entitled simply 'The Story of a Race', it recounted the victory of 66-1 outsider Russian Hero, an ex-hunter whose dam had been bought for £25 and whom only Cayton of the communist *Morning Post*, for somewhat obvious reasons, was bold enough to make his selection.

Russian Hero's owner-breeder Fernie Williamson was a tenant farmer of land owned by the Duke of Westminster at Cotton Edmunds, Christleton, near Chester, and had reputedly had £10 on him at 300-1. True, the horse had won three races that season, but he had also fallen on two of his last three starts. Nonetheless, ridden by the little-known Leo McMorrow, he outstayed Lord Bicester's Roimond and the fancied Royal Mount, with Lord Mildmay on Cromwell, the favourite, back in fourth.

Batchelor related how the race had attracted 'as huge a crowd as had ever thronged Aintree ... Not all were English. All round the course could be found Irish priests, hoping – of all things – for the success of Cromwell!

'There were Americans too ... One of them viewed Becher's Brook with disenchantment. "It looked tougher in the newspapers", he kept grumbling. He wouldn't have admitted for a half-share in *Oklahoma!* but he obviously expected spikes on top and the shaft of a coal mine on the landing side.

'Some thirty minutes before the start our strangers to Aintree are seeking the roof of the Enclosure for the view of the National for which they have paid £2 17s 6d apiece. In vain! A policeman, polite as the executioner who asks pardon for his deed, bars the road. The Reserved Enclosure is full to overflowing. This means the visitors must scrum behind the bookmakers near the rails. In this swarming crowd many are lucky if they see more than the hindquarters of the horses plunging away at the start, with a later glimpse of the caps of the jockeys flashing by.

'But now the horses are backing and sidling and tip-toeing forward into line. There near the inside is the favourite, his rider wearing the light blue and white hoops which down the course gleam like mother of pearl. There is Roimond, bearing Lord Bicester's black jacket, gold sleeves and red cap. Further down the line is Cloncarrig, carrying a little ball of muscle in green, with gold seal back and front, gold sleeves and Gordon tartan cap. The champion jockey, Bryan Marshall, wears Miss Paget's blue and yellow on the beautiful bay, Happy Home.

'O'Ryan is on the skittish Acthon Major who showed the whites of his eyes in the paddock. At the gate his purple and sea-green colours see-saw defiantly and execute skirmishing movements on either flank. But at last he is edged into line, not far from where McMorrow sits like a statue on Russian Hero, in Fernie Williamson's black and white livery. A tumbled heap of jewels in the pearly light.

'And then they are off to a royal start. The thud and thunder sound down the course ... and a howl from the first fence starts the news on the bush telegraph that Stone Cottage has turned a somersault under the very nose of Leap Man.

'Acthon Major is showing now that that little bit of temperament in the paddock and at the starting gate was nothing more than an eagerness to be up and at 'em. He shows his heels to another outsider, Astra. Not far behind is Roimond, classic in movement and a model for young jumpers with Aintree ambitions. Cloncarrig is still there in the first flight, and stride for stride with him goes Wot No Sun, fighting to get his head in front, with more dash about him than anything else at this stage. So they come to Becher's on the first round of the course.

'Half a dozen fences later, some of the ambitious have paid the price. Acthon Major has gone, and the bold Cloncarrig. It is Roimond now, moving with his champion's action, with Wot No Sun at his withers. So they come down towards the Chair fence and the water jump.'

Batchelor reported that Roimond and Wot No Sun had led them out onto the second circuit, with Royal Mount in third followed by Cromwell, Monaveen and Russian Hero. Monaveen fell when prominent at the nineteenth and Wot No Sun capsized at Becher's. Six horses either fell or were brought down at the Canal Turn.

'And so they come to Valentine's. That is where Bora's Cottage lies dead with a lot of the little money buried with him. The name Cottage has a magic ring in these parts, and while you watched the Punch and Judy show opposite Lime Street station after breakfast a horsy half-pint probably offered you this horse as the infallible winner in return for a double whisky (Irish preferred).

'In a little while now, the field swings into full view again, and a bookmakers' chorus, jubilant as an Abbey choir at a victory service, sets up a paean to Russian Hero. There is cut-and-thrust with Roimond and Royal Mount over the last two fences – and then history has been made.'

Batchelor's account did not relate the exploits of another 66-1 outsider, the remounted Perfect Night, trailing in last of the eleven finishers with his 24-year-old amateur partner, Derek Ancil.

Like the winner, Perfect Night was an ex-hunter chaser. In 1948 he won one at Towcester and was third in Cheltenham's Foxhunters', ridden by Peter Harvey, son of the owner. He failed to finish in that year's Liverpool Foxhunters', which was then still run over the full Grand National distance of four miles 856 yards.

Soon afterwards, Perfect Night was sold and joined Ronnie Horton's yard at Middleton Stoney, near Bicester. Derek was the stable's amateur rider and rode the horse to victory at Wincanton and Towcester in October 1948, then was last of six finishers in the Grand Sefton. Following a good third to Royal Mount at Sandown came disappointing efforts at Fontwell and Birmingham, but his connections felt he was entitled to take his chance in that season's Grand National.

'Lord Mildmay told me that he was going to follow me because mine was a good jumper,' said Derek. 'Unfortunately, we were half knocked over at Becher's first time. I did the unforgivable thing of remounting, as the owners had had a good bet about him getting round.'

Derek was born on 28 July 1924 in Redhill, Surrey, where the Ancil family then farmed, but in 1927 they returned to their native Oxfordshire. When he developed an interest in racing, his father paid 60 guineas for a horse called Dusky Chimes, who became Derek's first winner when landing an incident-packed novices' chase at Wincanton on Boxing Day 1946, a race in which the only other finisher was twice remounted.

He turned professional at the start of the 1949/50 season but had to wait until 1954 for his next Grand National mount, long shot Triple Torch. 'He was known by all the jockeys as Cripple Torch,' laughed Derek. 'He wasn't the best of jumpers but he got as far as the Chair.'

No Response, his 1955 partner, departed at the seventh fence, while Domata, trained by Frank Cundell, gave him a good ride until falling four out in 1956. However, an even better one awaited the following year, a horse owned by Colonel Bill Whitbread named Athenian.

Derek reflected on what might have been: 'It's an extraordinary thing that one of the best rides I had round Aintree was on Athenian, who was such an in and out performer. He was a very brave horse but he used to run away with you and he fired himself at those fences. I wouldn't say he was a bad jumper but he was a cocky horse who didn't try to put himself right at the fences because he thought he could bulldoze his way through. But you can't do that at Liverpool.

'He was trained by Gerald Balding, father of Toby and Ian. He said to me "I know you'll go off in front but you want to take a pull at him somewhere, otherwise you won't last home." It was after the Canal Turn second time round before I could really catch hold of him. I think he got a bit annoyed with me because I was trying to hang onto him and he fell four out. He was going so well and might easily have won but for falling. I know I was going better than the winner, Sundew, at the time and mine always got the trip so I suppose I should have let him bowl on.'

Following the sudden death of Gerald Balding later that year, Colonel Whitbread placed his horses with Peter Cazalet. Although Derek won on Athenian at Hurst Park, he insists that the horse wasn't right when falling at the nineteenth fence in the next year's National.

He had enjoyed a lengthy association with Peter Thrale's Mr Gay prior to riding him in the 1959 Grand National, including victories in the Hurst Park National Trial and two Withington Chases at Birmingham. However, they were brought down at Becher's first time.

He did not ride in the 1960 National won by Merryman II, ridden by Gerry Scott. But the following year Scott was sidelined with a broken arm. Amateur rider Charlie Scott (no relation), who had won the Liverpool Foxhunters' Chase on Merryman, was on standby but trainer Neville Crump was keen to engage an experienced professional.

Derek recalled: 'Neville Crump rang me and said, "Do you want a good ride in the National?" I went up to Middleham and schooled Merryman three days before the race. He was a super jumper. Neville said "Don't worry about his weight, he'll get the trip. Just keep him out of trouble."

'Unfortunately, he was kicked at the start. It was a nasty one but I really don't think it made any difference. The weight beat him and that's all. He carried 11st 12lb whereas Nicolaus Silver only had 10st 1lb, which is a big difference over four and a half miles. If he'd had a few pounds less I think he would have won.'

By then he was combining riding with training at his Middleton Stoney yard. He relinquished his jockey's licence at the end of the 1961/62 season, ending a career that had brought almost 250 winners, including the Hennessy Gold Cup, the 1955 Scottish Grand National on Bar Point and the 1958 Grand Sefton Chase on Tiberetta.

Knucklecracker was his standard bearer for the 1962/63 season. Derek had trained and ridden him to win all his first four starts of the 1960/61 campaign, culminating in the Hennessy Gold Cup. He again won his first four races in 1962/63 before finishing third to Neville Crump's pair Springbok and Rough Tweed in the Hennessy. Tragically, he broke a hind leg at the water jump on his next start in the Rhymney Breweries Chase at Chepstow.

Derek subsequently moved his training operation to Thorpe Mandeville, near Banbury, and saddled Kellsboro' Wood to finish eighth behind Highland Wedding in the 1969 Grand National. He retired from training at the end of the 1980s to concentrate on his two farms, one at Thorpe Mandeville, and the other at Middleton Stoney, but retained his racing involvement through having horses with Kim Bailey, Frank Jordan and Mark Wilkinson. He died on 17 July 2010 at the age of 85.

Russian Hero, the winner of that 1949 Grand National, never won another race in 27 tries, although he once came within a head of doing so at Leicester. He ran in the next three Grand Nationals, twice falling at the first fence. After retirement he spent two seasons in the hunting field, partnered during one of those by Anne, Duchess of Westminster, who would later become the owner of Arkle and Last Suspect. He lived out the rest of his days at Fernie Williamson's farm before having to be put down, aged 25, in January 1965.

'The great race over, thousands stream from the course,' concluded Batchelor's report.

'First into the road bordering Aintree is an Irish priest. He sees facing him a blind man with a banner: "Christ Alone Will Save." Behind, the cheers are going up for – of all names – Russian Hero. The Irish priest looks like a man whose ideology has had a stab in the back; and just at the moment when he happened to be off duty.'

Date: Saturday 26 March 1949 Going: Good Value to Winner: £9,528 10s

Horse	Owner	Trainer	Age / weight	Jockey	SP
1 Russian Hero	Mr W F Williamson	G R Owen	9-10-8	L McMorrow	66-1
2 Roimond	Lord Bicester	G Beeby	8-11-12	R Francis	22-1
3 Royal Mount	Mrs M Harvey	Maj J B Powell	10-10-12	P J Doyle	18-1
4 Cromwell	Lord Mildmay	P Cazalet	8-11-3	Lord Mildmay	6-1fav

Distances: 8 lengths, 1 length, 5 lengths. Time: 9 mins 23 4/5 secs. 43 ran

Winner trained at Malpas, Cheshire

1950

TONY GRANTHAM
The first royal jump jockey

Tony Grantham talks with Princess Elizabeth and the Queen following one of Monaveen's victories.

THERE WAS A sense of eager anticipation as royal colours were seen in the Grand National for the first time in 42 years. There had been no royal runner in the world's most famous steeplechase since King Edward VII's horse Flaxman had finished fourth in 1908. Eight years earlier, when he was still Prince of Wales, he had won the Grand National with Ambush II, but the royal family's subsequent racing involvement had been exclusively on the Flat.

At the end of the war National Hunt racing was still very much the poor relation and the prospect of any direct royal involvement appeared remote. Luckily, it had an ardent supporter in Lord Anthony Bingham, second Baron Mildmay of Flete, the leading amateur rider in each of the first five post-war National Hunt seasons. It was he who, while staying as a guest at Windsor Castle for the 1949 Royal Ascot meeting, first suggested to Queen Elizabeth, as she then was, that she should buy a steeplechaser.

The Queen asked Lord Mildmay to find her a good-quality chaser which she could own in partnership with her daughter, HRH Princess Elizabeth, and send it to be trained by Mildmay's great friend Peter Cazalet at Fairlawne, in Kent.

Mildmay came up with an eight-year-old gelding called Monaveen, who had been leading the field in that year's Grand National when falling at the nineteenth fence. He was owned by Dal Hawkesley, a West Ham greyhound trainer, and trained at Epsom by Peter Thrale.

Monaveen's first owner had been a County Meath farmer named George Flood. Legend has it that George considered Monaveen so full of spirit that he had put him in a milk float for a year to tame him. He was then bought by James Raftery, of County Galway, who thought so much of the horse that he named his house after him and sent Monaveen over to England to be trained by Peter Thrale.

But Monaveen couldn't settle down to life in an English racing yard. He went right off his food and began to mope, almost as if he was pining for his Irish homeland. He ran badly in both starts the spring of 1947, making no show in a hurdle race and falling in a novice chase. Raftery eventually became disillusioned and sold Monaveen to Hawkesley.

Gradually he began to improve, winning a couple of minor chases at Huntingdon and Wye in the spring of 1948. In December that year he beat the useful chaser Freddy Fox by four lengths over three miles at Kempton and connections quickly realised that they had a Grand National contender on their hands.

He was ridden in the 1949 Grand National by Cazalet's stable jockey, Tony Grantham, who was substituting for Vince Mooney, Monaveen's regular pilot, who had broken a collarbone when falling in the Topham Trophy on the Wednesday before the race (Liverpool was a four-day meeting that year).

Born in 1921, Tony was the son of Tom Grantham, a well-known Sussex horse dealer and livery man. He rode as an amateur before the war, in point-to-points and under Rules. During the war he spent four years in the army and saw action in both Palestine and Egypt.

Afterwards he continued as an amateur and began to ride a good number of winners, which led to the inevitable tap on the shoulder from the stewards, who gave him the option of turning professional or giving up race riding. It was an easy decision to make.

His first Grand National mount was on Lord Mildmay's second string, Ultra Bene, in 1948, falling at the third fence. His second was the aforementioned ride on Monaveen.

'He was a very free goer,' Tony recalls of Monaveen. 'He liked to be out in front and he'd jump his way there. I tried to hold him up but he gained three or four lengths at a fence.

'He was an easy horse to ride. He liked to gallop on and was a very good jumper, had a great spring in him. I just had to sit there and make sure I was ready when he was going to take off.'

Monaveen made his debut for his new owners at Fontwell Park on Monday, 10 October 1949. Partnered by Tony and watched by the Princess, he had no difficulty in beating two moderate opponents. The following month, the Princess flew to Liverpool accompanied by Princess Margaret to see Monaveen run in the Grand Sefton Chase. Jumping faultlessly, he led over the last fence but was passed by Freebooter on the run-in and finished second, beaten eight lengths.

He then won at Sandown later that month, and his next appearance was in the inaugural running of the Queen Elizabeth Handicap Chase at Hurst Park on New Year's Eve. Following a sustained duel with Wot No Sun, the royal runner drew clear to beat Freebooter by six lengths amid tumultuous applause. He returned to Hurst Park on 11 February 1950 to win the George Williamson Chase.

Tony had ridden Monaveen in all five races and would do so again in that year's Grand National. In addition to having become the first royal jump jockey, he was enjoying his best season and his final score of 41 winners would place him fourth in the jockeys' table.

The King and Queen were both at Aintree – the first time they had attended the Grand National since 1937 – and were accompanied by the Princesses Elizabeth and Margaret. Lord Mildmay was there too – riding in it – reunited with Cromwell, on whom he'd finished third and fourth in the previous two years.

As at Hurst Park, Monaveen duelled for the lead with Wot No Sun from the outset. Coming back onto the racecourse they were still duelling, but at the fourteenth fence Monaveen blundered badly, shooting Tony up around his ears. Somehow he managed to regain his balance.

Freebooter made an equally bad mistake at the very next fence, the Chair, leaving Jimmy Power clinging round his neck but, again, the jockey made an amazing recovery.

Acthon Major and Wot No Sun took them out onto the second circuit but it was a 33-1 shot, Angel Hill, that led over Becher's. Shagreen fell at the next fence when lying second, then Angel Hill capsized at the Canal Turn, leaving Cloncarrig and Freebooter out in front, ahead of Acthon Major, Wot No Sun and Monaveen.

At the second last fence, Cloncarrig stumbled and came down. This left Freebooter out on his own and he stormed home 15 lengths clear of Wot No Sun, with Acthon Major third. A distance behind these, Rowland Roy ran on to deprive Monaveen of fourth place.

'Monaveen landed in front over the first, having took off about fifth or sixth, so I let him bowl along,' says Tony. 'At the fourteenth fence he just didn't jump high enough. He was on his nose. It definitely made a difference between finishing fifth and being placed. I wasn't really able to get back into the race after that. It was just about completing the course.

'But the royal family were pleased to see him get round and that he'd run so well.'

After the race, the Queen wrote to Cazalet describing the thrill Monaveen had given her. 'The next thing,' she said, 'is to try to win a Grand National, if not next year the year after that.'

Monaveen began his 1950/51 campaign by finishing fifth in Hurst Park's Grand Sefton Trial, and then finished fifth in the Grand Sefton itself. But his third race of the season was to be his last.

On Saturday, 2 December 1950, he started 9-4 favourite for the Queen Elizabeth Chase, the race in which he had defeated Freebooter the year before. The Queen flew from Sandringham to London airport and then travelled on to Hurst Park.

Monaveen was one of three leaders approaching the water jump on the second circuit. He fell heavily, struggled to get up but could not do so. He had broken a leg.

'He dropped one leg short of the landing,' Tony recalls. 'I can still remember looking down and seeing it. He just took off too soon, which he was apt to do, and you can't do that at the water.'

After the race the Queen said that she hoped that the news of Monaveen having been destroyed had not been included in the radio broadcast of the race. She was certain that Princess Elizabeth, who was in Malta, would have been listening and been greatly upset.

As it happened, the news did not go out on the radio broadcast, only on television.

As the Queen left the course her car became stuck in the mud, and the crowd, running to the rescue, pulled and pushed it free. There were cries of 'Hard luck, your Majesty' as she drove away.

It was a tragic end for the royal chaser, but his death was not Fairlawne's only tragedy that year. On Friday, 12 May, Lord Mildmay had gone for his customary early morning bathe in the sea off his Devon estate at Mothecombe, near Modbury. He never returned. News of the 41-year-old amateur's death plunged the racing world into mourning.

Tony cracked several ribs in Monaveen's fatal fall and thus missed the winning ride on Queen Elizabeth's Manicou in the 1950 King George VI Chase. It was a remarkable performance by the French-bred five-year-old entire, having only his third race over fences.

'Manicou was a completely different type to Monaveen,' he says. 'He was a full horse and he looked like one, with big quarters and a lovely neck. He always had a lovely shine on his coat. He was too classy for a chaser, really.'

He made up for the disappointment of missing Manicou's 'King George' victory by winning it the next year on Statecraft, owned by Lord Mildmay's sister, Helen Mildmay-White.

Prince Brownie, in 1951, was his fourth and last Grand National ride. 'I remember thinking that this was my best chance of winning the National. He was a good horse, Prince Brownie, a former point-to-pointer from the West Country. I'd won on him a few times, including the Valentine Chase over the National fences. I was one of five that fell at the Canal Turn. I jumped straight into the back of one of the fallers – I think it was Glen Fire; I couldn't avoid him.'

A painting of Gay Donald jumping a fence at Cheltenham hangs over the fireplace of Tony and Sally Grantham's home outside the village of Kilmurry, near Sixmilebridge, County Clare. It's a reminder of the horse that gave him his biggest victory, in the 1955 Gold Cup. Owned by Philip Burt and trained by Jim Ford at Cholderton, near Salisbury, Gay Donald was the 33-1 outsider of nine runners, but, belying his SP, he took command at the fourth fence and went on to win as he liked, scoring by ten lengths from Halloween and with Four Ten third.

'He just out-galloped and out-jumped the others,' says Tony. 'He jumped his way to the front, I let him keep the lead and he enjoyed it. At the top of the hill I thought I must have gone the wrong way because I couldn't hear any other horses. I looked round and they were still coming up the hill and I was turning to go down it.

'He was a big-topped horse, a real chaser, but there was always a bit of an "if" about one of his legs and it finally gave out at Lingfield in December that year. That finished him; he came back eighteen months later but he was never as good. Jim Ford patched him up well but you can't replace the legs.'

Tony won on him at Windsor before lining up for the 1957 Gold Cup, in which he hit the fence after the water and was pulled up lame.

He was twice runner-up on Gay Donald the following season, the second occasion being behind Hart Royal at Windsor on the first day of February 1958, but Fred Winter rode him when he beat Kerstin in Sandown's Grand International Chase three weeks later. By then, Tony Grantham had ridden his last race, on a horse called Orphan Boy at Wincanton.

A troublesome back, an accumulated legacy of previous falls, led to him calling time on his riding career on the advice of Jockey Club physician Bill Tucker. Later that year he married Sally and took over his father's livery yard at West Grinstead. Then in 1982 they moved to Ireland.

'I was always coming over here bringing horses and I liked the way of life here,' he says. 'The traffic in England was getting terrible, while these roads were very quiet.'

Adds Sally: 'We bought point-to-pointers off Tom Costello and had a wonderful ten years of point-to-pointing and hunting with the Clare and the Limerick. We won a lot of point-to-point races before selling them on to trainers in England.'

Gay Donald's Cheltenham Gold Cup was Tony's biggest victory but he states without hesitation that riding for the Queen, for the royal family, was his proudest achievement. After all, he was the first royal jump jockey.

Date: Saturday 25 March 1950 Going: Good Value to Winner: £9,314

Horse	Owner	Trainer	Age / weight	Jockey	SP
1 Freebooter	Mrs L Brotherton	R Renton	9-11-11	J Power	10-1jtfav
2 Wot No Sun	Capt T D Wilson	N F Crump	8-11-8	A P Thompson	100-7
3 Acthon Major	Mrs J S Gorman	W Easterby	10-11-2	R J O'Ryan	33-1
4 Rowland Roy	Mr A G Boley	F Walwyn	11-11-7	R Black	40-1

Distances: 15 lengths, 10 lengths, a distance. Time: 9 mins 23 3/5 secs. 49 ran

Winner trained at Ripon, Yorkshire

1951

BOB McCREERY

A National won on eggs and stout

First fence fallers (left to right) Paddy Fitzgerald, Bryan Marshall, Dick Francis, Pat Taaffe, Bob McCreery, Jack Dowdeswell and Michael Scudamore. Bending down is Mick O'Dwyer.

JUST THREE OF the 36 starters completed the course in one of the most astonishing Grand Nationals for years. At each fence the horses came tumbling down; onlookers visualised none getting round. Nickel Coin and Royal Tan were the only two not to fall. The third, Derrinstown, named after a County Kildare village, fell at Becher's second time but was remounted.

Jeffrey Royle had originally purchased Nickel Coin for 55 guineas as a yearling. To his great regret, he sold her a couple of years later, but his son Frank bought her back for him, using part of his army gratuity as payment.

She was put into training with Jack O'Donoghue at Reigate, Surrey, and thrived on a diet of stout and eggs. Her rider, 34-year-old Johnny Bullock, was born in Walsall and served with the Paratroopers during the war.

With 33-1 shot Barnes Park having won the Lincolnshire Handicap the previous Saturday, bookmakers had another happy weekend as 40-1 Nickel Coin became only the third (and last) mare to win the National in the twentieth century.

The race got off to an appalling start. About two-thirds of the runners were in line, with the remainder milling around in a jumbled mass, when the starter, Leslie Firth, released the tape. Amazingly, no false start was called, setting off a frantic scramble as jockeys rushed to make up the lost ground. The mad-dash panic resulted in eleven horses, almost a third of the field, crashing out in a first fence pile-up.

Thereafter, almost every obstacle took its toll, trapping fancied candidates and complete outsiders alike. Freebooter was brought down at the second; Shagreen fell at the fifth. Only Morning Cover went at Becher's but five crashed out at the next. The favourite, Arctic Gold came to grief when leading at the Canal Turn, as did three others, while the second favourite, Cloncarrig, was baulked by loose horses and was unable to jump the fence. Four more went at Valentine's, including Roimond and Queen Of The Dandies, leaving just seven still standing.

With stable-mates Russian Hero and Dog Watch both departing at the Chair, it was the Vincent O'Brien-trained Royal Tan and Nickel Coin who led three outsiders, Derrinstown, Gay Heather and Broomfield, over the water and out for the second half of the race. Gay Heather and Derrinstown fell at Becher's then Broomfield departed at the next, leaving Royal Tan and Nickel Coin as the sole survivors. Both Derrinstown and Gay Heather were remounted but the latter refused at the very next fence.

Royal Tan blundered badly at the last jump, effectively handing victory to Nickel Coin who went on to win by six lengths. Derrinstown eventually completed a long way behind, the only other horse to pass the winning post.

Among those caught up in the first fence chaos was 66-1 outsider Stalbridge Rock, the mount of a 20-year-old amateur named Bob McCreery. Being the son of noted soldier-rider Dick McCreery, who twice won the Grand Military Gold Cup, it was to be expected that Bob would follow in a military career. But things don't always go as planned.

Says Bob: 'I was due to go in the army for two years' service but, much to everyone's surprise, I failed my medical. When I was a child I'd had a kidney removed and that failed me. It wasn't a great disappointment to me I have to say!

'My father was working for the United Nations on the military commission in New York at the time, so there was nowhere for me to go because I was expected to be in the barracks. That's really how I started in racing because I got a "job", if that's the right word, with a friend of my father's, Major Derek Schreiber, who had a small point-to-point yard on Salisbury Plain.

'Father had restarted racing in Vienna while commanding the Eighth Army there. He brought home from Austria a horse with the unoriginal name of Jumbo, who had won steeplechases in Italy and Austria just after the war. He sent him to Major Schreiber and I qualified him for point-to-points. On my first ride in a race I won a point-to-point on him at Larkhill.

'After I'd failed my medical, my father thought I should go to Oxford University. I took the entrance exams, passed them and went to Oxford – for one term. Every morning during that term I drove my motor cycle from Oxford to East Everleigh and rode out for George Bowden, who I'd met while with Major Schreiber. George was a very nice guy . He'd won the Welsh Grand National as a jockey but he struggled as a trainer. Like so many other small trainers with six or eight horses, it was a battle. East Everleigh was very different then to the place where Richard Hannon now trains. It was a tiny little yard with prefabricated boxes.

'After I'd been riding out for him for about six months, he allowed me to ride Alacrity in a race at Taunton in November 1949, my first ride under Rules. I was eighteen and the horse was nearly seventeen, so you could see which was the more experienced. He fell that day but George allowed me to ride him again two weeks later in a selling chase at Wolverhampton. By a total fluke he won by a short head, beating a horse trained by Gerry Wilson.'

The following season Bob rode Coral Boy to victory in the 1951 United Hunts Challenge Cup at Cheltenham's National Hunt Meeting. Four days after that he finished third on Harry Dufosee's Stalbridge Rock in the Hurst Park Grand National Trial. All eyes now turned to the real thing at Liverpool.

'Harry lived about two miles from my father, who by then was back from America, retired and living in Somerset, near Wincanton. I rode out for Harry every morning. Stalbridge Rock was a small but very tough horse, although size-wise he wasn't perhaps the right type for Aintree.'

He doesn't recall much of the shambolic start but knows exactly what led to his first fence departure. 'As always, everybody was keyed up at the start. The people who were left were trying to catch up and we all went much too fast. My horse was going at what I'd call hurdle pace. He flew the fence but wasn't used to the drop and over-jumped, just knuckled over. I don't think he touched the fence at all.

'Some great riders fell there, including Dick Francis and Bryan Marshall. There was a fair bit of cursing from people who had much higher expectations than I. We were all terribly disappointed but it happens to the best.'

Bob went on to enjoy happier times aboard Stalbridge Rock, scoring an appropriate victory in the Lord Stalbridge Gold Cup at Wincanton, then getting up close home to land the 1953 Welsh National by a neck.

He only rode in the Grand National once more, falling three out on Cloncarrig in 1953 when lying in third place. By doing so, Cloncarrig earned himself the unenviable record of being the only horse to fall in six consecutive Grand Nationals. Although he had run and fallen in every National since 1948, he was a far better Aintree horse than his record suggests, having won the Molyneux Chase twice (1947 and 1949) plus the Becher Chase in 1950.

'He wouldn't have won,' says Bob of Cloncarrig's sixth and final National attempt. 'Mont Tremblant was second and Irish Lizard third. I might have finished second; I would certainly have beaten Irish Lizard. Cloncarrig won the Becher and the Molyneux but not the National, the reason being that he didn't really stay. When I fell with him, I wanted to jump back up so that I could finish the course – only five finished that year – but he was out on his feet, his knees were wobbling, so I just led him back.'

Bob went on to share the 1955/56 amateur riders' championship with Danny Moralee and then won the title outright with 23 winners the following season. During that time he rode for George Beeby and won the 1957 Cotswold Chase (now the Arkle Challenge Trophy) for him on Ballyatom.

Overseas successes included Sweden's International Chase at Malmo, an amateur riders' hurdle in Madrid and a Flat race at Deauville. However, no triumph at home or abroad gave him more pleasure than winning a Newbury novice chase on the Queen Mother's Young Rajah in January 1962, his sole victory in the royal colours.

During that same season he struck up a partnership with Ryan Price's Granville, winning three novice chases, including the Henry VIII, run for the last time at Hurst Park.

'I was with Ryan Price for two years near the end of my riding career,' he recalls. He was a genius with horses, the best judge I ever met. I was with him when he bought two Grand National winners.

'We went to Ireland to look for a Grand National horse for Nat Cohen. I rode Kilmore over a couple of fences on a farm. Ryan said "What do you think, Bobby?" I replied "He's very small; I don't think he's big enough for Aintree." "Bollocks", he retorted, "he's made for Aintree. Balance, that's what he's got." Of course, he was a beautifully balanced horse and Ryan was absolutely right.

'I was also with him when he bought Anglo. He found him at a farm near Huntingdon and I must admit I wasn't very taken with him either. Unfortunately, Ryan lost the horse to Fred Winter when his licence was withdrawn after the trouble with Rosyth in the (1964) Schweppes Hurdle.'

Bob's retirement from the saddle, after more than 150 wins under both codes, coincided with his purchase in 1963 of Moreton Paddox, in the Warwickshire village of Moreton Morrell. He turned it into a stud and three years later purchased the modest three-year-old filly Camenae for 1,200gns. She became the dam of High Top, winner of the 1972 Two Thousand Guineas. He sold the stud in 1980 and moved his breeding operation to the family's Stowell Hill Stud in Somerset, close to the Dorset border. There Camenae went on to become the grand-dam of 1989 French and Irish Derby hero Old Vic.

For many years Bob was the energetic chairman of the Thoroughbred Breeders' Association and was a driving force in the creation of the European Breeders' Fund. In 2001, in recognition of his work, he was honoured by the TBA as the recipient of the Duke of Devonshire Bronze, the organisation's most prestigious trophy.

Date: Saturday 7 April 1951 Going: Soft Value to Winner: £8,815

Horse	Owner	Trainer	Age / weight	Jockey	SP
1 Nickel Coin	Mr J Royle	J O'Donoghue	9-10-1	J A Bullock	40-1
2 Royal Tan	Mrs H M Keogh	M V O'Brien	7-10-13	Mr A S O'Brien	22-1
3 Derrinstown	Mr P Digney	G Flood	11-10-0	A Power	66-1

Only 3 finished

Distances: 6 lengths, a bad third. Time: 9 mins 47 2/5 secs. 36 ran

Winner trained at Reigate, Surrey

1952

JOHN FOSTER
Foster brothers

Left to right: Jimmy Power, Mick O'Dwyer, Clive Straker, Francis Carroll and John Foster return without their mounts.

JOHN FOSTER WAS the eldest of four brothers who plied their trade over jumps during the fifties and sixties. John (born in 1934), David (1935), Gerald (1937) and Eric (1939) were four of ten children, six boys and four girls.

'Our parents and grandparents were all Somerset farming people,' says John. 'Growing up on the farm we all had to ride because it was our sole form of transport. We rode in pony clubs and gymkhanas in Somerset but only four of us went into racing. We each started with Major Bay Powell at Aldbourne, near Marlborough.

'I started there in December 1948, aged fourteen. I'd done a bit of pony racing, so I wasn't quite as raw as fourteen might suggest. I hadn't officially left school then but somehow the guvnor wangled an arrangement with a retired schoolteacher in the village whose husband was our head lad. So I got away with riding out and doing the horses in the morning, then going to school between two and four in the afternoon.'

He had his first ride on Golden Earth at Folkestone in July 1949, finishing second. His mother and father hired a taxi from Bridgwater to Folkestone, setting off at 4.00 a.m. to make sure of being there to watch his debut. His next ride, Red Royal at Bath on 31 August, was his first winner. The horse had only recently arrived from Ireland and was having his first start in Britain. His starting price of 25-1 supposedly reflected his chance, yet he made all and hung on by half a length.

He rode seven winners on the Flat but his weight was rising fast. The 7st 4lb of 1949 had become 8st 4lb a year later, and by 1951 he was struggling to do nine stone. His future lay over jumps.

'That didn't worry me, as I'd done show jumping and hunting as a kid. But I had a great love for the Flat because of the people I'd ridden gallops with, such as Gordon Richards, Frank Durr and Tommy Gosling. They'd give you a hard time, they'd give you a rollicking, but you knew they were good. I've always said through life that you're only as good as your tutors and, if you're with them long enough, it'll rub off.'

His first winner over fences came on Baire at Stratford on 3 January 1952; the second on Brighter Ingle at Newbury later that month; the third on Newpark, again at Newbury, in February.

Also in those first weeks of 1952, he came in for the ride on a strapping grey gelding called Hal's Venture, finishing third on him at Hurst Park, then fifth behind Legal Joy at Newbury. His next race would be that year's Grand National and John would be the youngest rider in the race. His owner, Charles Olliff-Lee, and trainer, Major Powell, were in buoyant mood, for they had just won the Lincolnshire Handicap with Phariza, so they went to Aintree the following week harbouring hopes of landing the Spring Double.

Three days before the race, John had his first taste of riding over Aintree's fences in the Topham Trophy, finishing sixth on Brighter Ingle. He still remembers the first time he jumped Becher's. 'You're coming down to it as a seventeen-year-old; you've read and heard and even had nightmares about that almighty drop. So I shut my eyes when I got inside the wing, shouted "Go on" and hoped for the best. He landed and went three strides the other side before I opened my eyes and thought "I've made it".'

Now he all was set for the Grand National itself. His local newspaper heralded the occasion, whilst pointing out a potential snag: 'If Hal's Venture, ridden by 17-year-old North Newton, Somerset, boy John Foster, wins the Grand National at Aintree on Saturday, the local villagers, who will be on the horse to a man, will be faced with a problem of where to celebrate. For North Newton has no village pub. The population of Newton is 604. The oldest inhabitant told the *Evening World*, "we will manage. We make some pretty good farmhouse cider around here and we'll have a good supply on tap if the news is good on Saturday afternoon."'

Alas, there were to be no celebrations in North Newton that night, for Hal's Venture fell at the first fence.

Although the going was good, visibility left much to be desired, heavy rain and thick mist obscuring much of the course for spectators. Following the farcical start of the year before, which resulted in eleven horses getting no further than the first, the stewards had warned the riders not to set off too fast.

Their words had no effect. Several of the 47 runners false started and charged the tape, leading to a long delay while it was repaired, with tensions heightening by the minute.

The Embankment enclosure, overlooking the first three National fences and constructed from rubble and debris left over from the racecourse's wartime occupation, was in use for the first time. Spectators situated there were to witness similar first-fence carnage to that which had occurred twelve months earlier.

'He was a quirky old character,' John says of Hal's Venture. 'He'd jump nearly every fence perfectly but always take one or two by the roots. My instructions were to line up somewhere inside to middle, set off and get a good position over the first, otherwise the others would bring us down. The trouble was, almost everyone else was given the same orders.

'We were all going ninety miles an hour down to the first. My horse went in much too fast and stood off. One horse fell, another horse fell and suddenly, before you knew what happened, it was all arms, legs and horses and we were just one big pile. There's ten of us gone at the first. I wasn't hurt, so I leant over the rails and waited for them to come round again.'

The thousands of listeners tuned to the radio would have had little more idea of what was going on than those jockeys stood by the first fence. It was the year when Mrs Topham, having been unable to resolve a dispute over copyright with the BBC, decided to stage her own broadcast with an ill-prepared and make-shift team of amateur commentators. The resulting ineptitude was a farce to be reckoned with and, thankfully, never to be repeated.

When the field reached the first fence on the second circuit it was the top three in the betting, Teal, Legal Joy and Freebooter that led the way, though the latter was to fall at the Canal Turn.

Legal Joy and Teal were still together at the last fence but Teal drew clear on the run-in to win by five lengths, giving trainer Neville Crump and jockey Arthur Thompson their second Grand National victory, following Sheila's Cottage's triumph four years earlier. Teal's stable companion Wot No Sun finished a poor third, with Uncle Barney fourth.

In his early life, Teal had passed through many hands, twice being sold for £35, before being bought by Harry Lane, a construction magnate from South Shields.

A fortnight after Liverpool, John won on Newpark at the annual Beaufort Hunt fixture. Later that year, Newpark gave him an experience he'd never forget when winning a three-mile chase at Devon and Exeter amid stair-rod rain and a thunderstorm after his sole rival had refused at the first fence.

Two months after that Haldon monsoon, John rode Brighter Ingle to finish third in the Molyneux Chase and also finished third on Baire in the Grand Sefton, both over the Grand National fences.

Baire was an extraordinary horse in that, despite being an entire, he ran 88 times over jumps in six seasons. John rode him in 31 races and either won or was in the frame in 24 of them. He was John's second Grand National ride in 1953, when he fell at the fourth fence. The following season, his owner, Michael Marsh, set up his own yard at Stratford-on-Avon and trained Baire himself. John rode him again in the 1954 Grand National but only got as far as the second.

Despite having had three Grand National rides before he was twenty, John never rode in the race again. After spells with Gerald Balding at Weyhill and Pat Daly at Upper Lambourn he moved to Devon and rode for Les Kennard. From there he joined Collumpton trainer Jack Cann, then subsequently freelanced.

'I didn't really want to come down to the south-west because it was very small in racing terms then and you had to be at Lambourn if you wanted to get on. It's very different now of course. But then I met my wife, June, got married in January 1959 and after that I didn't want to venture back up to Lambourn.'

By this time the three younger Foster brothers were all riding winners over jumps. David headed north to ride for Joe Hartigan at Tarporley and scored his biggest success on Eternal in the 1960 Lancashire Chase at Manchester.

Gerry joined permit holder Tommy Palmer, who ran a garage and trained a few horses at Callington, in Cornwall. He struck up a good partnership with a grey steeplechaser called Midstream, winning seven times on him and enjoying his own thrill of riding round Aintree when finishing sixth in the 1960 Molyneux Chase.

Eric rode a total of seventeen winners and, although there were no big ones, he did have the satisfaction of beating two of his brothers when winning a steeplechase at Buckfastleigh on Whit Monday 1958 on Nugget. John finished second on Sea Captain and Gerry was fourth on the favourite, Tatler III. That was as close as they came to a Foster family one-two-three.

John's career in the saddle came to a crashing end in an Ascot novices' chase on 7 February 1968, when a horse called River Dee was one of five fallers at the first fence. He received head and back injuries and spent three weeks in Ascot hospital. He was later advised that another fall would have serious repercussions and decided that the only sensible option was to call it a day. He had ridden 118 winners altogether, 111 of them over jumps.

Unlike some, he was not stuck for something to do. He had combined riding with running a livery yard at Cullompton, breaking in and schooling horses. He also stood two stallions at stud there.

He later bought ten acres of smallholding at Brompton Ralph where he added pig farming, albeit on a small scale, to his itinerary. That was sold in 1988, since when he has lived in Wellington. For four years he rode out for Martin Pipe, where his National Hunt jockey son Martin was then based.

Martin Foster, champion conditional jockey in 1990/91, emulated his father by riding in three Grand Nationals, twice on Paco's Boy for Martin Pipe in 1993 and '94, and finally in '96 when completing the course in fourteenth place on Lucinda Russell's Greenhill Raffles.

John always went up to Aintree with his son and, of course, told him how much easier the fences looked than when he was riding over them.

'Martin was a better rider than all of us brothers,' he acknowledges. 'But then, you're only as good as your tutors. If he hadn't been better than me, I wouldn't have done much of a job teaching him!'

Date: Saturday 5 April 1952 Going: Good Value to Winner: £9,268 12s 6d

Horse	Owner	Trainer	Age / weight	Jockey	SP
1 Teal	Mrs H Lane	N F Crump	10-10-12	A P Thompson	100-7
2 Legal Joy	Miss D Paget	F Walwyn	9-10-4	M Scudamore	100-6
3 Wot No Sun	Capt T D Wilson	N F Crump	10-11-7	D V Dick	33-1
4 Uncle Barney	Mr L Michaelson	H Clarkson	9-10-4	J Boddy	100-1

Distances: 5 lengths, a bad third, 10 lengths. Time: 9 mins 20 3/5 secs. 47 ran

Winner trained at Middleham, Yorkshire

1953

SAM McCOMB
From Aintree to Ontario

Blinkered Punchestown Star (Sam McComb) with Grand Truce (centre) and Roman Fire in the 1953 Golden Miller Chase at Cheltenham.

'WE'VE HAD TWELVE inches of snow here since lunchtime,' says Sam McComb in a trans-Atlantic phone call one mid-December night.

'Here' is Stevensville, eight miles from Fort Erie, Ontario. It's a fifteen minute drive from Buffalo – when it's not snowing, that is. Snow is something that the people put up with in Canada, a country where a white Christmas is the norm rather than the exception.

But it's home to Sam; has been for over fifty years, ever since British National Hunt was swapped for Canadian Flat.

'In truth, I was way too light to ever have been a jump jockey,' he acknowledges. 'I weighed less than eight stone and I had to have a couple of lead pads to make the weight up. I must have been just about the lightest man to have ridden in the Grand National since the war.'

Sam McComb was born in 1929 at Dunmurry, on the outskirts of Belfast. His father had a dairy business and Sam's first contact with horses was driving the milk cart. 'It was an awful life, delivering milk seven days a week. In addition, I was small and very light and I got fed up of being beaten up by the other kids, so I ran away from home.'

He spent six months with trainer Cecil Brabazon at the Curragh, followed by a five-year apprenticeship with Frank Boland at Killala in County Mayo. The stable star at that time was the 1947 Grand National runner-up Lough Conn, and Sam had the responsibility of galloping the horse at home. His first winner was for Boland, a filly named Lonely Polly in a mile-and-a-half Flat race at Ballinrobe on 13 April 1948.

'If I'd been smart enough I'd have gone straight to England,' he reflects, though he eventually did so and spent two years with Fred Rimell at Kinnersley. Rimell provided him with his first winner over jumps in Britain, Punchestown Star, a steely grey gelding by Bidar, in a novice riders' chase at Cheltenham on 16 April 1952. That was the first time he had ridden the horse. There would be another 31 occasions, including a brace of Grand Nationals.

By the start of the 1952/53 season Punchestown Star had moved to Jack Lea's stables at Wythall, on the south-west outskirts of Birmingham. Stable jockey Jim Edmunds rode him in his first four starts, including when last of nine finishers in the Molyneux Chase over part of the Grand National course.

Sam was also on the move by this time. He had struck up an acquaintance with a two-mile chaser named Gold Hyacinth, trained by Harry Whiteman at Upper Lambourn. Whiteman had telephoned Fred Rimell seeking a 7lb claimer and Sam's name had been put forward. Wins at Hereford and Perth, plus a quick hat-trick aboard Whiteman's novice hurdler Lancehead, cemented the partnership and Sam found himself in the position of stable jockey.

The relationship was to become more than just that of jockey and trainer. Whiteman had two daughters, Joan and Audrey - and romance was in the air between Sam and Audrey.

Meanwhile, Sam had renewed his partnership with Punchestown Star, finishing second on him at Cheltenham, Warwick and Worcester.

'Punchestown Star's owners, Mr and Mrs Greenaway, were from Dudley and were two of the nicest people you could wish to meet,' he recalls. 'The horse was just a plodder; no speed. He just plodded along in his own time. In the Worcester race, Johnny Bullock and I had it between us turning for home, but Johnny outrode me all the way to the line and beat me a neck.'

Hindered by a slipping saddle, Sam and nine-year-old Punchestown Star finished fourth at Wolverhampton in their final start before the 1953 Grand National, for which they were rated among the '66-1 others'. But those National dreams were almost over before they had begun.

The day before the race he was leading the field on Lancehead with four left to jump in the Liverpool Hurdle when horse and rider went their separate ways, leaving Sam with concussion and broken ribs. Patched up and conscious again, he was released from hospital only after valet Joe Ballinger vouched to look after him. If 'looking after him' constituted letting him ride in the world's most famous steeplechase the following day, then it could be said he did as he was told.

'You don't think about nerves when the starter sends you on your way,' insists Sam, 'but as I was coming to the first it seemed as though my horse was getting smaller as the fence was getting bigger. I thought: "Holy smoke, I should have stayed at school and got an education instead!"

'There were a couple down at the first and you could hear the jockeys shouting as others fell going down to Becher's.

'I misjudged Becher's, I was going forward when I should have been sitting back, but fortunately the horse did everything right. There were more problems alongside me at the Canal Turn but we kept going. Then, at the second after Valentine's, a loose horse cannoned into me and I went flying into the wing of the fence.'

Michael Scudamore on Ordnance had led from the outset and they were still in front when falling at the 20th fence, leaving Early Mist, the mount of Bryan Marshall, to inherit the lead running down to Becher's.

From that point on, nothing ever looked like catching Early Mist, who went on to win in runaway fashion, finishing 20 lengths clear of Mont Tremblant, with Irish Lizard four lengths further back in third.

Early Mist had formerly been owned by James V Rank but following his death in January 1952 the horse was acquired by Vincent O'Brien for 5,300 guineas on behalf of Dublin businessman Joe Griffin. This was to be the first of three successive National winners trained by O'Brien.

During the 1953/54 season Punchestown Star and Sam combined to win a three-mile handicap chase at Worcester and dead-heated for another at Warwick, though arguably their best performances were in defeat, when finishing second to Crudwell at Worcester, third to Irish Lizard in the Fred Withington Chase, and fourth to subsequent Gold Cup winner Four Ten at Cheltenham.

Sam and Audrey celebrated Grand National Day 1954 by announcing their engagement. Although Punchestown Star was again listed among the 66-1 rank outsiders for the Aintree marathon, Sam was hopeful of a good ride round to complete a memorable day.

'We were up with the leaders for the first circuit, along with Pat Taaffe on Coneyburrow and Derek Leslie on Sanperion. Then, when Pat's horse dropped his hind legs in the water, I found myself in front for a short while. I thought that mistake had finished Coneyburrow and I couldn't believe it when he came cruising past me again going out onto the second circuit.

'By Becher's Brook for the second time, Punchestown Star wasn't going anywhere and I was just trying to finish the race. Unfortunately, he bowed a tendon three out and I had to pull up. If I'd persisted I'd have finished him off there and then.'

It was a race marred by tragedy. The celebrations of Royal Tan's connections were overshadowed by the deaths of four horses, including the giant Coneyburrow, who had fallen four out. Sam's realisation of Punchestown Star's injury at least ensured that there wasn't a fifth fatality.

After he had broken down, Punchestown Star was given time to recover but he was never the same again. Sam rode him four more times the next season, all unplaced, then after three more lacklustre efforts he was finally retired. Poor Punchestown Star met a sad end, being gored to death by a bull that was sharing the same paddock.

He did, though, have a full brother who would duly enhance the family's credentials. He was called E.S.B., reputedly named with the initials of his sire and dam, being by Bidar out of English Summer, and destined to win the 1956 Grand National in the most dramatic of circumstances.

The aforementioned Gold Hyacinth proved a good friend to Sam, winning nine races together, the last in May 1955 when landing the Ledbury Handicap Chase on Hereford's Whit Monday card for the third year running. An injury-hit 1956/57 campaign yielded just three winners, a Stratford novices' chase on Clanyon, and victories at Birmingham and Liverpool on future Champion Hurdler Bandalore.

'Clanyon was the best I rode over fences. He was a tough little horse. You never knew when he'd take off; he really stood back at his jumps, yet the only time he fell with me was when he slipped up on the flat after jumping a fence at Ludlow. He was owned and trained by a super gentleman, Mr Johns-Powell at Bonvilston, near Cardiff.'

Sam won three times on Clanyon during the 1957/58 campaign. The following season they teamed up to win the Victory Chase at Manchester. This was to be his last British winner.

'I had my last ride in England on Clanyon in the Jerry M Chase at Lingfield in February 1959. By the time he won the Topham Trophy the following month [with Grenville Underwood riding] I'd left the country.'

The move to pastures new came about when the British Bloodstock Agency was looking for somebody to represent them on a one-year contract in Canada promoting British horses. Sam decided it to give it try. The lifestyle suited him well and when the year was up, he, Audrey and their young daughter Susan decided to settle there.

Sam could ride comfortably at 110lbs (7st 12lb) and quickly adapted to riding the left-hand ovals. He gained his first success on Thermonuclear at Fort Erie racecourse, Ontario, and went on to amass some 500 winners, including many of the top Canadian stakes races.

His major victories included the 1961 Jockey Club Cup aboard Prompt Hero, beating top American jockey Eddie Arcaro on Wise Command; the 1965 Prince of Wales Stakes (the second leg of the Canadian Triple Crown) on Good Old Mort; and the 1967 Canadian International Championship on He's A Smoothie. He also rode He's A Smoothie in that year's Washington DC International at Laurel Park, setting the pace for most of the way and turning for home alongside Fort Marcy and Damascus before tiring to finish fourth.

The one major prize that eluded him was the Queen's Plate, Canadian racing's most prestigious race. He was placed in it three times, including on Langcrest in 1964. He won several good races on Langcrest, including the Manitoba

Derby and two Kingarvie Handicaps, but he was destined to be second best in that 1964 Plate, for the horse that beat him would eventually become a racing legend. His name was Northern Dancer.

'I retired at the end of 1968 to take up training but I got conned into making a comeback the following year by an owner who got me drunk one night. When I came round from the hangover the next day, Audrey said "Do you remember anything from last night? You said you'd ride one more race." So I rode the horse in a maiden race on the grass. It finished second at 50-1!

'I finished riding in the fall of 1969. Ironically, I broke my finger in the starting stalls on my final ride, while the horse I actually trained won the race, ridden by an apprentice.'

Sam trained his share of winners and had a dozen horses based at Fort Erie. And when they put slot machines in, prize money there tripled, so he wasn't complaining.

His favourite horse, One Purpose, raced until he was fourteen. 'After he'd retired he was used as an outrider's pony in a commercial where a jockey jumps from one horse to another. The horse earned $750 a day for a week's work. I was working twice as hard as I ever did yet the horse was making more money than me!'

Date: Saturday 28 March 1953   Going: Good   Value to Winner: £9,330 10s

Horse	Owner	Trainer	Age / weight	Jockey	SP
1 Early Mist	Mr J H Griffin	M V O'Brien	8-11-2	B Marshall	20-1
2 Mont Tremblant	Miss D Paget	F Walwyn	7-12-5	D V Dick	18-1
3 Irish Lizard	Lord Sefton	H Nicholson	10-10-6	R Turnell	33-1
4 Overshadow	Mrs J A Wood	C Magnier	13-10-4	P Taaffe	33-1

Distances: 20 lengths, 4 lengths, 6 lengths. Time: 9 mins 21 3/5 secs. 31 ran

Winner trained at Cashel, County Tipperary, Ireland

1954

GEORGE SLACK
Three times second

Royal Tan (far side) holds off the late thrust of Tudor Line.

THERE WAS NO hint of regret, no tinge of envy. If there were, the photo that adorned the veranda wall at the Slacks' comfortable bungalow at Colsterworth, near Grantham, would have been taken down long ago. Instead, it hung as a reminder of one of the closest Grand National finishes of all. Royal Tan and Tudor Line, two horses battling stride for stride, captured in the same motion, their jockeys in synch, whips raised in identical fashion, seemingly inseparable. Such a pity that one had to lose.

George Slack passed away in March 2003, aged 79. I had met him in December 2001, the year he and wife Peggy had celebrated their golden wedding anniversary.

'I thought he was ghastly when I first saw him,' laughed Peg. 'I was at teacher training college in London. It was my twenty-first birthday party and we needed a spare man, so I sent a telegram home for my brother [Vic Speck, a successful jump jockey] to come up. He brought George with him. He was wearing a Prince of Wales checked suit – I thought I'd never seen anything so loud in all my life – and he went home and told my brother he was going to marry me.'

Peg had previously maintained that she 'would never, ever marry a jockey.' It was a statement born from harsh reality. She was only five when her father, Billy Speck, died five days after having his kidneys crushed in a fall from a poor selling chaser at Cheltenham in April 1935. Among the most stylish and popular jump jockeys of his time, Speck had excelled round Liverpool, winning the Stanley Chase and Champion Chase on Double Crossed, plus a hat-trick of Becher Chases on Thomond II. He rode Thomond II to third place in the 1934 and '35 Grand Nationals and was twice runner-up on him to Golden Miller in the Cheltenham Gold Cup. The famous Gold Cup finish of 1935 provided a duel every bit as memorable as that of Royal Tan and Tudor Line. But within a month, Speck was dead.

All the popularity counted for nought after he succumbed to his injuries. Peg recalled: 'In the first few months after he died, my mother was inundated with people wanting mementoes. Then it all very quickly dried up and nobody wanted to know her. She was very bitter and didn't want anything more to do with horse racing after that.'

It was two years after Billy Speck's death that a young George Slack entered racing. Born at Threapland Hall in Cumberland on the last day of March 1923, he was the son of a sporting farmer who stood a stallion at stud. George rode show jumping at local shows before becoming apprenticed to John Cockton – a friend of his father's – at Little Stukeley, near Huntingdon.

He had a couple of rides on the Flat in 1940 but broke a thigh when schooling the following year, necessitating the deferment of his military service. It was May 1947 before he rode his first winner, a 20-1 shot named Skipper, trained by Harry Marshall at Winterfield in Yorkshire, in a two-mile handicap chase at Wetherby.

His first two Grand National rides came courtesy of Gallery, trained by William 'Rip' Bissill. In 1949 they were brought down three out by the riderless Cloncarrig. In 1950 they departed at Becher's first time.

George rode Gerry Wilson's Morning Cover in 1951 but again got no further than Becher's. However, he enjoyed a far better ride the following year when Printer's Pie, also trained by Wilson, put in a clear round to finish sixth of the ten finishers.

By this time George was riding for Charlie Hall, who trained at Towton, near Tadcaster. Coupled with the job of stable jockey came a retainer to ride Clifford Nicholson's horses. These included Stormhead, on whom he won the 1952 Emblem Chase at Manchester.

It was Hall who supplied his 1953 Grand National mount, Witty. George had already won the Eider Chase and the Haydock National Trial on him and recalled: 'He was a good horse but he had a screw loose. He got into trouble if you asked him to do anything quick. If you gave him a kick and a slap down the shoulder, he'd miss. He'd gallop forever and always had a chance at four miles-plus, but at Becher's second time he hit the fence hard and I didn't survive. He didn't fall, it was rider unseated.'

At the start of the 1953/54 season Nicholson brought Paddy Farrell over from Ireland to be his retained jockey. Although George was still able to ride all of the other horses in the yard, on Hall's suggestion he accepted a retainer from Ripon-based Bobby Renton.

The new partnership made the best possible start at Liverpool's November

meeting, winning two of the three races over the National fences, the Molyneux Chase with Little Yid and the Becher Chase with Freebooter. For good
measure, George also landed the November Hurdle on Neville Crump's Blackpool, a lucky spare ride replacing the injured Peter Chisman, who had broken
a collarbone at Newcastle.

George came in for another 'spare' that season, stepping in for the sidelined
Fred Winter on Bill Wightman's Halloween in the Cheltenham Gold Cup.
Halloween ran his customary gallant race, finishing third to Four Ten.

The opening day of the 1954 Liverpool Spring Meeting brought further
success for the Renton-Slack partnership when Little Yid won the Topham
Trophy. Little Yid, one of relatively few twins to make a successful racehorse,
was a true Aintree specialist, winning the Molyneux Chase three times as well
as finishing first and second in the Topham. Camp confidence ran high for the
Grand National prospects of another horse from Renton's yard. His name was
Tudor Line, a nine-year-old chestnut gelding by King Hal, owned by Mrs Edna
Truelove and set to carry 10st 7lb.

Said George: 'The first time I sat on Tudor Line was at Ayr in January 1954
when he won a two-mile chase. The next time I sat on him was at Sandown
when he won again over two and a half. Then Bobby Renton sent him to Cheltenham for the Mildmay of Flete and he won that, despite meeting the last
fence wrong and diving through it. He was unbeaten that season prior to the
National, three runs, three wins. I really fancied him, even though he hadn't
run over more than two and a half miles.

'He hit the first fence very hard. He didn't get high enough and nearly fell.
After that mistake he started hanging to the right. I think he'd just frightened
himself at the first fence; they were a bit harder than he thought. I started on the
inside but I finished up jumping Becher's towards the outside.

'I lost ground at the Canal Turn because he was still going out to the right.
The leaders were already jumping Valentine's Brook and I was really worried
until I noticed that Royal Tan and Irish Lizard were also back with us. After that
he straightened himself up and we began to improve our position. I think we
jumped the water around fourteenth. He picked up on the second circuit and
we were about fourth jumping Becher's.

'I went second to Pat Taaffe on Coneyburrow at the fourth last, but Pat's
horse fell and broke his back. I was left in front and at the third from home I
thought I'd win, although I knew Bryan Marshall wasn't far behind on Royal
Tan. Tos Taaffe, Pat's brother, was with me on Churchtown but his horse burst a
blood vessel, so I was left to go on again over the second last. Then Bryan came
past me between the last two as though he'd beat me ten lengths.

'Bryan jumped the last about two and a half lengths in front of me. My horse
was tired and ran down the fence; he was hanging, meeting it all wrong and,
instead of putting in a short one, he went skew-whiff. He jumped to the right
and I gave him a slap down the shoulder to wake him up.

'When we got to the Elbow I saw Royal Tan's backside wobble. You know a horse is getting tired when that happens. I gave Tudor Line a good smack and from there I thought we might catch him.'

Gaining with every stride, Tudor Line relentlessly closed the gap. Royal Tan was stopping fast and conceding 14lb to his pursuer. The two chestnuts were giving all they had left and, with 50 yards to go, Tudor Line was at Royal Tan's quarters and gaining inch by inch.

'When we passed the post, Bryan looked across at me and asked "Did you win?" I said "No, I didn't," to which he replied "Well I don't think I did, so it's got to be a dead heat." Those were Bryan's words.'

The judge decreed that the winning post had come just in time for Royal Tan. In the absence of a photo finish he declared the official winning distance to be a neck, but it was never as much as that.

'Royal Tan was stone cold,' concluded George. 'It's my belief that had anyone but Bryan Marshall been on him, we would have won.'

Alex Bird's autobiography *The Life and Secrets of a Professional Punter* makes great play of the fact that victory for Tudor Line would have netted him around half a million. Bird also alludes to Bobby Renton's decision to leave the pricker off for the race, this being a small brush that 'was always fitted to Tudor Line's bit to stop him jumping to the right, which he had a habit of doing.' He insists that the absence of the pricker made the difference between victory and defeat. It didn't.

The reality is that Tudor Line had never worn a pricker. George was adamant about that. The late Jimmy FitzGerald, who looked after the horse at the time, confirmed the jockey's assertion.

Said George: 'When you ride a horse for the first time, the first thing you do is look what sort of bridle it's got on. I never saw Tudor Line wear a brush pricker. Fred Winter once said to me "That's a right-handed horse running on a left-handed track", yet he'd won round Ayr and Cheltenham.

'Tudor Line lay down for three days after the National. Bobby wanted to give him one more run as soon as he could to let him forget about Aintree, then get him out to grass. So he ran him in a three-mile chase at Wetherby's Easter meeting, where Tim Molony on Bramble Tudor beat me half a length.'

Five days later, George gained a measure of compensation for his Aintree defeat when winning the Scottish Grand National on the Herbert Clarkson-trained Queen's Taste. This was the second of Queen's Taste's three triumphs in the race which, until its move to Ayr in 1966, was run at Bogside.

Tudor Line's 1954/55 campaign was inevitably geared towards Aintree in March, yet there was to be an unusual beginning. Conscious of the fact that the horse had not won over hurdles, Renton started him off in a novices' hurdle at Wetherby at the start of October. But the horse fell and fractured his skull.

'He met it wrong and ignored it,' George told me. 'He was a big, strong horse and he tried to kick it out of the way but it didn't work. It took three men to lift him into the box and it was eight o'clock before he could be removed from the racecourse. He didn't run again until Cheltenham's New Year meeting when he finished third.'

After the Cheltenham race, Renton took Tudor Line to Manchester for the Lancashire Chase over three and a half miles. He also ran the mare No Response, ridden by Derek Ancil. Despite conceding from 12lb to 34lb to his ten rivals, Tudor Line put up a fine performance, getting up close home to beat No Response by a neck.

'I got up in the last couple of strides,' recalled George. 'He'd carried a fair weight and when I got off him, Bobby said "We've probably left our National there", yet he ran him again in the Great Yorkshire Chase the following week – that was more likely to have lost him the National.'

Tudor Line finished a well beaten seventh in the Great Yorkshire, his last start before Liverpool.

The going was soft for the opening day, which saw Clifford Nicholson's Stormhead win the Topham Trophy in the hands of Paddy Farrell, while George emerged unscathed from a fall on Renton's Sunavon at the fence after Becher's. By Saturday, however, the official going description was changed to heavy. It was barely fit for racing and, for the first time, the water jump was omitted due to the area around it being waterlogged.

Tudor Line had 11st 3lb to carry and started 10-1 third favourite behind Paddy Sleator's Irish raider Copp at 7-1 and the 1953 hero Early Mist at nines. Fourth in the betting at 100-9 was Vincent O'Brien's Quare Times, who revelled in the conditions and romped home by twelve lengths from the luckless Tudor Line.

'It was too wet to be holding, so I don't think the ground was against him,' reflected George. 'There was standing water and they'd dolled us to the outside parts of the last two fences. Quare Times simply galloped through it as though it was hard ground.

'After Tudor Line had finished second in his second National, Bobby said that he wouldn't be going back a third time. I told Bobby that I wouldn't run him in the National again but he deserved to be a winner round Aintree, and he'd win the Sefton.'

Tudor Line began his 1955/56 campaign with a second place behind Lochroe in the Grand Sefton Trial at Hurst Park. He was made a warm 7-4 favourite for the Grand Sefton itself but, after being in contention approaching two out, he faded to finish fifth.

'Both years before the National I rode work on Tudor Line at Ripon racecourse, yet in all the time I rode for Bobby Renton the only time I went to Oxclose [Renton's yard] was after Tudor Line had finished second in his first National. And that was to have my photograph taken on three horses, Little Yid, Tudor Line and Freebooter, for the *Great Horses of the Year* book.

'I never rode a school on his gallops. The only work I rode for him was at a racecourse after racing.'

It was a schooling fall at Catterick that so nearly ended George's career, on 4 January 1956.

'I rode a little horse called Scottish Sea. Tim Molony went up to school with me. Bobby told us to jump the four fences in the straight. I said to Tim "Don't get near a wing with that fellow because he'll lug out with you. He isn't a bad jumper but he does pull."

'We jumped the first fence down by the five furlong start. Tim then took a pull because he thought he might be run away with, leaving me in front. Mine just caught the top of the second and fell. It was an easy fall but he kicked me across the ankle. Molony pulled up before the next fence and came back. As I lay there rubbing my ankle he said "Come on, get up, you're all right." I went to sit up but I couldn't. My arm had gone.'

Not only had George dislocated and shattered his left shoulder, but the muscles and nerves were also injured. He spent a month at Harrogate General Hospital with his arm in a splint and underwent eleven operations. The bone became diseased and, eventually, was removed altogether. He was left with no shoulder joint, just muscle and fibrous tissue.

He was out of action for 21 months, missing the whole of the 1956/57 season. He resumed at Stratford in October 1957 but had to wait nearly eight weeks before riding his first winner back, Incompatible at Haydock. By then Jumbo Wilkinson was riding the Renton horses, making the comeback an uphill struggle.

But his luck changed at Cheltenham in 1958 when he rode Stan Wright's Bandalore to victory in the Champion Hurdle, getting up on the run-in to beat Dave Dick on the favourite, Tokoroa, by two lengths.

Two days later he went close to landing the Gold Cup when, riding Polar Flight, he was involved in a sustained duel with Stan Hayhurst on Kerstin over the last two fences. But in the end it was the mare that battled on to deny Polar Flight by half a length.

He then came in for the mount on Tiberetta in the Grand National. He'd ridden her on her previous start, finishing second to course specialist Cement City at Wolverhampton in bottomless ground. Alan Oughton was Tiberetta's usual partner but he was claimed to ride Eagle Lodge for Matt Feakes. Hating the soft going, Tiberetta nonetheless battled on to finish a distant second to Mr What, the third time George had been runner-up in the world's most famous steeplechase.

His 1959 Grand National partner was Bobby Renton's grey gelding Glorious Twelfth, who had finished fourth behind Sundew two years earlier, but they were brought down at Becher's first time round.

The rides dried up during what was to be his last season, 1960/61. His sole winner came courtesy of Pat Moore's juvenile hurdler Rosebud at Market Rasen on Boxing Day. With only 42 rides all season, George journeyed to Aintree in March 1961 as a mere spectator to watch the race in which he had three times finished second. But when Terry Biddlecombe injured a wrist in a fall from Tokoroa in the Mildmay Chase on the Friday, John Lawrence (now Lord

Oaksey) put him on standby to ride Kingstel for his father-in-law Ginger
Dennistoun. Could there be one last hurrah?

'He'd only won a novice chase at Wolverhampton,' recalled George, 'and that
was more than two years ago.

'Ginger arrived at the racecourse stables about twenty past eight on Saturday
morning and asked me what I thought of the horse. I said "He's alright. What
do you want him to do?" He replied "Nothing. Put him back in the stable." I
said "You don't want me to canter him, then?" He said "No; if he sees those
fences the shock will kill him!"

'I had a super ride to Becher's but he picked Becher's to miss out. Something
kicked me and knocked me unconscious. When I came round in the ambulance, my legs were strapped together so I asked what that was for. They said
"You've broken your leg". I said "No I haven't. I broke the other one and I know
what that feels like".

'That was my last ride, I retired that day. I'd only gone up to watch the
National and I ended up with a ride in it.

'I'd already got a farm at Saxby, near Melton Mowbray, mostly stock, a herd
of cows; we lambed ewes and sold them at the breeding sales. After nine years
there we moved to a bigger farm at Gunby, three miles from Colsterworth, and
had that for twenty years. We gave up in 1988 when I reached sixty-five.'

While he was off injured in 1956/57 he was invited to assist the judge at
Huntingdon races. Once he retired, Huntingdon's Clerk of the Course wrote to
Weatherbys seeking permission to grant him a judge's licence. He duly became
the first former jockey to officiate as a judge. He later served both as judge and
starter at Garthorpe, his local point-to-point course.

George had video recordings of the highlights from his years in the saddle,
though he rarely watched them. Not that the Grand Nationals were too painful
to recall; not a bit of it.

'I had three memorable rides round Aintree and enjoyed every minute,' he
insisted. 'I consider myself lucky to have partnered such good horses.'

Date: Saturday 27 March 1954 Going: Good Value to Winner: £8,571 10s

Horse	Owner	Trainer	Age / weight	Jockey	SP
1 Royal Tan	Mr J H Griffin	M V O'Brien	10-11-7	B Marshall	8-1
2 Tudor Line	Mrs E Truelove	R Renton	9-10-7	G Slack	10-1
3 Irish Lizard	Lord Sefton	H Nicholson	11-10-5	M Scudamore	15-2fav
4 Churchtown	Mrs M V O'Brien	M V O'Brien	9-10-3	T Taaffe	10-1

Distances: neck, 10 lengths, 6 lengths. Time: 9 mins 32 4/5 secs. 29 ran

Winner trained at Cashel, County Tipperary, Ireland

1955

REX HAMEY
Everything was muddy and wet

Rex Hamey on Clearing, his 1955 Grand National mount.

'A LOT OF them thought he was Irish but he was born in Grantham,' says Rex Hamey of his father. 'Even the local paper, the day after he'd won the National, had him down as "the Irish jockey Tim Hamey".'

Christened James Henry Hamey, he was a leading Cheltenham-based jockey of the 1920s and 30s, winning the Gold Cup in 1926 on Koko and the 1932 Grand National on Forbra. However, in an era when the names of cross-country jockeys (as they were often referred to) were not as familiar as their Flat racing counterparts, the newspapers continually referred to him as Tim rather than Jim, leading Hamey to adopt the 'if you can't beat 'em, join 'em' philosophy.

Son Rex was born at Bishops Cleeve in 1929. Among his earliest memories is that of walking to Cheltenham racecourse in 1935 and witnessing the epic Gold Cup duel between Thomond II and Golden Miller. But his scrapbooks bear witness to sporting achievements of a different kind, both on the wing for Cheltenham Rugby Club and as a county standard 100/220 yards sprinter. However, as the son of a Grand National winning jockey, racing was always going take precedence over rugby and athletics.

After the war, Tim Hamey trained a string at Moat Farm on the Prestbury Park estate. He supplied Rex with his first winners on Sahara, who scored twice over Newton Abbot's 1950 Easter meeting.

Rex's first two Grand National rides ended in disappointment. Frenchie Nicholson's Irish Lizard had been one of ten first-fence casualties in 1952, while in 1954 his father's Hierba was was prevented from jumping the Chair when loose horses forced him into the left-hand wing. But in 1955 he came in for a ride with more than an outside chance, the Willie Stephenson-trained seven-year-old Clearing.

Clearing belonged to Maurice Kingsley, owner of triple champion hurdler, Sir Ken. Rex had ridden him just once before, when second to Tudor Line in the Victory Chase at Manchester in January 1953.

The weather leading up to the 1955 Grand National had been so wet that there were serious doubts about whether the race would take place. The stewards held an inspection at 11.00 a.m. and gave the go-ahead with the proviso that the water jump would be omitted, as the ground around it was virtually waterlogged. Not that the remainder of the course was much better.

Vincent O'Brien had won the last two Grand Nationals with Early Mist and Royal Tan, and many believed that his representative Quare Times, winner of the National Hunt Chase at Cheltenham the previous season, had an outstanding chance of making it three in a row. But as the ground got heavier and heavier, the trainer's confidence steadily waned.

'It was a horrible day,' recalls Rex. 'Everything was muddy and wet. Willie Stephenson didn't even want me to canter Clearing on the morning of the race. As we were going down to the start, a lot of mud was being kicked up and it was coming down in a sort of shower. The reins on his bridle were worn and the mud made them very slippery.

'I intended to go down the middle. Clearing wasn't a fast horse out of the gate but they didn't go particularly fast. He was easy enough to guide and you felt balanced over all the obstacles. You could put him where you wanted at a fence and you knew he'd measure it and jump it, which was a nice feeling, though it was a battle to keep his head off the ground when he landed at the drops.

'I was never going well enough to win. I was trying to get placed. Up to the Canal Turn second time he was holding his position and I hadn't been too worried. But from the Canal Turn I could never get hold of him to push him forward because of the slippery reins. The leaders were twenty lengths in front and I was never really in contention from then on. You can't pick up in heavy ground and a horse can't bounce off dead ground.

'We finished seventh. There's a possibility that I might have finished closer if I'd been able to give more assistance.'

Up front, O'Brien's pessimism proved unfounded as Quare Times, ridden by Pat Taaffe, revelled in the heavy going. In front at the Canal Turn, he was headed briefly by the previous year's runner-up Tudor Line, and by Carey's Cottage, the mount of Tos Taaffe, Pat's brother. Once in the straight, however, Quare Times took command and came home twelve lengths clear of Tudor Line, with Carey's Cottage third.

In spite of the desperate conditions, thirteen of the 30 runners completed the course and none of the fallen horses or riders was injured.

A fortnight later, Clearing and Rex were reunited in the Welsh Grand National at Chepstow. Running a fine race without quite being good enough, Clearing finished third, beaten only a length and a half by Monaleen and Sundew.

Remarkably, Clearing and Rex took part in their third Grand National within a month, the Scottish version at Bogside. The good ground was in their favour but they were brought to a halt when Arthur Thompson's mount Much Obliged fell in front of them five out.

It was 7 January 1956 before a horse named Yes To-day broke a sequence of 57 losing rides to get Rex off the mark for that season. Two weeks later he doubled his tally by winning the Mildmay Memorial Chase on Linwell.

A royal victory had looked on the cards at the last fence, where the Queen Mother's Devon Loch went into a narrow lead. But Linwell, carrying just 9st 9lb, dug deep and regained the lead with 60 yards to go and then repelled the strong late challenge of the favourite, Wise Child. Devon Loch could finish only third. It was not the last time he would flatter to deceive his royal owner. His Grand National collapse was but two months away.

The hard-pulling Athenian was Rex's mount in that infamous 1956 Grand National. Gerald Balding had recently bought him in Ireland for Colonel Bill Whitbread, along with the previous year's third, Carey's Cottage. Rex recalls: 'Ted Greenway rode him in the Kim Muir at Cheltenham. He ran away with him going to the start and in the race, so it wasn't with any confidence that I set out in the National.

'My father rode Grakle in the 1929 Grand National, the first time that he'd worn the cross nose-band they later named after him. Grakle was a hard-pulling horse but my father told me that once he'd got him round the first circuit he dropped the bit, came back to him and gave him a super ride on the second circuit. I was hoping Athenian would do the same but he never took off at the twelfth.'

The following year Rex rode the American challenger Monkey Wrench. 'Well balanced but too slow,' was the rider's verdict, having pulled him up at halfway.

He had married the daughter of Upton-upon-Severn trainer Jack Yeomans in 1956 and thereafter rode as stable jockey. Yeomans turned out plenty of winners, despite the fact that few, if any, of his horses had cost more than 160 guineas. Star of the yard was the grey gelding Branca Doria, bought at Ascot for just 45 guineas, on whom Rex won the valuable November Hurdle at Liverpool in 1960.

Another high-profile victory came his way the following month aboard Willie Stephenson's Vivant in Cheltenham's Fred Withington Chase. Vivant would now be aimed at the 1961 Grand National and Rex would have the mount.

Campaigned in the highest company throughout that season, Branca Doria had finished sixth in the Champion Hurdle, fourth in the County Hurdle and fifth in the Imperial Cup all in the space of ten days. He started third favourite for the Liverpool Handicap Hurdle, the opening race on Grand National day, but fell at the last flight, resulting in four broken ribs for Rex and a missed Grand National ride. David Nicholson was given the late call up on Vivant and was up there when parting company at the Chair.

Vivant ran in the following year's Grand National but was well out of contention when Rex pulled him up three out. He returned for a third attempt in 1963 but departed at the Canal Turn first time round in unusual circumstances.

Recalls Rex: 'We went into the Canal Turn with a horse on the inside of us. Having been there before, Vivant knew where he was. He landed and turned but the horse on the inside of us went straight on. My horse ducked under the other horse's neck, and that horse's head came over Vivant's neck and swept me off.'

By then his career was nearing its end. He'd suffered the downs – crushed vertebrae incurred in falls at Towcester and Nottingham – but enjoyed the ups, none more so than when riding Bud Flanagan's last winner, Stenimonk at Newton Abbot in August 1961. He still treasures the hand-written letter Flanagan sent him and recalls being invited to take his sons to see the Crazy Gang show for free at Victoria Palace.

Rex brought his own curtain down at the end of 1963, having ridden his last winner on Willie Stephenson's Pappa Three Ways at Southwell on 14 December. He took over as manager of Stephenson's Tudor Stud at Buntingford, seven miles south of Royston, and stayed there for sixteen years before moving back to the Cotswolds, where he became involved in preparing the submission for a minimum wage for stable staff.

Convinced of racing's need to modernise itself, he joined the staff of Witney College, setting up racing industry courses and lecturing thereon. Titled 'The Science and Husbandry of the Thoroughbred Horse', the courses dealt with varying facets of the racing industry, such as breeding, training and racecourse management. In 1982 he published his first book, *Working With Horses*.

He ran the courses until reaching retirement age of 65 in 1994. He then went to Dubai for six weeks and ended up staying five years.

The move came at the invitation of a Dubaian businessman who wanted to breed horses to race in Dubai. 'He'd bought some mares in foal,' explains Rex. 'I'd gone for a six-week all expenses paid holiday but he needed someone experienced with broodmares and rearing foals, so I agreed to stay for six months.

'It was called Al Aweer Farm, located 30 kilometres from Dubai city in the middle of a desert. It had started as a date farm and we had to pump water up from 100 metres down. There were sixteen horses when I arrived. The sixteen grew to 150, a mix of Thoroughbreds and Arabs.

'I left Dubai at the end of 2000. At the age of 72 I thought that was long enough.'

He is now back in Cheltenham, a mere stone's throw from the racecourse. His years of experience in the breeding industry, coupled with his appreciation of the analysis of proteins and nutrients, made him an expert in his field.

Date: Saturday 26 March 1955 Going: Heavy Value to Winner: £8,934 10s

Horse	Owner	Trainer	Age / weight	Jockey	SP
1 Quare Times	Mr W H E Welman	M V O'Brien	9-11-0	P Taaffe	100-9
2 Tudor Line	Mrs E Truelove	R Renton	10-11-3	G Slack	10-1
3 Carey's Cottage	Mr D J Coughlan	T J Taaffe	8-10-11	T Taaffe	20-1
4 Gigolo	Mrs M Milne Green	J S Wight	10-11-3	R Curran	100-6

Distances: 12 lengths, 4 lengths, 2 lengths. Time: 10 mins 20 3/5 secs. 30 ran

Winner trained at Cashel, County Tipperary, Ireland

1956

GEORGE MILBURN
The mystery of Devon Loch

George Milburn aboard Gentle Moya.

ONE PIECE OF Grand National footage is guaranteed an airing each time the race comes round. It's black and white sports newsreel at its most dramatic. The voice of Bob Danvers-Walker captures the moment:

'Into the final straight with victory in sight for Devon Loch. He's clear away from E.S.B. and Gentle Moya. Only 40 yards to go, Devon Loch can't lose … but he's slipped, he's down … '

E.S.B. and Dave Dick were thus gifted the 1956 Grand National a few strides from the winning post and the mystery of the Queen Mother's horse's sensational collapse is still debated whenever the National is discussed.

People asked Dick Francis, Devon Loch's jockey, about it ever after; likewise the late Dave Dick was quizzed about the mystery throughout his life. But not many asked George Milburn, rider of the runner-up.

Gentle Moya was George's first Grand National ride, though he was not devoid of course experience, having partnered her to victory in the Grand Sefton earlier that season. He had also finished third on Wise Child in that year's Topham.

Born in Corbridge, Northumberland, in August 1932, George grew up among horses, his father running a successful livery stable and riding school. He trod the traditional path of rural shows, pony club, show jumping, hunting and point-to-pointing, followed by occasional rides under Rules in hunter chases.

His first winner was at Hexham on the Saturday of Whitsun 1953, riding Hurgill Lad for local permit holder Max Smith. The second came ten days later at Sedgefield, a special meeting held on Coronation Day. A few hours after the crowning of Queen Elizabeth II, George steered Bristol Fashion to victory in the day's big race, the Coronation Handicap Chase.

'I took agriculture at university in Newcastle,' he says. 'I graduated in 1953 and my father went to see Major [Calverly] Bewicke, to ask if he'd got a vacancy for me on the farm as manager or assistant manager. He said that I could be his assistant farm manager and I could also ride as an amateur for him.'

But George was so successful in that first season (1953/54) that he was obliged to turn professional when the next one started.

Among the horses in Major Bewicke's Shawdon Hall Stables, to the west of Alnwick, was Gentle Moya, a bay mare by Steel-point, owned – and usually ridden – by John Straker. He won several races on her, including Newcastle's Eider Chase, and rode her in two Grand Nationals, falling at the first in 1954 but finishing sixth behind Quare Times the following year. He was due to partner her again in 1956 but was prevented by injury. Having won the Grand Sefton on her, George was the logical replacement.

'She was a lovely ride; all you had to do was steer her. You could settle her in where you wanted. She was very clever and made few errors jumping. She'd pop short, she'd stand off; you didn't have to organise her.

'My idea, especially with so many runners, was to jump off and try to get up there with the leaders to keep out of trouble.

'The race went well; I was always handy and the mare jumped like a buck, except that she made a bad mistake at the Canal Turn second time. It knocked the stuffing out of her and I could never get her going again. My chance of winning had gone by the time we crossed the Melling Road. We were cut for speed but she kept plugging on at one pace. Over the last I was ten lengths behind E.S.B. and he was ten lengths behind Devon Loch. I would have been third if Devon Loch hadn't spread-eagled.

'I saw it happen. He just dropped, hind legs out, forelegs forward, then got up and stood there. Francis was off the horse and standing beside him, so Dave Dick had to swerve past him, whereas I was about twenty lengths behind and had time to pull round.

'Everybody's got ideas about what happened, whether it was the crowd, or he saw the water jump, or baulked at a shadow. Personally, I don't think it was any of them.

'The following season Devon Loch ran four times, won twice and was second twice, all in races of two-and-a-half or three miles. Probably his best effort was in the King George VI Chase at Kempton, but it wasn't a good race that year, because I finished third on Wise Child who was just a north-country handicapper.

'Then in January I rode Green Drill in the Mildmay Memorial Chase at Sandown. Dick Francis had just retired so Arthur Freeman rode Devon Loch. He finished fourth and I finished seventh or eighth but quite close up, five lengths behind Devon Loch. We passed the winning post and were pulling up when he did exactly the same thing he'd done at Liverpool. Not as bad, but he went down and then got straight back up on his feet. I don't think anyone noticed from the stands because we pulled up right behind a building at the side of the track, just after the winning post.

'I think it was muscular cramp, a muscular problem that overtook him when he was getting very tired. They were both long-distance races, Liverpool four-and-a-half miles and Sandown's was three miles five. I don't think it had anything to do with crowds or shadows or anything like that. I think it was purely some form of cramp, a muscular seizure that he got when fatigued. After that Sandown race he never ran again.'

George came within a length of winning the 1957 Cheltenham Gold Cup on Kerstin, being outgunned in the closing stages by Michael Scudamore on Linwell. Kerstin was to have her day twelve months later but with Stan Hayhurst in the saddle. George and Stan were both stable jockeys to Major Bewicke, enjoying an amicable arrangement whereby each rode for different owners.

George and Gentle Moya were reunited for the '57 Grand National but trailed home last of the eleven finishers, after which the mare was retired. Luckily, Bewicke had a ready-made Aintree replacement in Lord Cadogan's Green Drill, although the two horses could not have been more different.

'Green Drill was a big, rangy horse, whereas Gentle Moya was a stockily built, compact mare,' George recalls. 'Green Drill was the hardest I ever rode. You were pushing, kicking and scrubbing before you got to the first fence. He was as idle as could be; you just had to keep at him.'

George and Green Drill went off as lively 28-1 outsiders for the 1958 Grand National and finished third behind Mr What and Tiberetta. His delighted owner later wrote to George: 'I have not forgotten how brilliantly you rode Green Drill in the National. I am absolutely certain that no other jockey could have done what you have with that horse.'

The following year they were put out of the race at the Canal Turn second time round, but finished sixth on their third and final attempt in 1960.

George's next Grand National ride was on the former hunter chaser Duplicator in 1962. 'He was very hard to hold. I told all the lads down at the gate, "I won't be able to hold him so if I go on in front, for God's sake don't chase me". There was an Irishman named Frankie Shortt [on Fredith's Son] who took no bloody notice and he kept having a go and chasing me on. At every fence he kept disappearing and then he was back again. By the time we got to the nineteenth, a big ditch, about twenty yards before we got there, I felt my horse heave a deep breath and he never left the ground, went head over tail and that was the end of our race.'

Rainbow Battle was his final Grand National mount in 1965. 'I was riding for Ken Oliver by then,' says George, 'but he didn't have a runner in the race. Bill Shand Kydd had bought her to ride in the National but had broken his collarbone the week before, so I filled in. I'd never even seen the horse until I went into the paddock. When I saw her I thought she was just a pony. When I cantered her to the start I was up among her ears, her neck was so short.

'I felt sure I'd be on the floor because she wasn't at all robust. We jumped off and I got nicely settled in, went to the first and pinged it. Went to the next, same again. She never put a foot wrong all the way. I never looked like winning but I had a super ride round and finished fourth.'

Around that time Ken Oliver had taken possession of a bay gelding called Arctic Sunset. George rode him in all his races during the 1965/66 campaign, culminating in victory in the Cotswold Chase at the Cheltenham Festival. The following season they finished a close third to Drinny's Double and Pawnbroker in the 1967 Two Mile Champion Chase.

As September 1967 loomed, George realised that, at 34, he was in the autumn of his riding career. 'I had it in my mind that I was going to ride that season because I had Arctic Sunset and I thought I could win a Gold Cup on him. I was going to pick my rides; I wasn't going to do anything silly.

'I went down to Market Rasen at the start of September for one ride for Ken and I won. Then I went to Sedgefield a week later and had a ride there [unplaced]. I was already fired up to go to Perth as usual, then Ken rang me up and told me that Arctic Sunset's owner didn't want me to ride him. He wanted Barry Brogan. Ken said it wasn't his decision but if he wouldn't let Brogan ride it, the owner was going to take the horse away. I said "Fair enough Ken, I'm finished". Simple as that; I never rode again.'

George had had a smallholding while still riding and, after announcing his retirement, built up a poultry farm for egg production. He subsequently bought a fruit and veg shop in Alnwick, then added a delicatessen. 'I ran both businesses for quite a while, then I sold the poultry farm and concentrated on the shop. I ran the shop for twenty years until I decided to retire in 1994.'

But the word 'retirement' didn't extend to racing. 'I still go racing quite a lot,' he says, 'and I've always been involved in point-to-pointing. I was clerk of the scales at three point-to-points and starter at two others, so I had five jobs in the spring, all of which I thoroughly enjoyed.'

Date: Saturday 24 March 1956 Going: Good Value to Winner: £8,695 5s

Horse	Owner	Trainer	Age / weight	Jockey	SP
1 E.S.B.	Mrs L Carver	F Rimell	10-11-3	D V Dick	100-7
2 Gentle Moya	Mr J J Straker	C Bewicke	10-10-2	G Milburn	22-1
3 Royal Tan	Prince Aly Khan	M V O'Brien	12-12-1	T Taaffe	28-1
4 Eagle Lodge	Mr N A Mardon	M Feakes	7-10-1	A Oughton	66-1

Distances: 12 lengths, 4 lengths, 2 lengths. Time: 10 mins 20 3/5 secs. 30 ran

Winner trained at Kinnersley, Worcestershire

1957

SIR PIERS BENGOUGH
A very special place indeed

Charles Dickens and Major Piers Bengough jump the last fence to win the 1970 Grand Military Gold Cup.

SIR PIERS BENGOUGH loved being at Aintree on Grand National day. He attended for the last time shortly before his death, aged 75, in April 2005.

'It's always been a wonderful racecourse,' he said when I'd met him three years earlier. 'The atmosphere is unique, different from the Cheltenham Festival. The anticipation all around gives one a great thrill.

'Riding out on Grand National morning, seeing all the horses, some just trotting round, others cantering up the straight; the connections having a look round; the chat, the excitement; that's when the real atmosphere begins to build up.

'And whenever I was riding there I'd be thinking "I can't have any breakfast; I've got to do ten stone!"'

'It is a very special place indeed.'

His other favourite racecourse was Sandown Park, home of the Grand Military Meeting, for so long a traditional part of the jumping scene. And back in 1957, when Colonel Bengough was a mere captain, juggling his amateur rider career with military duties, he rode in both the Grand Military Gold Cup and the Grand National too.

He belonged to the Cavalry Regiment, the 10th Hussars, which boasted a long tradition of soldier riders, both in racing and on the polo field. Graduating via hunting and point-to-points he rode out for Alec Kilpatrick, who trained at Collingbourne Ducis, near Marlborough, and had his own tradition of grooming soldiers in the art of race riding.

'I rode Eastern Chance for Alec in that 1957 Grand Military Gold Cup,' he recalled. 'He was a horse that never really got three miles and wasn't quite fast enough for two miles. Alec clearly thought I'd ridden a very moderate race to finish third. When I got off and said "Doesn't stay", he made some non-committal remark and walked away. I was a bit depressed and, clearly, he was upset.

'As I was leaving the racecourse I passed the members' bar and saw the old boy at the bar by himself having a drink, so I thought I'd go and make amends. He was sitting there with the evening paper. I said "Sorry". In sheer rage he picked up the paper and hit me across the face with it. I was slightly surprised, but more so when, almost immediately, he said "Will you ride one for me in the National?"

'The horse was Go-Well. I'd never ridden him but I'd seen him when riding out my own horse in the morning. The next time I was down there I got on him. He took a hell of a hold, a very strong horse, difficult to ride. I then found out that Alan Lillingston had been offered the ride but had got off it because he'd got the chance of a better one. As it turned out, Alan's fell at the first and I fell at the third.

'My lasting memory is the excitement and atmosphere of the paddock before getting up. Once I'd got onto the horse I felt it was up to me and the buzz of what was going on was rather forgotten.

'I remember the start very well because I was pretty concerned whether I was going to get run away with. Because he took such a hold, I didn't want to be up in the front so I thought I'd try and jump him off behind the front line. I elected to go down the middle as I didn't think that going up the inner was a sensible thing for an amateur to do.

'The tapes went up and before I knew where I was, I was in the first third of the field. Being such a wide racecourse with the runners spread right across, it's not the easiest thing in the world to tuck your horse behind something, shut out the daylight and get him settled. I think that's perhaps why I fell so early on.

'He jumped the first brilliantly. At the second fence I think he couldn't believe they were quite as big as that. By the third, you are going at such a speed that, if you don't get your stride right at the ditch, you have little chance of clearing it. You might scramble over and get away with it but Go-Well landed on his nose and down he went.

'I remember walking back towards the start, standing with a number of jockeys and trying to see the rest of the race.'

Armorial's fourth-fence fall had left the massive Sundew in front, and, despite barging holes through some of the fences, there he stayed, coming home eight lengths clear of Wyndburgh to give Fred Winter his first Grand National victory.

Sundew was one of just ten horses trained by Frank Hudson at his Botley Hill Farm stables, on the outskirts of Henley-in-Arden. Sadly, later that year, Sundew broke a shoulder at Haydock Park when falling at the water. He was buried on the course, near to where he met his end.

Sir Piers achieved 'the ultimate aim for a soldier rider' when winning the 1960 Grand Military Gold Cup on his own horse, Joan's Rival. He trained regimental horses whilst stationed in Germany in the early sixties and rode over jumps and on the Flat.

'Those in command were very understanding. I used to save up all my leave, come back to England at the beginning of March and stay until the middle of April. I tried to cram in as much riding as I could in that period. When I was stationed in England it was reasonably easy to take the odd day off to go race riding.'

Then along came a horse named April Rose. 'I bought him through Eddie Harty, who was Alec Kilpatrick's stable jockey at the time, primarily to win the Grand Military Gold Cup,' he said. 'To have a chance of winning that race is probably the limit of a soldier rider's horizon and it became a feature of my life.'

April Rose could finish only third in the 1965 Grand Military Gold Cup but then gave his owner-rider the thrill of completing the course in that year's Grand National, coming home eleventh of the fourteen finishers.

'Even if you finish that far back in the National, there is still a sense of achievement that you wouldn't find in any other race. April Rose wasn't the easiest ride because he was never on the bridle and therefore quite hard work. He wasn't the best of amateur rides in that sense but he was a brilliant jumper. He had the most economical action jumping a fence, he would hardly pick his legs up, yet somehow the Liverpool fences suited him. He was quite a funny horse in the stable. He always looked as if he was going to attack you from one end or the other.'

The following season he rode April Rose to finish fourth in the Becher Chase but pulled up three out in the 1966 Grand National. A third attempt the following year ended with a fall at the third fence. 'If you study the film of Foinavon's National,' he pointed out, 'I'm afraid you'll see April Rose as one of those running down the twenty-third fence and causing the mayhem that followed.'

The 10th and 11th Hussars combined in 1969 to become the Royal Hussars, and that newly created regiment was soon to bask in the glory of Major Piers Bengough's 1970 Grand Military Gold Cup triumph on his latest acquisition, Charles Dickens. Horse and rider (promoted now to rank of Lt. Colonel) went on to complete a hat-trick of Grand Military victories.

Having been appointed Colonel-in-Charge of the Royal Hussars, he discovered that staying in shape while commanding the regiment had its difficulties. 'It was hard work. Because of one's commitments as a Commanding Officer it wasn't easy to keep fit. I had soldiers on duty in Northern Ireland, Hong Kong and Belize, so one was on the move quite a lot. I used to wait until it was dark before going for a run round the barracks so, hopefully, the soldiers wouldn't see me.

'We had a doctor named David Chesney, who was actually a very good jockey. Because he was a horseman I managed to get him transferred to my regiment, so whenever I went into the gym to try and keep fit I insisted that the regimental medical officer, David Chesney, was also in the gym with an oxygen mask in case I passed out!

'Interestingly, the last time I rode in the Grand Military Gold Cup was in 1973 on Nether Edge, when Sandown was closed for renovations and the race had been transferred to Kempton. David Chesney was riding a horse belonging to someone else in the regiment. He jumped out of the gate and went, I thought, far too fast, so I sat thinking he was going to come back. But he never did come back and I finished second, beaten twenty lengths. So getting him transferred to my regiment probably wasn't the best solution as far as my winning another Grand Military Gold Cup was concerned!'

Charles Dickens, meanwhile, was being prepared for a tilt at the 1974 Grand National. Andy Turnell was entrusted with the mount and gave him a great ride to finish third to Red Rum and L'Escargot, beaten just a short head for second place.

'Andy rode him brilliantly,' said the proud owner. 'The saddle slipped jumping the Chair and, by the end of the race, his girths were back round his stomach. To a certain extent it stopped him breathing. The consequence of that was it strained his heart.

'Sadly, we never got him into the unsaddling enclosure. After the race the horse staggered and we rushed out to where they pull up. He was very distressed. The jockey took the saddle off and I told the stewards' secretary that I didn't want him to collapse in the unsaddling enclosure. We kept him walking, walking, walking, for about an hour.

'We gave him a year's rest, then had him tested. The vet could find nothing wrong so [trainer] Michael Scudamore ran him twice the following season. He went for two miles and stopped, so I had him as a hunter. Charles Dickens was a splendid horse and I was lucky to have one like that.'

Sir Piers left the army in 1973 after 26 years' service. That same year he founded Arrow Farm Stud, in the Herefordshire village of Canon Pyon. During the 1970s he served as Senior Steward of the Jockey Club, sat on the Horserace Betting Levy Board, and was a director at Cheltenham, Hereford and Ludlow. From 1983 until 1997 he was Her Majesty's Representative at Ascot.

During the Royal Meeting his duties focussed on making certain that the Queen and her guests were properly looked after and that the day's racing went without any hitches.

However, there was one occasion when Royal Ascot protocol took second place, this being when Cabochon carried Sir Piers' 'black, silver sleeves and green cap' colours to victory in the 1991 Ascot Stakes.

'That was a dream come true,' he told me. 'The Ascot Stakes was the last race on the card in those days and I was in the Royal Box shouting my head off. Everyone looked rather surprised because it wasn't the usual thing.

'One of my jobs as soon as racing was over was to organise the Queen's car outside the Royal Box. The Queen was wonderful and said "Go down to the winner's enclosure, Piers, don't worry about me." So I ran like a scalded cat, fighting my way through the crowd to get down to the winner's enclosure for a very happy and exciting occasion.'

But of all the various boards and committees he served upon, none gave him greater satisfaction than his long-standing association with the Grand Military committee. When I'd met him in 2002 he'd expressed his pleasure that the previous year's Gold Cup winner and third had both been ridden by Sandhurst cadets.

'That must be encouraging for the future. After all,' he concluded self-mockingly, 'you don't want too many old Lt-Colonels bumping about!'

Date: Friday 29 March 1957 Going: Good Value to Winner: £8,868 10s

Horse	Owner	Trainer	Age / weight	Jockey	SP
1 Sundew	Mrs G Kohn	F Hudson	11-11-7	F T Winter	20-1
2 Wyndburgh	Miss R M Wilkinson	P Wilkinson	7-10-7	M Batchelor	25-1
3 Tiberetta	Mr E R Courage	Owner	9-10-0	A Oughton	66-1
4 Glorious Twelfth	Mr H J Joel	R Renton	8-10-1	B Wilkinson	100-8

Distances: 8 lengths, 6 lengths, 8 lengths. Time: 9 mins 42.4 secs. 35 ran

Winner trained at Henley-in-Arden, Warwickshire

1958

PETER PICKFORD
They wouldn't leave him alone

Peter Pickford on Hart Royal, his mount in the 1957 and 1958 Grand Nationals.

PETER PICKFORD RODE just short of 200 winners during a 20-year career that spanned the fifties and sixties, including back-to-back victories in the Lancashire Chase and the 1957 County Hurdle on Flying East.

'Father was a huntsman,' he recalls. 'I was riding ponies when I was five. Lord Willoughby de Broke hunted with the pack and advised my father to send me into racing. So I went to Harvey Leader at Newmarket when I was thirteen and a half, even though the school leaving age was fourteen then. I managed to ride five winners on the Flat, the first two at Wolverhampton on successive days.'

Zero was the first, on 10 June 1946, followed by 33-1 outsider Fionchra the next day. The following month he won on Zero at Newmarket, a driving finish in which the first four were separated by two short heads and half a length, the result being determined by one of the first photo finish prints, the system having been introduced that year.

He weighed just 4st 7lb when starting out but eventually became too heavy and 'went jumping', joining 'Rip' Bissill's yard at Aslockton, Nottinghamshire. His first winner under National Hunt Rules came on Redcross Girl for owner-trainer John Rose, at Market Rasen on Easter Monday 1951.

The following season he won a Doncaster selling chase on Column, trained by Bissill for Sir Arthur Pilkington of the Pilkington glass family. He was placed on him in similar contests at Newcastle and Manchester.

Column was no more than a veteran selling chaser and was one of eleven horses that had got no further than the first fence in the 1951 Grand National. Nonetheless the owner was keen to run him at Aintree again in 1952 and Peter would keep the ride. Although dismissed as 100-1 no-hopers they managed to complete the course in eighth place, well behind the placed horses but ahead of two other long-shot finishers.

He remembers: 'Column was a good old jumper. I'd only ridden two or three winners at the time. I lay up early but he couldn't keep going. He never looked like winning but gave me a good, safe ride and I was quite pleased to get round.'

He had to wait five years for another Grand National ride – but at least this one was a live contender. He was called Hart Royal. Peter was his regular jockey and rode him to win his first chase, at Towcester in November 1955. Later that season they finished second to Gold Cup winner Four Ten in the Golden Miller Chase at Cheltenham.

'Hart Royal was the best I rode over fences. Although Ian Lomax held the licence, Rosemary Lomax [his wife] did all the training. Her father owned him at first and won two or three point-to-points, then they sold it to a local farmer named Les Denton.

'He liked it very heavy and he liked to make the running. He was a hard ride because you had to push and kick him along but he kept responding.'

Hart Royal won three times during the 1956/57 campaign, including when making all to win the valuable Lancashire Chase at Manchester, and went into the Grand National as the 100-7 fourth favourite. But his race ended at the very first fence.

'He over-jumped,' says Peter. 'He took off but didn't get his front feet down properly, slid along the ground and I was still on his back, and then he just rolled over. It was a long way after the fence.'

Hart Royal returned to winning form at Windsor in February 1958, beating former Gold Cup hero Gay Donald. Gay Donald then reversed the form when landing Sandown's Grand International Chase next time out. However, Hart Royal bounced back to win at Haydock, his last start before the 1958 National, for which he was the 18-1 joint third favourite, alongside Irish challenger Mr What and behind the previous year's runner-up Wyndburgh and sixth Goosander.

In 1958 the Grand National was sponsored for the first time, by Irish Hospitals Sweepstakes, resulting in the winner's prize being almost £5,000 more than the previous year. Peter Pickford reckoned Hart Royal had a good chance of landing the sponsors' money.

'I thought he would win, to be quite honest,' he says. 'I had a lot of faith in the horse. But I think that fall there the year before probably upset him because he didn't run very well the next time.

'The race didn't suit him because they wouldn't leave him alone; they took him off his feet. In three-mile chases they didn't go so fast but in the National they always went like hell over the first two. That soured him a bit and he didn't like it. They didn't sort themselves out until after Becher's first time and they rode a sensible race from then on, but they'd gone so fast over the first two, it didn't suit him. He jumped the fences all right but in between them he was sulking; he wasn't getting hold of the bridle and going on.'

The form book states simply 'baulked Becher's second time' but Peter elaborates. 'He didn't actually refuse. I was a long way back and going so slow when I was coming to Becher's, and what with that drop, I more or less pulled him up. He probably would have jumped it from a standstill but you want to be galloping so they can spread themselves over it.'

Meanwhile, Irish raider Mr What had jumped into the lead at Becher's, and there he stayed. Despite his jockey, Arthur Freeman, putting up 6lb overweight and despite trying to smash his way through the last fence, Mr What ploughed through the gruelling conditions to come home 30 lengths clear of the gallant mare, Tiberetta. Green Drill finished a further 15 lengths back in third, followed by Wyndburgh, Goosander, E.S.B. and Holly Bank, those being the only finishers.

Although he'd won the Troytown Chase at Navan, Mr What was effectively little more than a novice. Indeed, he'd struggled to win a weak Dundalk novice chase barely six months earlier. His owner, David 'Tone' Coughlan, was managing director and chairman of a firm of chemists and also a director of Tuam Racecourse.

Hart Royal came out of the Grand National well and headed to Manchester nine days later to dead-heat with Dovetail in the Lancashire Chase, which had been moved from earlier in the season to an Easter Monday slot.

Although eleven years old in 1959, Hart Royal remained in good form, coming second in Cheltenham's Fred Withington Chase, winning the Trial Chase at Leicester and finishing a creditable fourth behind Roddy Owen, Linwell and Lochroe in the Cheltenham Gold Cup, ridden on that occasion by Dave Dick as Peter had broken his collarbone three days earlier.

Reunited with Peter, he won Worcester's richest race, the Royal Porcelain Chase, by ten lengths. They then attempted to bag a third Lancashire Chase but could only finish third behind E.S.B. and Badanloch.

Hart Royal only ran twice the next season but he and Peter enjoyed one final victory together at Windsor in March 1961.

Later that month, Peter rode Carrasco for Bryan Marshall in the Grand National but fell at Becher's first time. However, his final Grand National ride was more rewarding, on front-running Peacetown in 1965.

Prominent throughout, they disputed the lead with Rondetto from halfway down to Becher's. 'He always made the running,' says Peter. 'He jumped the last about fifth but I didn't knock him about. There was no point because he'd done his best, so I just let him run up to the winning post. The owner was so pleased that he gave me another tenner for not knocking him about.'

He ended that 1964/65 season with a career best score of 22 winners, including two on novice chaser Choreographer, owned by Bryan Jenks and trained by Jack Bissill. In November they came within a half-length of beating top-class Dunkirk in the Mackeson Gold Cup. Choreographer also gave Peter his final ride over the Grand National fences when completing the course in the 1966 Topham Trophy.

He retired during the 1967/68 season, in which he rode just four winners, three of them courtesy of novice chaser Moison in the opening month. 'I was 38 and going round on bad horses, horses that other people didn't want to ride, so I couldn't see a lot of point to doing it.

'I was very lucky; I'd never really hurt myself,' he says, recalling that his worst injury had been a broken arm sustained in a fall at Leicester in November 1961, which sidelined him for three months.

After retiring he ran a pub just outside Swindon for eight years, then went in with a friend in a bookmaker's business. They had three shops in Swindon and 'turned over a lot of money' but as they leased rather than owned the properties, it was a struggle to break even.

Three hip replacements later, he is now retired and lives with his wife June in the village of Aldbourne, midway between Swindon and Hungerford. They have three sons – David, Gary and Andrew – each of whom has their own businesses, with Lambourn-based Gary being one of the country's top farriers.

Peter still goes to Cheltenham every year, and just maybe his mind goes back to that County Hurdle victory on Flying East; or perhaps to his rides on Hart Royal and Choreographer.

'Racing,' he reflects, 'was more fun then.'

Date: Saturday 29 March 1958 Going: Soft Value to Winner: £13,719 10s

Horse	Owner	Trainer	Age / weight	Jockey	SP
1 Mr What	Mr D J Coughlan	T J Taaffe	8-10-6	A Freeman	18-1
2 Tiberetta	Mr E R Courage	Owner	10-10-6	G Slack	28-1
3 Green Drill	Lord Cadogan	C Bewicke	8-10-10	G Milburn	28-1
4 Wyndburgh	Miss R M Wilkinson	P Wilkinson	8-11-3	M Batchelor	6-1 fav

Distances: 30 lengths, 15 lengths, 15 lengths. Time: 10 mins 1.2 secs. 31 ran

Winner trained at Rathcoole, County Dublin, Ireland

1959

JOHN HUDSON
Turmoil

John Hudson on Turmoil at a snowy Hall Bank.

Foxes who prowl in the graveyard to howl,
Take heed of his grave as you go;
Else to your surprise John Peel will arise,
With a shriek and a wild Tally Ho!

THE TINY CUMBRIAN village of Mealsgate, just a couple of miles from Wigton, was home to the Hudson family for many years. Farmer Tom Hudson, born in the parish of Caldbeck and a direct descendent of local hunting legend John Peel, owned a 200 acre dairy farm there at Hall Bank. In addition to having a mixed herd of 100 Friesian and Ayrshire cattle and 200 sheep on the farm, he also trained a single-figure string of racehorses.

He'd held a trainer's licence since 1956, having started out with a permit. Prior to that he'd trained a few point-to-pointers. Most of the Hudson runners were partnered by his son, John, who had turned professional at the start of the 1956/57 season after riding five winners as an amateur.

This is proper northern jumping country, land made famous by the late Gordon Richards at nearby Greystoke in the Cumbrian fells. From there he sent out a brace of Grand National winners in Lucius (1978) and Hallo Dandy (1984). But back in February 1959, Farmer Tom had two National candidates of his own.

Sundawn III had romped to a 12-length victory over Liverpool's Mildmay course two months earlier. Turmoil had put up an equally impressive performance when winning Newcastle's Eider Chase and had finished third over the National fences in the 1958 Topham Trophy. Both horses had proved rare bargains.

That Sundawn III ever amounted to anything was little short of remarkable. There was nothing wrong with his breeding, for he was a son of Union Jack, winner of the 1938 Northumberland Plate and sire of most of the jumpers in Cumberland. But nobody wanted him. Originally sold at a farm sale for 15 guineas, he was passed on for one guinea profit and then sold twice more, at one time being intended for use as a police horse in Lancashire.

Eventually he was bought by a young Cumberland farmer, Len Skelton from Low Ireby, who proceeded to win five point-to-points on him, including the John Peel Cup. Put into training with Tom Hudson, he won a couple of novice chases in the autumn of 1958 prior to his Liverpool victory.

Turmoil had had a more conventional start, winning a novice hurdle and a novice chase for Tadcaster trainer Charlie Hall. But he had bad shoulders, so following those two victories his owner decided it was a good time to sell. Joe Watson, a Cumbrian farmer, picked him up at Stockton sales for 180 guineas.

John Hudson took up the story: 'Joe Watson had Union Star in training with us. He'd been my first winner at Sedgefield in 1955, so that's how we came to get Turmoil. We started him off in two-mile races but we were cutting his throat to get him to go at two-mile pace. It took us a full season to realise that he was really a stayer who needed soft ground. Once we got him settled and he got soft going, he stayed forever. He was a horse you'd got to wait with; you'd have to let him warm up.

'Joe Watson didn't have his own racing colours. He used to use ours – scarlet and grey horizontal halves, white sash and black cap. He was a shy sort of fellow. When he went racing he'd keep out of the way, never came near you. He'd be given an owner's complimentary ticket for lunch but he'd never use it. He preferred to bring his sandwiches instead.'

With the fields and gallop frozen hard and covered with four inches of snow, Tom Hudson improvised by taking his Grand National hopes to exercise on the sands at Skinburness. He also constructed two Aintree-style fences from a couple of hedges.

John recalled: 'Shortly before the Eider Chase, Mr and Mrs Geoffrey Kohn, the owners of Sundew, visited the yard. They'd come up with the intention of buying Sundawn but the owner wouldn't sell. When they saw Turmoil, Mr Kohn said "I like the look of that." We said "Come and see him run at Newcastle." The ground was like a bog and he cantered in, so the next day Mr and Mrs Kohn bought him to run in the Grand National and said I could still ride him.'

Turmoil was transferred straight away to Alec Kilpatrick's yard at Collingbourne Ducis, near Marlborough. Tom Hudson still had Sundawn III but there was never much doubt as to which of the two horses John would ride. Turmoil looked by far the better prospect. And when Jimmy Power rang up for the ride on Sundawn III, the decision was finalised.

Sundawn III was a forlorn 100-1 outsider and was one of eight casualties at Becher's first time round. Turmoil started as a lively 20-1 chance and fared much better.

'It was good ground on Grand National day and that wasn't Turmoil's going,' recounted John. 'It was all against him. The aim was to hold the horse up so we started off at the back.

'All went to plan on the first circuit and we started to creep up after halfway. There were so many riderless horses. We were still running on from Becher's but at the Canal Turn there were six loose horses, three on either side of me. The three on the outside ran down the fence, straight across my path and I had nowhere to go. I think there were three or four of us put out of the race at that fence.

'But for being baulked by the loose horses, he'd certainly have finished. The further he went the better he went, he was just starting to warm up. I think I'd have finished in the first four.'

Just four horses got round that year, with Oxo and Michael Scudamore beating a stirrupless Tim Brookshaw on Wyndburgh. After Brookshaw's right iron had broken on landing over Becher's second time round, he had kicked his other foot from the remaining iron and ridden the remainder of the race without stirrups.

Oxo had jumped the last fence four or five lengths clear of Wyndburgh but Brookshaw was not prepared to concede defeat without a fight and Wyndburgh began to eat into Oxo's lead on the run-in, but he was still one-and-a-half lengths behind by the time Oxo reached the winning post. The previous year's winner, Mr What, finished third, followed by the only other finisher, Aintree specialist Tiberetta, finishing in the frame for the third consecutive year.

Turmoil recovered quickly from his exertions and, partnered by John, reappeared three weeks later in the Golden Miller Chase at Cheltenham. The day had dawned with firm ground but incessant rain throughout the morning rendered it soft by the time the race started. That suited him just fine. Taking the lead from former Gold Cup winner Gay Donald five out, Turmoil ran on to win in a canter by 15 lengths.

Afterwards, however, things went rapidly downhill, as John recalled: 'After Cheltenham he ran in the Whitbread Gold Cup. He didn't run very well and he was never really the same horse after that race. Next season I rode him in the Grand Sefton but we fell at Becher's. It was a dry autumn with fast ground from August to nearly Christmas. It didn't suit him and he was ruined by running on it.

'He didn't really like Liverpool either. He jumped it but he found the fences too big for him. The first time, when he was third in the Topham Trophy, he jumped really well but the more he ran there, the less he liked it. He hated the drop fences because they hurt his shoulders.

'I think he lost his nerve completely after the Grand Sefton. Alec Kilpatrick wasn't very happy when I told him he didn't like firm ground or Liverpool. He never asked me to ride him again.'

Perhaps Kilpatrick should have heeded the jockey's words, for Turmoil's form tailed off disastrously. He fell in that year's Hennessy Gold Cup and fell twice more the next season, pulling up or finishing last on all his other starts.

The horse was subsequently bought by Mrs Daphne Brackenbury from Newton Abbot, whose husband John held a permit on her behalf. She trained him on the moors and he went out to exercise accompanied by a pack of dogs. He forgot he was a racehorse and thrived in his new environment. To aid his ageing legs, Daphne hit upon the idea of standing him in the cold Dartmoor streams.

Turmoil did manage to win her a race, a three-mile chase at Plumpton in January 1964, ridden by her 18-year-old son, also named John.

At the time the Brackenburys ran the Ring o' Bells pub in North Bovey and that victory had an unusual sequel, as the younger John Brackenbury relates: 'By coincidence, HMS Turmoil was docked in Plymouth, and a good portion of the crew backed him. So they hired a bus from Plymouth to North Bovey on the Saturday night and didn't leave the Ring o' Bells until God knows what time. It was a great night.'

Turmoil ran twenty times for the Brackenburys, his final race being at Wincanton in October 1964. He lived to a ripe old age before succumbing to a heart attack.

John Hudson had his second and final Grand National ride in 1965, on the former hunter chaser Nedsmar. He was owned and trained by Miss Eden Pearson, although, as women were not then empowered to hold a trainer's licence, he was initially listed as being with her father, Jack. When she married Wigton farmer Bob Graham he took over the licence, though his wife still trained the horse.

'Mrs Graham wanted to run him in the 1965 Grand National because she thought it could well be the last,' John told me. 'There was a lot of talk and bluffing going on at the time regarding the future of the race, but a lot of people thought that it would be the last one.

'On his day he was a good horse but he was heavy shouldered. He could only run three or four times a year at most because of the weakness in his shoulders. Soft ground was okay but he didn't like it dry. I knew he would struggle to get round because the ground on Grand National day was dry. He was a genuine 100-1 shot and didn't have any realistic chance. The idea was to be up there from the start and see how he went.'

Nedsmar was up with the leaders jumping the first fence. He made a slight mistake at the fourth and started to lose his place. Then at Becher's he jumped violently to the left, taking a spectacular fall and bringing down three others in the process.

'His right shoulder was starting to go as we came to Becher's, that's why he dived to the left to try and save it. It was an awful looking fall and I was lucky really. I got up and walked away from it. The only damage was that I needed three stitches in a foot after a horse had trod on it and ripped my boot open.

'Funnily enough, twelve months later I was in a barber's shop getting my hair cut. The barber was looking at a magazine and said "Here, have a look at this horrible fall." I looked and said "Hang on a minute, that's me!" I hadn't seen it until then.'

John's next visit to Aintree was when winning over hurdles on Costa Rica on the last day of 1965. He won on him again at Haydock the following week.

He rode just one more winner, Gilthwaite in a Catterick selling chase on New Year's Eve 1966. By then a regime of rigid dieting had begun to take its toll. His final ride, Night Guard at Kelso on 1 May 1968, finished last. His career as a jockey over, he left racing and worked for Pirelli tyres for the next twenty years.

Meanwhile, Tom continued to combine training with farming until retiring from both in 1974, after 45 years at Hall Bank. He died in the spring of 1984, in his 81st year.

When I first met John Hudson in 1999 he hadn't sat on a horse for over ten years, yet sitting in the front room of his Mealsgate house, with its magnificent view of the Solway, the memories come flooding back when he took out his scrapbook. Aintree memories, of Turmoil, of Sundawn, of Nedsmar. Oh yes, and Costa Rica too. Even selling hurdlers count when they pass that famous winning post in front.

A total of 33 winners in thirteen years had hardly set the racing world alight. He was typical of the band of journeyman jockeys who rode moderate horses around the northern jumping tracks in the fifties and sixties. But to me, he was more than that. I'm not ashamed to say that John Hudson had been my all-time racing hero for forty years.

When he died in lamentably tragic circumstances in the summer of 2008, just a couple weeks after I'd spoken to him for what was unknowingly the last time, I grieved at the loss of someone I was proud to call a friend.

Some say you shouldn't meet your heroes. You put them on a pedestal and they often disappoint. But I'm glad I met John Hudson.

He didn't disappoint.

Date: Saturday 21 March 1959 Going: Good Value to Winner: £13,646

Horse	Owner	Trainer	Age / weight	Jockey	SP
1 Oxo	Mr J E Bigg	W Stephenson	8-10-13	M Scudamore	8-1
2 Wyndburgh	Mrs J K M Oliver	J K M Oliver	9-10-12	T Brookshaw	10-1
3 Mr What	Mr D J Coughlan	T J Taaffe	9-11-9	T Taaffe	6-1 fav
4 Tiberetta	Mr E R Courage	Owner	11-10-9	A Oughton	20-1

Distances: 1½ lengths, 8 lengths, 20 lengths. Time: 9 mins 37.2 secs. 34 ran

Winner trained at Royston, Hertfordshire

1960

STAN MELLOR
As seen on TV

Stan Mellor takes the last on Wayward Muse to win the Ainsdale Chase over the Mildmay fences at Aintree in January 1964.

THE FIRST BBC-TELEVISED Grand National brought a rare victory for the favourite when Miss Winifred Wallace's former hunter chaser Merryman II galloped home well clear of his rivals. The 13-2 market leader was trained by Neville Crump and ridden by stable jockey Gerry Scott, who rode the Aintree marathon with a heavily strapped collarbone, having broken it in two places at Doncaster just twelve days earlier.

The bitter east wind made for a cold day and the crowd appeared to be smaller than usual. The withdrawal of the top-weight Kerstin meant that the field lacked a horse of Gold Cup calibre, with only three carrying more than 10st 12lb. Just 26 runners lined up, the smallest field for 40 years, the several no-hopers including Irish Coffee, ridden by his 50-year-old owner, Mr W St George Burke.

The blinkered Tea Fiend went straight to the front and still led jumping the water, where 17 of the 26 runners were still standing. As Tea Fiend led them down towards Becher's, Merryman II moved into second place, just in front of Lord Leverhulme's Badanloch, then came Green Drill, Mr What, Cannobie Lee, Eagle Lodge, Team Spirit, Sabaria and Clanyon.

Mr What fell at Becher's, as did Team Spirit, having been baulked by Cannobie Lee, who refused. Merryman II made his only mistake here, landing too steep, and for a couple of strides his fate hung in the balance, but Gerry Scott sat tight.

Tea Fiend relinquished the lead soon after jumping Becher's and Merryman II and Badanloch led the survivors over the Canal Turn. From Valentine's onwards, these two had the race between them. But after jumping the fourth last fence, Merryman II began to stride steadily away, passing the post 15 lengths clear.

Always up in the first half dozen, Badanloch stayed on stoutly to finish second. Clear Profit finished strongly and passed Tea Fiend on the run-in to take third place. Behind them, Sabaria was fifth, Green Drill sixth, Arles seventh, with Skatealong, who had refused three from home but jumped it at the second attempt, last of the eight finishers.

'I didn't really have a chance of winning,' acknowledges Badanloch's rider, Stan Mellor. 'The only hope I had was when Gerry's stumbled slightly at Becher's second time. For just one moment I thought "That's it, he's gone". He was always going slightly better than me but I had a very good ride. No complaints; I was beaten fair and square by a very good horse.'

The son of a Manchester timber merchant, Stan had started his racing career in 1952 as a 15-year-old amateur at George Owen's Cholmondeley Stables in Malpas, Cheshire. It was a good place to start, for Owen, a man short on words but long on reputation, had already set Dick Francis and Tim Brookshaw on their way to champion jockey status. Stan was hoping to be the third such graduate.

Owen supplied Stan's first winner, Straight Border, in a Wolverhampton selling hurdle on 19 January 1954. Later that year, he also provided him with his first ride over the Aintree fences, Pearl's Choice, who finished seventh in the Molyneux Chase.

Stan finished sixth on his first Grand National ride, aboard Martinique in 1956. Following a couple of 'did not finish' efforts on outsiders Never Say When and The Crofter in 1958 and '59, he enjoyed his first victory over the course when Roy Whiston's Fresh Winds landed the 1960 Topham Trophy.

Two days later came that second place finish on Badanloch in the Grand National. They tried again the following year but trailed in eighth behind Nicolaus Silver, trained by Fred Rimell and ridden by Bobby Beasley.

'I used to ride for Fred Rimell,' says Stan, 'and he invited me to the Adelphi afterwards to celebrate. So I drove home to Cheshire, put my dinner jacket on and headed for the Adelphi.

'On my way there I got stopped by a policeman for speeding. He came up to me with a very straight face and he was going to book me. He got out his notebook and asked my name. I said "Stan Mellor". Not a flicker. But I thought he might be a sport so I said "I rode in the National today."

'"Where did you finish?" he asked. "Eighth," I replied, which I thought was pretty good.

'"You know your trouble son?" he said. "You went too slow this afternoon and too fast tonight."'

Stan's 1962 Grand National mount was Stanhope Joel's classy chestnut Frenchman's Cove. He looked to be close enough to play a part in proceedings when being brought down at the nineteenth fence. 'It was the only time I ever got brought down from behind,' he recalls. 'Willie Robinson on Team Spirit fell when just behind me and his horse's head and neck got entangled in my horse's hind legs, and down we went.'

Even so, he is adamant that he would not have won. 'The ground was too soft and he was never really going. He may not have been in love with Aintree; he was a bit too flashy a jumper.'

Good ground was Frenchman's Cove's forte, as he demonstrated when winning the 1962 Whitbread Gold Cup with Stan on board. He would have ridden him in the 1963 National had he not been seriously injured two days before the race.

A field of 41 turned out for the inaugural running of the Schweppes Gold Trophy, a richly endowed handicap hurdle on Liverpool's opening day card. Stan rode one for Derek Ancil called Eastern Harvest and recalls: 'The ground was a bit soft, quite poached, and everyone was going for a bit of good ground. I was lying handy up there when he grabbed at the second hurdle and fell. I was in the path of all the runners. My nose and everything above it was all right, but the cheekbones and jawbone were broken and I lost six teeth.

'It was a bad time to have happened because I'd been champion jockey for the last three seasons and I was going to be champion again. It was the bad winter of '62/63 and the only good thing about it was that I was twenty winners ahead and I thought there wouldn't be enough of the season left for them to catch me. But the Aintree fall put the kibosh on that and Josh Gifford caught me and beat me by six.'

Dave Dick came in for the National ride on Frenchman's Cove. Anchored by top weight of 12 stone and on unfavourable soft ground, he was never in the race and beat only two of the 22 finishers.

There was no Grand National ride for Stan in 1964 and he didn't have much of one the following year when Ayala, the winner in 1963, exited at the very first fence. In 1966 he rode Vultrix but was out of contention when pulling up four from home.

Later that year Stan achieved perhaps the most famous victory of his career, when Stalbridge Colonist beat Arkle half a length in the Hennessy Gold Cup. He maintains that Stalbridge Colonist was unlucky not to win the 1967 Cheltenham Gold Cup and blames himself for his narrow defeat by Woodland Venture. 'I shouldn't have picked my stick up on him but, being the Gold Cup, I did. It was foolish. I should have kept changing hands.'

Three weeks later came that most extraordinary of all Grand Nationals, in which Popham Down and another riderless horse ran across the fence after Becher's on the second circuit, causing mayhem and enabling only the 100-1 outsider Foinavon to jump it at the first attempt. Stan was riding The Fossa, on whom he'd won the 1965 Grand Sefton, and ended up in the thick of it.

'I came off, went straight over Popham Down, and landed on the fence. I thought that wouldn't be a healthy place to hang around, so I jumped down and ran. Ironically, there was a picture in the following day's papers with the caption 'John Lawrence and Stan Mellor running to catch their mounts.' We weren't; we were running away from them!'

After the race, a story emerged that Stan had ended up remounting the wrong horse and continuing. However, as is often the case, comments get distorted. Here's what really happened: 'I was the only jockey that didn't find his horse. I genuinely did try but I'd gone the wrong way. I saw this horse going down towards the Canal Turn and it looked like my blue saddlecloth. I ran to catch him but, when I got there, it wasn't my horse. When I got back I told the press that I'd run down to the Canal Turn but it was the wrong horse. That's all I said, I didn't say I'd got on it. But the story got round that I had. Then it became expanded to where I'd finished the course before realising it wasn't the right horse.'

The Grand National had not been a lucky race for Stan. His 1968 mount, the well-fancied French Kilt, could finish no nearer than fourteenth. Then in 1969 he picked up a 'spare' on Game Purston for bookmaker John Banks.

'I was just pleased to get a ride. Game Purston was an old horse by then and he hadn't got a lot of foot on the first circuit, but on the second circuit he started to motor.

'When I came to the big ditch, the third fence second time round, Hove was stuck in the fence with David Nicholson still sat on him. I was directly behind so I pulled to the left to miss him. Game Purston jumped the fence well but, as he came down, I hadn't quite got far enough away and my right foot caught Hove's shoulder.

'As I rode to the next fence, I looked down and saw the foot sticking out at right angles. I pulled up, got off, landed on my good foot, shooed the horse away and sat down feeling sorry for myself, waiting for someone to come and get me. Eventually, an ambulance arrived.

'When I got back to the ambulance room it was choc-a-bloc full of injured jockeys. I came in on a stretcher but there was nowhere to put me, so they stuck me underneath the bed and I lay there waiting for attention. Somebody said to my wife, Elaine, "Stan's in the ambulance room." She came in, had a quick look round, didn't see me lying under the bed, went back out again and said "He was going well when I last saw him. The windy bugger must have bottled out!"

'When I got to hospital they put the foot back, pinned it in and I went home the next day. But I didn't ride again until the start of the following season.'

His next Grand National ride, The Beeches, was one of eight third-fence casualties in 1970. His final attempt, in 1971, also ended with a first-circuit fall, this time on Fulke Walwyn's Lord Jim at the eleventh.

On 18 December 1971, Stan Mellor became the first National Hunt jockey to ride 1,000 winners when a five-year-old grey gelding named Ouzo won the Christmas Spirit Novice Chase at Nottingham. Six months later he ended his riding career by winning on Arne Folly (his 1,035th) at Stratford on the penultimate day of the 1971/72 season.

Even though the Grand National, Gold Cup and Champion Hurdle had all eluded him, he nonetheless assembled an impressive list of major prizes during his 18-year career. In addition to those already mentioned, the list included Cheltenham's Two Mile Champion Chase, the Mackeson Gold Cup, Mildmay Memorial Chase and two King George VI Chases. It's a list notable for its lack of big hurdling prizes but perhaps that's not too surprising.

'Riding over fences was what I had to offer,' he says. 'I was more of a horseman than a jockey. I'd done show jumping for five years and had a good eye for a fence. I think if I could do anything better than anybody else, it was to give a winning chance to a horse that needed help. A lot of those were novice chasers. In those days the horses weren't schooled so well and you had twice the number of falls, but I won streams of novice chases.'

Awarded the MBE for services to racing in 1972, Stan had been the first chairman of the Jockeys' Association and also used to represent the jockeys on the Injured Jockeys' Fund committee.

Training was a natural second career and he was soon on the Grand National trail. He came closest with Royal Mail, third behind Aldaniti and Spartan Missile in 1981, and with Lean Ar Aghaidh, who occupied the same place behind Maori Venture in 1987.

'Lean Ar Aghaidh was one-paced but a very good jumper. He liked fast ground and just flowed along at his own pace. Had it been fast in the 1987 National, I'm sure he would have won, but from Valentine's to the second last the ground was soft. He'd gone to the front but, instead of getting on with business and striding away, he shortened his stride and was treading water. Then he hit two out and, by the time they came to the last, a couple had sneaked up behind him and they did him for speed up the run-in.

'After the race – and it was an extraordinary thing to say – I said that he hadn't had a hard race and I'd run him in the Whitbread three weeks later. He'd come back from the National as fresh as paint and I knew he'd done nothing from Valentine's to the second last.'

The trainer's confidence was justified when Lean Ar Aghaidh made all under Guy Landau to land the Whitbread Gold Cup by five lengths. It was Stan's second Whitbread, following the victory of Royal Mail in 1980 – a victory that had its own remarkable story.

'Royal Mail was brought down in that year's Cheltenham Gold Cup and came back with a fractured lower jaw. On the Monday after the race, his lad, James Devaney, put a head collar on him and rode him down the road. We kept him working by riding him out in a head collar. Then, when the jaw mended, we put a Kineton noseband on so that it didn't interfere with his lower jaw. We got him right for the Whitbread six weeks later, which he won.'

Just as he embarked on his training career, ladies' races were introduced to the racing calendar. Elaine wanted to ride in them and, naturally enough, asked her husband for advice on what to do and how to ride a finish.

'I realised then,' says Stan, 'that I'd ridden for eighteen years and never really thought about it. In all that time I'd never had so much as a two-minute conversation with anyone on riding. I didn't know what to say. I'd certainly never analysed it inasmuch as I could relate it to somebody else.'

This gave him the incentive to combine training horses with training jockeys. His courses on jockeyship proved highly successful.

'I was no stylist at all,' he admits, 'but I didn't teach them to ride like me!

'In the first half my career I had plenty of courage. In the second half I had plenty of knowledge. I tried to get the knowledge into the young jockey, instead of him taking years to acquire it through trial and error. One of my objectives was to bring out their individuality, to coach them to find their individual talents and encourage them to do what they do well.'

He decided not to renew his trainer's licence when it expired in February 2002. His last runner was Storm Tiger, at Aintree on 28 October 2001. He finished third, so Stan once more stood in the spot where he had greeted both Royal Mail and Lean Ar Aghaidh on their return to the unsaddling enclosure after their respective Grand Nationals. It was a fitting place to end a training career.

When I first thumbed the racing pages as a child, Stan Mellor was about to become champion National Hunt jockey for the third consecutive season. I grew up watching that forceful drive as he lifted his mount over a fence. It was a style that never changed.

And yes, I was stood by Stratford's final fence on that Friday night in June 1972 when, on Arne Folly, he did it for the very last time. You don't forget moments like that.

Date: Saturday 26 March 1960 Going: Good Value to Winner: £13,134 10s

Horse	Owner	Trainer	Age / weight	Jockey	SP
1 Merryman II	Miss W H S Wallace	N F Crump	9-10-12	G Scott	13-2fav
2 Badanloch	Lord Leverhulme	G R Owen	9-10-9	S Mellor	100-7
3 Clear Profit	Mr B Sunley	R Newton	10-10-1	B Wilkinson	20-1
4 Tea Fiend	Mr J D Pickering	G R Owen	11-10-0	P G Madden	33-1

Distances: 15 lengths, 12 lengths, 12 lengths. Time: 9 mins 26.2 secs. 26 ran

Winner trained at Middleham, Yorkshire

1961

BILL REES
The Queen Mother's jockey

Magic Tricks (Joe Coates) leads The Rip (Bill Rees) over the water at Lingfield in January 1964. The Rip went on to win by 10 lengths.

BORN IN 1934 and raised amid tales of Aintree and Cheltenham glories, Bill Rees was always destined to be a jockey. His father, Lewis Bilbie Rees, more commonly known by his second name, had won the Grand National in 1922 on Music Hall. His uncle Frederick Brychan Rees, popularly known as Dick, had done likewise aboard Shaun Spadah the year before.

Dick had been the more successful of the two, being champion jockey five times in the 1920s. Together they dominated the National Hunt Festival of 1928 when Dick won the Gold Cup aboard Patron Saint and Bilbie the Champion Hurdle on Brown Jack. The following year Dick landed both those races within the space of 40 minutes, winning the Champion Hurdle aboard Royal Falcon and the Gold Cup on Easter Hero.

Bill began his career with Sam Armstrong but did not much care for Newmarket and so became apprenticed to Walter Nightingall at Epsom. His first winner came on Gold Sandal for Lambourn trainer Fred Templeman in a one-mile apprentice handicap at Salisbury on 24 August 1950, surviving an objection from the runner-up on grounds of crossing. By the time his five-year apprenticeship finished in 1953, rising weight dictated that he would follow his elder brother Michael, who was already established as a National Hunt jockey. Bill rode his first winner over hurdles for Snowy Parker on Canberra at Wye in March 1953.

It was Parker who provided him with his first experience of the Grand National course, courtesy of a horse named Pelican Star in the 1955 Becher Chase. When Bill saw the Aintree fences he was far from confident of getting round, but the horse adapted well and finished fourth.

His first Grand National mount came when Fulke Walwyn asked him to ride Felias in 1957. The horse had been bought by the *Daily Sketch* specifically to run in the National and Walwyn had only recently acquired him from northern trainer Jack Ormston. But there was to be no scoop for the *Sketch*, for Felias was brought down at the eleventh.

His 1958 Grand National ride came on Lawrie Morgan's Colledge Master, a top-class hunter chaser who had won the Liverpool Fox Hunters' Chase and was destined to win it again. But there is often a wide gulf between good hunter chasers and proven handicappers and Colledge Master was well in arrears when being pulled up after a circuit.

By now Bill was riding for Bob Turnell, who supplied his third Grand National mount, Vigor in 1959. Horse and rider went their separate ways in a melee at the Canal Turn second time round, ending up on opposite sides of the fence.

Earlier that month Bill had seen the Cheltenham Gold Cup snatched from his grasp when Turnell's six-year-old Pas Seul fell at the last when holding a narrow lead from Roddy Owen and Linwell. But he was compensated the following year when Pas Seul atoned for his fall by winning the 1960 Gold Cup from Lochroe.

Sixteen days after that Gold Cup triumph, he rode Aintree veteran Eagle Lodge in the Grand National, standing in for his injured brother-in-law, Alan Oughton. Bill likened his nimble-footed technique to that of a ballet dancer and maintains that he gave him the best of all his Aintree rides until pulling up two out.

Royal trainer Peter Cazalet asked him to become his stable jockey for the 1960/61 season following the retirement of Arthur Freeman. He accepted the offer and was rewarded with a personal best tally of 52 winners, including the Topham Trophy on Mrs A. T. Hodgson's Cupid's Charge. The victorious owner, trainer and jockey teamed up again in the Grand National two days later with the well fancied Scottish Flight II.

There had been some significant developments since the previous year's Grand National. Firstly, the approach to twelve of the fences had been made more inviting by constructing a one-foot wide apron on the take off side, thus altering the shape of the fences and meaning that the jumps would be taken at an angle of 50 degrees instead of 65 degrees. Only the open ditches retained their upright shape, reflecting their origin as natural hedges. The modified fences had been introduced at the 1960 November fixture, which featured three races over the National course – the Molyneux, Becher and Grand Sefton – and the improvements had met with full satisfaction from the riders taking part.

In December 1960, Mrs Mirabel Topham announced that the 1961 Grand National would be worth over £20,000, the result of Schweppes Ltd joining the Irish Hospitals Trust as co-sponsors. Schweppes would provide £7,500, Tophams £7,000 (including a gold trophy value £600) and the IHT £5,000.

Another new departure was that the top weight would from then on be 12 stone instead of 12st 7lb.

Three weeks before the race and after much speculation, it was announced that the three Russian entries, Epigraf II, Grifel and Reljef, would be coming to Aintree. Officials in Moscow had threatened to withdraw the horses when it was realised that they would have to carry automatic top weight of 12 stone. The decision came at the end of a day-long conference and was confirmed by Grigori Nechitoremko, Chief Inspector of Horses at the Soviet Ministry of Agriculture. The horses and their escorts would travel by train via Poland, Germany and Holland and thence by boat to England.

Reporters gathered at Moscow Hippodrome got the impression that the debate whether to run or not had been a contentious one. One Hippodrome veteran remarked: 'Our horses do not stand a chance.'

The three Russian horses had their first experience of English fences at Haydock ten days before the race. The fences were specially built up and topped with spruce for their practice. Epigraf II, their main hope, was more impressive than Reljef and Grifel, though the work was done at a slow pace. Unfortunately, Epigraf was subsequently ruled out of the race.

Though confident that their two remaining runners would acquit themselves well, the Russian delegation insisted that their initial entry was purely experimental and resolved to return the following year, adding that Russian horses would become a permanent feature of the great race. Four days before the National they turned up at Aintree fully equipped with cine-cameras – shots from which would be shown in cinemas throughout the Soviet Union – and a wooden pole, marked in inches, to measure the fences.

Uliy Gulin, their interpreter, said: 'We shall very likely be building fences in Russia equivalent to those at Aintree and our entries next year will be larger.'

On the opening day of the meeting the Russian party watched the Topham Trophy at Becher's, where the pacemaker, Draw Well, took a crashing fall. Undeterred, Vladimir Prakhov, their champion jockey, who was originally due to partner Epigraf II but would now ride Grifel, said: 'We still think that the big obstacles of the Grand Pardubice are worse.' Alas, it was all a bit of an anti-climax, for neither Reljef nor Grifel survived beyond the first circuit and, despite all the Soviet optimism, no Russian horse has since been sent to tackle the Grand National.

Says Bill of his ride on Scottish Flight II: 'I thought he might get left behind if they went a bit quick, because he was a bit slow in the early stages of a race. So I jumped off quickly on the inside and was amazed to find myself in front for a few seconds going to the first. Then the race settled down and he was always going quite nicely.'

The front-running Fresh Winds, partnered by Roy Edwards, soon established a long lead, which he maintained until falling at the nineteenth fence.

As the field came back towards the 'racecourse proper', the destiny of the 1961 Grand National lay between four horses: Nicolaus Silver, O'Malley Point, Scottish Flight II and the previous year's winner Merryman II.

Nicolaus Silver and Bobby Beasley jumped the second last a length ahead of Merryman II, but the latter's 11st 12lb burden began to tell going to the final fence. Nicolaus Silver jumped it in front and drew away to win by five lengths. Merryman II was eased in the last few strides and just held on to second from O'Malley Point, with Scottish Flight II fourth.

Nicolaus Silver was owned by Jeremy Vaughan, a 30-year-old company executive from Bridgnorth. He and trainer Fred Rimell had bought him for 2,600 guineas at Dublin sales, outbidding another English trainer, Ivor Herbert. The owner's father, Douglas Vaughan, had owned First Of The Dandies, runner-up to Sheila's Cottage in the 1948 race.

'I always thought I had a chance but once Nicolaus Silver started to assert himself, I could see I wasn't going to get to him,' comments Bill. 'Scottish Flight always found a little bit right at the end of a race but he just didn't find enough.'

It was a fair effort nonetheless and Bill was looking forward to an additional bonus, having asked his sister-in-law to put £20 each-way on for him. 'Unfortunately,' he says ruefully, 'she didn't stipulate fourth place and so I didn't get my money, which was a bit of a letdown.'

Bill relished his role as royal jockey and was to ride more than 50 winners for the Queen Mother. They included a treble on 9 December 1961, when Laffy, Double Star and The Rip all won steeplechases at Lingfield.

The Queen Mother had another good chaser in Silver Dome. Bill rode him three times at Aintree, finishing second to Team Spirit in the 1963 Grand Sefton and third in the 1964 Topham Trophy before he finally gave his owner her first victory over the Grand National fences in the 1964 Becher Chase.

'He was a bit wild and pulled hard,' Bill recalls. 'He used to get so low at his fences. How he got round Aintree I'm still not quite sure, because he did used to hit a fence very hard. He was a good horse on his day but he suffered from a weak heart and in the end he died of a heart attack.

'Now Laffy,' he continues, 'was a smasher. I loved that little horse. He was the most wonderful jumper if conditions were right, but he used the get the wind up if the ground was slippery. If he felt his feet going he didn't take off.'

After Bill had won three chases on Laffy during the 1961/62 season it was decided to go for the Ulster National at Downpatrick. It had been 56 years since the last royal runner at Downpatrick, King Edward VII's Flaxman in 1906. But for what were termed 'political reasons', Bill found himself replaced by an Irish-born jockey, Willie Robinson. The notion of putting up a jockey from County Meath in the Republic for a race run in Northern Ireland was indeed a strange one. It worked, with Robinson defying the effects of an earlier fall to bring Laffy home in front, but the decision annoyed Bill and still rankles to this day.

He rode Laffy in the 1964 Grand National, the Queen Mother's first runner in the race since Devon Loch's debacle eight years earlier. Laffy started as one of the four 100-7 co-favourites but did not get beyond the fourth fence. 'I fell off him, no question about it,' he admits. 'God, he hit the fence so hard. Aintree's fences frightened him – he fell again at Becher's when he was loose.'

The Rip was his Grand National mount the following year. 'The Rip was a lovely horse but just missed being top class. He gave me a good ride in the National, finishing seventh. I fancied him a bit but he wasn't quite good enough. I wasn't going to win at any stage of the race.'

He rode The Rip in Sandown's Gallaher Gold Cup in November 1965, finishing fourth behind Arkle, Rondetto and Mill House. Seven days later he rode Colonel Whitbread's Dunkirk to victory in Cheltenham's Mackeson Gold Cup, then run over two miles. The royal jockey was at the height of his career.

But sometimes, that's when it all goes wrong. And for Bill it went wrong with a vengeance.

It was decided to pitch Dunkirk against Arkle in the 1965 King George VI Chase. Recalls Bill: 'I'd ridden him in the Stone's Ginger Wine Chase at Sandown over two and a half miles, when I'd told Peter [Cazalet] that he'd never win unless we held him up. I did hold him up but it nearly killed me to do it, so it was decided that the best way to ride him in the King George was to make the running.

'I let him run and he was always going reasonably well, but going to the last ditch, when Arkle moved up to me, he started to wobble and I think he might have suffered a heart attack. He just crashed through the fence and that was it.'

Dunkirk's fatal fall resulted in a smashed right thigh for Bill. He spent four months on his back with the leg in traction. It was November 1966 before he made his comeback.

Four months and fifty-odd rides later, there had been plenty of seconds and thirds but still no winners. At last he rode the Queen Mother's Oedipe to victory at Windsor, his first success for sixteen months. But jubilation was short-lived, for the very next day brought a fall from the hurdler Lochmore at Fontwell, breaking the same thigh in the same place.

With David Mould by then firmly established as the royal jockey, Bill went freelance when he eventually returned but found it tough and struggled to achieve double figures for the remainder of his career. He did, however, have four more Grand National mounts.

In 1968, Edward Courage's San Angelo, despite having been kicked at the start by the eventual winner Red Alligator, ran well enough to finish twelfth. The following year he finished fourth on Paul Mellon's grey The Beeches.

In 1971 he substituted for the injured Johnny Haine on Charter Flight, the previous year's Topham Trophy winner, and he had his final Grand National ride on Limeburner in 1972. Both were pulled up on the second circuit.

With rides ever harder to come by, Turnell suggested that he put his name on the Jockey Club's interview list for the post of assistant starter. In what represented an enlightened change of policy by racing's governing body, both Bill and fellow jockey Gerry Scott were accepted for the job.

He had his last ride on Jim Joel's Arctic Bow in the Jim Ford Challenge Cup at Wincanton on 22 February 1973. The final paragraph of his time as a jockey epitomised the triumphs and tragedies of National Hunt racing. Arctic Bow gave him a victorious farewell, coming home fifteen lengths clear of his sole rival, Black Secret, but shortly after passing the post, without any warning, the horse collapsed and died of a ruptured spleen.

The following week Bill commenced his new career. He spent eleven years as an assistant before becoming a full time starter, earning the respect of the jockeys and acquiring a reputation for being one of the best in the business.

He released the starting tape for the last time at Sandown in January 1999, when, to mark his retirement, a handicap hurdle was named in his honour. It was an appropriate venue to sign off; the course where he'd ridden so many of the Queen Mother's finest steeplechasers.

Date: Saturday 25 March 1961 Going: Firm Value to Winner: £20,020 2s 6d

Horse	Owner	Trainer	Age / weight	Jockey	SP
1 Nicolaus Silver	Mr C J Vaughan	F Rimell	9-10-1	H Beasley	28-1
2 Merryman II	Miss W H S Wallace	N F Crump	10-11-12	D Ancil	8-1
3 O'Malley Point	Mr A Elliott	W A Stephenson	10-11-4	P A Farrell	100-6
4 Scottish Flight II	Mrs A T Hodgson	P Cazalet	9-10-6	W Rees	100-6

Distances: 5 lengths, neck, 6 lengths. Time: 9 mins 22.6 secs. 35 ran

Winner trained at Kinnersley, Worcestershire

1962

GORDON CRAMP
An artist in the saddle

Melilla (left, Gordon Cramp) jumps alongside Vain-Wax (David Mould) at Plumpton in October 1963.

ONE OF LIFE'S grafters, Gordon Cramp was born into a racing world. His father was not only travelling head lad to Lewes trainer George Poole at the time of Shaun Spadah's 1921 Grand National victory; he was also the town's bookmaker.

Gordon began his apprenticeship with Lewes trainer Bob Maxwell, then joined George Beeby when Maxwell retired in 1948. He spent nine months at Beeby's Compton yard, which then housed Lord Bicester's top-class chasers Silver Fame, Roimond and Finnure.

Two years with Matt Feakes was followed by a stint of National Service in the King's Troop, and then a further year at Feakes' Rhonehurst stables at Upper Lambourn.

In 1955 he returned to Lewes and spent the next fifteen years as head lad cum stable jockey for Tom Gates. It was for Gates that he eventually rode his first winner, on Sandstorm IV in a Plumpton novices' chase on 25 September 1957.

The best horse he rode for Gates was the grey hurdler Lunar Prince, whose wins included a ten length trouncing of Invader at Hurst Park in March 1962. Within a few days of that victory, Gordon was offered a ride in the Grand National.

He takes up the story: 'David Ellison, the most sporting owner you could wish to meet, rang me up and said "I've bought a horse to run in the Grand National. Would you be interested in riding her?" I accepted without hesitation.

'Though I'd had thirty or forty rides over hurdles that season, I hadn't had a ride over fences. I phoned Frank Muggeridge, who was training at Lewes racecourse at the time, and managed to get a ride on his selling chaser Pelican's Pay at Fontwell on the Monday before the National, but that was my only ride over fences before Melilla.'

Trained at Cirencester by Jim Bowie, Melilla was a true 100-1 outsider, her sole victory having been gained in a Wincanton novices' chase. She had qualified for the Grand National by finishing a well-beaten third in the 1961 Becher Chase.

'We travelled up the day before in David Ellison's Sunbeam Talbot. It took us eight hours,' laughs Gordon. 'As I hadn't ridden at Liverpool, Jim Bowie arranged for me to see Bryan Marshall for advice on how to ride the track.

'Bryan asked "Has she got a chance?" I replied "Realistically, no". He told me to go middle to outer, adding "You'll soon know if something is falling in front of you because you'll see the tail go up".

'Sure enough, as I was approaching one of the fences, well back, about eight lengths off the couple in front of me, both their tails went up, so I moved to one side, jumped it and they were both on the floor.'

Rain had marred the first two days of racing, which had taken place on soft ground. By Saturday morning the course had dried out fairly well but as the crowds began to arrive the skies darkened again. A combination of heavy rain and sleet for two hours before the race resulted in sodden ground, yet despite the gruelling conditions only three of the 32 runners failed to negotiate the first circuit, with Irish raider Fredith's Son and northern challenger Duplicator leading the field past the stands and back out into the country.

Duplicator and Team Spirit both fell at the nineteenth fence, the latter bringing down the favourite, Frenchman's Cove. At the Canal Turn, Fredith's Son was in front of another Irish-trained runner, the 100-1 shot Gay Navarree, followed by Nicolaus Silver and that Aintree perennial Wyndburgh.

Gay Navarree, the mount of amateur rider Tony Cameron who would go on to represent Ireland in the Tokyo Olympic Games, took over at Valentine's and led the tiring Fredith's Son back on to the racecourse, but by the second last fence he had been joined by the twelve-year-old triumvirate of Kilmore, Wyndburgh and Mr What.

Kilmore and Fred Winter hit the front approaching the last, jumped it well and drew clear on the run-in to beat the luckless Wyndburgh, runner-up for the third time, by ten lengths, with Mr What the same distance away third. Behind them came Gay Navarree, pacemaking Fredith's Son, Dark Venetian and the previous year's winner Nicolaus Silver. Seventeen runners, just over half the field, completed the course.

Kilmore was owned in partnership by film distributor Nat Cohen and Hatton Garden jeweller Ben Rosenfeld. Neither owner was present as they were both reported to be ill in bed with heavy colds. They watched the race on television.

Gordon thoroughly enjoyed his first Grand National ride on Melilla. 'My only worry was falling off at the first. Once I'd jumped the first, it was brilliant. She jumped the Chair so well that I nearly went over her head. Otherwise, there were no problems and I took her on to the one before Becher's second time. She'd got tired by then so I pulled up her up.'

He rode Melilla in all her races the following season, by which time Tom Gates was training her. With all-weather gallops still a thing of the future, the Lewes trainers coped with the 1962/63 freeze-up by clubbing together to erect a large indoor ring, close to where Towser Gosden then trained.

By way of relieving the boredom of what was to be two and a half racing-less months, Gordon took up oil painting as a hobby and found that he wasn't too bad at it. One or two owners got to hear about his hidden talent, liked what they saw and asked him to paint their horses. In five weeks he completed twelve paintings. An exhibition was organised in a local pub.

He rode Melilla again in the 1963 Grand National, confident of a good ride, though without a winning chance. He got most of the way round but did not finish.

'I remember jumping the Canal Turn and Valentine's second time round. Then I looked up and saw this loose horse walking across the take-off side of the ditch. There were about five of us baulked there. We ended up on top of the loose horse and Melilla put her head through the fence.

'I took my feet out of the irons, jumped down, and Melilla fell off the other horse. They opened up the side and we walked out. The five of us then cantered our horses back. There was some confusion because the stewards initially thought we'd completed the course.

'Melilla was a lovely old mare, round as a barrel. She wasn't brilliant but, even if she was legless, she still picked up. She ended up in Castle Point, Schull, in County Cork. I still have a photo taken of her in retirement in 1973.'

In the 1966 Grand National he rode Monarch's Thought, also owned by David Ellison and trained by him under permit, getting as far as the Chair before refusing. Gordon later landed a Lingfield selling chase on him in March 1967, his first win for 21 months.

Ellison then upgraded Monarch's Thought to the 1967 Whitbread Gold Cup, taking on Mill House, Woodland Venture, What a Myth and several other top-class chasers in what must rank as one of the strongest Whitbreads ever run.

Recalls Gordon: 'Monarch's Thought was a 100-1 selling chaser against three past or future Gold Cup winners. I thought "What can I do to make some show?" So I led them past the post after the first circuit, having taken the lead from Mill House, who flew past me again down the back straight. It was about the only thing I could have done to put him in the race at some point. But David was thrilled to bits; you'd have thought he'd won it.'

His fourth and last Grand National ride, in 1968, was also his shortest. Portation, owner-trained by Ellison, was baulked and put out of the race at the Canal Turn first time round by the riderless What a Myth, who had fallen at Becher's.

A broken hand, the result of a fall at Plumpton in April 1969, ended Gordon's riding career. With a total of 36 winners to his name he was never a top jockey, but that brought other advantages in that he was able to spend more time learning about stable management.

He trained for two seasons at Failand, near Bristol, turning out a dozen winners, including a double at Newton Abbot in August 1970. He spent eighteen months as second travelling head lad to Michael Jarvis and then joined Roddy Armytage as head lad. His highly successful fourteen-year stay, from 1974 to 1988, coincided with some of the best chasers in the country, such as the gigantic Straight Jocelyn, dual Scottish National winner Barona, and Sir John Thompson's team of Prince Tino, Tuscan Prince, Proud Tarquin, Lean Forward and Princely Bid.

From there, Gordon moved to Philip Hobbs in Somerset before settling as head lad to Peter Cundell at Compton. His wife, Daphne, became the stable's secretary, as she had been for both Armytage and Hobbs. And when Cundell was brought in as the technical adviser for the BBC television series *Trainer*, Gordon's artistic talents were once more in demand.

'Peter bought ten horses for the series. The horses, their rugs, bridles, saddles, sheets and rollers were my responsibility. I like to think that everything on the horses looked right. Those ten horses were in 23 episodes, featuring as year-lings, two-year-olds and older horses. I used to do the make-up on them. I'd paint stars on some, take markings off others, and paint their legs white using a water-based aerosol.'

After thirty years without having had time to indulge in his favourite hobby, Gordon at last found time to pick up his paint brushes again at his West Ilsley home. He paints water colours of local cottages for the village fetes.

And his mind's eye can still paint a picture of those Grand Nationals. 'All three horses, though they weren't world-beaters, gave me four good rides.'

'I've had a good life in racing,' he concludes. 'There were lots of jockeys like me, who didn't ride every day but still earned enough to get a mortgage. I was a small fish in a very big pond.'

Date: Saturday 31 March 1962 Going: Soft Value to Winner: £20,238 15s

Horse	Owner	Trainer	Age / weight	Jockey	SP
1 Kilmore	Mr N Cohen	H R Price	12-10-4	F T Winter	28-1
2 Wyndburgh	Mrs J K M Oliver	J K M Oliver	12-10-9	T A Barnes	45-1
3 Mr What	Mr G V Keeling	R Ward	12-10-9	J Lehane	22-1
4 Gay Navarree	Mr J F Hoey	R A Hoey	10-10-0	Mr A Cameron	100-1

Distances: 10 lengths, 10 lengths, 4 lengths. Time: 9 mins 50.0 secs. 32 ran

Winner trained at Findon, Sussex

1963

PADDY CONNORS, CLIVE CHAPMAN *and* GENE KELLY
The Earl Jones Trio

Gene Kelly (left) and Paddy Connors.

EARL JONES RAN three horses in the 1963 Grand National. He wasn't an Earl at all; it was merely his Christian name, although many people assumed he was and addressed him with appropriate deference.

The late journalist and paddock commentator Clive Graham, a great friend of Earl's, was once asked whether Jones was a member of the British aristocracy. Graham replied bluntly that Earl was no lord, and his only claim to fame was that he drank like one.

Born in Cork in 1917, Jones had served his apprenticeship with Jack Ruttle in Ireland, coming to Britain in 1939 for 'a bit of a holiday'. The 'holiday', which included war service with the Royal Army Ordinance Corps, was to last almost fifty years.

He rode his first British winner, Queen Of The Dandies, at Wincanton on Easter Monday 1947. Within two years he was combining riding with training at Roel Stables, Guiting Power, near Cheltenham.

In October 1958 he rode one of his string, Good Gracious, to win a four-year-old hurdle at his local track. The mare blossomed when put over fences the next season, winning four of her first five starts.

But the stable star at that time was Forty Secrets, who gave Jones his biggest success when winning the 1962 Welsh Grand National in the hands of Josh Gifford.

Both Forty Secrets and Good Gracious were aimed at the 1963 Grand National. They were to be joined by Holm Star, a horse with a dismal completion rate over fences prior to that season, but whom Jones had improved sufficiently to win two minor chases and to finish fourth in the 1962 Grand Sefton.

Working for Jones at that time was a young Irishman named Paddy Connors. The son of jump jockey Davy Connors, he hailed from Naas in County Kildare and had served his apprenticeship with Paddy Prendergast. He spent a year with George Beeby at Compton before joining Jones.

His first winner, Hamoun, came in a handicap hurdle at Stratford on 5 April 1962. His second, Conor's Choice in a Cheltenham selling chase, followed six months later. Soon after that came the big freeze, wiping out all British racing from 22 December 1962 to 8 March 1963, bar a single day at Ayr in January.

Jones's stable was luckier than most, as Paddy recalls: 'We had a farmer up the road who chain-harrowed a field for us every morning. There were half a dozen riding out and two of us carried shovels to get into the gateways, where the snow had drifted overnight. We left the shovels by the gate, rode out, picked them up again afterwards and led the horses back home.'

When racing resumed, Paddy finished third on Good Gracious behind Ayala in the Worcester Royal Porcelain Chase. Jones agreed that he could ride her in the Grand National.

With Josh Gifford committed to riding the tearaway Irish import Out And About for Ryan Price, Clive Chapman was booked for Forty Secrets, while Gene Kelly came in for the ride on Holm Star.

Clive Chapman was born in London in 1934 but, shortly after his father was killed in the war, the family moved to Folkestone where his mother ran a guest house.

He began his career in 1949 as a 15-year-old apprentice with Captain Cecil Boyd-Rochfort. He won two stable lads' boxing titles but left racing after four years and signed up as a 'regular' in the army because he didn't think he would make the grade. However, when he came out three years later, he was keen to get back into the sport.

Returning to Folkestone, he first joined Doug Marks's Lanslade Stables, near Ashford, before moving to Chris Nesfield, who had just started training at Charing. His first winner came on a horse called Mushtara in a Plumpton selling chase in November 1956. Frenchman Rene Emery was Nesfield's first jockey at the time but he struggled to ride at below 10st 10lb and Clive duly inherited the mantle.

By the early 1960s he was well established. He won Chepstow's Rhymney Breweries Chase on Reprieved in 1960 and the following year's Imperial Cup aboard Fidus Achates. The 1961/62 season was numerically his best with 30 winners, including a four-timer at Fontwell's Whitsun meeting.

Having turned freelance, the 1962/63 freeze-up was a financial disaster. Every week without racing cost him £100 income. At least being based in Folkestone had its advantages in that, during the summers, he worked as a steward on the Folkestone-Bologne Channel steamer to supplement his earnings.

Gene Kelly hails from the village of Minworth, Sutton Coldfield. His father worked for the Birmingham Teme and Rea District Drainage Board, which is where Gene began his working life as an errand boy.

By the end of the war he was apprenticed to Joe Lawson at Manton, where he looked after High Stakes, winner of 34 races. When called into the army for National Service, he weighed only 7st 10lb. He was sent to Egypt and while there won the United Services flyweight and bantamweight championships.

He rode his first winner for Winterbourne trainer Charlie Cooper, getting up close home on Star Of April in a two-mile chase at Worcester on 16 October 1954.

In 1956 he had his first ride in the Grand National, on the 66-1 outsider Polonius, a horse that had been bought for £25 and a cartload of hay. The owner's son, Colin Hailstone, usually rode him but was laid low with pneumonia, which he'd caught after diving into a pond to rescue a young calf. Unable to extricate himself and the calf from the water, he had been forced to endure a cold and soaking couple of hours before help arrived.

Recalls Gene: 'Polonius was a horse you dared not move on, you had to be quiet as a mouse. At Liverpool he was hopping round, just a dream, when a loose horse brought me to a standstill on the second circuit.

'After that I was often close up for good rides in the National but was always having to depend on the misfortune of somebody else. In 1957 I rode Tiberetta for Edward Courage at Birmingham and was to ride her in the National on condition that Eagle Lodge ran. Eagle Lodge was to be ridden by Alan Oughton but he struck into himself on the morning of the race. Quite naturally, Alan claimed the ride on Tiberetta and she finished third.

'The next year the Courages had second claim on George Slack after Bobby Renton. Three days before the race, Bobby's horse went wrong so George rode Tiberetta and finished second.

'When the French horse, Imposant, came to this country in 1961, I was given the job of schooling him at Hurst Park. I was going to ride him at Aintree if his regular jockey wasn't available. Alas, he was.'

Gene won twice over the Mildmay fences during the 1961/62 season on Pat Upton's Dancing Rain. The obstacles on the Mildmay course, introduced in 1953 and named in memory of that most popular of amateur riders Lord Anthony Mildmay, were smaller versions of the Grand National fences and an ideal trial for the real thing. They were dispensed with in favour of traditional birch fences in 1975 with Aintree's Spring Meeting becoming an all jumping fixture two years later.

Gene continues: 'In 1963 I was due to ride Ayala for Keith Piggott but his leg kept filling up. Meanwhile, Earl Jones wanted me for Holm Star. Josh Gifford had won on him and told me I really ought to ride Holm Star but warned me to drop him out for the first mile or so because he broke blood vessels.

'Earl was chasing me to ride him but I told him I couldn't let him know for sure because I was hoping to ride Ayala. On the Saturday before the National, Earl knocked at my door and said "Holm Star. He runs. You ride him." He put £100 on the table and walked out. When I got to Sandown races that afternoon, Keith Piggott came up to me and said "Ayala's leg's gone down. He runs." I told him what had happened with Earl Jones so Keith asked me to go round the weighing room and find him a jockey who'd ridden in the National and could do ten stone.

'I went to Joe Guest and Owen McNally but they'd already got rides and couldn't get off. After going round asking everybody, the only person in the weighing room who hadn't got a ride, had ridden in the National and could do ten stone was Pat Buckley. I asked him what his form was at Liverpool and he replied "I rode the favourite last year for Neville Crump, my only ride, and fell at the first." I said "Come with me, and don't tell Keith Piggott that!"'

Says Paddy Connors of the Earl Jones trio: 'Good Gracious was the smallest of the three but a good, honest mare. Forty Secrets was a very hard puller. I'd ridden him one foggy day at Leicester earlier that season. I thought I had the race won going to the last, then Ian Balding came out of the mist and beat me. Holm Star was probably the ugliest horse you could ever look at, with great big ears and a huge, common head.

'I'd never been to Aintree before. I walked round the track with Taffy Salaman and thought the fences didn't look too bad at all. I'd got halfway round when I spotted a line of flags over on the other side. I said, "There's something wrong here; let's go over and have a look where all those flags are." It was then I found that I'd been walking the Mildmay Course!

'It doesn't worry you too much, riding in the National, as long as you try and treat it as just another race. You know the fences are there and they're big. A steward comes in, gets up on a box and tries to tell everybody not to go too fast, but it's a complete waste of time. They just jump off and go, because everyone's trying to get a position.

'It's a sprint going to the first. All I can remember is the sound of the horses' hooves touching the grass as they landed. The third, the open ditch, was the biggest fence I'd ever seen. When you've jumped the first few you try to sort a position out. I was handy enough, on the inside of middle.

'She jumped the fifth great. Then at Becher's, she just got in a bit close and the drop caught her out; she couldn't find her front legs and came down. I wasn't hurt. While I was still lying on the ground, a reporter came over to me and asked what happened!'

Gene Kelly got further: 'Holm Star was popping along beautifully without me doing anything. You couldn't put a fence in the wrong place for him, even round Liverpool. As we were going into Valentine's second time, there were two horses, one on either side; they both ran in and pinched me and mine stopped dead.'

As predicted, Out And About had stormed off in front and there he stayed until after the Canal Turn on the second circuit. But by then he was a tired horse and being pressed by French Lawyer, Carrickbeg and Hawa's Song over Valentine's. Two fences later, Out And About fell, interfering with Carrickbeg.

As they came back onto the racecourse with two left to jump, Hawa's Song, Springbok, Ayala and Carrickbeg were several lengths clear of the toiling French Lawyer and the improving Team Spirit. Springbok weakened quickly between the last two and it was Carrickbeg who jumped the final fence in front of Ayala.

At the Elbow, Carrickbeg led by two lengths and looked sure to win, but he weakened close home and the 66-1 outsider Ayala, ridden by 19-year-old Pat Buckley, got up in the last fifty yards to deprive John Lawrence and Carrickbeg of Aintree glory. And Gene Kelly was left to reflect upon missing the chance of being on the winner, and of having put Buckley in for the ride.

Forty Secrets was the only one of Jones's trio to get round, trailing in last but one of the 22 finishers. Said Clive Chapman: 'I was up in the first four when, at the last jump first time round, the one before the Chair, he skidded along on his belly and went from fourth position to right out the back. After that I kept going just in case anything happened up front. I had a good ride round and if it hadn't been for that mistake on the first circuit I'm sure he'd have been in the first three.'

Good Gracious ran twice more that season, finishing last at Cheltenham and pulling up at Towcester, before being retired to the paddocks. Holm Star finished last in the Welsh Grand National then left Jones's yard to be trained by Fred Rimell.

Reunited with Josh Gifford, Forty Secrets won his next start, the Sunday Express Chase at Cheltenham, but then fell in the Scottish National. Paddy rode him in the 1963 Whitbread Gold Cup but was forced to pull up on the second circuit when the saddle slipped back over the horse's quarters.

Looking back on the second half of that decimated 1962/63 season, Paddy is convinced that Jones's ability to work the horses on the chain-harrowed fields every day during the freeze-up worked against him in the long run.

'The farmer did a great job and the gallops were absolutely brilliant; we could work our horses to the fullest. But when racing restarted, they'd all gone over the top. We'd worked them and worked them, thinking we'd got one up on the other trainers whose horses were stood idle in their boxes. But three months was too long to be working horses hard. They'd got really fit during the freeze, then gone over the top and we couldn't win a race with them for the rest of the season.'

In 1964 Earl Jones moved his string to Hazel Slade stables, from where Tom Coulthwaite had sent out three Grand National winners. He put in a loose school and laid down one of the first all-weather gallops in the country to supplement the existing grass gallops on nearby Hednesford Common.

Soon after, Paddy Connors suffered a serious motor bike accident, which kept him out of the saddle for several months. Mariner's Signal gave him a victorious comeback when landing the Astbury Trophy at Wolverhampton's 1966 Christmas meeting.

After nine years with Jones, he joined Bob Clay at Shareshill, near Wolverhampton. Although Clay held the licence, he concentrated more on farming while Paddy looked after the training side and continued to ride. They enjoyed their biggest success when Esban, owned by the exuberant singer Dorothy Squires, romped home in the 1973 Scottish Grand National with Jimmy Bourke on board.

In the early 1980s, Paddy took out a permit and trained a couple at Old Longdon Hall Farm, Rugeley, but when Jones retired and sold his yard to Guiseppe (Joe) Fierro, Paddy found himself back at Hazel Slade as Fierro's trainer.

He left after three years and joined local vet and breeder John Newcombe at Brownhills, where his life revolved around Irish Draught and Shire horses.

At the time of the 1963 Grand National Gene Kelly was riding regularly for Nickel Coin's trainer Jack O'Donoghue, whose Reigate stables housed the Queen Mother's chaser Gay Record.

'I was first asked to ride him at Hurst Park. When I got there I had three white fivers in my pocket. I didn't know if I'd ever get to put the royal colours on again so I went to the three photographers, got one to take a photograph of me in the paddock, another to take one of me cantering down to the start, and the third to take a photo of me jumping the first, just in case we didn't get to the second. We finished fifth.'

He recalls his first win in the royal colours on Gay Record at Sandown Park on 17 November 1961. It was also the first time he'd met the Queen Mother. As a career highlight it could not be surpassed and the memories of the reception in the unsaddling enclosure, with the Queen Mother being there to greet her winner, remain as vivid as ever.

He won twice more on Gay Record that season, breaking the Windsor three-mile track record by almost nine seconds on the last occasion, despite having twisted a plate into the shape of a letter S. Gene still has that very plate, given to him as a memento of an outstanding performance.

He reflects: 'Gay Record had so much ability. I would love to have ridden him in the Grand National. Nobody knows better than me just how good that horse was.'

Gene rode Gay Record in 24 races, winning five, the last being at Sandown in November 1963. When Gay Record became the Queen Mother's 100th winner at Folkestone on 20 October 1964, it was Bobby Beasley who had the ride. Gene was recovering from four fractured vertebrae and seven broken ribs, sustained a week earlier in a second-fence spill at Worcester.

He was heartbroken at missing the ride on the Queen Mother's hundredth winner but was delighted to be invited to party at the Savoy to celebrate the century. 'It was gone one o'clock in the morning and they were already starting to lay the tables for breakfast when I had the honour of dancing with the Queen Mother. She really was some mover, a wonderful dancer.'

Despite the specialist's warning that the next fall would aggravate the Worcester injury, Gene carried on riding. He went more than 50 rides before suffering another fall, the one that ended his career, on a horse named Yvan II in a hurdle race at Chepstow in February 1965.

Says Gene: 'I said to the specialist "Will you get me ready for the National?" He said he'd do his best. He let me sweat on it for a few days and then he said "Mr Kelly, what about the National?" I replied "I think we'd better forget it".'

Afterwards he worked for many years as the UK Sales Manager for Constant Laboratories, a Liverpool-based company supplying an equine nutritional product called Convital. He also ran a saddlery business.

Home for Gene and Diana Kelly is in the Worcestershire village of Willersey, on the outskirts of Broadway. For the last 25 years they have bred and shown black rams and run a large closed flock of Lleyn Peninsula sheep. Diana and son Adam judge at the major county shows.

'I was very lucky,' he concludes. 'I had the best out of racing. It was good fun and you just can't buy the comradeship that I experienced back in the days of the white fiver.'

Clang! The starting stalls swing open and the horses burst from the gates…all except one. The jockey endeavours to galvanise his mount into action but to no avail. Unperturbed, he looks down at his recalcitrant steed, then lights up a Hamlet cigar.

It was an advertisement seen by millions. The man on board was Clive Chapman.

The success of that TV ad, first shown in 1973, would lead to a second career in television and films for the former jockey.

Two weeks after the 1963 Grand National Clive rode his only winner in the Queen Mother's colours aboard Super Fox at Plumpton's Easter meeting. Being based in Kent, he regularly rode out for royal trainer Peter Cazalet, whose Fairlawne stables were located in nearby Tonbridge.

A broken neck at Wincanton in December 1966 left him in a plaster cast down to his waist for six months. After that he found it tough going. He rode his final winner on Another Surge at his home course, Folkestone, on 2 October 1969, before suffering head injuries in a Boxing Day fall at Huntingdon. The Jockey Club doctors would not allow him to ride again.

'They said I was punch drunk, which I probably was,' he admitted. 'Over a period of fifteen years, the concussions from falls caught up with me.

'I wanted to stay in racing, so I travelled horses, taking them to Australia by ship. We took six horses at a time and it took a month to get over to Sydney.'

Then in 1972 came something out of the blue. It began innocently enough, a quiet dinner with Clement Freud and his trainer Tim Finch. During the meal, Freud, whose television partnership with bloodhound Henry advertising dog food was a performance made in Ad Heaven, asked Clive if he'd ever done commercials. He offered to get him an equity card.

Twelve months later, to the background of the second movement of Bach's Suite for Orchestra No. 3 in D Major, better known as 'Air on a G String', Clive Chapman lit up that famous Hamlet cigar.

The ad proved so popular that it led to further commercials for Jacob's Club biscuits and Kellogg's Corn Flakes and quickly helped him establish a new career in show business. Working under his second Christian name of Ira – it was his father's name – he enjoyed regular TV appearances during the seventies and eighties alongside the likes of Cannon and Ball, Little and Large, Dick Emery and Dave Allen, plus a part in the film *Love Story*.

Magazine advertisements brought him further recognition, as did a Dick Turpin TV special starring Richard O'Sullivan, in which Clive had to be pulled off a horse while riding through the woods.

'I had three parts in the film *Cleopatra* – a Greek soldier, a courtier and a Syrian slave. Then my agent got me quite a lot of work with *The Two Ronnies*. I doubled for Ronnie Corbett riding horses and motor bikes, falling off and rolling down the cliffs. It was trick photography but Ronnie didn't want to do the stunts.'

He made a belated return to race riding in the mid-1980s, taking part in Arab races.

In June 1985, almost sixteen years since his last winner, he rode Magic Lord to victory at Newton Abbot. He continued to ride in Arab races for the next five years until a fall at Towcester resulted in six broken ribs and retirement.

Clive Chapman died in May 2006, aged 71, following a short illness.

As for Earl Jones, the highlight of his career came at the 1968 Cheltenham Festival, when his £210 purchase Jolly Signal landed an enormous gamble in the County Hurdle and The Hustler took the Cotswold Chase. In 1974 he won a second Welsh National with Pattered, a 25-1 chance, ridden by Ken White.

Jones always liked a tilt at the ring but the failed coup of novice hurdler Nemon at Wolverhampton in March 1978 had a horrific sequel when he was 'kneecapped' in a brutal gangland-style ambush. His attackers riddled him with a hundred shotgun pellets.

Within a year of that assault, Jones suffered a stroke, from which his recovery was both slow and painful. Though he returned to training, it was with a much reduced string. Roy's House was his final winner, in a Wolverhampton novices' chase in November 1986. Following the death of his wife, Bridie, in 1988, he handed in his licence after 40 years, during which he had sent out some 500 winners.

He returned to Ireland, settling in Waterford on the south coast, where he died, aged 85, in June 2003.

Date: Saturday 30 March 1963 Going: Soft Value to Winner: £21,315 7s 6d

Horse	Owner	Trainer	Age / weight	Jockey	SP
1 Ayala	Mr P B Raymond	K Piggott	9-10-0	P Buckley	66-1
2 Carrickbeg	Mr G Kindersley	D Butchers	7-10-3	Mr J Lawrence	20-1
3 Hawa's Song	Mr W Stephenson	W A Stephenson	10-10-0	P Broderick	28-1
4 Team Spirit	Mr R B Woodard	F Walwyn	11-10-3	G W Robinson	13-1

Distances: ¾ length, 5 lengths, 6 lengths. Time: 9 mins 35.8 secs. 47 ran

Winner trained at Lambourn, Berkshire

1964

JOHN KENNEALLY
There's a different roar

Purple Silk (far side) is caught close home by Team Spirit, accompanied by riderless Lizawake.

THE *PETERBOROUGH EVENING TELEGRAPH* summed it up. 'The hearts of hundreds of racing fans beat extra quickly on Saturday afternoon, as they saw the Market Deeping horse Purple Silk pipped on the post in one of the most thrilling Grand National finishes. Racing over the distance for the first time, he led from the moment he jumped the last fence in the world's toughest race until he was overtaken by Team Spirit's sensational finishing burst during the last fifty yards.'

Whenever John Kenneally watches the recording of that 1964 Grand National he recalls the details of a master plan carried out to perfection for four and a quarter of those stamina-sapping four and a half miles.

'It was heartbreaking,' he says. 'I fancied Purple Silk so much; it was my life's ambition.'

Such an ambition seemed a million miles away in the late 1930s at his family's farm near Cappaquin, County Waterford. There were plenty of animals around, though not all were horses. He learned to ride on an old sow called The Bonn.

'She was a very clever pig,' he recounts. 'My mother used to boil pots of potatoes to feed the pigs. After she'd boiled one pot she put it outside to cool off while she boiled the next one. The Bonn figured out that if she knocked those pots over, they'd get cool quicker, so she always helped herself. My mother would see her and rush out the door with a stick. The Bonn would wait until mother took the last step and then go scooting off.

'So mother used to tell me to put The Bonn in the little field, out of the way. It's difficult trying to get a pig going in one direction when she doesn't want to, so I started to ride her. The dog got very excited and was hanging on her ear, knocking pots and pans all over the place.'

John graduated from sows to ponies, then went hunting and flapping. He began his racing career with trainer Tim Hyde, who had ridden Workman to win the 1939 Grand National.

He eventually left Hyde to join Vincent O'Brien. 'He had Cottage Rake, Royal Tan and Early Mist then,' he recalls. 'I really loved it there, it gave me great confidence. But I wanted to be a jockey and Vincent was changing over from jumpers to Flat horses and I knew there'd be no opportunity there, so I came over to Britain, aged eighteen.'

A short spell with Tom Pettifer at Letcombe Regis was followed by stints with Jack Anthony and John de Moraville. He then spent two years with Solly Parker at Rhyl, in North Wales, and rode his first winner for him, Evening Paradise, in a Manchester selling hurdle on the Saturday of Easter 1955.

In 1957 John moved east and joined Market Deeping trainer George Vergette. Although he had more horses than Parker, there was no immediate guarantee of rides, for Geoff Mann was his stable jockey at the time.

'George Vergette was a great man to ride for,' says John. 'He'd been a good jockey and a very fine finisher, but he was a horseman as well as a jockey. But I made a big mistake shortly after going there. I'd started to get more and more rides, then Geoff Mann, who was also his head lad, left and Vergette talked me into being his new head lad. That restricted me for getting outside rides. I loved it, but I knew afterwards it was a mistake.'

He did, however, have an outside ride on the Eric Cousins-trained Wood-brown in the 1963 Grand National, completing the course in eighteenth place.

The Vergette yard housed a number of useful performers during the early sixties, including hurdlers Red Holly, Red Flush and Golden Sailor, but none was more promising than Purple Silk. John won on him over hurdles at Southwell and Cheltenham and in a novice chase at Wolverhampton in February 1962.

In the spring of 1963 he rode Purple Silk to victory at Doncaster and was then second in Cheltenham's Golden Miller Chase. With John unable to do 9st 7lb, Clive Chapman rode him in the Whitbread Gold Cup, where he finished runner-up to Hoodwinked. His 1963/64 campaign would be geared towards the Grand National.

Purple Silk was owned by Tom Beattie, who also owned Long Eaton grey-hound stadium. The horse came to the 1964 Grand National in great form on the back of victories at Leicester and Wetherby. John really fancied his chances.

'I knew from when he was a three-year-old that he was a National horse.

He wasn't the easiest of horses to know. He wouldn't jump a fence at home, so before the National we schooled him over hurdles with Red Holly and Red Flush.'

Grand National day started tragically when a plane crashed near the Canal Turn, killing all five occupants. Among them was the television personality Nancy Spain, who was to have been a guest of Mirabel Topham.

The wide openness of the race was reflected by the fact that four horses shared favouritism at 100-7 – making the 1964 National, according to betting guru John McCririck, the most open race ever recorded. Five more, including Purple Silk, were priced at 100-6, with Team Spirit and Willie Robinson, making their fifth successive attempt to win the National, at 18-1.

Purple Silk's handicap weight of 10st 3lb was always going to be a struggle for John. He had been on a controlled diet for six weeks before the race and finally weighed out a pound overweight at 10st 4lb.

'I told George Vergette how I would like to ride him. I wanted to go down to Becher's in the first half dozen to keep out of trouble. Then after Becher's I'd take a pull and give him a nice long breather. I'd be quite happy to pass the stands in the first dozen. After that, start making ground gradually, jump Becher's second time in the first six and then start riding a race on him.

'I rode him exactly that way, with the exception that I didn't want to strike the front until after the Elbow because I knew what sort of a character he was. When he ran out of fences and ran out of horses he thought he'd done enough.'

As expected, front-runners Peacetown and Out And About set off at a cracking pace. Purple Silk got a good start and was with the leaders at the first fence. He took the fifth in third place, jumped Becher's superbly, then settled in behind the leaders. Everything was going to plan.

Out And About and Peacetown still led the field a merry dance approaching the Chair, with Team Spirit in third, himself clear of the pack. On TV, commentator Peter O'Sullevan exclaimed, prophetically, 'I've never seen Team Spirit lying up so close before in the National!'

John rode into the Chair just behind Paddy Farrell on Border Flight. He heard the crash and knew that the horse had made a terrible mistake.

By the time the field reached the seventeenth fence, Out And About had shot his bolt, leaving Peacetown clear in front. By Becher's, Purple Silk had moved up and when Reproduction fell at the next, breaking Robin Langley's arm in the process, John found himself going well in second place.

'The only trouble I had was when Peacetown carried me wide at the Canal Turn. Going to the fence I was trying to pull Purple Silk round, like he'd jumped it first time, but when Peacetown went straight on, he instinctively cocked his jaw and followed the leader. I could see he wanted to jump straight, so I dropped my hands and let him go. That left me on the outside following Peacetown into Valentine's. It was here that he made his one mistake. He was more interested in watching what Peacetown was doing than measuring his fence up. He really hit that one and he was clever to stand up.'

Peacetown still led at the second last, ahead of Purple Silk, Team Spirit, Eternal and the weakening Springbok, this quintet being clear of the rest. A loose horse, Lizawake, slightly hampered Purple Silk, causing John to switch inside him.

'I was upsides at the last, exactly where I'd planned to be, but Peacetown was just about finished. He was renowned for jumping out to the right and he did so at the last. That left me in front with nobody there to lead us and no option but to kick on.'

Hugging the inside, Purple Silk passed the Elbow two lengths clear of Team Spirit, who had riderless Lizawake alongside on his right. Peacetown had drifted wide to the stands side rails.

'I was aware from the roar of the crowd that Team Spirit was there. You couldn't help but hear it, especially at Aintree. There's a different roar between cheering a winning horse and an exciting finish. I knew there was something coming at me, but I also knew I was going as fast as I could.

'When he appeared I picked my stick up and gave Purple Silk one good smack, but he never lengthened his stride one iota. Some people criticised me for not using the whip more, but I knew the horse. If I'd hit the horse in front, I think he'd have stopped. If he hadn't have been left on his own after the last fence, I'm certain he would have won.

'If the loose horse had come with me, I suppose I would have won. If the loose horse hadn't been there at all ... well, who knows? Team Spirit didn't quicken until the last fifty yards but I think my fellow was dying by then. I don't think he quite got home.'

Team Spirit won by half a length. Had the pound overweight made the difference?

'The one thing I didn't want to be was weak. I was at a weight that I felt strong at. I don't think I was tired in the finish. There was no reason for me to be tired because I was still on the bridle going to the last. I wasn't pushing; I was just getting there as the race was unfolding. I just wanted a lead to the Elbow and, of course, it didn't happen.

'It was very disappointing to be beaten like that. Then when I came in I learned that Paddy Farrell had broken his back in the fall from Border Flight. That was the lowest point for me, on top of just having got beat.'

John and Purple Silk returned to Aintree that autumn, finishing second in the Grand Sefton, beaten two lengths by Red Thorn. Purple Silk injured a leg shortly afterwards and was off the course for over a year. He failed to finish in all three of his comeback races at the start of 1966 and that looked to be the end of his career. However, he was later bought by Mrs P. A. Feeney and sent to Ryan Price, who nursed him back to win at Lingfield in March 1968. He was second at Ascot on his next start but never ran again.

John had one more Grand National ride, in 1967, on the 66-1 outsider Lucky

Domino. He was an honest enough campaigner on the northern circuit, with two Durham Nationals to his credit, but he did not enjoy the Aintree experience and was well behind when falling at the nineteenth.

At the end of that season John gave up his constant battle with the scales to set up as a salaried trainer at Clipsham Hall, near Oakham, where the gallops were located along a disused railway track. That came to an abrupt end when his employer went broke. After that came a brief spell as assistant to Doug Marks followed by a longer association with David Arbuthnot as head lad / travelling head lad.

Disillusioned with racing and looking for a secure future, he set up as a partner in a Newbury-based taxi company, Cabco, which allowed him the freedom of being able to work the hours he wanted.

It also allowed him the opportunity to go racing, to meet old friends, and to reminisce about old times; such as the day when Purple Silk so nearly won the Grand National.

Date: Saturday 21 March 1964 Going: Soft Value to Winner: £20,280

Horse	Owner	Trainer	Age / weight	Jockey	SP
1 Team Spirit	Mr J K Goodman	F Walwyn	12-10-3	G W Robinson	18-1
2 Purple Silk	Mr T Beattie	G Vergette	9-10-4	J Kenneally	100-6
3 Peacetown	Mrs F Williams	G R Owen	10-10-1	R Edwards	40-1
4 Eternal	Lt Col R G Fenwick-Palmer	Owner	13-10-2	Mr S Davenport	66-1

Distances: ½ length, 6 lengths, 3 lengths. Time: 9 mins 46.8 secs. 33 ran

Winner trained at Lambourn, Berkshire

1965

JIM RENFREE
A Cornish farmer's son

Dark Venetian and Jim Renfree are led from the paddock by Beccy Brackenbury on their way to the start for the 1965 Grand National.

'CORNISH FARMERS ARE hard men and he was the hardest of the hard,' said Jim Renfree of his father. 'He was a strong man in every way. He used to wrestle; he was never thrown. He spent the war as a reconnaissance observer in the air force, where average life expectancy was about three weeks because the Germans were shooting them all down. He survived that. He had tremendous nerve.'

Alfred Renfree, known as Fred by all who knew him, fathered a son and two daughters. In 1932 he bought Bush Farm in Saltash. He farmed a herd of cattle, grew rhubarb in the days when there wasn't much fruit about, and always had horses around the place. All three children learned to ride on Dartmoor ponies.

'Father used to buy 25 Dartmoor ponies at a time and we'd ride them two miles to school and back to break them in,' continued Jim. 'As each one was sold, we'd ride another, until we were left with the bad ones he couldn't sell. And they were bad – I'd get thrown off every day. Then, when I went to grammar school I had to ride them five miles each way. I never learned anything, except how to fall off a horse!

'I was taking part in gymkhanas and flapping races by the time I was nine. You get a lot of race riding experience in gymkhanas. That's how I got to be very good at turning bends. The bread and butter racecourses, such as Wye, Buckfastleigh and Newton Abbot, were all sharp and a man who could turn bends had a tremendous advantage. It was surprising how many jockeys didn't seem to know that. You could wait behind them and go on their inside.

'When I was sixteen I started riding point-to-points over banks. If you went too fast, they overjumped and fell. There was no such thing as going through a bank. It was solid earth. Hence, when I went on to ride under Rules, steeple-chasing held no fears for me.

'Father took out a permit around 1950. We only had two horses and neither of them was a real racehorse. I used to come last every time, even though I tried my heart out. My breeches were made by a local tailor. They were so tight around the knees that I couldn't reach the stirrups, so I had to shorten my irons to be able to reach them. They were so big around the waist I had to hold them up with braces. My silks were so baggy that if I tucked them into my trousers, they'd fill with air. These hideous clothes handicapped me terribly – it looked as though there was a barrage balloon going round on the back of a horse!

'One day the stewards called us in and asked us whether we ought to be running these horses as they were never going to get anywhere. Father didn't really have an answer. Anyway, he got Johnny Bullock to ride one of them next time. Whereas I used to come about twelve lengths last, scrubbing like hell for every stride of the race, Johnny only rode him passing the stands, putting on a bit of a show, and finished 25 lengths last. Father put me back on again after that.'

Eventually, they found a horse capable of winning a race, a handicap chaser called Golden Kippers, who gave Jim his first success at Buckfastleigh on 23 May 1953. From the mid-1950s onwards, while retaining his amateur status and riding mainly for his father, Jim was the leading jockey around the tight little right-handed circuit that was Buckfastleigh and enjoyed conspicuous success at the other south-west courses.

Fred Renfree had a good eye for a bargain. He would often pay next to nothing for a seemingly hopeless case and turn it into a winner. War Whoop cost £75 yet Jim won three novice hurdles in a row on him. John O'Groats was bought cheaply at Ascot Sales and Jim won six times on him in his hurdling days. Over fences he won the Senior Service Trophy at Sandown for Syd Dale.

'Being a Cornish farmer, father didn't want to spend any money,' recalled Jim, 'so he didn't encourage me to turn professional because, if I did, he'd have had to pay me. My mother felt it was such a comedown to be a professional jockey. I thought it sounded all right to me but I didn't want to let the family down, so I stayed an amateur.'

Jim was not the only Renfree riding at the time, for sister Jenifer was the national champion lady point-to-point rider five times in the 1950s. She won 41 times on the extraordinary East Cornwall pony Lonesome Boy, who, despite standing no more than 15 hands, won 65 races, 53 of them in succession, between 1950 and 1959.

Although her father held the licence, it was Jenifer who unofficially trained the Renfree horses. When she married David Barons in 1961 and took up training on a public scale at Kingsbridge, she and jockey brother Jim combined to great effect. Two horses in particular brought them into the limelight. One was Staggered, who scored eight times over fences during the 1963/64 season.

The other was a front-running mare named Volant. In just eight months between March and November 1963, she ran 17 races, won 15 and was second in the other two (she was found to have been in season on the two occasions she lost). She won over hurdles and fences, signing off by winning the Ansells Brewery Chase at Worcester and the Middlesex Chase at Kempton. Jim rode her in all bar one of her races – and there's a story about the one he missed.

'I won on her at Newton Abbot on a Friday and she was entered there again the following day. I had to go "up country" to Plumpton on the Saturday so David Nicholson was asked to ride her. She was a mare you couldn't move on. If you did, she'd get completely muddled, but if you sat still and left her alone, she'd ping her fences lovely. David asked me how to ride her but, being a bit canny and not wanting to lose the ride, I didn't exactly tell him right. I told him he'd have to push her along a bit. She won, but she went terrible for him. The more he rode her, the harder she hit the fences. I was thrilled!

'Her owner, Bill Scott, wasn't too pleased with David's ride and said in his broad Cornish accent, "We won't be needin' 'e again" and refused to pay him.'

After narrowly losing out to Stephen Davenport for the 1963/64 amateur riders' title, Jim finally turned professional the following season. Among the horses in the Barons yard was the bay mare Dark Venetian, who had completed the course in both the 1962 and '63 Grand Nationals.

Dark Venetian was originally trained by Richmond Sturdy before being bought by Charlie Stuck, a Plymouth bookmaker who also owned a football pools business. Stuck's ambition was to own and train a string of racehorses. Money was no barrier but being a bookmaker was, for bookies were then not permitted to own racehorses or to hold a trainer's licence. Undaunted, in 1960 he had purchased Crossways Stables at Yelverton, South Devon, bought himself eighteen horses, registered his wife as their owner and installed National Hunt jockey Mick James as his private trainer. The enterprise made a good start, highlighted by the 25-1 victory of Fidus Achates in the 1961 Imperial Cup.

Despite the success of that first season, there was a falling out between owner and trainer, with Bob Bassett taking over the licence for the 1961/62 campaign, while his son, Dave Bassett, combined the job of stable jockey with farming 60 acres at West Woodburn, near Tiverton.

Paddy Cowley took the mount on Dark Venetian in the 1962 Grand National with Bassett electing to ride stable companion Politics. Both horses completed the course, finishing sixth and sixteenth respectively.

Dark Venetian won three races around the Devon courses in the early part of the 1962/63 season before the worst winter since 1947 wiped out virtually all British racing between Christmas and the second week of March. She reappeared a fortnight before the 1963 Grand National to beat Vivant in the Coventry (now the Racing Post) Chase at Kempton and finished ninth in the National itself, partnered this time by Dave Bassett.

She scored twice in the opening weeks of the 1963/64 season when trained by Jim Bowie at Cirencester. Normally a front runner, she had for once come from well off the pace to beat Taxidermist a short head in a sponsored chase at Fontwell, then won the West of England Champion Challenge Trophy at Devon and Exeter. However, her form then deteriorated and a change of owner and trainer had failed to induce any improvement. Despite having shown nothing for more than a year, Barons aimed her at the 1965 Grand National.

Racing had been rocked the previous summer when Mrs Mirabel Topham announced that she was selling Aintree racecourse to a building developer, Capital and Counties, whose stated intention was to redevelop it for housing. The course's former owner, Lord Sefton, who had sold the land to Tophams Limited in 1949, successfully brought an injunction on the grounds that it breached covenants in the 1949 sale, which restricted the use of Aintree to racing and agricultural purposes only during his (Sefton's) lifetime. However, this was cold comfort because nobody could actually force Tophams to continue staging the race itself.

Consequently, 112 entries were received for what, according to Mrs Topham, was to be the last Grand National at Aintree. The presence of Mill House gave an uneven look to the handicap, for he was set to concede lumps of weight to his lesser rivals. Following his subsequent defection, in accordance with the rule then in force, all the weights were raised, thus the minimum weight would be 10st 13lb. (In those days all the bottom weights were automatically lumped together on 10st, there being no such thing as a 'long handicap'.)

On a perfect, bright March afternoon, the Scottish-trained former hunter chaser Freddie, the new top weight with 11st 13lb, was backed down to 7-2 favourite, ahead of the Queen Mother's The Rip at nines. Rondetto and Kapeno were both 100-8, with Vultrix and the American challenger Jay Trump, now trained by Fred Winter, at 100-6. Out of form Dark Venetian was a 100-1 long shot among the 47 runners.

Yet it was Dark Venetian that led over the first fence, alongside habitual front-runner Peacetown, with Phebu, Freddie, Nedsmar, Pontin-Go, Vulcano and Brown Diamond all close up. Ayala, the winner in 1963, was the only faller there.

'The National looked easy to me,' reflected Jim. 'I'd been riding over banks since I was sixteen so I was used to the drops. And as it was four and a half miles, they weren't going to go very fast.

'I remember lining up four or five off the inner. Then I did completely the wrong thing by going off too fast. That was the way I was used to riding. I was always in the first two or three around the sharp west country tracks. Most of us west country riders rode pretty well to the front and that is not the way to ride the Grand National.

'It was so easy to get to the lead and jump the first in front. Everything was fine early, delightful, and I was still in front at Becher's, which felt like a hell of a drop. I caught it just right and we were floating. My word, that did seem big.

'The truth is, I was very tense until the Canal Turn. When I got over that, I thought everything was all right and felt it was time to settle down and think about the remaining three and a half miles of the race.

'Maybe I relaxed too much, goodness only knows. At the fence after Valentine's her legs collapsed when she landed, simple as that. No feeling that it was going to happen until I was actually on the ground. But oh, the interminable time it took the horses to go over me was amazing. It seemed like four hundred rather than forty. Amazingly, I wasn't stepped on. As I was way out in the country, I managed to catch another loose horse and rode it back.

'Paddy Cowley and Dave Bassett had both ridden her along steadily early on, which would have suited her. It took me a long time to learn that you had to wait in the Grand National. It's a race you've got to ride in once to realise what it's all about.'

Phebu, attended by two loose horses, led Peacetown and the rest of the runners approaching the thirteenth, where the riderless Red Tide ran across the fence and cannoned into Phebu, who had nowhere to jump and fired Jimmy Morrissey over to the landing side.

Rondetto, who had made rapid improvement from the rear, jumped the Chair ahead of Peacetown and this pair led the field out onto the second circuit and down towards Becher's. Rondetto remained in front until the fifth fence from home where he knuckled over on landing, leaving Freddie in front of Jay Trump. From thereon, the race lay between them.

Following a tremendous battle up the run-in, with both horses giving their last ounce of courage, it was 27-year-old amateur Crompton 'Tommy' Smith from Littlebury, Virginia, who went on to win on Jay Trump, beating Pat McCarron on Freddie by three-quarters of a length. Mr Jones, ridden by another amateur, Chris Collins, was twenty lengths further back in third. For former champion jockey Fred Winter, in his first season as a trainer, it marked the start of an outstanding second career.

In the weeks before the race, the BBC had focussed on two horses as part of the build-up to its Aintree coverage. The two it had chosen were Jay Trump and Freddie. It proved to be an inspired choice.

Jim rode Dark Venetian in that year's Welsh Grand National, finishing third behind Norther. He hung up his boots at the end of the following season.

'The fences started to look bigger. I was nearly 35 and not enjoying it any more. I was down at the start at Windsor one day and I thought "I've got two lovely kids at home. What the hell am I doing this for?" Then, to add insult to injury, I fell off.'

With 300 acres' worth of Bush Farm and 35 milking cows to look after, Jim had plenty to occupy his time. Together with his German-born wife Irene, he also ran a popular and busy riding school for sixteen years, combining it with bed, breakfast and evening meal.

He took part in midnight steeplechases at 55, but otherwise rode very little. 'In my late sixties,' he confessed, 'when I put my foot in the stirrup, the saddle came down instead of me going up!'

In 2002, while holidaying in Lanzarote, he was struck down by a staphylococcus bug, a form of bacteria which may have been in his body for many years. An abscess quickly developed on his spine, swelling and pressing it sideways and destroying the spinal cord. The local doctors failed to identify the problem or send for a specialist in time, with the result that he was left partially paralysed.

It was an ironic twist, considering that he'd spent twenty years riding over banks and fences and emerged without so much as a broken collarbone. Nonetheless, though wheelchair-bound, he continued to adopt a positive outlook on life right up until his death, aged 77, on 2 July 2010.

Date: Saturday 27 March 1965 Going: Good Value to Winner: £22,041

Horse	Owner	Trainer	Age / weight	Jockey	SP
1 Jay Trump	Mrs M Stephenson	F T Winter	8-11-5	Mr T C Smith	100-6
2 Freddie	Mr R R Tweedie	Owner	8-11-10	P McCarron	7-2fav
3 Mr Jones	Mr C D Collins	W A Stephenson	10-11-5	Mr C Collins	50-1
4 Rainbow Battle	Mr W Shand Kydd	C Bewicke	9-10-13	G Milburn	50-1

Distances: ¾ length, 20 lengths, 1½ lengths. Time: 9 mins 30.6 secs. 47 ran

Winner trained at Lambourn, Berkshire

1966

PAT McCARRON
All about Freddie

Freddie (right, Pat McCarron) jumps the Chair alongside Norther (Peter Jones) in the 1966 National.

FOR THE SECOND year running, Fred stood beside the winner while Freddie stood in the place reserved for the runner-up.

The Fred Winter-trained Anglo beat owner-trainer Reg Tweedie's Freddie, but in a very different manner from the pulsating duel in which Jay Trump had beaten him the year before.

With the exception of Arkle and Mill House, Freddie was by now probably the most popular chaser in training. He was named after Freddie Ringwood, a vet and uncle of the breeder, Miss Bina Ringwood, from County Offaly. Mr Ringwood had been called out to treat the young foal who was suffering from a potentially life-threatening stoppage of the bowel. In lieu of payment he suggested: 'You'd better name him after me.'

Freddie was trained on Tweedie's 1,000-acre Middlethird Farm, located midway between the Borders villages of Gordon and Greenlaw, within ten miles of Kelso. He started out by being hunted with the Duke of Buccleuch's hounds and made a winning debut at its point-to-point at Friars Haugh in 1962. He graduated to hunter chases the following year and went on to win the 1964 Foxhunter's Challenge Cup at Cheltenham, ridden by Alan Mactaggart.

The day before Freddie's Foxhunters' triumph, Londonderry-born Pat McCarron had won the Champion Hurdle on Magic Court, beating 1960 winner

Another Flash by four lengths. The 26-year-old jockey was enjoying easily his best season.

He had been involved with horses all his life, breaking in hunters and show jumpers with his father before going into racing. He served a four-year apprenticeship on the Flat with Harry Blackshaw at Middleham and rode his first winner on a two-year-old filly called Mary Eleanor at York in May 1953.

Pat was offered the ride on Freddie the following season and, on 9 January 1965, they scored a thrilling short-head victory over Vultrix in the Mildmay Memorial Chase at Sandown.

From then on, however, Freddie's build up to the 1965 Grand National had been a troubled one. Tweedie, who had been a leading amateur rider and finished fifth in the 1940 National, intended to run him next in Doncaster's Great Yorkshire Chase but heavy snow resulted in atrocious road conditions and he decided not to risk the long journey. Freddie was then declared to run in Haydock's Grand National Trial four days later but that meeting was abandoned through frost. That left Newcastle's Eider Chase as his next objective but he bruised a foot two days before the race and could not run.

'He was a very straightforward horse to ride,' recalls Pat of Freddie, 'and very intelligent. When you placed him at a fence he had enough intelligence and was good enough to do it himself. You didn't have to adjust his stride, you didn't have to get him to lift off.

'He and I used to work well together. I don't know whether he read my thoughts or I conveyed something to him but he was particularly good. You'd put him at a fence and if he was a little bit wrong, without too much trouble he'd get his stride right and he'd jump. He was the bravest horse I've ever ridden. You could ask him to stand off and he'd answer you. He did everything you wanted him to.

'I had some brilliant leaps out of him in the '65 National and he stayed on well under a lot of weight. But to be beaten on the run-in, it lives with you for a long, long while afterwards. Little things stick in your mind. After the Elbow where you straighten up for the winning post, I was gaining a bit on Jay Trump, then the lad who was riding him, Tommy Smith, started to push. I was delighted because I could see his horse curling up under him. I thought then I was going to win it. But I think Tommy got tired because he put his hands down, and as soon as he did that, the horse ran on.'

In contrast to the previous season, his 1965/66 preparation went far more smoothly. Fourth on his first two starts, he then finished a game second to Arkle in the Hennessy Gold Cup.

Recounts Pat: 'Freddie was getting a lot of weight from Arkle at Newbury and I thought the only thing I could do was to jump off and make the running, make use of his stamina, knowing that Freddie would get the trip. But when the tapes went up, Jimmy FitzGerald on Brasher decided he was going to take Arkle on. The pace was suiting me, we were going fast enough and I didn't want to increase it any more. I decided to sit on their tails, let Jimmy do the work and take an interest later.

'I was happy enough on the first circuit. Going down the back side second time round, maybe a mile out, I thought I'd make my move and take them on, but for some reason I just could not find a gear with him. We were going flat out. Coming round the final bend, Arkle just pulled away. Obviously, Jimmy's horse got tired and I was running on at the death but I just couldn't get anywhere near Arkle. It didn't work out as I thought it would and, in retrospect, perhaps I should have taken him on.'

Despite being beaten three-quarters of a length by Johnnie Walker (who was receiving 17lb from Freddie) at Ayr on 3 January, Ladbrokes made him 8-1 favourite for the Grand National. Soon after that, a single bet of £4,000 to £500 saw his odds clipped to 7-1 and cut again to sixes.

Despite all the gloom-laden forecasts of twelve months earlier, the Grand National was still with us in 1966. However, its reprieve looked no more than a stay of execution, with Mrs Topham insisting that this year's race would be the last staged at Liverpool. The autumn fixture with its long-established Molyneux, Grand Sefton and Becher Chases had been held for the final time in 1965. Now the death knell sounded more loudly than ever before.

The 109 horses entered for what threatened to be the final Aintree National included one from Japan, Fujino-O, owned by Kazuo Fujii and sent to be trained by Fulke Walwyn in his preparation for the race. By an American sire, Bric A Brac, out of an Australian dam, he had won 22 of his 38 races since 1962, including four successive victories in the twice-yearly Nakayama Daishogai Kyoso, a two-and-a-half mile chase over 2ft 6in high fences that ranked as Japan's version of the Grand National.

Fujino-O's former trainer, Teruo Hashimoto, described him as 'a born steeplechase genius' and forecast that he would finish in the first five. It looked a very bold statement considering that the horse would be lumbered with automatic top-weight of 12 stone, as he had not run three times in Britain or Ireland and was therefore ineligible for a handicap rating.

When the 1966 Grand National weights were announced at the end of January, Walwyn's Cheltenham Gold Cup winner Mill House was set to carry 12 stone, alongside Fujino-O.

While Neville Crump expressed himself happy with the 10st 8lb to be carried by his runner Forest Prince, Freddie's owner-trainer was disappointed with his allocation of 11st 7lb, 3lb less than in 1965. 'I think he's been given 2lb too much,' Tweedie said. 'I expected What A Myth [11st 4lb] to be above my horse.' The bookmakers agreed and eased his price half a point from 6-1 to 13-2.

Three days after the weights had been announced, Freddie, ridden as usual by Pat McCarron, scored an impressive victory in the Great Yorkshire Chase and his odds were reduced to 4-1. A subsequent defeat at Kelso on 5 March did little to discourage his supporters and on Grand National day he headed the betting at 11-4, the shortest priced favourite since the war. The Aintree betting market was all about Freddie.

Meanwhile, Japanese invader Fujino-O had finished a well-beaten sixth on his one start in this country, in the Mildmay of Flete Challenge Cup at Cheltenham. Not surprisingly, he was a 100-1 no hoper, with Jeff King being given the dubious responsibility of riding him.

Another huge field of 47 lined up, yet the race was devoid of dramatic incidents and its story is simply told. Forest Prince, with his rider Gerry Scott sporting the same colours worn by previous winners Kirkland (1905) and Glenside (1911), was in front from the first fence until the second last, where he was collared by the 50-1 outsider Anglo. Anglo then drew right away to win by twenty lengths from Freddie, who deprived Forest Prince of second place on the run-in. The Fossa finished fourth.

As in the previous year, Freddie had stayed on the inside throughout, but the concession of 21lb to Anglo on rain-softened ground proved too much. Anglo found a turn of speed which Freddie simply could not match.

'He jumped superbly all the way but just couldn't find it on that long run-in,' recounts Pat. 'The horse felt really well in himself and everything went great; he'd done everything right. The ground was a bit on the sticky side in places and I think it was an accumulation of that and the weight that beat him.'

Anglo had started his racing career as Flag of Convenience but was later bought by Stuart Levy, a director of Anglo Amalgamated Films Inc., hence the change of name. The winning jockey, 22-year-old Tim Norman, from Dawlish in Devon, was having his first ride in the race and had been fortunate to escape serious injury in a car crash less than 48 hours earlier. The stitches in his face were there for all to see.

As for Fujino-O, he got as far as the Chair before refusing. His owner was evidently satisfied with the performance, for he stated the following day that the horse's half-brother, Fujino Chikara, would also be joining Fulke Walwyn's team.

Freddie's 1966/67 campaign was not geared exclusively to the Grand National. He won the Joan Mackay Chase at Ayr in October and scored a remarkable victory in November's Gallaher Gold Cup at Sandown. Despite jumping like a reluctant novice throughout the first circuit, he improved as the pace increased in the second half of the race, but between the last two fences he was floundering in fifth place and looking well beaten. Yet somehow he found the fighting spirit to wear down the four leaders, passing each, one by one on the run-in and turning certain defeat into unbelievable victory.

As Audax (John Lawrence) remarked in that week's *Horse and Hound*: 'Not even Arkle could have been a more universally popular, supremely deserving winner.'

He returned to Ayr on 2 January and beat his sole rival by 30 lengths, then ran moderately in the Great Yorkshire Chase but stormed back to winning form over three and a half miles at Wetherby.

Carrying top weight of 11st 13lb in the 1967 Grand National, he was a victim of the infamous 23rd fence pile-up. Having jumped what remained of the obstacle at the third attempt, all chance of victory had gone and he trailed home seventeenth of the eighteen finishers.

'I wasn't going too well,' Pat acknowledges. 'We were plodding along round the inside, where I always liked to go. I looked up after jumping Becher's to measure the next fence, the smallest, when, suddenly, horses were milling all over the place, running back and forward across the fence. To my imagination it looked as if they were drawing the curtains.

'It stopped him dead. I went back, had another go, and still got stopped. It was only on the third attempt that we managed to find a little room on the inside and get through.'

Freddie ran four times in the first part of the 1967/68 season but the spark was no longer there and he was duly retired. He had more than played his part.

He was not only a hero in Scotland but, as Vian Smith remarked in his biography *A Horse Called Freddie*, 'he went into the affections of men and women in England, Wales and Ireland, few of whom had ever owned a horse, many of whom had never seen a racecourse, but all of whom liked a fighter.'

Pat McCarron continued to ply his trade as a tough northern jump jockey, though he only rode in one more Grand National, falling at Becher's on Swan-Shot in 1972. He announced his retirement, aged 34, at the end of that season and took over his father-in-law's haulage business.

'I'd just planned to run it for a while until my father-in-law recovered from illness, but I ended up buying the business and carried on doing it for more than thirty years until I retired and sold it in 2006,' he says.

'I'd love to have had some involvement with racing, but I chose the haulage business instead. Or rather, I didn't choose it; it chose me.'

Date: Saturday 26 March 1966 Going: Soft Value to Winner: £22,334 5s

Horse	Owner	Trainer	Age / weight	Jockey	SP
1 Anglo	Mr S Levy	F T Winter	8-10-0	T Norman	50-1
2 Freddie	Mr R R Tweedie	Owner	9-11-7	P McCarron	11-4fav
3 Forest Prince	Mrs D Thompson	N Crump	8-10-8	G Scott	100-7
4 The Fossa	Mr R Greatbach	F Rimell	9-10-8	T W Biddlecombe	50-1

Distances: 20 lengths, 5 lengths, 20 lengths. Time: 9 mins 52.8 secs. 47 ran

Winner trained at Lambourn, Berkshire

1967

JOHN LEECH, STAN HAYHURST and PADDY BRODERICK
Foinavon

*Rutherfords (11, John Leech)
and Kirtle-Lad (Paddy
Broderick) lead over the Chair.*

*AND RUTHERFORDS HAS been hampered and so has Castle Falls. Rondetto
has fallen, Princeful has fallen, Norther has fallen, Kirtle-Lad has fallen, The
Fossa has fallen; there's a right pile-up. Leedsy has climbed over the fence and
left his jockey there; and now, with all this mayhem, Foinavon has gone off on
his own. He's about fifty, a hundred yards in front of everything else. They're
all pulling up, having a look now to see what's happening at the fence. Aussie
is jumping over it, Quintin Bay is climbing over it. And as they go now to the
Canal Turn, er, well the one that's going to the Canal Turn happens to be Foinavon.*

That passage of Michael O'Hehir's immortal, incredulous, machine-gun
commentary took precisely 31 seconds, during which horse after horse came
to a standstill in the ever-increasing melee. In that time the winner of the 1967
Grand National was decided and the fate of the losers settled in one of the most
extraordinary races ever run.

The white-blinkered Foinavon was an unconsidered 100-1 chance. Even his
owner and trainer did not fancy him and neither saw much point in making the

journey to Aintree. Trainer John Kempton went to Worcester instead, where he rode another of his string, Three Dons, to victory in a novices' hurdle. Owner Cyril Watkins opted to stay home and watch the race on television, hoping to catch a brief glimpse of his black colours with the red and yellow braces before they dropped out of range of the cameras.

Predictably, Foinavon, having been prominent over the first few fences, was toiling among the backmarkers as they went out onto the second circuit. Rutherfords, Castle Falls, Princeful and Kirtle-Lad led the way.

Aboard Rutherfords that day was 29-year-old John Leech, having his third Grand National ride, and by far his best.

The first two, a pair of 100-1 shots, hadn't amounted to much. Coleen Star in 1965 had been one of a number of unlikely candidates taking part mainly for the sake of competing in what was then thought by many to be the last Grand National. Says John: 'He refused at the fence after Becher's but, to be honest, I didn't give him a lot of help. It amazes me that he got over the fences he did jump without falling.'

In Haste was John's mount in 1966. He jumped well enough but got tired after a circuit and was pulled up. His rider enjoyed a far better day five weeks later, when winning the Scottish Grand National for Selkirk trainer Bobby Fairbairn on African Patrol. It was the first time the race had been held at Ayr, following the closure of Bogside twelve months earlier. John finished that 1965/66 season as the leading northern rider with 39 winners from 176 rides.

The Cheshire born and bred jockey had come a long way since his three-year apprenticeship with Ernie Davey at Malton and his spell of National Service. 'I went into the veterinary corps to be with horses but they said 'we don't need horsemen, we only want dog handlers', so I was shipped off to Singapore for two years.

'When I came out of the RAVC in 1958 I went jumping. I started with George Owen but I wasn't getting many rides. Then I went north to John Dixon and rode five winners that season [1960/61]. When he decided to concentrate on farming, I joined Harry Bell and was with him for two and a half years. I was riding fifteen winners every season, when Bobby Fairbairn asked me to ride for him as stable jockey.'

As well as the Scottish National they also won the Great Yorkshire Chase with Spear Fir in January 1967. A fortnight after that victory, John partnered the Tim Molony-trained Rutherfords at Wetherby, finishing second to Freddie. After the race, Molony asked him to ride Rutherfords in that year's Grand National.

Castle Falls was a spare ride for Stan Hayhurst. Charlie Hall trained him for Clifford Nicholson but Pat McCarron, Hall's stable jockey, was on Freddie.

Stan was born in Durham in September 1933, served a four-year apprenticeship with Major Verly Bewicke and rode his first winner for him, Carpact at Hexham on 30 October 1950.

He served two years of National Service with the RAVC in Kenya at the time of the Mau Mau uprising, a movement that launched an armed struggle against British rule. He had one ride while in Kenya, in a hurdle race on Grand National day 1956. He listened on forces radio to Devon Loch's collapse and Dave Dick going on to win it, with George Milburn finishing second on Gentle Moya, trained by Major Verly Bewicke.

After leaving the army later that year, Stan and George shared the rides at Major Bewicke's Shawdon Hall yard. Among the stable stars at that time was Kerstin. George rode her in the 1957 Cheltenham Gold Cup, failing by a length to peg back Linwell. Stan took over during the 1957/58 campaign and he and Kerstin galloped up that famous hill to Gold Cup glory, winning by half a length from Polar Flight.

Sixteen days after winning the Cheltenham Gold Cup, Stan had his first ride in the Grand National on Wise Child. 'He wasn't a bad little handicapper but he didn't have a lot of scope and he just didn't jump the fences. We stopped at the big ditch going down to Becher's second time,' he recalls.

He rode Kerstin in the 1959 Grand National. Despite having to shoulder top weight of 12 stone, the formbook relates that she was in touch with the leaders when being brought down at Becher's second time round.

Stan explains what happened: 'Mick Batchelor rode a horse called Mains-town for Stewart Wight. Ideally, you need to jump Becher's at a slight angle to get right for the twenty-third. Batchelor came swanning along on my inside and jumped into me. There's a photograph of us falling and we both went identi-cally. In fairness to the mare, she slid along the ground on her knees and belly but never turned over.

'I was five or six lengths behind Michael Scudamore on Oxo [the winner] and going very easily, and the one thing we always knew was that she would stay. Everyone has their own story don't they, but I do think that was my unlucky year.'

It was eight years before Stan's next Grand National ride, on Castle Falls in 1967.

Paddy Broderick, 27-year-old rider of Kirtle-Lad, was enjoying a Grand National ride as good as his first one on Hawa's Song four years earlier.

'I hit the front on Hawa's Song coming over the Melling Road back on to the racecourse,' he recounts, 'but John Lawrence came past me [on Carrickbeg] running away to the second last. Then Pat Buckley came past me going to the last on Ayala and he's under hard pressure. How he won I do not know because he had no chance when he passed me. My horse tired from the last but we held on to finish third.'

Paddy's second Grand National mount, Supersweet, though little more than a novice, jumped round safely to finish twelfth of fourteen in Team Spirit's year, while Major Hitch, his ride in 1966, fell at the nineteenth.

West Meath-born Paddy had started out with Cyril Bryce-Smith at Kells. He describes it as: 'A five-year apprenticeship at half a crown a week, one suit in five years and not a brain in my head!'

He rode his first winner aged fourteen on Pipe Band in an apprentices' race at Navan on 19 June 1954. But it was neighbouring trainer Charlie McCartan who was instrumental in arranging the link with Bishop Auckland trainer Arthur (W.A.) Stephenson seven years later.

Paddy's big race victories for Stephenson included the 1964 Welsh Grand National on Rainbow Battle and the 1966 Mackeson Gold Cup on Pawnbroker. However, the partnership that mattered most to him was that forged with head lad Nan, who had been at Stephenson's Crawleas yard since way back when he operated in the world of hunter chases and point-to-points. Nan and Paddy were married in June 1968.

'Really,' says Paddy, 'there was only the one head lad – and that was 'W.A.' himself. In the morning Nan would feed some of the horses and he would feed the rest. He was a hard man but you couldn't say he was a bad man, because he expected everybody to do the same as him.'

It was during the 1966/67 season that Paddy teamed up with Stephenson's Kirtle-Lad. The horse rattled off four wins in five starts before finishing third behind Highland Wedding in Newcastle's Eider Chase. He lined up for the 1967 Grand National a quietly fancied 28-1 shot, backed down from 33s shortly before the race.

A group of four – Kirtle-Lad (Broderick), Rutherfords (Leech), Castle Falls (Hayhurst) and Princeful (Roy Edwards) – led the field past the stands and out into the country. This same quartet was still in front approaching Becher's.

Hayhurst: 'My instructions were to jump him off outside, let him settle, then second time round go where you want, which is how it worked out. We jumped Becher's first time in the first six and quietly popped along in company with John Leech on Rutherfords. We were in a handy position and going very nicely but it was still a long way from home and I didn't know if he would stay.'

Leech: 'I was having a good ride. I let the horse enjoy himself and was jumping well and keeping out of trouble. There were loose horses all around us. As we were going out on the second circuit, Paddy Broderick tried to chase them off onto the Mildmay course but they didn't go. Instead, they carried on and were jumping away in front of us. I remember going to Becher's and thinking "God, I hope those things don't stop here or we'll all get killed." They jumped Becher's and I said to myself "Oh, we'll be alright now."'

Broderick: 'John Leech, Roy Edwards and Stan Hayhurst led me over Becher's and I was just on their tails.'

Hayhurst: 'Along the line of five fences to Becher's, Popham Down, who had fallen earlier, went straight, never deviated. I feel sure it was a shock to him when he landed over Becher's. Unfortunately, at the next fence he ran in to me, I hit him and collided with Rutherfords.'

Leech: 'The loose horses ducked into the left-hand corner, then ran back across the fence. Rutherfords braked, so did everyone else, and I came off. I went off his right-hand side, kept hold of the reins, swung round in front of him and I thought I was lying in the bottom of the fence, waiting to get myself kicked to death. In fact, I'd just about rolled under the wing.'

Broderick: 'Poor John, he was a very lucky man how he wasn't killed, because his horse stuck his toes in so fast as the loose horse went across him. By the time he got out of the way there were other loose horses coming round and I'm going for a gap that's closing. I got stuck between horses on top of the fence. I couldn't get out.'

Hayhurst: 'I landed on top of the fence, then the horse of Francis Shortt's [Aussie] came and literally pushed my fellow over.'

Leech: 'When I looked up, it was mayhem, with jockeys running round looking for their horses.'

Broderick: 'My horse is stuck on the fence and with the horses all piling up around me, it's getting tighter and tighter. I rolled off onto the landing side of the fence and pulled him off. I'm shouting to the ambulance man stood by the fence "Give-us-a-leg-up, give-us-a-leg-up", but he just stood there looking at me, dumbfounded.'

Hayhurst: 'I came off and landed like a sprinter on my hands and knees and thought, "Get out of here." We didn't know what was happening at the time behind us, but Pat Buckley's horse [Limeking] had slid to the ground and was lying prone across the fence. The boys sitting on horses on the take off side could weigh things up much easier. All I saw was this melee on the inside and Castle Falls underneath the fence with his feet in the air. It was chaotic. There was a natural grandstand right round there to the Canal Turn and, with all the horses refusing and stopping, the noise was deafening.'

Leech: 'Paddy was the unluckiest. He'd remounted and was leading Foinavon's pursuers going to the Canal Turn but his horse was lame.'

Broderick: 'I was the first to remount, not that far behind Foinavon. I got to the next fence but my horse had gone lame behind; he'd pulled a muscle in his hindquarters and he refused there.'

Hayhurst: 'I never saw Foinavon. The first I realised was when Terry [Biddle-combe] on Greek Scholar walked over what was left of the fence, which was two foot by then, and shouted, "Come on lads, there's only one gone on." All of Clifford Nicholson's ran with a white breastgirth and the reins had got stuck behind it, so it wasn't just a matter of jumping back on. So I just lobbed round, jumped through a few gaps and finished fourteenth.'

Leech: 'I remounted Rutherfords and carried on. It wasn't until I was three fences from home that I suddenly thought, "I suppose I am on the right horse." Luckily I was and he finished sixteenth.'

Broderick: 'I think if Kirtle-Lad hadn't gone lame I would have won. The only reason Foinavon got over was that he was so far behind, he had plenty of time to pick his way through.'

Foinavon and jockey John Buckingham doggedly made their way over the remaining fences and plugged on up the run-in, passing the post fifteen lengths clear of Honey End, with Red Alligator third and Greek Scholar in fourth.

John Leech rode Princeful in the 1968 Grand National, finishing ninth. He hung up his boots in 1970, then trained for two seasons at Wigton, in Cumberland. 'I trained a winner, had a few placed. The horses looked well but the next season they all started coughing, so I thought I'd get out while I still had something left.

'I broke in horses and kept them at livery. Then one day, the Jockey Club rang me to ask if I'd like to do a bit of part-time starting at Carlisle at Easter and Cartmel in August. I did that for five years before they asked me to go full-time.'

That was in 1979. He was a full-time starter for 23 years, retiring at the end of the 2002 Flat season, but continued to officiate as starter on a part-time basis until bowing out at Bangor-on-Dee in February 2008.

Stan rode Castle Falls again in the 1969 Grand National. 'I led from the twelfth to the fourteenth but there wasn't the same feel,' he says. 'He wasn't the same horse that he'd been in 1967. We finished second last.'

He had his final ride at his local course, Sedgefield, on 31 May 1973, aboard Ken Oliver's Arctic Explorer in a two-mile chase. 'I had a newsagents business by then with my mother- and father-in-law at East Herrington, on the outskirts of Sunderland. We sold it in 1974 and moved to Consett, home of the steel company.

'Unfortunately, in 1981 the steel works closed and decimated the business. We'd had a good "counter save" with people coming off night shift and others going on day shift. That stopped; a third of the business literally went overnight. We still had the deliveries but the "counter save", which is the easy part, just disappeared.

'We hung on until 1987, then my wife Patricia and I decided we'd have a change of direction, so we started a livery yard – point-to-pointers, hunters, breaking, schooling young horses, that sort of thing. We got out of that when arthritis caught up with me. You need full strength for breaking in those big five-year-olds. If you've got bad shoulders you can't handle them like when you were younger.'

Stan and Patricia live in West Woodburn, located on the edge of Northumberland National Park. He has acted as a steward at Sedgefield, Hexham and Newcastle and is also involved with local point-to-points.

Paddy Broderick also had one more Grand National ride, completing the course on Harry Lane's Limetra in 1969. He continued to ride plenty of winners during the early 1970s.

By the summer of 1974 he was approaching his 35th birthday. Injuries had restricted him to just nine winners the previous season and it seemed that retirement beckoned. But then, along came dual Champion Hurdle winner Night Nurse.

'By a long, long way the best horse I ever rode,' he insists. 'From the first time I sat on his back at Peter Easterby's he jumped the same way, brilliant. We started off in three-year-old hurdles at Market Rasen in August and he wins on the bridle. He was such a good jumper as a three-year-old; he'd gain two lengths at every hurdle, so I used to let him lob along on the bridle and just keep hold of his head. I couldn't see any sense in stopping a horse when he's jumping like that; you're losing the lengths you've gained.

'That first Champion Hurdle [in 1976] on firm ground was just a canter, he won on the bridle – but then he loved fast ground. He was unbeaten in all eight starts that season, including the Irish Sweeps Hurdle and the Scottish and Welsh Champion Hurdles.

'I'd stopped riding over fences by then because I had such a good horse and I didn't want to fall on something stupid.

'The horse wasn't right the next season until the Champion Hurdle. The ground was soft that year, so I walked round on the morning and picked all the best ground. It takes a good horse to win on firm ground and soft and I think that second Champion Hurdle win in 1977 was his greatest performance because of the ground and the condition he was in all the time up to the race.'

How ironic, then, that the horse who had given him his greatest triumphs should also be responsible for ending his career. It came in a crashing fall in the William Hill Christmas Hurdle at Kempton in December 1977.

'We were going to the last upsides Beacon Light and Dramatist; it was touch and go. I asked for a long one and he came up for me, but he never got there. That's all I can remember.

'I woke up in the ambulance room, dazed and not quite sure where I was. They took me to hospital for a check up. I was black and blue all over but I thought I'd better get home and see my own doctor, so Night Nurse's owner, Reg Spencer, drove me to just south of Wetherby where I'd left my car, then I drove home from there.

'Once I'd seen the x-rays I knew I'd never ride again. It was the second serious head injury I'd had [the first, in a fall from Dashing White Sargeant on rock hard ground at Uttoxeter in 1967, had left him unconscious for twelve days] and the Jockey Club's brain specialist told me how bad it was.'

For a time after Night Nurse's fall, Paddy lost his sense of balance. Even today he has to be careful. In April 2000 he and Nan moved south to Newmarket to be closer to their daughter, Alison.

As a 'regular' on the Injured Jockeys Fund's holidays in Tenerife, Paddy has nothing but praise for the organisation that has done so much for so many for so long.

But there's give and take in this life, and Paddy, along with Stan, John and fellow stalwarts of the northern weighing room in the 1960s, also did much for so many. Let it not be forgotten that when the Farrell-Brookshaw Fund, the precursor of the IJF, was set up in 1964, it was they who championed the cause.

Date: Saturday 8 April 1967 Going: Good Value to Winner: £17,630 15s

Horse	Owner	Trainer	Age / weight	Jockey	SP
1 Foinavon	Mr C P T Watkins	J Kempton	9-10-0	J Buckingham	100-1
2 Honey End	Mr C Pugh	H R Price	10-10-4	J Gifford	15-2fav
3 Red Alligator	Mr J Manners	D Smith	8-10-0	B Fletcher	30-1
4 Greek Scholar	Mr J Thornton Jnr	D Smith	9-10-13	T W Biddlecombe	20-1

Distances: 15 lengths, 3 lengths, 8 lengths. Time: 9 mins 49.6 secs. 44 ran

Winner trained at Compton, Berkshire

1968

DAVID ELSWORTH
Major Pearn's long shot

David Elsworth
(left) with
Tony Pearn and
their Grand
National hope
Chamoretta.

ONCE AGAIN, WE were assured that this would definitely be the last Grand National. The bizarre events of twelve months earlier which vindicated the theory that big outsiders could still win, coupled with the desire to be a part of what might be the end of an era, served to encourage the connections of many a no-hoper.

Consequently, in 1968, a mixture of high-class chasers and unlikely candidates competed to be the final name on the winner's roster. They included several victims of the previous year's twenty-third fence pile-up plus the main beneficiary, Foinavon.

Among the genuine outsiders was Chamoretta, owned by Major Tony Pearn of the Royal Marines. He'd been commissioned in 1942, aged seventeen, and took part in the Normandy and South of France landings. After the war he was posted to Hong Kong where he rode winners on the Flat. It was while passing round the celebratory champagne after scoring a double there one day that he met his future wife, Heather.

By 1948 he was on active duty in war-stricken Palestine, returning to England later that year. Being posted in Portsmouth gave him the opportunity to ride out at weekends for Captain Ryan Price, who was then based at Lavant, near Chichester. Although steeplechasing was his first love, he also competed in other equestrian events, being placed fourth in the cross-country phase of the 1951 Badminton Three-Day Event on Bambridge Boy.

He didn't have any racing colours when making his debut in point-to-points in the early 1950s so he rode in a Royal Marines rugby shirt. He developed his colours from the shirt – navy blue, yellow, green and red hoops (the yellow and green being narrower than the rest) on a white background being the Royal Marines belt in the correct proportions. He added a navy blue collar and cuffs to represent the link between the Marines and the Royal Navy, with a yellow cap to signify the colour of the Duke of Albany's regiment, the forerunner of the Marines.

In 1955 he bought a horse called Waking, a winner of point-to-points and a Folkestone hunter chase, to ride in the following year's Grand Military Gold Cup. After a couple of 'rider fell off' efforts, he won the three-mile Jack of Newbury Chase on him but finished second to Cottage Lace in the Grand Military itself. He also rode Waking to win at Plumpton in January 1957 and then achieved a long-held ambition when riding him in that year's Grand National.

By doing so, 32-year-old Captain Anthony Pearn became the first (and so far only) Royal Marine to ride in the great race. On arriving at Aintree he was heartened to find around a dozen 'good luck' telegrams pinned to the weighing room notice board, including from fellow naval officers who all planned to invest a few shillings each-way.

Realistically, not even his most loyal friends and supporters expected him to win, hence he felt no pressure, though as the race drew nearer, the sense of excitement and anticipation increased. He recalled the occasion as being 'a great thrill and a very moving experience.'

Alas, the experience was short lived, as Waking was brought to a halt at the fifth fence when the riderless Armorial, who had fallen when leading at the previous jump, refused, causing Hart Royal to cannon into him and swerve off to the right, directly in front of Waking at the very moment he was about to take off.

Afterwards he received another telegram, this time from his troop sergeant: 'Send 60 shirts soonest!'

The following season, the now Major Pearn again finished second in the Grand Military Gold Cup, this time on Le Voyageur. By then he was based at Camberley and combining race riding with military duties was a complex task.

'I only entered my horses on days which I knew I could get off,' he recalled in conversation one day at Taunton. 'However, I wanted to run Le Voyageur in the Lord Stalbridge Gold Cup at Wincanton and I couldn't get off, so I got Fred Winter to ride and he won the race.

'On another occasion, I asked Fred to ride one for me in a three-mile chase. He was surprised to see me there when he got into the parade ring. "Why aren't you riding?" he asked, "I only ride as your substitute." I replied "I've four sons and school bills to pay next month. If I ride him, I think the horse will win. If you ride him, I *know* it'll win," whereupon he said "Well, I've been given some bloody funny instructions by owners, but I've never been asked to educate their children before!'"

Major Pearn made three more attempts to win the Grand Military Gold Cup but never quite managed it, the nearest coming when finishing fourth on Tulla-herin Lord in 1960. But some years later, while serving in the Caribbean in 1967, he was notified of a horse due to be sold at Ascot, a mare named Cham-oretta, a daughter of that great Aintree mare Tiberetta.

Tiberetta, who was bred, owned and trained by Edward Courage, had finished third, second and fourth respectively in the 1957-58-59 Grand Nationals and won both the Becher Chase (1957) and the Grand Sefton (1958) over the National fences. Chamoretta, born in 1960, was her first foal, one of seven who would go on to become multiple winners over fences. They comprised Spanish Steps, who won the Hennessy Gold Cup and was in the frame in two Chel-tenham Gold Cups and three Grand Nationals; Tamoretta, Trajan, Quintus and Mafia King, who between them won 20 chases; and Lictor, who, despite being by the sprinter Right Boy, inherited his dam's stamina and won the Topham Trophy over the Grand National fences.

In addition, Tiberetta's full-sister Tiberina was the dam of Neapolitan Lou, Lira, San Angelo and Saccone, who between them won 29 races for the Courage family. Lira became the dam of Cover Your Money, who in turn produced Red Marauder, the 2001 Grand National winner. This was a proper steeplechasing family.

Chamoretta had herself won three chases during the 1965/66 season, including one at Sandown, and had only twice been out of the frame in 14 races when carrying the famous Courage maroon and yellow halved colours. However, her form tailed off the following term and she was placed only once in eight starts.

Major Pearn bought her and sent her to Neville Dent's yard at Brockenhurst, hopeful that she would give her new owner a good, safe ride in his final crack at the Grand Military Gold Cup in 1968. Unfortunately, Dent was unable to get a race into her beforehand and a hurried preparation meant that she went to Sandown not fully fit, hence her owner-rider was obliged to pull her up in the closing stages.

Chamoretta reappeared five days later in the Kim Muir Chase at Cheltenham, where she trailed home last of seven finishers. Ten days after that she took her place in the line-up for the 1968 Grand National, where she was partnered by a 5lb claimer David Elsworth, who had not ridden a winner all season.

He had served his apprenticeship with Alec Kilpatrick from 1955-58 and had been riding over jumps for twelve years but had mustered just eleven winners in that time, the first having come on Rathronan in a 35-runner novices' hurdle at Cheltenham on 15 November 1957. His first three winners had taken him eight years to achieve, yet it was he who came in for the ride on Chamoretta, wearing Major Pearn's Royal Marines colours.

'She was a wonderful looking mare but she must have had some kind of problem because she hadn't run for nearly a year when Major Pearn bought her,' recalls David. 'When I rode her at Liverpool I doubled up as the horse-box driver and drove her all the way up there. She had ten stone so I had to go light.

'We were 100-1 shots and I was going to play it by ear for the first circuit. In the second half of the race, thinking back to Foinavon twelve months earlier, I thought anything could happen.

'She reared and whipped round when they jumped off and so I was right at the back going to the first fence. We began to get into the race going to the Chair. Then, at the water, Bassnet, Foinavon and a couple of others fell and it had a domino effect and I ended up having to go right, right and even more right. I managed to jump the water just inside the wing, on the stands side, which put me way at the back again.

'But we went on and by the time we came to the last ditch we were staying on really well. There were two horses in front of us, the grey Forecastle, and Vultrix, who was Terry Biddlecombe's mount. One of them refused and the other one thought that was a good idea so he refused too and I went right in behind them and got baulked, and I found myself straddled across the fence.

'I immediately stepped off and led her along the ditch, and that was the end of our National adventure. She would have finished very well and would have run much better had we had a bit more luck.'

Red Alligator, a luckless third the previous year, had taken the lead at that same fence, the fourth last, and he led Different Class and Rutherfords across the Melling Road and into the straight. He jumped the last two fences five lengths to the good and galloped on strongly to win by 20 lengths from Moidore's Token and Different Class, giving 20-year-old Brian Fletcher a first Grand National victory on his second ride in the race.

Owned by John Manners, a butcher and farmer, Red Alligator was out of Miss Alligator and thus a half-brother to Anglo, the winner two years previously. Not since Emblem and Emblematic won for Lord Coventry in 1863 and 1864 had one mare produced two Grand National winners. Remarkably, Red Alligator's sire, Magic Red, had barely stayed six furlongs!

'That evening,' continues David, 'Clement Freud was looking for a celebrity for a programme called *The Simon Dee Show*, which was *the* big show on Saturday night on the BBC. He wanted a jockey to go to the Manchester studios. The winning rider, Brian Fletcher, was unavailable and Clement couldn't get anyone else to go, so I got the job and got what was quite a substantial fee for those days.

'I was chauffeured there and appeared on the show, which was quite a big thing for a young man. When I went back home I was the celebrity for a week because I'd appeared on *The Simon Dee Show*.'

He rode Chamoretta in her next race, at Plumpton on Easter Monday, finishing fourth in the Abergavenny Challenge Cup. Bob Davies then took over for what was to be her last start under National Hunt Rules, at Newton Abbot, when she again finished fourth.

Major Pearn sold Chamoretta soon after, something he deeply regretted later, feeling that she was 'the ideal type of dam to produce a real National sort.' She was bought by Fiona Forbes, who rode her in all her ten point-to-point races in 1969, winning the Surrey Union Ladies' Open at Tweseldown and never finishing out of the first four.

In her final season, in 1970, Chamoretta ran six times, recording two wins over the Easter weekend in ladies' opens at Parham and Hackwood Park. She finished second once, third once and fourth twice in her other starts. The 1971 *Hunter Chasers and Point-to-Pointers* annual commented: 'A superb jumper, a model of consistency.'

Major Pearn left the Royal Marines in 1969, after 27 years' service, becoming Joint Master of the East Devon Foxhounds. He strived in vain to win the Grand Military Gold Cup, his last runner being Bearys Cross, who was brought down in 2000.

As for David Elsworth, the two seasons following the 1968 Grand National were the most successful of his riding career, with five winners in 68/69 and a career high of nine in 69/70 including a double at Wye. But the following campaign yielded only two, courtesy of an Easter Monday brace at Newton Abbot, with his final three victories being achieved in the 71/72 season.

He retired having ridden a total of 30 winners. He'd hardly set the world alight as a jockey and his early spells at training looked unlikely to do so either. He started as assistant to Lt-Col G R A Vallance – whose first name was Guy but was commonly known as Ricky, after the pop star Ritchie Valens – before taking out his own licence at the start of the 1978/79 season.

David's achievements as a trainer have far outstripped those as a jockey, becoming one of the few to reach the top both on the Flat and over jumps. Classic and Group One successes rank alongside those in the biggest of steeplechases, and he has trained two of the most popular horses of all time.

Desert Orchid's big race triumphs, which included four King George VI Chases, a Whitbread Gold Cup, Irish Grand National and, unforgettably, that 1989 Cheltenham Gold Cup, elevated him to a household name, a status equalled perhaps only by Red Rum and Arkle in modern times.

Persian Punch, with his three Jockey Club Cups, a pair of Goodwood Cups, two Lonsdale Cups and a Doncaster Cup, became the most popular of all Flat race stayers.

In The Groove won an Irish One Thousand Guineas in 1990, along with that year's Juddmonte International and Champion Stakes, plus the 1991 Coronation Cup, while Seattle Rhyme landed the 1991 Racing Post Trophy.

Many of the big handicaps have also come David's way, including the Cambridgeshire, Lincoln, Royal Hunt Cup, Wokingham and Ayr Gold Cup.

Barnbrook Again won back-to-back runnings of the Queen Mother Champion Chase, while at Newbury, Jamesmead won the 1988 Tote Gold Trophy, and Ghofar the next year's Hennessy Cognac Gold Cup.

And of course, there's Rhyme 'N' Reason. In 1988 he won his trainer the biggest prize of all – the Grand National.

David Elsworth continues to train successfully, based nowadays at Newmarket, focusing predominantly on the Flat.

Tony Pearn died in 2005 aged eighty, following which his second son, John, took over the distinctive Royal Marine racing colours in which his father had won the Royal Marines Cup at Cowdray Park's point-to-point six times and finished second in five Sandown military races.

Happily, they are still in active service, for the Major's granddaughter, Alice Pearn, has worn them to victory in point-to-points and was placed in an Exeter hunter chase in 2010.

Date: Saturday 30 March 1968 Going: Firm Value to Winner: £17,848 10s

Horse	Owner	Trainer	Age / weight	Jockey	SP
1 Red Alligator	Mr J Manners	D Smith	9-10-0	B Fletcher	100-7
2 Moidore's Token	Miss P Harrower	J K M Oliver	11-10-8	B Brogan	100-6
3 Different Class	Mr Gregory Peck	P Cazalet	8-11-5	D Mould	17-2fav
4 Rutherfords	Mr J Bonnier	N F Crump	8-10-6	P Buckley	100-9

Distances: 20 lengths, neck, 12 lengths. Time: 9 mins 28.8 secs. 45 ran

Winner trained at Bishop Auckland, County Durham

1969

JEFF KING
Rondetto & Co.

Jeff King, widely acknowledged as one of the great jump jockeys.

SOME SAY HE was the best jockey never to be champion. Many say it was because he called a spade a bloody shovel, rather than tell an owner what he wanted to hear. But Jeff King will have none of that.

'I'd never have been champion no matter how much bullshit I'd given them, because the job I had as Bob Turnell's stable jockey I shared with Johnny Haine. There was no chance of being champion with two of you sharing the job.

'If I'd had it on my own, or Johnny had had it on his own, we'd have had a chance of being champion jockey, for sure, but it was still a great job.'

Born in 1941, Jeff started his racing career with Sir Gordon Richards at Ogbourne Maisey, just north of Marlborough, and had a few rides on the Flat. 'I got heavy quick,' he says. 'In those days an apprentice needed to do 6st 7lb. I had a job to do 7st 12lb!'

A National Hunt career beckoned, leading to him joining Sir Gordon's neighbour, Bob Turnell. His first winner came on Pilgrim Father in a Warwick selling hurdle on 30 January 1960.

'Bill Rees was stable jockey when I went to Bob's. Johnny Haine was the apprentice and Andy [Bob's son] was still at school. Bob was a terrific man, a tough old bugger but a very, very good trainer, as straight as a die, and I had a lot of respect for him.

'When Bill moved to join Peter Cazalet, me and Johnny shared the rides as joint stable jockeys. Everyone asked how hard it was to do that but it just worked itself out. The ones you rode first time, you probably stuck with them. There were only a few where there was any swapping about.'

Among the Turnell's horses was former Cheltenham and Whitbread Gold Cup winner Pas Seul. Jeff rode him in the 1964 Whitbread and recalls: 'He ran all right and he wasn't too far off them jumping the Pond fence, but he was an old horse and way past his best by then. But in his prime I think he was the second best horse, to Arkle, that I've ever seen.

'He was a very hard horse to train; he'd never eat in the winter, he hated the cold. That's why he had a good record in the Whitbread – it was in the spring and he always looked better by then. In the winter he used to look awful; he never carried any flesh, he used to look cold. I can remember the guvnor saying to Jack Beasley, who looked after him, "Jack, don't take that rug off him until the very last minute. I'm ashamed to see him in my name".'

One of Jeff's first big winners came on Red Tide in the 1964 Topham Trophy. He had his first Grand National ride two days later on Jim Joel's Beau Normand, a horse that, like many a Turnell inmate, successfully mixed hurdling with chasing. He refused at the eleventh.

The dark, almost liver chestnut Rondetto was Jeff's mount in the 1965 National. His first ride on the horse had been a winning one, at Wincanton in November 1962, since when they'd won several races together, including the 1965 running of the Stone's Ginger Wine Chase at Sandown.

'You couldn't hold a leg of him if he didn't want you to; you couldn't hold him by force. Some days he'd settle, some days he didn't and you just had to let him roll. The first day he arrived, the guvnor put a little lad nicknamed Sparrow on him, and he came pissing off past all of us. We used to canter in what we called the Windmill Field. We'd set off at the bottom by the windmill and come all the way round to the top. Rondetto came flying by, down the gallops and back up again. Bob went bananas. Sparrow got off and said "Well, you ride the bloody thing." So Bob rode him the next day, and he held him, but by Christ, his cheeks were puffing.'

Along with Peacetown, Rondetto led the 1965 Grand National field past the stands and out onto the second circuit. Says Jeff: 'The only reason I'd got to the front was that I had him in behind and he'd relaxed, but coming onto the race-course first time, two loose horses raced round the outside. You could see they were going to cause havoc and they started edging towards the inner, so I had to pull out. The minute he saw daylight he was off. So from coming onto the racecourse nearly last, he jumped the water in front.'

Rondetto and Peacetown maintained their lead down to Becher's and the Canal Turn. Rondetto landed in front over Valentine's but the next fence was where the dream ended, as the horse slithered to the ground.

'What made him fall, I'm certain, was that they'd knocked quite a lot of the fence out first time round, and he landed with his knees still bent. He didn't really do much wrong. He was expecting more of a drop on the other side but, because they'd taken the top out, there wasn't as much and he hadn't quite got his front legs right out. To me, he'd have definitely won. He'd hardly stopped pulling. He was a better horse than Jay Trump [the winner] around a park track, and he'd jumped super until then. Those Liverpool fences didn't frighten him.'

Rondetto's next race was the Gallaher Gold Cup at Sandown in November, when he finished second, splitting Arkle and Mill House, albeit twenty lengths behind Tom Dreaper's great champion, who was then at the height of his powers. Rondetto won at Lingfield and at Ascot but his season ended early when he chipped the back of his knee in a second last fence fall at Kempton in February. Thus Jeff was left without a 1966 Grand National mount. He got one, but it was an unlikely pairing.

'Fulke Walwyn mentioned riding the Japanese horse, Fujino-O. He said I'd have no chance because he wasn't even handicapped; he had automatic top weight of twelve stone. I rode him in the National Hunt Handicap Chase at Cheltenham. He was a lovely little horse but he was still an entire, he still had a pair of balls. And he was small, so he didn't want to get them too near those fences at Liverpool.

'Fulke said "The Japs would love you to ride him; I'll give you two hundred quid." Well, two hundred quid then was a lot of money. I didn't give him a definite yes, just that it should be all right now that Rondetto had hurt himself.

'Not long afterwards, Fred Winter asked me to ride Anglo [the eventual winner], but Tim Norman had won on him at Windsor and was booked to ride him. I knew he'd be bloody gutted if I climbed on it now. To be honest, I didn't think Anglo would win a National anyway; I thought he was a windy old bastard, so I stuck with Fulke's horse.

'In the paddock, apart from having twelve stone he had lucky charms hanging all over his bridle. I said to Fulke, "Bloody hell, he's got enough weight as it is without weighing his head down as well." Fulke said, "Look, if you could just get him past the stands once, they'll be over the moon."

'He was never going to fall but I shouldn't have gone and jumped the Chair. Going to it there were three or four loose horses. I was just going to pull up when they all pissed off up one end of it, so I thought, perhaps I could just get him over it. Once you're over the Chair, you've only got to hop over the water.

'So I went at it and, at the last second, I could feel the poor little bugger think, "Shit, I can't get over this", and he stuck the brakes on. He went straight into the front of the fence, his bridle hooked on one of the blackthorn stakes inside it, and he was left hanging there. His feet didn't even touch the ground because it was such a deep ditch in those days. I leaned up his neck and pulled the ring off and he fell down into the ditch. I've got a photo of him being led out of the ditch. You can only see a bit of his back above the guard rail.'

Later that year Jeff won Cheltenham's Massey-Ferguson Gold Cup on Jim Joel's precocious five-year-old chaser The Laird. The combination followed up at Kempton over Christmas, initiating a double for Jeff, completed by Dormant in the King George VI Chase. That 1966 renewal is mostly remembered for being Arkle's last race, the one in which he suffered his career-ending pedal bone injury. Leading over the last fence, he was collared close home by Dormant and beaten a length.

'You knew there was something wrong with Arkle,' the winning rider reflects. 'Dormant was an ignorant old shit of a horse. He used to gallop through fences. Turning for home I thought I might just about be third, and then Woodland Venture tipped up with 'Biddles' [Terry Biddlecombe] and I thought I was going to be second. Then, all of a sudden, I realised that Arkle wasn't going anywhere, and Dormant always did used to quicken at the end.'

Rondetto was back for the 1967 National but Jeff wasn't. He was off with a fractured skull, incurred at Huntingdon on Easter Monday, so Johnny Haine had the ride. They were right there with the leaders at the twenty-third fence when the 'Foinavon' pile-up occurred, ending their participation in the race. It was the very same fence that caught out Rondetto the following year, when reunited with his usual partner.

In between those two Grand National attempts, Rondetto and Jeff scored a famous victory in the 1967 Hennessy Gold Cup, scraping home by a head from Stalbridge Colonist in a dramatic finish which saw the first four separated by less than a length.

'He was past his best by then,' the jockey reckons. 'The reason he won was he just wouldn't give up. He was flat out turning for home; I certainly didn't think I'd win, and then, as he got further up the straight and they weren't getting any more away from him, you could feel him think, "I'll have these bastards". He flung himself at the last, got a length or two, and just got there. He was a magic little horse.'

Having failed to complete in three previous attempts and now at the advanced age of thirteen, Rondetto was a largely ignored 25-1 chance for the 1969 Grand National. But it proved to be a good year for the old timers. Just as in 1962, when a triumvirate of twelve-year-olds filled the first three places, so once again the combined ages of the first three home totalled thirty-six.

Going to the second last fence, twelve-year-old Highland Wedding, who had jumped into the lead at the Canal Turn second time round, was being pressured by eleven-year-old Steel Bridge, with Rondetto and the near-white The Beeches the only others still in with a chance.

Just for a moment, Jeff, though barely able to see through a huge black eye acquired in a fall in the Topham Trophy two days earlier, still felt Rondetto may have something in reserve, but it wasn't to be. Highland Wedding, owned by American Tom McKay and Toronto banker Charles Burns, stayed on stoutly under Eddie Harty to score by twelve lengths from Steel Bridge, the mount of Richard Pitman, with Rondetto running on to claim third place, just a length behind the runner-up.

'I had a lovely ride,' Jeff reported afterwards, 'and it was only old age that beat Rondetto.'

They returned in 1970 for a final attempt at the great race, but this time they were among eight casualties claimed by the third fence. The rider recalls: 'The year he finished third he wasn't quite as good as he could have been because he'd had a dodgy joint all season. The next year he was definitely better. I rode him for ten minutes on Grand National morning and he was like a nutcase. He was so well, he was too fresh. That's the reason he came down at the third. He was going like a nutter and hurled himself at the fence and his arse overtook his head.'

Rondetto and Jeff had one more race together, finishing fourth at Stratford in May 1970, after which the horse was retired. But Jeff still had plenty of ammunition at the Turnell yard, including The Laird.

Since winning the Massey-Ferguson as a five-year-old, The Laird had matured into a top-class chaser and had been unlucky not to win two Cheltenham Gold Cups. The first of these was in 1968, when he'd failed by a neck to peg back Fort Leney, the mount of Pat Taaffe, with Stalbridge Colonist just a length further back in third.

'If you'd run that race ten times he'd have won eight of them for certain,' insists Jeff. 'He put in a massive leap at the last and landed a bit heavy, then with the roar you get from the crowd at Cheltenham, he just sort of dwelt. He didn't put the brakes on but in those sorts of races you don't need to do any more than just dwell for a second. Fort Leney would have led me a length at one stage up the run-in and The Laird only got beaten a neck. Another three strides and I'd have won half a length.

'The following year he was a certainty but I got brought down at the top of the hill. I followed Pat McCarron on a horse called Dicky May, which you'd have sworn blind would have been the safest conveyance in the race. He went arse over head at the fence at the top of the hill first time round. I actually went to jump back on him, that's how much of a certainty I thought he was, but he had a puncture wound in his shoulder where something had galloped on him. I promise you, he would have won a minute that year.'

The following season The Laird could only finish fifth behind 33-1 shot L'Escargot in the Gold Cup. However, the start of 1971 saw him back to somewhere near his best, landing a hat-trick of victories in Ascot's Whitbread Trial, Kempton's Coventry Chase and the Cathcart at Cheltenham. His next race was the Grand National, for which he was the 12-1 third favourite, but he got no further than the second fence. Says Jeff, succinctly: 'He jumped it very big and came down on his head.

'The Laird was one of those horses that matured early. He won the Massey-Ferguson when he was five, carrying 10st 9lb and beating Ryan Price's Charlie Worcester, a seasoned old handicapper who had 10st 1lb, by ten lengths. Then after Christmas he won the Stone's Ginger Wine at Sandown with 11st 10lb, beating Hello Dolly, another of Price's, and she also only had 10st 1lb.

'He got on the floor a lot of times, that was the trouble. Bob always wanted him held up but I think he'd have been a better horse if I'd have let him roll, because he was brave and loved to stand off. To me, I often got him in trouble because I was trying to steady him and not going for a long one all the time. But he was the next best I rode, after Pas Seul.'

The Laird's second fence exit in 1971 prefixed two more Grand National falls for Jeff, with Fortina's Palace departing at Becher's second time round in 1972, and Ashville crashing out at the third the following year. Roman Holiday got to the third last fence in 1974 before Jeff pulled him up.

With only one completion in ten rides, Jeff's Grand National record looked indifferent to say the least, but his next three mounts all got round. It started with Money Market, who finished fourth in 1975.

'I really fancied Money Market. I thought he'd be terrific round there, but he jumped so good and big that he tired himself out. He finished fourth but he was legless from three out. He got home because of his guts but he was absolutely knackered.'

The ever reliable Spanish Steps came home sixth in 1976, as did What A Buck twelve months later, but Otter Way's participation ended with a first fence fall in 1978. 'He should never have gone there,' observes Jeff. 'He wouldn't have jumped round Liverpool if you'd put air balloons on him!'

The last of his fifteen Grand National rides, Casamayor in 1980, fell at the nineteenth. As a trainer his only runner was 500-1 outsider Spartan Orient in 1987. He remembers: 'Luke Harvey rode it and he fell off. I told him to go down the inner because he jumped left. For some unknown reason he pulled him out [at the twelfth fence], the horse ran left and nearly hit the rail as he landed. As he made sure he didn't hit it, he toppled Luke straight out the bloody side door!'

In 2005 Jeff King called time on his training operation at Broad Hinton stables, some six miles south of Swindon, thus ending a racing career stretching back over 45 years. But the link forged in his days as joint stable jockey to Bob Turnell remained, for the yard was taken over by Andy Turnell, the son of Jeff's Marlborough mentor.

Date: Saturday 29 March 1969 Going: Good Value to Winner: £17,849

Horse	Owner	Trainer	Age / weight	Jockey	SP
1 Highland Wedding	Mr T H McKoy, Jnr	G B Balding	12-10-4	E P Harty	100-9
2 Steel Bridge	Mr J L Drabble	Mrs B Lockhart-Smith	11-10-0	R Pitman	50-1
3 Rondetto	Mr A B Mitchell	R Turnell	13-10-6	J King	25-1
4 The Beeches	Mr Paul Mellon	R Turnell	9-10-1	W Rees	100-6

Distances: 12 lengths, 1 length, 12 lengths. Time: 9 mins 30.8 secs. 30 ran

Winner trained at Weyhill, Hampshire

1970

ROY EDWARDS
Up front out of trouble

· *Roy Edwards, rider of more than 500 winners.*

THERE WAS ONE thing you could guarantee when Roy Edwards was riding in a race – they'd go a good pace from the start. He always preferred to be up there with the leaders, keeping out of trouble.

From a Montgomeryshire farming family, Roy was riding by the age of four and spent his early years in gymkhanas and hunting with the North Shropshire before graduating to show jumping and point-to-points. His two brothers were also associated with horses, Charles being involved with show jumpers whereas Gordon found success in the point-to-point world. Their sister, Sheila Crow, was a leading point-to-point rider, as was her son Alastair.

Roy's first winner under Rules came on 5 January 1957, aged nineteen, in a Leicester maiden hurdle aboard Audition, trained by permit holder Wilf White at Malpas, Cheshire. White was better known in show jumping circles as the owner-rider of Nizefella, part of the Gold Medal winning team at the 1952 Olympic Games in Helsinki.

Having enjoyed considerable success as an amateur, Roy was 'asked' (a euphemism for 'ordered') by those in authority to turn professional at the start of the 1959/60 season. Having done so, he rode for Market Drayton trainer Roy Whiston who provided him with his first Grand National ride in 1961 aboard Fresh Winds, owned by Southport advertising chief Arthur Maiden.

Fresh Winds went straight to the front, led the field past the stands and was still leading when coming down at the nineteenth.

In September of that year Roy finished second on 21-year-old Creggmore Boy in a Ludlow selling chase. But the following week he fractured his skull in a first fence fall from Breaker at Woore and lay unconscious in hospital for ten days. Amazingly, he was back in action just six weeks later.

At the time, Roy and wife Susan were living at Park Farm, near Kidsgrove in the Potteries, where they ran a dairy farm to supplement the uncertain income from race riding. From there they moved to what was to become Blakeley Stud, near Hodnet in Shropshire. They bought it as a 75-acre farm with the intention of turning it into a stud but started with milking cows and then turned it over to arable, thus enabling Roy to continue his riding career.

His second Grand National mount came in 1963, aboard Chavara. Formerly trained by George Owen, for whom he won the Great Yorkshire Chase, he had joined Jack Peacock's Shropshire stable the previous autumn.

The *Sporting Chronicle's* front page headline read '*Chavara is the National Nap*' but the prophecy did not materialise. Though prominent throughout the first circuit, Chavara gradually weakened, eventually finishing twelfth of the 22 finishers.

Roy's preference for setting the pace was perfectly suited to the front-running Peacetown, his mount in the 1964 National. Having burnt off the other pacemaker, Out And About, after a circuit, Peacetown was clear of the field for the second half of the race. He was looking all over a winner when hitting the fourth from home and still held a commanding lead coming onto the racecourse. But by the last he had given everything and his tendency to jump right-handed proved costly. He veered over to the stands side rail as first Purple Silk and then Team Spirit went past. Peacetown kept going doggedly and held on to third place.

In February 1965 Roy suffered a serious fall at Birmingham which was to rule him out of that year's National. The fall itself was fairly innocuous but another horse landed on him and trod on his head. The damage comprised a broken cheekbone, fractured upper and lower jawbones, a broken nose, cracked forehead, a black eye and bruises. He was unconscious for two days and woke up to hear that the doctors wanted to take out all his teeth in order to operate. Somehow they were dissuaded from doing so when X-rays revealed that the jawbone fractures, while serious enough, weren't quite as bad as first feared.

During the 1966/67 campaign he teamed up with the Peter Easterby-trained Saucy Kit and rode him to victory in the 1967 Champion Hurdle. He finished fourth in that season's jockeys' table with 64 winners, a personal best, and was given a retainer by Lord Leverhulme to ride his horses the following season. He celebrated by winning the Rank Cup Chase at Killarney in July on Marvellous Tack, this being the only time he rode outside Britain.

His mount in the 1967 Grand National, Fred Rimell's Princeful, had been bang up there with the leaders when caught in that year's infamous twenty-third fence pile-up. Stable companion The Fossa was put out of the race at the same fence. Roy rode The Fossa in the following year's National, when he made most of the running until Valentine's second time before fading to finish fifth behind Red Alligator.

Saucy Kit's attempt to win a second successive Champion Hurdle in 1968 had floundered with a bad mistake at the second last flight but that was far from the end of Roy's association with the horse. Indeed, it was merely the beginning, for in 1969 he bought Saucy Kit and stood him as a stallion at Blakeley Stud. He then purchased two more stallions, Right Honourable Gentleman and the smart Sweeps Hurdle winner Normandy.

By now the stud was taking up ever more of his time. Nonetheless, in 1970 he found himself on the Grand National favourite, George Owen's Two Springs. He had won the Greenall Whitley National Trial on him the year before and had picked up further 'beer money' when landing the Whitbread Wales Trophy at Chepstow.

Despite having been beaten in the Haydock Park National Trial, Two Springs went to post at Liverpool the 13-2 favourite. Roy had been around for too long to feel any pressure associated with a leading fancy but there had been plenty of talk beforehand about the size of the third fence, the first open ditch. 'As big as a house,' was how one jockey described it. It certainly took its toll that year, claiming eight fallers, including Two Springs, who up to then had been getting a typical Edwards ride, right up there with the early pace.

'I don't know what went wrong,' he reflected. 'He went in to jump it perfectly but just didn't get there. I always said it was the biggest fence on the course.'

The fences continued to take their toll, with more than half of the 28 runners, including 1968 winner Red Alligator, failing to negotiate the first circuit. A 100-1 outsider, Villay, led the survivors past the stands and he remained in front until unseating his amateur rider Derrick Scott four fences from home, which left just seven still standing.

The Fred Rimell-trained Gay Trip, with Pat Taaffe deputising for the injured Terry Biddlecombe, took command over the second last and drew clear to pass the post twenty lengths clear of his toiling rivals, headed by the Irish pair Vulture and Miss Hunter, with Dozo in fourth. Former champion jockey Josh Gifford, having his final ride before retiring, completed the course in last place on Assad.

Roy and Two Springs resumed their partnership a fortnight later, finishing runner-up to The Spaniard in the Scottish National. Two weeks after that they combined to win the Midlands Grand National at Uttoxeter.

The following year, Roy rode Two Springs to victory in the Great Yorkshire Chase, beating The Laird by two lengths. He started a well-fancied 13-1 shot for the 1971 Grand National and ran creditably enough to finish sixth, without ever really getting into the race.

'He was a horse that loved to be up in front and that race was run very fast,' said Roy. 'I was further behind than usual and when I turned into the straight I was well back. I stayed on past others that were stopping, which made it look better than it was. In truth, I gave him too hard a race to win the Great Yorkshire. I think if I hadn't given him such a hard time at Doncaster, he'd have had that bit extra left for Aintree.'

By now Roy had decided that this would be his last season. He was riding as well as ever with more than 50 winners to his credit and had achieved a personal milestone when scoring his 500th winner on Pitznair at Warwick in January. But at 38 and with the three stallions generating good business at the stud, he decided it was time to stop.

He went out on a winner, aboard Ray Peacock's Miss Soundly at Uttoxeter on 1 June 1971. What better way to sign off – and the rousing reception he received as he entered the winner's enclosure left no doubt about the public's feeling for him at the course where he had been the leading jockey for many years.

Despite having broken 'every bone down my left side,' Roy counted himself fortunate at having been able to finish on his own terms, rather than having retirement forced upon him, as he had seen happen to so many of his weighing room pals.

For a time he combined running Blakeley Stud with training, his biggest success being achieved with Relevant in the 1974 Victor Ludorum Hurdle at Haydock.

Saucy Kit remained at the stud until his death in 1981, his produce including the prolific winning hunter chaser Flying Ace. Meanwhile, Normandy sired Bridge Ash, winner of the 1982 Midlands Grand National. The stud expanded over the years to comprise over 200 acres with its stallions including Seymour Hicks, sire of 1999 Cheltenham Gold Cup winner See More Business.

Roy Edwards died in December 2010 at the age of 77. When I'd interviewed him in 2002 he'd remarked that he'd like to slow down but wasn't quite sure how to go about it. But then, it was usually fast and furious back in the days when Roy Edwards led the field.

Date: Saturday 4 April 1970 Going: Firm Value to Winner: £14,804 10s

Horse	Owner	Trainer	Age / weight	Jockey	SP
1 Gay Trip	Mr A J Chambers	F Rimell	8-11-5	P Taaffe	15-1
2 Vulture	General R K Mellon	T Dreaper	8-10-0	S Barker	15-1
3 Miss Hunter	Mrs W Macauley	D Auld	9-10-0	F Shortt	33-1
4 Dozo	Mrs E W Wetherill	G Balding	9-10-4	E P Harty	100-8

Distances: 20 lengths, ½ length, 2½ lengths. Time: 9 mins 38.0 secs. 28 ran

Winner trained at Kinnersley, Worcestershire

1971

JIM DREAPER
Growing up with Arkle

John Cook brings Specify through on the rails to beat Black Secret.

THE POSTAL ADDRESS says Dublin, for Kilsallaghan is classed as Dublin. But Greenogue itself lies in County Meath, the importance of which is not lost on its community. It's at Greenogue that you will find the Dreapers.

For those who grew up during the times of Presley, the Beatles and Tom Dreaper, this is Graceland; this is the Cavern Club. It's a shrine to excellence; a temple to equine greatness.

Greenogue was home to Arkle, the one known simply as 'Himself'; and also to the marvellous Flyingbolt. It housed Fortria and Ben Stack, both Two-Mile Champion Chase winners; plus Gold Cup heroes Fort Leney and Prince Regent. Tom Dreaper trained them all.

'Arkle's box is number 7,' says Jim Dreaper, the legend's son, who hasn't made a bad fist of training in his own right since inheriting the licence. 'Flyingbolt was in box 22, round the corner out of the way. If someone came along and put their hand up, he'd bite it.'

James Thomas Russell Dreaper is standing between the house and the yard. Around him are gathered a dozen members of the West Midlands Racing Club. It is midsummer, 2003 and they have come to visit the yard that in the salad days of youth approximated to the absolute. The trainer tells them how the legend of Arkle began.

'Three three-year-olds were bought at the sales for the Duchess [Anne, Duchess of Westminster]. At that time there was the Westminster estate in the north-west of Scotland. There were three mountains on it – Arkle, Ben Stack and Foinavon. Those were the names given to the three horses.

'Initially, Foinavon looked as if he was going to be the proper horse, but he was a thief. Pat Taaffe got a fall off him one day at Baldoyle. It was a soft enough fall. Pat rolled away, picked himself up and looked back and there's the horse, sat like a dog, eating grass. That was Foinavon.'

The Duchess later sold Foinavon for 2,000 guineas and the horse left Dreaper's star-studded yard for that of little-known trainer John Kempton, located at Compton, near Newbury. Maybe it was Foinavon's laid back attitude that, in 1967, enabled him to sidestep the melee at the fence that would thereafter bear his name, coming home the unlikeliest of post-war Grand National winners.

'Arkle was broken in England,' continues Jim. 'When he arrived here we didn't think he was anything special. We were very surprised when he won [on his hurdling debut] at Navan at 20-1. Father had another runner in the race, Kerforo, owned by Mr Stafford from Wexford. Pat Taaffe was riding Kerforo, the favourite, and you could name your price Arkle and Liam McLoughlin. Arkle beat Kerforo going away.

'Any time after that when Mr Stafford had a runner, he'd ask, "Are you running anything else?" I think he'd had a few quid on Kerforo!

'I was at boarding school when Arkle was in his prime. It was a relatively small yard, twenty-five to thirty horses, and there was no secretary at the time. In the end, the secretary for the Duchess of Westminster's estate in Ireland came over two afternoons a week because there was so much fan mail. Letters would arrive addressed "Arkle, Ireland".'

Arkle's 27 victories included three Cheltenham Gold Cups, three Leopardstown Chases, two Hennessy Gold Cups, a Whitbread Gold Cup, a King George VI Chase and an Irish Grand National before his career was ended by a broken pedal bone, sustained during the 1966 King George at Kempton. For more than a year there were hopes that he would run again. All looked set fair when Arkle was entered in a hurdle race on the second day of the 1968 Fairyhouse Easter Meeting.

'He was fit enough to run but he wasn't a patch on what he had been,' recounts Jim. 'It would have been terrible to have made little of a horse like that. It's like a good footballer or cricketer who's well past his sell-by date.

'Arkle was everything he was painted as. A great horse obviously, but also a pet. He would allow anyone who came into the yard to sit up on him. But Flyingbolt was a vicious brute. He would bite you or kick you; he just didn't like people.

'Flyingbolt was a better horse, mind you, at his best. My father often thought it but, for many reasons, he just didn't like to say it.

'Pat Taaffe said that, at the height of their careers, if they were in a three-mile race on heavy ground, at level weights, he would ride Flyingbolt. On quick ground or at less than three miles, he thought he would probably stay with Arkle.'

Contrary to popular belief, the pair often worked together on the gallops.

'The work that was done here was never actually very meaningful,' comments Jim. 'It would be a mile and a half, and that's not going to tell you what's going to happen in a three-mile race.

'There were two gallops – our own gallop and a neighbour's gallop, which was up the back. They were both reasonably level gallops. It wasn't as though one was uphill or one was softer than the other. I know for a fact that, in one field up the back, Flyingbolt was always more impressive against Arkle. It didn't matter whether they went left-hand or right-hand but for some reason up there, Flyingbolt always worked best.

'It was always the worry because, when it happened that Flyingbolt had worked well, we wondered was Arkle not as good as he used to be? Was he not going well? Was there something wrong?'

Whereas Arkle was forced to retire when still in his prime, Flyingbolt eventually overcame the illnesses that had bedevilled his career and returned to action, without ever recapturing his former brilliance. Maybe it's the reason why he's not generally held in equal esteem, but that's not the case down at Greenogue. Says Jim: 'It would be mixed opinion here as to whether Arkle was any better than Flyingbolt.

'Flyingbolt suffered from brucellosis, a blood disease. It's mostly known as a cattle disease. He used to break out in sores and warts, and possibly that's why he was so ill-tempered all his life.

'My father used to farm this place. He kept cattle, bullocks and also heifers. Heifers, the females, were at one time accused of spreading brucellosis, and from that year on there were no more heifers kept here.'

Tom Dreaper won the Irish Grand National seven years running yet Aintree's always eluded him. Prince Regent humped 12st 5lb when finishing third to Lovely Cottage in 1946. The following year he carried his 12st 7lb burden into fourth place behind the unconsidered Caughoo. The closest Tom came to landing the great race was with a horse named Black Secret in 1971. Jim takes up the story.

'Every year my father would buy two, perhaps three, yearlings, bring them on at the farm, then break them as three- or four-year-olds; and they were what they were.

'Black Secret at the outset was an ugly duckling. He had curbs, he'd a wind problem, he had lots of things wrong. As an unbroken horse he was unsalable, so he had to go and prove himself. I'd just left school at the time and he was given to me to do my best on him. So he started as a point-to-pointer.

'He was a seriously obnoxious horse; very difficult. He was a horse who wanted to do his own thing. In fact, I openly admit I wasn't able to ride him. Sean Barker, who was second on Vulture in the 1970 Grand National, did the rough work on him.

'His point-to-pointing was reasonably successful, and with the racing he became more mannerly and I was able to ride him. Then he was sold to my Godmother, Mrs Carol Watney. The price was 1,500 guineas if Pat Taaffe was going to ride him or 1,000 guineas if I was going to ride him. Being a good, straightforward Quaker and not supposed to be involved with anything to do with gambling, she decided to go for the cheaper option!'

At Fairyhouse on Easter Monday 1969, five-year-old Black Secret made his debut under Rules. The race chosen was the T. Levins-Moore Memorial Hunters' Chase and, emanating from the Dreaper yard, he was inevitably sent off favourite. It wasn't a great start – he was one of the race's seven fallers.

Black Secret was back at Fairyhouse in November, winning an amateur riders' maiden hurdle with young Jim Dreaper in the saddle. Back over fences he was second to a future Cheltenham Gold Cup winner in Glencaraig Lady at Navan, and then won at Naas. He finished third in Cheltenham's Kim Muir and third again, behind Glencaraig Lady and his stable companion Proud Tarquin, in the John Jameson Cup at Punchestown.

The following season, 1970/71, Black Secret was near invincible, winning six of his first eight starts, including the Troytown Chase at Navan, and finishing second (to Proud Tarquin at Naas) and third (to Money Boat in the Kerry National) in the others. The 1971 Grand National was to be his next target, and connections were confident of him running a big race.

'Yes,' recalls Jim, 'we had a great chance. Everything seemed right on the day.'

'No,' he replies emphatically when asked if he had any qualms about the horse's ability to jump round. And then he pauses, reflects, and grins. 'I say that as if I mean it!' he laughs. 'Liverpool … it was always my ambition, not particularly to win it, but to get round.

'I'm walking the track on the Friday evening with Sean Barker and another jockey, Pat Black. Because I'd been so built up, I looked at the first and thought, "It's not that big", then the second one, "That's all right." We go down to the third and we're about fifty yards away and we see these two lads standing there clipping it. We get a bit closer and see that they're actually on a small tractor and trailer which is between the fence and the guard-rail. Pat said, "That's enough" – and we went back!

'The next day in the weighing room, just before the Grand National, I thought, "This is magic." Stan Mellor was there, Terry Biddlecombe, household names with their great craic, laughs and jokes. What did impress me was when Lord Someone-or-other came in and told us to take our time, and all of a sudden, things became very quiet.

'When all those household names went so deathly silent, I thought, "Maybe this is not such a wonderful idea." As I walked out to get up I looked at these great men, proper men, and right then I thought there were other places I might be better off.

'I'd been warned about the walking round. When you get up on the horse you think you'll feel okay, but walking round in the parade nothing seemed to be right. This leg was longer than that one, everything was wrong. It was just the tension of the whole thing.

'The race went fine bar for one bad mistake at the smallest fence on the track, the Foinavon fence. There was a hole in it when we came round the second time and horses naturally will go for the hole. Black Secret decided he was going for it. I was aiming for it when the horse beside me - at the last minute...bang, we collided. For ten strides I was hanging off him, nearly gone, and in hindsight that cost him more than he was beaten by. But every horse in the race probably had a different excuse.'

The mare Sandy Sprite, with Ron Barry on board, led over the last from Black Secret, Bowgeeno, Astbury and Specify. She may well have become the first mare to win since Nickel Coin twenty years earlier but, alas, she broke down on the run-in, leaving Black Secret in front.

Says Jim: 'I remember working hard and pushing him along. I was in semi-disbelief that I was still in there with a chance.

'He got to the front about halfway up the run-in, just before the Elbow. I thought I was going as well as Sandy Sprite, but then I didn't know at the time that she was breaking down. She started to hang, and she just pushed us out a bit.

'It suited Specify ideally because that's the sort of horse he was. He had to be produced late and the gap opened up for him perfectly and John Cook and Specify got up inside.'

Specify's late surge up the rails saw him pass the post a neck in front of Black Secret. Astbury was two-and-a-half lengths back in third, a length-and-a-half ahead of Bowgeeno, with the luckless Sandy Sprite only a neck further away in fifth.

Jim rode Black Secret just once more, finishing third in Punchestown's Conyngham Cup in December 1971. That was one of his last rides. 'For the previous year my father hadn't been in the best of health and wasn't doing as much as he had. He said to me "Are you going to train these horses or ride them?"

'In those days the season [in Ireland] ended on 31 December. It was just a matter of changing the name on the licence. Progressively he was doing less and less but he was always there for me to ask a question.

'Yes, I would like to have combined training with riding a few, but I was the wrong side of 10st 7lb so I was going to be a bit heavy. And if you're going to train them you need all the help you can get, rather than preventing them winning by riding them yourself.'

Jim had inherited a stable full of fabulous chasing talent. He was soon off the mark with Straight Fort winning the Express Chase at Sandown under Eddie Wright on 7 January 1972.

Sean Barker took over on Black Secret. He made the frame all season without winning, though connections were still very hopeful of his chances in the 1972 Grand National. He ran a fine race, leading over Becher's second time until approaching the second last, eventually dead-heating for third place with General Symons, five lengths behind the winner, Well To Do, and three behind the runner-up, Gay Trip.

Reflects Jim: 'He'd had a good year building up to that first National, but then he got to a stage where that was as good as he was and he wasn't able to defy the handicapper any more. He was there or thereabouts but just not able to win. I don't think Aintree affected him; I don't think it made him any worse.'

Black Secret returned to Aintree for the William Hill Grand National Trial in October 1972, trailing home last of the seven finishers. He won a minor three-horse race at Punchestown next time out but soon after was moved to Roddy Armytage's stable at East Ilsley, near Newbury. Partnered again by Sean Barker, he completed the Grand National course for the third time in 1973, finishing a distant tenth behind Red Rum and Crisp.

'Once the handicapper caught up with him there weren't that many options in Ireland,' explains Jim, 'so he was better off moving across to race in the UK, where there are more opportunities.'

Meanwhile, Jim's runners continued to dominate on both sides of the Irish Sea. At Cheltenham in March 1975, Lough Inagh won the Two-Mile Champion Chase, Brown Lad won the Lloyds Bank (now the World) Hurdle, and Ten Up, sporting the colours immortalised by Arkle, landed the Gold Cup. Before the month was out, Brown Lad had won the first of his three Irish Grand Nationals and, three days later, Our Greenwood won Liverpool's Topham Trophy.

Brown Lad had carried just 10st 5lb when winning that first Irish National but won it the following year with 12st 2lb, then carried the same weight to victory in 1978. He was also second in the 1974 and 1976 Cheltenham Gold Cups. Not bad for a horse that had been diagnosed with a heart murmur.

'I was lucky it happened,' reflects Jim, 'but it happened too soon. Father used to say "Horses win in spite of you, not because of you." If they're good horses they win, unless you've made a total horlicks of it, but there's great satisfaction to be had from winning a race with a bad horse.'

The small band of West Midlands Racing Club members had clung to his every word. What, they asked him, had been Tom Dreaper's secret?

'People would ask my father, "How much work do these horses take?" He would reverse it: "How little do they need?"'

It was time to leave the temple.

Date: Saturday 3 April 1971 Going: Good Value to Winner: £15,500

Horse	Owner	Trainer	Age / weight	Jockey	SP
1 Specify	Mr F W Pontin	J Sutcliffe	9-10-13	J Cook	28-1
2 Black Secret	Mrs J Watney	T Dreaper	7-11-5	Mr J Dreaper	20-1
3 Astbury	Mr B P Jenks	J Bissill	8-10-0	J Bourke	33-1
4 Bowgeeno	Mr V T Holt	T Forster	11-10-5	G Thorner	66-1

Distances: Neck, 2½ lengths, 1½ lengths. Time: 9 mins 34.2 secs. 38 ran

Winner trained at Epsom, Surrey

1972

BUCK JONES
The Otter and the Major

Buck Jones. who rode The Otter in three Grand Nationals.

THERE WAS NEVER much doubt that brothers Peter and Buck Jones would become jockeys. As the sons of dual purpose jockey Davy Jones, it was determined from an early age.

Davy had his first ride in 1925, his last in 1972 and rode out for Cheltenham trainer Jack Perrett until well into his eighties. He rode in three Epsom Derbies and in the 1938 Grand National, finishing sixth on Red Knight II. In 1945 he won the Cheltenham Gold Cup on Lord Stalbridge's Red Rower. Later that year, he finished second in York's Ebor Handicap, carrying 7st 10lb.

Peter, Davy's eldest son by two years, rode in four Grand Nationals, finishing fifth on Pontin-Go in 1964 and seventh on Norther two years later. He won the 1964 Molyneux Chase over the National fences on Leslie.

Peter's younger brother was christened Thomas Michael but was always known as Michael. He acquired his nickname 'Buck', after the cowboy character Buck Jones, soon after starting out as an apprentice with Sam Armstrong at Newmarket, where he was part of a small army of young hopefuls that included Wally Swinburn and Josh Gifford.

His first winner came in an apprentice race at Thirsk in September 1958, on a horse called Doctor Bother for Yorkshire trainer Tommy Dent. 'Tanked off with me going to start and tanked off with me coming back,' he laughs.

His only other Flat race victory was part of a father-son double at Salisbury the following year. Buck won the first race on the card, and then Davy won the second race aboard an odds-on shot trained by Keith Piggott.

Having graduated from Armstrong's apprentice academy, Buck followed Josh Gifford to the Findon yard of Ryan Price. Fred Winter was then Price's first jockey with Gifford as his number two and Paul Kelleway at three. There was plenty of competition for rides and Buck rode just seven winners over jumps in three seasons.

Come the start of 1964, Fred Winter was in his final season, with Gifford by now having assumed the role of stable jockey. But things were to change dramatically following Rosyth's sensational victory in the 1964 Schweppes Gold Trophy.

The Newbury stewards called upon Price and Gifford to explain the discrepancy in Rosyth's form as compared with his five previous runs that season. Not being satisfied, they referred the matter to the stewards of the National Hunt Committee who withdrew Price's licence for the remainder of the season and suspended Gifford until the end of March.

It's an ill wind that blows nobody any good and Epsom trainer Sid Dale inherited several of Price's string, with Buck coming in for the winning ride on Invader in Sandown's Imperial Cup. An hour later he partnered What A Myth, like Invader another former Price inmate now trained by Dale, to land a long-distance handicap chase.

The following Saturday, the day of the 1964 Grand National, he rode a treble at Worcester, losing his 3lb claim in the process.

'With Josh suspended and Fred Winter packing up, I rode sixteen winners in little over eight weeks,' says Buck. 'I was in the right place at the right time.'

In 1966 he had his first ride in the Grand National. His mount was the doughty Pontin-Go, who, when named Gay Navaree, had finished fourth in 1962 and on whom Peter Jones was fifth in 1964 under his new name.

'The old horse had had it by then but I was asked to have him up there and get a few mentions. He did it all on his own. He got to the Canal Turn and turned left; you didn't have to ask him, he'd been round so many times. He completed one circuit then dropped himself out. By the third fence second time round he'd had enough and refused.'

Earlier that season Buck had won a novices' hurdle at Cheltenham on a horse called The Otter, trained under permit by Major Richard Dening, then based at Molecomb, near Goodwood, but shortly to relocate to Cullompton in Devon.

'I'd started riding for him while he was at Goodwood, through a contact of one of Ryan Price's owners. He put me in for the ride on Elegant Mink at Fontwell, my first winner for Major Dening.

'He'd ridden the dam, Sealskin, himself in Germany. She produced some quite good horses, including Moleskin and Highland Seal, as well as The Otter and Elegant Mink. Sealskin's dam, Tarka II, was a full sister to 1948 Grand National winner, Sheila's Cottage.

'Major Dening was an eccentric permit trainer. He'd stand in the grandstand with a stopwatch and time the race, then if you got beat, he'd tell you if you went too quick!

'When I rode The Otter the first time over hurdles at Cheltenham, he won at 20-1. In the race before, Major Dening had run Moleskin, who was making his first start over fences. The old boy wasn't a betting man as such but he'd had a tenner each-way double. Moleskin finished second – to a future Gold Cup winner, Woodland Venture.'

The Otter won once over hurdles during the 1966/67 campaign, when ridden by Brough Scott, who also had the mount when he won the 1969 Mandarin Chase at Newbury. But Buck was reunited with him for all his races the next season. They included the 1970 Grand National.

'I was going well and thinking I had a great chance when falling at Becher's second time,' he recalls. 'I was upsides the eventual winner, Gay Trip, when The Otter got it wrong. He stood off a bit far and came down too steep. It was a long way out but I was going as well as you'd want to go and beginning to get a bit excited.'

Ridden by Buck throughout the 1970/71 campaign, The Otter won the Haydock Park National Trial but fell in the National itself at the fence after Valentine's, the tenth.

The following season, The Otter and Buck finished third in Sandown's Mildmay Memorial and were short-headed in Haydock's National Trial. They were to have one more attempt at the Grand National in 1972, when the race was sponsored by BP Limited, the first time it had had a sponsor since 1963.

There's a photograph of that year's Grand National – the frontispiece of this book – taken at the first open ditch on the second circuit, fence nineteen. It shows Peter Morris leading Nephin Beg out of the ditch and Buck Jones perched on top of the fence, his mount nowhere to be seen.

Recalls Buck: 'The horse was getting used to it by then. Nephin Beg impeded me a little but that was just enough to stop him. He dug his toes in, dropped into the ditch, I've gone straight onto the fence.'

By that stage of the race, the leaders had a familiar look about them, with the previous year's runner-up Black Secret having just taken up the running, closely pursued by his conqueror, Specify, last year's third, Astbury, and 1970 winner Gay Trip, this quartet being followed by Well To Do, General Symons and the fading Fair Vulgan.

In driving rain, General Symons headed Black Secret with two jumps remaining, but he in turn was collared by Well To Do, the mount of champion jockey Graham Thorner. Well To Do led over the last fence and stayed on to prevail by two lengths from Gay Trip, who found the concession of 22lb of weight just beyond him. Three lengths further back came the dead-heaters Black Secret and General Symons.

Well To Do's owner-trainer, Captain Tim Forster, had been bequeathed the horse by his late owner, Mrs Heather Sumner, who had died from cancer the previous June.

A three-mile steeplechase, the Well To Do Challenge Cup, was inaugurated at Towcester the following January in honour of the Aintree hero and, appropriately, Well To Do won the first running of his own race.

The 1972 Grand National was the last time Buck rode The Otter. He ran just four more races over the next two seasons, being pulled up in three of them. The old spark had gone and he was eventually retired.

Major Dening had a ready-made replacement in The Otter's half-brother Highland Seal, who, in 1973, beat Red Rum by five lengths in the Haydock Park National Trial and put himself firmly in the Grand National reckoning. But whereas Red Rum went on to snatch a dramatic victory in the final strides, Highland Seal hated the experience and was already tailed off last when being baulked and put out of the race at the Canal Turn first time round.

In 1970 Buck had moved to 85-acre Brook Farm at Albury, on the outskirts of Guildford. He started training but didn't want to give up riding so he combined the two until 1976 when he finally hung up his boots. He'd ridden exactly 100 winners, 98 of them over jumps.

The best horses he trained were Wayward Angus and Ebony Rock, both of whom won the Peter Ross Novices' Chase at Ascot. He never saddled a runner in the Grand National, although Wayward Angus was due to run in it but began coughing four days before the race.

He harbours fond memories of those three Grand National spins on The Otter, and of his slightly batty owner-trainer, Major Dening, there in the grandstand, stopwatch in hand.

Date: Saturday 8 April 1972 Going: Soft Value to Winner: £25,765.50

Horse	Owner	Trainer	Age / weight	Jockey	SP
1 Well To Do	Capt T Forster	Owner	9-10-1	G Thorner	14-1
2 Gay Trip	Mr A J Chambers	F Rimell	10-11-9	T W Biddlecombe	12-1
3= Black Secret	Mrs J Watney	J Dreaper	8-11-2	S Barker	16-1
3= General Symons	Mrs E N Newman	J Tormey	9-10-0	P Kiely	40-1

Distances: 2 lengths, 3 lengths, dead-heat. Time: 10 mins 8.4 secs. 42 ran

Winner trained at Letcombe Bassett, Berkshire

1973

PETER CULLIS
Riding the no-hoper

Peter Cullis enters Taunton's winner's enclosure on May Gate, his final ride.

IT WAS ARGUABLY the most famous Grand National finish of all, with Red Rum relentlessly overhauling an exhausted Crisp up that Aintree run-in to snatch a dramatic victory in the dying strides. But half a mile further back down the course there was drama of a different kind.

Four fences from home, two loose horses had careered up and down in the ditch on the take-off side, baulking six runners and preventing them from jumping the fence. While three of the riders elected to call it a day, those on Sunny Lad, Go-Pontinental and Mill Door turned their mounts back and negotiated the obstacle at the second attempt and went on to complete the course.

While Red Rum and the vanquished Crisp were returning to the unsaddling enclosure amid frenzied scenes and resounding cheers, Mill Door trailed in last of the seventeen to get round.

For Mill Door's veteran rider Peter Cullis, getting round had been the aim. By then he was in his mid-forties and had waited 28 years for a ride in the National. Time was fast running out.

Born in Southampton in 1930, his father, Tommy Cullis, was captain of the town's speedway team. He had been due to represent Britain in an international in Australia when his career was ended by a serious accident, in which lost an eye and broke a leg.

Peter's racing career began when, aged eleven, he was apprenticed to Major Fred Sneyd at Sparsholt. 'I rode out before going to the local school in Childrey,' he remembers. 'It had been arranged with the headmaster that I'd be late in, but every morning I had to hold out my hand and the headmaster would give me a crack with the cane, just to make an example to the other kids in case they were late.'

He had his first ride on Weathercock, who carried just six stone when unplaced at Salisbury in April 1945. Later that year, the same horse provided him with his first winner, again at Salisbury, on 21 September, four days after his fifteenth birthday.

In 1948 he rode outsider Special Scotch in Masaka's Oaks, although it was hardly a distinguished occasion, the pair being slowly away and finishing last of the 25 runners. However, increasing weight soon brought his Flat aspirations to an end.

Following two years' National Service in the King's Troop, he rode over jumps for George Spann, who trained at Russley Park, Marlborough. The best horse he rode for Spann was Polar Flight, runner-up in the 1958 Cheltenham Gold Cup. Peter rode him when he finished third to Lochroe in Hurst Park's Grand Sefton Trial in October 1957. He won on him next time out at Stratford but then fell at the first in the Emblem Chase at Manchester and was unceremoniously 'jocked off' by the horse's owner.

Peter had entertained hopes of a ride in the 1957 Grand National. 'I was supposed to ride Wild Wisdom for Luther Bridge. Luther had ridden him the year before and had won a lot of money for getting round. We walked the course together and when we got to the Chair, he said to me "That's too big for you to jump. I'd better ride him again", so he did. I went bloody crackers but he assured me I still had plenty of time.'

Wild Wisdom fell at Valentine's first time round, while Peter waited for another opportunity. It was to be a long wait. He managed a spare ride on Uncle Bones in the 1960 Topham Trophy and was brought down at Becher's. Four years later he rode Lively Hopkins in the Topham but again failed to complete. By that time, he was a forgotten man.

In 1960 he had broken his neck in a fall from novice chaser Curling Iron at Kempton's Christmas meeting. Afterwards he found it hard to rekindle his riding career and managed only six winners during the whole of the 1960s. He retired but came back. He retired a second time after a horse named Pirodome had given him his first winner for four years at Stratford on the penultimate day of the 1970/71 season. Again he came back.

Pirodome was to prove a good friend to Peter, providing him with his only winners in each of the next two seasons. But it was another horse that, in 1973, finally brought the chance of a Grand National ride.

Mill Door was among the least distinguished Grand National runners of post-war years. A chestnut gelding by Cacador, he had pulled up and finished last twice in three Irish bumpers, but won a point-to-point there. Bought at Ascot September sales for 250 guineas, he managed to scrape home in his hunt race at the Cambridgeshire point-to-point in 1971. He was again sold at Ascot later that year for 170 guineas.

His new owner was Elwyn Birchall, who lived at Hartlebury, near Kidderminster. He campaigned him in point-to-points in 1972 and was rewarded by a lucky win in an adjacent and a more convincing victory in an open novices' race. Upgraded to hunter chases and partnered by Don Weaver, he managed a remote fourth behind Credit Call in that year's Liverpool Fox Hunters' Chase.

Under the regulations then in place, any horse finishing in the first four in a race over the Grand National fences was thereby qualified for the National itself. Hence the 1973 Grand National would be his aim.

Three weeks before the race, making a belated seasonal debut, Mill Door finished tailed off last in a Huntingdon novice chase. While it did not bode well for his chances at Aintree, for Peter Cullis it represented the fulfilment of a dream.

'I knew Elwyn Birchall very well. I used to play cards with him in the pub and I'd ridden a couple of horses for him that were trained by Ray Peacock. He'd now got his own permit and he was thinking about giving Don Weaver the ride in the National but I spoke with him for about an hour and talked my way into riding Mill Door.

'I was nearly 43 and I'd half finished by then. I was working on the pipelines for BP oil and combining it with riding. I'd never ridden in the National and I was keen to get the ride on Mill Door as I was just about to pack up altogether.

'BP were sponsoring the race that year and I didn't dare tell anyone that I'd got the chance of a ride because I was frightened of BP making a fuss. They had their own company magazine and I could see exactly what was going to happen. They'd have had the cameras down straight away and I didn't want any of that. So I took a week's holiday and rode out for Martin Tate each day.

'I'd never ridden Mill Door before, so I suggested to Elwyn that it would be a big help if I sat on him.

'There was a point-to-point scheduled at Chaddesley Corbett on the same day as the National so I got hold of Martin Tate, who trained just around the corner from the course and asked if there was any chance of me jumping a couple of the fences. Martin said "Yes, but you must be gone by seven because I'm not allowed to use them – and make sure you tread the holes back in."

'So we got there at six o'clock on the Friday morning, I jumped two fences on him and trod all the holes back in. We were all set to go to Liverpool the next day.'

But that night in the early hours Peter woke up in agony and found he couldn't see out of one eye. He'd waited almost thirty years to ride in the world's most famous steeplechase and now he was half blind.

'In the morning I rang the doctor and went to see him at quarter to nine. I'd ridden out at Martin's the day before on a horse that had been clipped. He'd put his head up, stuck his ear in my eye and he'd left a hair stuck in it. The doctor managed to get the hair out and gave me some eye drops.

'We set off straight away for Liverpool and when we reached the car park, Freddie [Peter's wife] had to put the drops in for me. I told to her to be careful not to let anyone see. Then Bob Davies parked next to us and saw what was going on. He looked at me and said "With the horse you're riding, you'll be better off keeping your eyes shut anyway!"

'I was riding a horse with no chance and they all said he shouldn't be in the race. But I was confident he'd get round because, barring something knocking him over, the horse did jump well. I hadn't been paid anything to ride him but I was on a promise of £300 if I got round.

'I'd planned to jump off and just lob round behind. The tape went up and I went down the inner with Ken White on Rouge Autumn. By the time we got to the Canal Turn I was about tenth and I said to Ken, "Bloody hell, I shouldn't be here, I'd better drop back." It wasn't until then that I took a pull and started hunting round. I'd set off to ride a race on him!

'He kept popping, but when I got to the fourth last there was just nowhere to go. Astbury refused in front of me and stopped me. So I went back, tried again and popped it. I wanted to get round, otherwise I'd have got nothing.

'He got round and I got my £300. He gave me a brilliant ride, the thrill of a lifetime. When you think about it, there's a lot of top jockeys who ride fancied horses and never get round.

'When I got home on Saturday night, BP were on the phone. Weren't they upset! The chap said, "You've just ridden in the National. You work for us. Why haven't you said anything?" I replied, "Because of exactly what's happening now."'

The following morning they were round with the camera crew. They took pictures of me with the horse and published the story in the company's magazine.

'I went back to Martin's afterwards and he played hell with me. "Well, didn't you get me into trouble," he fumed. "Why's that?" I asked. "I trod all the holes back in".

'"Yes," he replied, "but the bloody horse had got bandages on and you left cotton wool on top of the fences!"'

Birchall sold Mill Door shortly after the race to a Mr Lipka, who had similar aspirations for his new acquisition – a tilt at the 1974 Grand National. He gave the horse an unorthodox preparation, finishing fourth in the Waveney Open point-to-point, before sending him to licensed trainer Robin Blakeney at Charing.

Jimmy McNaught was Blakeney's stable jockey and had the ride at Aintree. His aim, as with Peter Cullis, was just to get round. Last of the thirty survivors jumping the water, they plugged on until parting company five from home.

After more than thirty years in the saddle, Peter Cullis retired for a third and final time. It was on a winning note, at Taunton on 9 May 1975. Making the weight had become ever harder and he had spent five hours in the Turkish baths in order to do 11st 7lb on Martin Tate's selling hurdler May Gate.

He remembers it well: 'When I first stood on the scales in the baths I was 12st 4lb stripped. I didn't dare tell Martin. It was when I was coming back to the winner's enclosure that I decided that was it. I rang Freddie and told her to cancel my other rides. I'd retired on a winner. You can't beat that when you think about it.'

BP promoted Peter to the post of control supervisor on a pipeline. He moved from his Stourport home to live in South Wales, where he rode out occasionally for local trainer Bryn Palling. On retiring from BP he returned to the Midlands and now lives at Wolferlow, near Bromyard.

As for Mill Door, his owner, Mr Lipka, continued to campaign him in point-to-points and hunter chases. In 1975 he won a hunt race and an adjacent. He did finally achieve a placing under Rules, when last of three finishers in a Folkestone hunter chase. That was his last race.

Maybe he didn't go out on a winning note but he retired in one piece and, after all, third place in a hunter chase was some sort of moral victory. For even at his best, a one-paced point-to-pointer is all Mill Door ever was. Yet for Peter Cullis he provided an experience he would always remember.

Date: Saturday 31 March 1973 Going: Firm Value to Winner: £25,486

Horse	Owner	Trainer	Age / weight	Jockey	SP
1 Red Rum	Mr N H Le Mare	D McCain	8-10-5	B Fletcher	9-1jtfav
2 Crisp	Sir Chester Manifold	F Winter	10-12-0	R Pitman	9-1jtfav
3 L'Escargot	Mr R Guest	D Moore	10-12-0	T Carberry	11-1
4 Spanish Steps	Mr E R Courage	Owner	10-11-13	P Blacker	16-1

Distances: ¾ length, 25 lengths, 12 lengths. Time: 9 mins 1.9 sec. 38 ran

Winner trained at Southport, Lancashire

1974

KEN WHITE
Older and wiser

Ken White, who rode in eight Grand Nationals and won the Champion Hurdle on Comedy Of Errors.

WHEN RED RUM won his first Grand National twelve months earlier, the cheers and applause that reverberated around Aintree had been just as much for Crisp, the courageous runner-up. But this time the ovation was his alone. In winning the race for the second time by beating dual Cheltenham Gold Cup winner L'Escargot, he confounded those doubters who insisted that no horse could win carrying 12 stone, or that 'they're never as good again' after a National victory.

Going to the last, it seemed that L'Escargot might have Red Rum's measure but he was a spent force by the time they reached the Elbow and Red Rum drew away to win by seven lengths.

Charles Dickens, who had made so much of the running, stayed on spiritedly on the run-in and failed by only a short-head to snatch second place off L'Escargot in the Grand National's first ever photo finish. Then came Spanish Steps, fourth for the second successive year, ahead of Rough Silk, Vulgan Town and the previous year's fifth, Rouge Autumn, the mount of Ken White.

Born on a farm on the Croome Estate in Worcestershire, where his father 'always had a horse or two', Ken had served a five-year apprenticeship with Jack Yeomans at Hill Croome and rode his first winner on Trace in a mile-and-a-half maiden at Manchester on 16 April 1959. That was to be his only success on the Flat before switching to jumps.

His first victory under National Hunt rules came courtesy of Lean Sport, trained by Yeomans, in a Southwell selling hurdle on 30 March 1961. Two years later he had his first ride in the Grand National on rank outsider Solonace. 'I fell off at the third,' he ruefully admits.

In January 1965 he won Haydock's Tom Coulthwaite Chase on Game Purston, his first big race victory. Later that year he suffered a depressed fracture of the skull when a spare ride called Surcharge fell at Wetherby.

He was out of action for nine months, returning in August 1966 for the beginning of the new season. It started well enough with his old friend Lean Sport rattling off a Devonshire hat-trick in the space of a week. But two days after the third leg, Ken's mount Double L slipped up on the flat at Market Rasen. This time he fractured the front of his skull. Remarkably, he returned to action just six weeks later at Perth, riding Cortachy Sand to victory twice within 24 hours.

He finished the 1966/67 season with 34 winners, including the Welsh Grand National on Happy Spring. He completed the course in the Grand National itself on Game Purston, though only after three attempts to negotiate the demolished twenty-third fence, while Foinavon was setting up an unassailable lead.

'Game Purston had run in the 1966 Grand National,' Ken recalls, 'but I was injured so Paddy Cowley had the ride. I stood by the Chair to watch the race. When Game Purston came to it, he hit the fence and dropped back into the ditch, but Paddy was shot forward and cleared the fence on his own. I was left with the job of getting the horse out of the ditch.'

Ken won the 1969 Haydock Grand National Trial on Game Purston, along with that year's Midlands National on Happy Spring. He won the Haydock race again the following year on French Excuse, by which time he had been offered and accepted the post of second jockey to that horse's trainer, Fred Rimell.

French Excuse won the Welsh National on his next start in the hands of stable jockey Terry Biddlecombe, but Biddlecombe suffered a bad fall at Kempton just six days later which ruled him out of the 1970 Grand National. Pat Taaffe proved a winning substitute on Rimell's Gay Trip, while Ken took over on French Excuse, who went off as second favourite but fell at the Canal Turn first time round.

He rode The Pantheon in the 1972 National and was with the leaders when falling at the thirteenth fence. His next two rides, on Rouge Autumn in '73 and '74, would be his best.

Rouge Autumn had looked like developing into a useful hurdler at one stage, having been placed behind top-grade timber-toppers such as Drumikill and Celtic Gold. He fell on his chasing debut at Ludlow in March 1969 but improved to win the Oxfordshire Chase at Newbury the following season. However, his jumping was a cause for concern and he finished up on the deck in three of his next five chases, including being brought down at the second fence when Ken rode him in the 1970 Totalisator Champion Novices' Chase (now the RSA Chase) at Cheltenham.

Rimell then reverted Rouge Autumn to hurdles and it was November 1971 before he was asked to jump a fence in public again. Ken rode him to win a three mile five furlong chase at Sandown, after which they finished fourth in the Mildmay Memorial and second in the Great Yorkshire before winning Haydock's National Trial by a head from The Otter.

'He was a decent hurdler but when he started to jump fences he was quite desperate,' recalls Ken. 'He eventually got the message and I think he was cleverer than I was.

'When we schooled at Fred's, we had a big loose school and they used to go round there, with solid poles to get them pacing themselves and picking their feet up. Fred never believed in over schooling them with a jockey on.

'I wouldn't label Rouge Autumn as ungenuine. It was just that he looked after himself. When he wasn't racing he'd take the Mick and try and take off with you going down to the start. I had a job to stop him before the first fence. But then as soon as the tapes went up, you were punching and kicking, and as long as you kept doing that, he'd keep going. But I loved him and got on well with him.'

Ken rode Rouge Autumn throughout the 1972/73 campaign, during which he was third in Ascot's Kirk and Kirk Chase, fourth in Newbury's Hennessy Gold Cup and second in the Warwick National.

He was sent off a 40-1 outsider for the 1973 Grand National but belied his odds by running a fine race to finish fifth, always in the first half-dozen without ever threatening to play a part in the finish, in which Red Rum wore down the legless Crisp in the dying strides.

'I was pushing and struggling just to get a position, the pace was so fast, but he kept going,' says Ken. 'He was an out and out stayer. I'd originally thought he was a bit better than that because he'd won a decent hurdle race but I think he used to save a bit.'

Rouge Autumn managed to win an amateur riders' chase at Cheltenham that autumn and was thereabouts in three of his four other races during the season prior to the 1974 Grand National. Ken had already won that year's Welsh National on Pattered for Earl Jones and was looking forward to a second Aintree spin on Rouge Autumn, whose starting price this time was 28-1. He again ran respectably but this time could never get amongst the leaders.

'He was a year older and a bit wiser and he probably wasn't enjoying it so much,' reflects Ken of his mount's seventh place effort. 'He went and done his job but he just wasn't quite as sharp as the year before.'

Behind them in eighth came the gallant Duke of Alburquerque on Nereo, riding with a strapped-up collarbone – no mean performance for a man of 56.

Red Rum's second National win was the first double since Reynoldstown in 1935-36 and the first win under 12 stone since Reynoldstown himself carried two pounds more than that to the second of his two triumphs. The winning time of 9 minutes 20.3 seconds was more than 18 seconds slower than the previous year's record time, in which Crisp had set such a furious pace.

Rouge Autumn's owner, Bryan Jenks, gave the horse to his son Willie to train the following season. Ken rode him one last time over the Aintree fences, finishing seventh in the 1975 Topham Trophy.

Bill Smith had taken over as Rimell's stable jockey when Terry Biddlecombe left to ride for Fulke Walwyn. When Biddlecombe retired in 1974, Smith took over at Walwyn's and Ken was promoted to first jockey for Rimell. He established a great partnership with former champion hurdler Comedy Of Errors during the 1974/75 campaign, winning six in a row, including the Fighting Fifth, the Cheltenham Trial (subsequently the Bula) Hurdle, the Irish Sweeps and the Scottish Champion Hurdles, plus a famous eight-length regaining of his Champion Hurdle crown.

He rode Rimell's Junior Partner, a fancied 18-1 chance, in that year's Grand National but, disappointingly, got no further than the second fence.

Ken had the last of his eight Grand National rides on 66-1 outsider Perpol in 1976. Behind at halfway, he pulled his mount up two fences before Becher's. He hung up his boots and saddle at the end of that season due to a recurring shoulder injury.

He retired to his dairy farm at Drakes Broughton, just outside Pershore, but retained his racing connections as a permit holder. Gradually he found that he was getting more horses than cows around the place, so he said goodbye to the milking and took out a full trainer's licence.

Drakes Broughton was a tad too busy for training racehorses, so in 1981 he upped sticks and moved to the 37 acres of Little London Farm, one mile from the Shropshire village of Aston Munslow. He trained there for 15 years before relinquishing his licence.

But that wasn't the end of his racing involvement, for he kept his lorry and transported horses to the races, mainly for fellow Shropshire trainer Tim Forster, and did that for eight years.

He hasn't strayed far in retirement, living in Craven Arms, just a few miles down the road from Ludlow, where many of his 350-plus winners had been gained during an 18-year career that included the English and Scottish Champion Hurdles, Welsh Nationals, Midlands Nationals and a Topham Trophy, plus a brace of clear rounds on Rouge Autumn in the Grand National.

Date: Saturday 30 March 1974 Going: Good Value to Winner: £25,102

Horse	Owner	Trainer	Age / weight	Jockey	SP
1 Red Rum	Mr N H Le Mare	D McCain	9-12-0	B Fletcher	11-1
2 L'Escargot	Mr R Guest	D Moore	11-11-13	T Carberry	17-2
3 Charles Dickens	Lt Col P Bengough	M Scudamore	10-10-0	A Turnell	50-1
4 Spanish Steps	Mr E R Courage	Owner	11-11-9	W Smith	15-1

Distances: 7 lengths, short head, 8 lengths. Time: 9 mins 20.3 sec. 42 ran

Winner trained at Southport, Lancashire

1975

BILL SMITH

What a rotten day to turn up!

Bill Smith on Edward Courage's fine chaser Spanish Steps.

THE HAMPSHIRE VILLAGE of Hambledon once boasted its own racecourse. The final meeting under National Hunt Rules took place there in 1928, although it was used for point-to-points until 1952. The course was within the grounds of Grenville Hall, and it was from Grenville Hall's stables that Captain William Henry Poulett (later the 6th Earl Poulett) sent out The Lamb to win the Grand Nationals of 1868 and 1871.

A short but winding, single-track road drive from the village lies Kelanne Stud, where Bill Smith sits in an armchair and talks of Kelanne, the horse after whom the stud was named and on whom he won the Sweeps Hurdle at Leopardstown in 1971.

'It was only his second run for Bill Marshall, who was a past master at getting one ready for the day,' he recalls. 'It was the day after I'd got beaten half a length in the King George on Spanish Steps.'

Ah yes, Spanish Steps. That resolute chaser who ran in four Grand Nationals and made the frame in three; winner of sixteen races during ten consecutive seasons, including the Hennessy and Benson and Hedges Gold Cups, the Gainsborough and SGB Chases, and placed in a Cheltenham Gold Cup too.

Bred, owned and trained under permit by Edward Courage, Spanish Steps was a son of Tiberetta, winner herself of the Becher Chase and the Grand

Sefton over the Aintree fences and placed third, second and fourth in successive Grand Nationals. Like mother, like son.

Bill first moved into Kelanne Stud in 1975, the same year that Spanish Steps gave him his best ride in the National. He bought the remainder of the property before he retired from riding in 1984.

Between 1984 and 1990 he was employed as ambassador for the Maktoum family, a diverse role which included becoming the first man to ride a horse under lights at Dubai's brand new Nad Al Sheba racecourse, in order to ensure they worked properly.

In 1991 Sheikh Ahmed asked him to train some Arabian racehorses for him in Britain, which is what he's done since. He's been champion trainer five times and had winners all over Europe.

Born on 30 October 1948, the son of a professional road race cyclist, Bill Smith has come a long way since winning awards in the southern show rings at the age of twelve.

'It was rather sad,' he muses, 'because my father was a racing cycle specialist and had a shop in Chertsey. Every Sunday he'd have the lads round for club type activities, and in the morning I'd walk out, past all these lovely, lightweight racing bikes to go and ride a horse, which was a bit like a trainer's son walking past all the horses to go and ride a bike.

'I got into horses when I was about nine. I did show jumping as a kid and I would like to have been a show jumper but I didn't have the financial backing.'

Instead, he left school at fourteen, went to Fred Rimell's stables for one month, didn't like it, came home, and worked in Moss Bros at Southsea, near Portsmouth, for eighteen months, acquiescing with his parents' request to get a 'proper' job.

Moss Bros then was a very different type of store from what it is now, focussing on morning suit hire and army and navy kit. Young Bill's responsibilities included looking after the shop's tack area – yes, they sold horse equipment too – which eventually led to a customer inviting him to ride his point-to-pointers.

'I went to Cowdray Park's point-to-point and got a ride for Donald Underwood, on a horse called Beaumette. When Don asked me if I'd ridden before, I said "Of course." I didn't actually tell him that I hadn't ridden in a race.

'I got left twenty lengths at the start and fell off three out. I went over her head and took the bridle off with me, and she disappeared out the front gates of Cowdray Park, straight up Midhurst High Street with no bridle on. Don wasn't best pleased and told me so. It was about five years before I next had a ride for him, when I won a novice hurdle at Newbury on a horse called Mon Plaisir.'

He began riding under Rules as an amateur and had his first winner at Taunton on 28 November 1968, on Silver Meade for permit holder John Blake. He turned professional at the start of the following season and joined Bill Marshall, for whom he'd he had one ride as an amateur, finishing second on Mustardflower at Worcester in May 1969.

'When I was a kid I modelled myself on David Mould,' he admits. 'He was such a stylish jockey, both on and off the horse, and I was always 'moulding a Mould'.'

The link with Spanish Steps came through a meeting with Jack Morgan (Edward Courage's right-hand man) at Huntingdon. Johnny Cook was Courage's jockey but had broken a leg and a replacement was needed to ride Spanish Steps and his stable mate Royal Relief. The trainers Bill rode for had no chasers of that calibre so he took a retainer to ride both of them.

His first ride on Spanish Steps was a winning one, in the SGB Chase at Ascot in December 1971. Having looked beaten turning for home, he ran on to beat Charles Dickens, Royal Toss and Khan. The first time he rode Royal Relief was in Sandown's Stone's Ginger Wine Chase, which he also won. It was a good start.

Nine days after winning the SGB, Bill and Spanish Steps lined up for Kempton's King George VI Chase and finished second, beaten half a length by The Dikler, with Titus Oates third.

'The Dikler used to jump left-handed,' he recalls. 'He jumped into me and struck into Spanish Steps at the second last. It just affected his confidence going to the last.

'He was a brilliant jumper but I just couldn't get him right at the last and we popped and missed it. That was the half length we couldn't get back. He had quite a nasty overreach from where The Dikler had jumped into him.'

He finished sixth on Spanish Steps in the 1972 Gold Cup and was then fourth in Worcester's Royal Porcelain Chase, but it was almost two years before he rode him again.

'I'd just taken the job of first jockey to Fred Rimell in 1972. I won the Triumph Hurdle on Zarib for him and Royal Relief won the Champion Chase the same year. Then on April 27 I broke my leg going to the start at Devon and Exeter. The horse ran into the rails, I hit the concrete upright.'

He came back at the end of October and won the 1973 Champion Hurdle with Comedy of Errors. The following season they won the Irish Sweeps Hurdle but were beaten in the 1974 Champion Hurdle, finishing second to Lanzarote, the mount of Richard Pitman.

'He definitely wasn't right that year,' Bill insists. 'He was lathered up and sweaty at the start and he was gone at halfway. This was a horse you could cruise on, and he wasn't cruising. Lanzarote was a good horse but not as good a hurdler as Comedy of Errors. Richard Pitman always maintained he pinched the race, but Richard Pitman couldn't pinch a fat lady's bum!

'The two things that stand out about my job with Fred and Mercy Rimell are Comedy of Errors and me falling out with them. It was pretty much on the cards before Comedy of Errors got beat. I got on all right with Fred but not with Mrs Rimell. She, almost politely, said she didn't dislike me as a jockey but we never saw eye to eye. We just didn't gel.

'But I'd followed Terry Biddlecombe, who'd been there nine years, and Terry is a totally different character to me. Terry is big, loud and great fun, and I'm not like that.'

Biddlecombe was by that time stable jockey to Fulke Walwyn but had decided to retire after the 1974 Cheltenham Festival. Walwyn trained three of the seven runners in that year's Gold Cup. Ron Barry retained his partnership with the previous year's winner The Dikler, while Terry rode the Queen Mother's Game Spirit, and Bill came in for the ride on Charlie Potheen. They finished second, third and fourth respectively behind Captain Christy.

With Terry retiring and Bill in need of a job, having just split with the Rimells, he once again followed in Biddlecombe's footsteps and became Walwyn's retained jockey.

By then, Bill was back on Spanish Steps, who was now eleven years old. Thirty-five minutes after finishing fourth on Charlie Potheen in the Gold Cup, he and Spanish Steps were second in the National Hunt Handicap Chase. The next stop would be the 1974 Grand National and Spanish Steps went into the race as a live 15-1 chance.

'He had quite a bit of weight, 11-9,' says Bill. 'He couldn't get to them with that weight. I never really held out much hope of winning, and finished fourth.

'But my best memory of Spanish Steps was in the 1975 National, when he had a stone and six pounds less, 10-3.

'I'd won the Schweppes Hurdle in 1975 on Tammuz for the Queen Mother. He was number thirteen and Spanish Steps was number thirteen. Also, John Cook had won the Schweppes on Cala Mesquida and the National on Specify the same year.

'I was totally and utterly convinced I was going to win the National that year. I couldn't see defeat. He was in good form, carrying a stone and six less, the ground was right. I even changed hotels – I'm very superstitious!

'I wasn't much fun to be around for the three weeks before the National because I was so convinced Spanish Steps would win. I used to get quiet and serious before a big race; not the most even of tempers. I certainly wasn't very good company the night before the National.

'His dam, Tiberetta, had been second, third and fourth in the National, and she'd bred Spanish Steps, Quintus and Lictor, who all jumped round Aintree. They all had this hugely powerful jump.

'It's a funny place, Aintree, a law unto itself. Spanish Steps had that huge drive from behind; you could feel the power from the back end. He would over-pitch a bit. He'd go into a fence, almost drop his head and power into it and jump it. He was an amazingly good horse round there. I'd almost describe Spanish Steps as a navvy compared to Royal Relief, who was a very classy horse but couldn't jump round Aintree.

'One of Fred Rimell's horses spread a plate at the start. We all sat around on a rail. Jack and Tom Morgan were down at the start and they took Spanish Steps off me. Jack, 'Kingy' [Jeff King] and myself sat on a running rail and Jack produced out of his pocket a quarter bottle of Haig whisky. We all had a quick mouthful.

'I got back on, went to line him up, and he half whipped round, and he whinnied, which wasn't like him. I think the waiting around had got to him a bit and he was very geed up.

'He didn't give me the best of rides going down to Becher's first time and it took him until Valentine's to settle but after that he gave me a super ride, although he didn't jump as well on the first circuit as he had done the year before.

'Everything went pretty much according to plan but going out second time, when you start to get into the race, I wasn't finding it quite as easy as I thought it should be.

'Unfortunately, I never really got into a challenging position; I could never quite get to the leaders. In the end, L'Escargot and Red Rum beat me and I was about 25 lengths off the winner in third.

'I'd been so confident of winning but what I hadn't taken into account was that the two horses in the race that beat him would between them win four Grand Nationals, finish second in three, and had already won two Gold Cups. What a rotten day to turn up!

'Any "normal" Grand National, particularly of that era, Spanish Steps would have won in a canter, but he just happened to have had L'Escargot and Red Rum in front of him.'

Two years later, 1977, he had what he rates his worst Grand National ride, aboard Gay Vulgan.

'I'd won the National Hunt Handicap Chase on him. He was very like Spanish Steps; not very big, very powerful, great jump to him, but he absolutely hated it. I pulled him up at Becher's second time but I really should have pulled him up at the second fence. Some horses don't always jump the first few fluently, but he got worse and worse. He was a real disappointment because he was a very good horse.'

In 1982 Bill finished fourth behind Grittar on the ex-Irish trained Delmoss, who had joined Fulke Walwyn's stable at the start of that season. He'd run in the previous two Grand Nationals, falling at Becher's second time in 1980, when ridden by Gerry Newman, and getting no further than the fourth with Frank Berry in 1981.

'He was owned by a syndicate of Americans, one of whom was Jack Goodman, who'd owned Team Spirit. He wasn't a big horse, about 15.2. He had a terribly sensitive mouth and teeth, and he was crying out for a rubber bit because every time you caught him, his head went up, but because of what happened to Mandarin in the Grand Steeplechase de Paris [when his rubber bit had broken going to the fourth fence], Mr Walwyn wouldn't run them in rubber bits.

'Frank Berry came to me before the Grand National and said "What are you doing riding that? You're mad. I wouldn't ride it down to the start!"

'In the paddock, Mr Walwyn, who didn't normally give instructions, said, "The owners are all here, so pop him out the gate and let him run to the first so they can see him, because that's all they'll see of him!"

'The National is fast but not as fast as you think. You do go a hell of a gallop but the fences slow them up. What Delmoss could do was jump the fences like hurdles, and that's how he came to be so easily in the lead.

'He led until the second fence on the second circuit and he stayed on and only just got touched off for third. Mind you, the third horse, Loving Words, had fallen and remounted!'

Delmoss and Bill were reunited for the 1983 Grand National and led until the Chair, where they were badly baulked by some loose horses. They completed the course, albeit last of the ten finishers.

Altogether he rode in eleven Grand Nationals – from the first, seventh on Bright Willow in 1972, to the last, eighteenth on Fauloon in 1984 – and completed the course in eight.

'Self preservation has always been quite high on my agenda,' he laughs.

'The last one I rode, Fauloon, had had a crashing fall the time before and wasn't the bravest. We basically hunted round. I'm not saying that we didn't try very hard, but we certainly didn't do anything very brave that day!'

That season was Bill's last as a jockey. He retired after finishing third on Diamond Edge behind stable mate Special Cargo in an epic 1984 Whitbread Gold Cup, which produced perhaps the greatest of all finishes ever to be fought out on Sandown's run-in.

Diamond Edge had provided Bill with a Hennessy and two Whitbread Gold Cups. But he's uncertain whether he would have liked to have ridden him in the Grand National. 'He'd have either fallen by the third or given me a great ride,' he says. 'I'm not so sure about the great ride because he could miss a fence out. He really could walk through one.

'The horse I'd love to have ridden in the Grand National was Fort Devon. He'd won the Maryland Hunt Cup twice over timber. We came quite close to running him in it in 1978 but he broke a blood vessel.'

Maybe Fort Devon would have provided Bill with a Grand National winner, but Spanish Steps gave him two rides to remember. It was just bad luck that they happened to be the years of Red Rum and L'Escargot.

Date: Saturday 5 April 1975 Going: Good Value to Winner: £38,005

Horse	Owner	Trainer	Age / weight	Jockey	SP
1 L'Escargot	Mr R Guest	D Moore	12-11-3	T Carberry	13-2
2 Red Rum	Mr N H Le Mare	D McCain	10-12-0	B Fletcher	7-2fav
3 Spanish Steps	Mr E R Courage	Owner	12-10-3	W Smith	20-1
4 Money Market	Lord Chelsea	C Bewicke	8-10-13	J King	14-1

Distances: 15 lengths, 8 lengths, 12 lengths. Time: 9 mins 31.1 sec. 31 ran

Winner trained at The Curragh, County Kildare, Ireland

1976

KEITH BARNFIELD
The nomad and the decorator

Ormonde Tudor (centre, chevrons) is last away.

ORMONDE TUDOR MAY not have been the best horse to run in a Grand National but he has good claims to having been the most travelled. In eleven years of racing he had eleven different trainers!

The nomadic career of Ormonde Tudor began with four runs as a two-year-old for Mick Easterby in 1971. The 1972/73 National Hunt campaign saw him with Owen Brennan, for whom he was unplaced eight times over hurdles. He joined Paddy Cowley's string the following year, achieving three placed efforts from nine starts. After one run for Dick Holland, he began the 1975/76 season at the Pontesbury, Shropshire, stables of Rodney Bower.

It was for Bower that Ormonde Tudor finally got off the mark, winning a Tees-side Park (Stockton) selling chase in December 1975 and a three-runner handicap chase at Sedgefield the next month, ridden on both occasions by 7lb claimer Colin Brown. In between those victories he had finished sixth in the Bruce Carr Memorial Trophy at Market Rasen on Boxing Day, ridden that day by Keith Barnfield. It wasn't the first time he'd ridden the horse, nor would it be the last.

In contrast to Ormonde Tudor's wandering traits, Keith Barnfield's racing career was much more parochial. Home was always close to Cheltenham – and still is. He lives in Bishops Cleeve, just a couple of miles from the headquarters of jumping.

He was born on 3 March 1940 in the village of Dowdeswell, six miles from Cheltenham. Later the Barnfield family moved to Andoversford, where former champion jockey Gerry Wilson then trained. Keith joined his yard straight from school but when Wilson retired twelve months later, he moved to Frenchie Nicholson at Prestbury and stayed there for ten years.

He had his first ride at Towcester on Whit Monday 1958, but had to wait the best part of seven years for his first winner, Scarron, in a Cheltenham selling hurdle on 7 January 1965, trained locally by Jack Perrett.

Keith remembers: 'It was the first race on the card and the lads from Frenchie's didn't have time to get to the stands. I knew they'd all be congregating by the stile at the end of Frenchie's field and I thought "I'll show those chaps how good I am", so when I went past them I picked my stick up and gave the horse a couple of smacks. He shot to the front and was never headed!'

He won three times on handicap hurdler John's Nephew during the 1967/68 season, culminating in the Col. R. Thompson Memorial Hurdle, which, with £1,000 added, was then a decent prize for an Easter Monday at Market Rasen. That was the richest race Keith ever won, and the ten winners he rode that season proved to be a personal best.

His only retainer was with Bromyard trainer Stan Wright, who paid him the princely sum of £250 for first claim on his services for the 1968/69 season. But the arrangement got off to a bad start.

'I went the wrong way on a chaser called Mazo at Ludlow,' he admits. 'Turning into the straight I inadvertently went straight on to the hurdle track. When I got back I told Stan the horse was hanging and I couldn't stop him going down there. But I was caught out in the local pub the next evening when Frenchie walked in. He knew just what I'd done, because he told me he'd done the same thing there the year he was champion jockey.'

Although he was lucky with injuries, suffering just a couple of broken collar-bones, winners were few and far between. His last two came courtesy of Vale Royale for Bishops Cleeve permit holder George Hackling, in November and December of 1974. By then he was riding only occasionally and combining it with running his own painting and decorating business.

By 1976 his riding career was almost at an end. He was 36 and had held a licence for 18 years but had never ridden in the Grand National. Then along came Ormonde Tudor.

'He was a cunning old bugger,' says Keith. 'He wasn't a hundred per cent genuine and had his own way of doing things. His owner, John Kelly, was a lecturer at Manchester Polytechnic and a clever chap, inasmuch as he'd buy cheap horses and sell bits to other people. He was the head of the syndicate and used to keep shuffling the horses around different trainers.

'At the time he was Colin Brown's ride. I happened to be speaking to John Kelly at the races one day and he mentioned he'd got Ormonde Tudor in the National. I asked him if he'd got a jockey and, if he hadn't, I'd be happy to ride him. He said "Okay, take that as a booking," and that was that. Afterwards, Colin said to me "I thought I was going to ride that horse." I told him "You're younger than me, you've got more time!"

'Rodney Bower trained him when he ran in the National. Bill Hickling owned a share, along with John Kelly, and both their names appeared on the race card. *The Sun* summed up his chances – "This one wouldn't have any chance if he started before breakfast!"

'I lined up in the middle of the course at the back, close to The Dikler, Money Market and Sandwilan. I wasn't going to go mad; the plan was to hack around. But we only got as far as the first fence. It was unfortunate because he didn't really fall, he slipped up. It wasn't as though he made a bad mistake. The grass was long and lush and quite damp and when he landed he just skidded on his belly and then rolled over.

'I banged my elbow but it was nothing serious, so I leaned on the rail, watched the rest of the race, and then made my way back. I was disappointed. I would like to have gone one circuit at least. It would have been nice to have jumped Becher's but it wasn't to be.'

Only eight of the 32 runners were out of the race as Nereo, ridden by his 57-year-old owner the Duke of Alburquerque, led the way back onto the race-course and the thirteenth fence. But it was to prove unlucky thirteen for Nereo who came down there, giving the Duke a heavy fall and leaving him at the mercy of the following pack.

Golden Rapper led at Becher's second time round but nosedived in spectacular fashion and fired John Francome to the ground, leaving Churchtown Boy in front of Ceol-Na-Mara, Spittin Image, Sandwilan and The Dikler.

Half a dozen were still in with a chance at the second last fence, but there was only one that the cheering racegoers wanted to win. Red Rum, running in his fourth Grand National, was on the verge of a unique third victory and jumped the last in front. But no sooner had he set off up the long run-in than Rag Trade appeared at his side and quickened to go clear. Roared on by the crowd, Red Rum responded and fought back bravely and began to eat into Rag Trade's lead, but the 12lb weight concession proved just too much and he was two lengths behind at the winning post. Eight lengths further back in third came Eyecatcher, followed by the strong-finishing Barona, then Ceol-Na-Mara and The Dikler.

Rag Trade gave his flamboyant owner, Mr 'Teasy Weasy' Raymond, a second Grand National winner, thirteen years after the triumph of Ayala. It was a record breaking fourth victory in the race for trainer Fred Rimell, following the successes of E.S.B., Nicolaus Silver and Gay Trip.

Says Keith: 'I was 39 when I had my last ride. I went up to Perth for one mount, a novice chaser named Dad's Image. It pulled up and I thought "I don't want to bother any more". The painting and decorating side was expanding so I decided to concentrate on that.

'It may not be the most glamorous job in the world but it gave me a degree of freedom. I enjoy trout fishing and if I fancied taking a day off to do that, I could do. I used to ride out for Nigel Twiston-Davies on Saturday mornings, but I'm getting old and soft and I can't face the cold weather on top of that hill now!'

As for Ormonde Tudor, he continued his nomadic ways for six more years. After leaving Rodney Bower, he briefly joined John Gilbert, who trained at the back of Cleeve Hill. From there he moved to Rosemary Lomax in Wiltshire, winning three handicap chases for her early in 1978.

The 1978/79 season was spent up in Middleham with Squeak Fairhurst, for whom he won three more races. The next two seasons saw him trained by Chris Wildman at Larkhill and John Long near Canterbury. Finally, he was sent to the Taunton yard of former jump jockey Tony Andrews and it was for him that he ran the last of his 95 races, pulling up at Hereford on Easter Monday 1982.

Ormonde Tudor may have been a moderate horse but he gave Keith Barnfield his one and only chance of taking part in the Grand National, even if he didn't get beyond the first fence.

Date: Saturday 3 April 1976 Going: Firm Value to Winner: £37,420

Horse	Owner	Trainer	Age / weight	Jockey	SP
1 Rag Trade	Mr P B Raymond	F Rimell	10-10-12	J Burke	14-1
2 Red Rum	Mr N H Le Mare	D McCain	11-11-10	T Stack	10-1
3 Eyecatcher	Mr J R Bosley	Owner	10-10-7	B Fletcher	28-1
4 Barona	Mr W H Whitbread	R Armytage	10-10-6	P Kelleway	7-1fav

Distances: 2 lengths, 8 lengths, 3 lengths. Time: 9 mins 20.9 secs. 32 ran

Winner trained at Kinnersley, Worcestershire

1977

RON ATKINS
R.A.

Ron Atkins, wearing that famous skull cap.

THE WALLS OF the Leathern Bottle, midway between Guildford and Horsham, were bedecked with reminders of its landlord's riding days. Over the fireplace hung a framed photograph of him winning on True Song at Cheltenham in 1976. But this was no exhibition of vainglory by a former jockey wanting to remind people how stylish he was. The nature of the man reveals that there was far more to it than that.

One wall showed spectacular falls, unseated riders and refusals. Some were of himself, others of weighing room colleagues. Another wall displayed Injured Jockeys Fund Christmas cards. Both were reminders, as if needed, that National Hunt racing is a dangerous occupation.

Ron Atkins was never a conformist. The fashionable King's Road garb, long hair stylishly over his collar, the initials 'RA' emblazoned boldly in white on his skull cap, the perceived upstart who dared to question the status quo, was never going to cut the mustard with racing's 'establishment'. Some of jumping's top trainers offered him the position of stable jockey, subject to a sergeant-major-ish 'get yer 'air cut' proviso, but Ron didn't want to know about that. He was his own man. Still is.

With some 400 winners to his credit, there were few stronger in a driving finish than Ronald Anthony Leonard Atkins. Hardly surprising, given that boxing was so nearly his chosen sport.

He was born in Stonebridge Park, Willesden, in 1943, the son of a cobbler with a shoe shop opposite Wembley Stadium. As a lad he helped his dad repair shoes and he left school in 1958 with the intention of becoming a boxer, having already fought as a flyweight for clubs in Acton and Hendon. It was only when he moved to box for Crawley that horses first entered his life.

'In those days Crawley was out in the country,' he says. 'I went out with a girl from there who had a pony. The only horse I'd ever seen before pulled a rag and bone cart.

'Through nothing but dare-devilment I learned to ride the pony, fell off a few times, and had a bit of fun.'

His dad was put in touch with Winchester trainer Les Hall, who had a vacancy going for an apprentice. Ron joined Hall, one of the shrewdest trainers of the post-war era, at the end of 1958 and served five years there.

He had his first ride in public for Hall, on 33-1 outsider Princess Pretty in a 36-runner straight mile maiden at Newbury in April 1960. It was not an auspicious start. 'Coming to the final furlong, Bill Rickaby was in front of me and gave his horse four or five cracks of the whip. His horse ducked, mine clipped heels and I came off. I woke up in Newbury Hospital with the old man [Hall] giving me a bollocking!'

Falling off on the Flat wasn't the best beginning for a future jump jockey, which rising weight dictated would be his destiny. His first winner came on Tudor Meteor at Plumpton on 15 February 1964, for Tony Cobbett, who held the trainer's licence for local vet Donald Underwood. Although he rode one more winner that season, there was none the next and only five the season after that, but his career took off during the 1966/67 campaign. It was around that time that he made the acquaintance of a horse called Foinavon.

'I'd had the odd ride for his trainer, John Kempton. Two months before the National, I rode Foinavon at Kempton Park and finished second, only beaten a length, to Josh Gifford [on Loyal Fort]. He ran in a bitless bridle and after the race I suggested to John that had the horse worn a rubber bridle as opposed to a bitless one, I would have been able to get a better hold of him. It had already been mooted that I might ride him at Aintree, but John's father tore me off a strip about the bit, so we begged to differ.

'The horse's name was then booted around the weighing room as eight or nine jockeys were offered the chance to ride him. Eventually, John Buckingham came to me and asked me what I knew about Foinavon, as he'd just taken the ride on him. I thought he'd jump round but that's about it, so I told him "There's nothing wrong with the horse but you'll be lucky if you get anywhere." It's a fairy tale from there!'

By now the trademark white 'RA' on the black skullcap was featuring more and more at the business end of races. But the reason for the appearance of this particular motif was not solely down to self-publicity.

He says simply: 'My helmet kept getting nicked!

'At first, like a lot of jockeys just starting out, I used to borrow gear. Once I'd ridden a few winners, I bought my own saddle, breeches, boots and helmet. Although I had my name inside my helmet, it went missing a couple of times, and I had to think of a way to stop it. Also, I remember hearing a racegoer say "All you jockeys look the same when you've got your colours on; nobody can tell you apart", so I tried to think of a way in which I could stand out from the crowd. How could I make them know it's me? So I decided to paint my initials on the front. Initially, it was quite small, because it was all a bit tongue in cheek, but then I made it more prominent. Loads of the lads copied me. I've still got the helmet too.'

He acquired a reputation for giving a horse a good ride and rode for a number of small trainers and permit holders. It was one of the latter, Brian Trafford, who provided him with his first Grand National mount, Some Slipper in 1968. He ran well enough for a 66-1 shot, finishing thirteenth of the seventeen finishers. But riding outsiders in the great race wasn't for him.

'After that,' he says, 'I vowed that the next one I'd ride in the National would have a winning chance. So I made a point of being somewhere else on National day, where I could pick up a winner or two.'

Some decent hurdling prizes came Ron's way during the early seventies, including the John Skeaping on William Pitt, plus the Ackermann Skeaping Trophy on Moyne Royal and Kempton's 'KP' Hurdle on Rabble Rouser. He finished fourth in the 1973 Champion Hurdle on Donald Underwood's Mon Plaisir, just four days after they had finished second to Lanzarote in the Imperial Cup.

In 1977 the Grand National ride he had been seeking finally arrived, albeit in fortuitous circumstances. Fred Winter's stable jockey, John Francome, took a heavy fall from a horse called Navigation at Liverpool the day before the race, resulting in a badly swollen leg that left him unable to get his boot on. The date was Friday 1 April, but the chance to ride Winter's Grand National runner Pengrail was no April Fool joke.

Recalls Ron: 'I was staying at the Bedford Lodge Hotel at Southport with some of the other jockeys. Micky Cullen, Fred Winter's head man, came over on the Friday night and said that that Fred wanted me to ride Pengrail. I must admit, I thought it was a joke at first. I was delighted. Micky, John and Fred all thought the horse would win; so did I. But it wasn't to be.

'There were no problems going to the first. We'd popped off, bowled along, had a good clear look at the fence, not travelling too fast, not doing anything wrong. He stood off and had a go at the fence, but he just brushed through the top of it. Although you see all this fern coming off, it's blackthorn in the fence, stiff as broom handles, and about 3ft across the top. He left his hind legs in the top of the fence, couldn't get them out; the fence stopped him dead, so he landed right on his head. And that was it. Six others went at the fence. Micky Cullen told me later that the horse's eyes were closed for a fortnight afterwards.'

At the same fence next time round, leader Boom Docker decided he'd had enough and refused. This left Andy Pandy clear on the run down to Becher's. Still a good ten lengths ahead, Andy Pandy crumpled on landing over Becher's, leaving Red Rum in front. It was earlier than jockey Tommy Stack would have liked but, nonetheless, he turned for home with Churchtown Boy as his only serious challenger. But even that challenge evaporated after he made a mistake at the second last fence.

The cheers grew to roars when Red Rum cleared the last and then reached a crescendo as he drew further and further clear on the run-in. Red Rum's historic third Grand National victory had been achieved by 25 lengths. He truly was the King of Aintree.

Churchtown Boy held on for second, six lengths ahead of Eyecatcher, third for the second successive year, with The Pilgarlic fourth.

By that time, Ron was combining riding with training from a yard at Elstead, Surrey. He enjoyed a fair measure of success, notably with Rushmere, who won over hurdles and on the Flat. However, he now admits that, at 35, he started training too soon. After six years he gave up for financial reasons, citing non-payment of bills as his downfall. He bought a restaurant, which he named 'Chasers', complete with three and a half acres of land, just a couple of miles from Newton Abbot.

'The plan was to get the business off the ground, then put some boxes up and train again. Because I'd taken over the restaurant in April, I didn't get round to applying for my jockey's licence when the new season began in August, so everyone jumped to the conclusion that I'd retired. I hadn't, I was just late in applying for my licence because I'd been so busy at the restaurant.

'I was at the races one day when Martin Pipe suggested I rode out for him, which I did. Later he asked me if I'd still got my jockey's licence. I hadn't, so I quickly took it out again and rode for two or three more years. The funny thing was that, although I wasn't pushing or chasing rides, the number of rides started to increase. At 42 years of age, my phone kept ringing. I had more fun in those last couple of years than I'd had for the previous ten.'

Although he subsequently sold the restaurant, there was still plenty on the menu for Ron when he finally stopped riding, aged 43. During his long career in the saddle, he had put a lot back into making a tough game a little less hazardous for his weighing room colleagues. That work was not about to stop.

Besides being vice-president of the Jockeys' Association for 21 years, working with Peter Smith and his successor, Geoffrey Summers, he had been the Association's first inspector of courses. He was also responsible for instigating the Jockeys' Pension Fund scheme.

'I rubbed some of the "old school" up the wrong way initially,' he admits. 'It wasn't in any way malicious on my part. It was just the fact that I didn't speak their language and they didn't understand mine. However, we succeeded in getting a lot of avenues opened up for us. In the latter years of my role as inspector of courses, I was well respected.'

Relations with those in authority have mellowed considerably since those early days. He acknowledges that toeing the party line may well have brought him lucrative opportunities, but has no regrets about being his own man.

'When I look back, perhaps I should have bitten my tongue, but that was me. That's the way I was. It didn't do me any harm at the end of the day.'

No harm at all. And no amount of cavalier devil-may-care-ism can hide the significant contribution that Ron Atkins has made to the plight of jockeys past, present and still to come.

Date: Saturday 2 April 1977 Going: Good Value to Winner: £41,140

Horse	Owner	Trainer	Age / weight	Jockey	SP
1 Red Rum	Mr N H Le Mare	D McCain	12-11-8	T Stack	9-1
2 Churchtown Boy	Mr B Arnold & Mr J Watkins	M Salaman	10-10-0	M Blackshaw	20-1
3 Eyecatcher	Mr J R Bosley	Owner	11-10-1	C Read	18-1
4 The Pilgarlic	Mrs G Poole & Mr A Poole	F Rimell	9-10-4	R R Evans	40-1

Distances: 25 lengths, 6 lengths, 8 lengths. Time: 9 mins 30.3 secs. 42 ran

Winner trained at Southport, Lancashire

1978

RICHARD and JAMES EVANS

Make sure you get round!

*James Evans (left) and
Richard Evans*

SIBLING RIVALRY HAS long played a part in Grand National history. In 1978 Richard and James Evans were about to play theirs – and land a wager in the process.

Richard, elder of the two brothers by ten years, had set his race riding career in motion when buying Marchairy out of a Stratford seller for 280 guineas. Marchairy duly became the first winner for his then amateur rider when landing a handicap hurdle at Towcester on 16 October 1965, trained under permit by his father, Glynn.

'I think Marchairy benefited from coming to mugs like us because we didn't really know how to train a racehorse,' laughs Richard. 'He was a windy old so and so with a legacy of bad legs but he put his best foot forward for us.'

From childhood days Richard's racing hero was George Owen, who not only trained Russian Hero to win the 1949 Grand National but had also turned three amateur riders – Dick Francis, Tim Brookshaw and Stan Mellor – into champion jockeys. He thus considers it an honour to have had the chance to ride for him. The best horse he rode for Owen was Lord Leverhulme's Casbah, on whom he won the Wills Hurdle at Haydock.

It was Lord Leverhulme and Owen who had provided Richard with his first Grand National mount, Brian's Best in 1971. They got no further than the first fence, being brought down in a five-horse pile-up. Says Richard: 'It was a great disappointment. I was so looking forward to riding in the National, but I learned nothing. I remember going into the fence and I remember being on the floor after it, but what happened in between I can't recall.'

The 100-1 no-hoper Permit was Richard's 1972 Grand National ride. Six years earlier he'd run in Charlottown's Derby but by now his best days were behind him. Even so, he gave a creditable account of himself until falling at the second Canal Turn.

The following year he rode Proud Percy, trained by Jack Berry, and winces at the memory. 'I was highly delighted to have a ride in the race but Proud Percy was a hairy one. It wasn't a question of *if* he'd fall; it was a question of *when*. I remember turning into the straight on the first circuit – I'd been lucky to get that far because he'd belted everything. There was a huge roar as we came towards the Chair and that completely broke his heart. He took off from inside the ditch and banked the fence. There was then a point when I realised that the ejector button had to be pressed, so I went straight over his head, then another horse kicked me while I was on the ground and broke my wrist.'

The Tunku, another 100-1 shot, was his partner for 1974. He was trained by Ginger McCain, who could have been excused for having weightier matters on his mind, for he was also saddling Red Rum and Glenkiln for Noel Le Mare. As Red Rum made his way triumphantly up the run-in, Richard was heading back from the eighteenth fence where he'd pulled up.

Four attempts but no clear rounds. However, his next National ride would change all that.

The Pilgarlic was a half brother to dual Gold Cup winner and 1975 National hero L'Escargot. He'd won three hurdle races for Paddy Sleator in Ireland before being put over fences in 1974/75. In seven starts that season he was only once out of the frame. After winning his first two races the following season he was bought by Fred Rimell who introduced him to British racegoers in January 1976 at Ascot, where stable jockey John Burke steered him to victory.

Richard first rode him at Wolverhampton in December of that year, finishing second. They were second again at Ludlow, The Pilgarlic's final start before the 1977 Grand National. Rimell also trained Andy Pandy, who started 15-2 favourite and was in front when falling at Becher's second time round, leaving Red Rum clear to record an unprecedented third National triumph from Churchtown Boy and Eyecatcher, with 40-1 shot The Pilgarlic chasing them home in fourth place, eight lengths behind Eyecatcher.

'I'd been rowing away from the Canal Turn,' says Richard. 'It wasn't as if he got tired but he just stopped trying, got less competitive. If there'd been a loose horse to beat he'd have gone and beat it, but the other three had got the better of him, so he plodded on to finish fourth. Having said that, I was over the moon and I couldn't wait to get home to watch it on telly that night.

'He was a wonderful ride. He knew exactly what was going on, where every foot was landing. He took no chances, no silly risks whatsoever, which was ideal round Aintree. I always steered down the middle on him. I was never an "inner" man; couldn't see any sense in that at all.

'If there were forty runners, he'd have been about thirty-fifth at Becher's first time. By Valentine's the horses who'd gone quick early on were coming back, whereas mine hadn't done a stroke and was just warming up. By the time we came to the Chair we were back in the race. That's the way it was every year. You couldn't make him go a yard faster because he wouldn't. He just kept jumping and galloping.

'The '78 National, when he finished fifth to Lucius, beaten only three lengths on firm ground, has to have been his best performance. I remember coming to the Elbow and he really went to compete, changed his legs and went. It was unlike him to do so but he put his ears back and I thought "I'm going to win it".

'We were four abreast, Lucius, Sebastian, Coolishall and ourselves, but the light went out as quickly as it had come on. Had the ground been that bit softer and the others dying a bit, he could have gone a length up and kept going, but Lucius and the others kept trying and he thought "Bugger this". Then Drum-roan came past us close home. I was so disappointed to finish fifth – at one stage I was going to win it and then I'm out of the frame. I was gutted for the horse because he'd run the race of his life to be only three lengths off winning, yet we didn't even get to unsaddle in the winner's enclosure.'

Lucius had prevailed by half a length and by so doing prevented Sebastian V from becoming the first Scottish-trained winner. The fast-finishing Drum-roan finished third, just ahead of Coolishall and The Pilgarlic. Lucius was the luckiest of all spare rides for Bob Davies, who was substituting for the injured David Goulding.

At least Richard had the consolation of seeing his brother James come home thirteenth of the fifteen finishers on Lean Forward.

Richard explains: 'I'd been to a sporting dinner the week before and I was offered odds of 25-1 for James and myself to both get round. Lean Forward and The Pilgarlic were both safe jumpers and had pretty good potential for jumping round, so I had £25 on. I can only admit that now – at the time I'd have been warned off for betting!

'The bet was struck so it was worth a lot to me for us both to finish. I don't think James took much regard of it because he jumped off and went like the clappers. I remember going past him coming down to Becher's second time and calling out to him "Make sure you get round!"'

The Pilgarlic and Lean Forward were both half-brothers to Cheltenham Gold Cup winners. Whereas The Pilgarlic was a half-brother to L'Escargot, Lean Forward was out of that prolific dam of winners, Leney Princess, who had produced the 1968 Gold Cup hero, Fort Leney. As with all of the mare's offspring, Sir John Thomson owned Lean Forward. Formerly trained by Jim Dreaper before joining Roddy Armytage at East Ilsley, the horse's best days were left behind in Ireland, where his many victories included the 1974 Leop-ardstown Chase.

'By the time he came over to England he was on the way down,' says James, 'but I managed to win a handicap at Plumpton on him and he gave me great rides in the Whitbread and the Hennessy without being quite good enough to get placed. We finished third in the 1977 Topham to Churchtown Boy. He'd never fallen and I just didn't feel I could get him on the floor, no matter how badly I rode him.

'We really thought he had a chance of being placed in the National. I wanted to give him a clear run. I knew that if he saw the fences, we'd be okay. Whereas The Pilgarlic took a long time to get warmed up, my old horse had a bit of pace. He liked to be handy and see a bit of daylight, so I jumped off in the middle. There was a huge bunch to my left on the inner and another huge bunch on the outer. He really belted the first because we were going a bit quick to try and get a position. That must have put the wind up him because he cleared everything else by at least a foot!

'Going to Becher's second time, Richard's starting to move up and we're both not far off the pace but Lean Forward was getting a bit tired. I do remember Richard passing me and telling me to make sure I got round. I nursed him home from the Canal Turn and we finished thirteenth but I had a fantastic ride.'

That was to be Lean Forward's last race. He was retired and afterwards went team chasing.

James was then at the peak of a career that had started while still at school. He joined Martin Tate as an amateur and rode his first winner for him on Miralgo Joe at Uttoxeter on 12 October 1974. Richard was then Tate's stable jockey but when he broke his thigh in February of that season, Tate offered James the chance to ride all his horses, providing he turned professional.

'Although it was a bit earlier than I'd intended, I turned pro on the strength of that. Obviously, with Richard coming back the next season, I needed to sort something out over the summer, so I joined Roddy Armytage and ended up riding for him for two or three years.'

James rode freelance during the 1978/79 season, picking up his second Grand National ride on Steve Nesbitt's Red Earl, who refused when in arrears three out. Richard and The Pilgarlic put in their customary clear round but once again finished fourth, beaten less than eight lengths behind Rubstic.

Although still only 22, that was effectively James's last season in the saddle. 'Freelancing had become economically impossible. Petrol prices had doubled, and valet fees, insurance and saddlery were all rocketing and I didn't have the money to keep up. I'd had five great seasons, rode 77 winners and it was a lot of fun, with my rides at Liverpool being the highlights. I didn't want to struggle for rides; I didn't want to beg.

'I went to Trent Polytechnic in Nottingham and did a four-year degree course in estate management and surveying. I kept my jockey's licence for the first two years, rode for a couple of friends and had a few spares for permit holders at local meetings.'

After qualifying from university, he and a partner opened a chartered surveying and estate agency business in Stratford-upon-Avon. He subsequently bought a farm at Mickleton and developed the property to provide boarding kennels plus a couple of holiday cottages, later taking out a permit with three horses in training.

The Pilgarlic finished third in the 1980 Grand National, but it was Ron Hyett in the saddle with Richard being sidelined by a broken ankle, incurred at Devon and Exeter. Richard retired in the autumn of that year. There was plenty to keep him and wife Sue occupied at their Oxstalls Farm home, on the outskirts of Stratford-upon-Avon.

'We'd had a small stud with one stallion for about four years before I retired. I found it was getting more and more difficult going off to Plumpton for one ride when there were six mares to be covered in a day. I could see the direction I wanted to go in and it was far more worthwhile my staying home where I could build up the stud. It was a decision easily made. We finished up with three stallions, the best known of which was The Brianstan.'

With Stratford being a popular area for visitors, they converted some of the farm buildings into accommodation and set about providing bed and breakfast. The B&B business thrived and expanded to the size of a small hotel; then in 1998 they bought the Foxhunter pub in nearby Snitterfield, which was managed by their son, Sam. They have latterly wound down those activities to focus on the 50-acre stud.

James has now graduated to having a full trainer's licence, while Richard also remains actively involved in racing, officiating as a steward at local meetings.

As for The Pilgarlic, he was acquired by Terry Biddlecombe who dispatched him to the hunting field. He gave amateur rider Nigel Twiston-Davies what he describes as the 'perfect ride' when finishing fourth in the 1981 Liverpool Fox Hunters' Chase.

He had his final start, aged fourteen, at Towcester on 28 May 1982. Biddlecombe then gave the horse to Riding for the Disabled, where he finished his days in happy retirement.

Date: Saturday 1 April 1978 Going: Firm Value to Winner: £39,092.50

Horse	Owner	Trainer	Age / weight	Jockey	SP
1 Lucius	Mrs D A Whitaker	G W Richards	9-10-9	B R Davies	14-1
2 Sebastian V	Mr R M C Jeffreys	C Bell	10-10-1	R Lamb	25-1
3 Drumroan	Mrs G St John Nolan	Owner	10-10-0	G Newman	50-1
4 Coolishall	Mr & Mrs P W Harris	P Cundell	9-10-0	M O'Halloran	16-1

Distances: ½ length, neck, 2 lengths. Time: 9 mins 33.9 secs. 37 ran

Winner trained at Greystoke, Cumbria

1979

JOHN FRANCOME
Rough And Tumble

John Francome and Rough And Tumble take the third last fence.

FOLLOWING SEVERAL NEAR misses with runners-up Macmoffat, Wyndburgh, Freddie, Moidore's Token and Sebastian V, a Scottish-trained horse finally won the Grand National. Rubstic, a first runner in the race for John Leadbetter, was the horse that broke Scotland's hoodoo. On arriving back at the Roxburghshire village of Denholm, he was welcomed home by a kilted piper.

A pile-up at the Chair resulted in nine runners – more than a quarter of the field – being put out of the race. Seventeen, half the number that had started, survived beyond the first circuit, and just seven of those were left as Rough And Tumble led them back on to the racecourse and over the second last.

Going to the final fence Rough And Tumble was joined by Zongalero, with Rubstic at their shoulders. On the run-in, Rubstic came on the outside to collar Zongalero and win by a length and a half, with Rough And Tumble in third, a length ahead of The Pilgarlic. Wagner, Royal Frolic and the tailed off 200-1 shot Prime Justice were the only others to complete the course.

Sadly, two horses lost their lives, namely Kintai, a casualty of the carnage at the Chair, and the favourite, Alverton, who broke his neck when falling at Becher's second time, just 16 days after having won the Cheltenham Gold Cup.

Owned by former British Lion and Scotland rugby international John Douglas, Rubstic had come to Aintree having never fallen in any of his 60 races.

He was a first ride in the race for Maurice Barnes, whose father Tommy had finished second on Wyndburgh in 1962.

Third placed Rough And Tumble, a 14-1 chance, was partnered by the reigning champion jockey John Francome, who was having his fifth Grand National ride. The first, on Cardinal Error in 1972, hadn't lasted long. Along with dual Gold Cup winner L'Escargot they were baulked and put out of the race at the third fence.

'I was still claiming at the time,' recalls the seven times champion jockey. 'Fred Winter had two runners; the other was Lime Street, ridden by Richard Pitman. Fred just said, "Make sure you go round the inside." Cardinal Error wasn't the best jumper in the world and I think the only reason I got the ride on him in the first place was because he wasn't particularly safe.

'I'd had a go round the National fences two days before, finishing fourth on a really good old horse of Ken Cundell's called Regimental in the Topham Trophy.'

In 1975 he rode Rag Trade and got round, albeit finishing last of ten. 'He didn't look particularly great down at the start,' he reflects. 'I think I did really well to get him round, truth be told.'

The following year his mount was the ex-Irish-trained Golden Rapper, a lively 28-1 shot who had won Leopardstown's Harold Clarke Chase seven weeks earlier, beating Davy Lad, a future Cheltenham Gold Cup winner, by ten lengths. This was his first run in Britain for his new trainer Fred Winter.

'He was a prize in a newspaper,' says John. 'The winner of the competition got the horse to run in the National.

'When I walked into the paddock my heart sank because he was barely 16 hands high. Anyway, he jumped immaculately, never put a foot wrong; went all the way round the inside first circuit and halfway down the far side. Jumping Becher's second time round, absolutely still running away, loads of horse underneath me, hadn't touched a twig, and then for some reason he just didn't put his landing gear out.

'I've got a picture of him at home; his nose is an inch from the ground and he's still got his front legs tucked up like he's over the top of the fence. I couldn't tell you now why he decided not to put his feet out in front of him – he'd already jumped it once. His nose hit the ground a split second before mine.

'Golden Rapper had a good chance of winning; he was really going well. It was a bit like Andy Pandy's fall with John Burke the following year, and he was going every bit as good as him. That was his day. He was primed for the day. We were still a long way from home at that point but there's no doubt that he was travelling ominously well.'

John guided Lord Browndodd round to finish seventh in 1978, and then came the aforementioned third place on Rough And Tumble behind Rubstic and Zongalero.

'I'll tell you how good a ride Rough And Tumble was,' he says. 'At the time Ricky Dormer bought him he was an eventer. Fred Winter's daughters, Diane and Jo, evented him. He was tiny, smaller than Golden Rapper, but he had a good jump in him and a big heart. Ricky came down to buy a horse and Fred didn't have anything else to sell him so he sold him the girls' eventer, and he never looked back.

'His asset was that he was a good jumper. You could go all the way round the inside on him. He used to get his feet up by his ears over the top of the fence. He was a really moderate horse; he was slow, almost too slow to go eventing, but he could jump and it stood him in good stead.

'The year he was third he led at the second last. I think if the ground had been better he might have won but it dragged the bottom out of him and he ran out of steam. I think we both did. I was tired from helping him and he was tired from helping me. He was rolling around drunk by the time he jumped the last.'

Twelve months later, John gave the Mildmay-White family's Uncle Bing one of the great Aintree rides to land the Topham Trophy. The ground that day was soft but incessant rain had rendered it heavy by the Saturday.

Only four of the 30 runners got round in that year's National, the quartet toiling home at long intervals. Rough And Tumble finished second, beaten 20 lengths by Ben Nevis. Observes John: 'I found a bit of decent ground going to the second last, but bar for Ben Nevis falling twice up the run-in he was never going to beat him. It was rather ironic because I'd schooled Ben Nevis at Newbury the weekend before.'

In 1981 he rode So for Michael Oliver and again completed the course, finishing tenth. 'I must hold the record for riding the smallest horses round there,' he muses. 'I almost missed him in the paddock; he was obscured by somebody's dog!

'Not only was So small, he was a bad mover as well. He went down to the start like his front legs were tied together. I should have been given a knighthood for getting that horse round.'

Rough And Tumble was back in 1982 but refused at Becher's second time round. That year's winner, Grittar, was John's mount in 1984 when coming home tenth. His final Grand National ride was Edward O'Grady's Drumlargan in 1985, who was pulled up before Becher's second time having broken a blood vessel.

He'd already decided that the 1984/85 season would be his last. Eight days after riding Drumlargan he landed a four-timer at Huntingdon's Easter Monday fixture. The following day at Chepstow he took a fall from The Reject, recognised the warning sign and announced his retirement there and then.

So ended a career that had yielded a record total of 1,138 winners, plus 13 abroad, including a Cheltenham Gold Cup on Midnight Court, a Champion Hurdle on Sea Pigeon, a brace of King George VI Chases and two Hennessy Gold Cups.

Not bad for someone who admits that as a kid he was never interested in racing. 'I couldn't have named one trainer or one jockey and always turned it off and went outside when it came on TV.'

Instead he focussed on show jumping, becoming a member of the winning GB European Championship team. But with little money to be made in show jumping and Lambourn being just down the road, he diverted into racing after his father had arranged an interview at Fred Winter's. He stayed there for sixteen years, with outstanding results.

From his first winner on Multigrey at Worcester on 2 December 1970 to his 1,000th on Observe at Worcester in February 1984, to the last on Gambler's Cup at Huntingdon, there are many respected observers who insist that there has never been a more complete, all-round jump jockey than John Francome.

He commenced training but with his 'cheeky chappie' personality and quick-witted responses he was an obvious candidate to follow Richard Pitman, his stable jockey predecessor at Fred Winter's, into television. Sure enough, Channel 4 Racing's Andrew Franklin invited him to sit in as a pundit for a weekend over Christmas.

'I was between training and building another yard,' John recalls, 'so I thought I might just do it for a bit. Twenty years later I'm still doing it!'

Date: Saturday 31 March 1979 Going: Good Value to Winner: £40,506.25

Horse	Owner	Trainer	Age / weight	Jockey	SP
1 Rubstic	Mr J Douglas	J Leadbetter	10-10-0	M Barnes	25-1
2 Zongalero	Mr D Montagu	N Henderson	9-10-5	B R Davies	20-1
3 Rough And Tumble	Mr L Dormer	F Winter	9-10-7	J Francome	14-1
4 The Pilgarlic	Mrs G Poole	F Rimell	11-10-1	R R Evans	16-1

Distances: 1½ lengths, 5 lengths, 1 length. Time: 9 mins 52.9 secs. 34 ran

Winner trained at Denholm, Roxburghshire

1980

BROD MUNRO-WILSON
Corinthian spirit

Brod Munro-Wilson and Coolishall on the beach at Climping, near Arundel.

TO BE BRANDED a cad is a rarity in this day and age. The actor Cardew Robinson played the part to perfection during the 1960s and pretty much made the word his own.

Of course, there's a world of difference between a cad and a bounder. A cad may be regarded as someone of good breeding who indulges in ungentlemanly conduct, whereas a bounder implies an ill-bred person of loose morals who commits a horsewhip-able offence. The arrival of the pill largely put an end to bounderism.

Broderick Giles Edward Munro-Wilson was described as a cad by Mr Justice Otton in a 1993 court case, in which he was sued for harassing his former fiancée. 'You have made disparaging remarks about a woman you once loved, and you, with your background, social standing and education, I would expect you, even now, to behave like a gentleman. You have not. You have behaved like a cad.'

'It was just so ridiculous,' scoffs Brod. 'It was a totally trumped up charge and Judge "Rotten" Otton comprehensively misread the case. If someone had lied to you, taken money from you and smashed up your car, as the result of which you called her a stupid little tart, I defy any man in England with half an ounce of red blood in his veins not to have said that.'

Not for the first time, he turned round an unfavourable situation to his own advantage, revelling in the sobriquet and ending up with his own 'cad slot' on GMTV.

'I thought, well, if I'm a cad, I'm the king of cads, and I completely turned everything on its head as a massive send-up. As a result, Richard and Judy, which was *the* breakfast television show in those days, invited me on and I had a fantastic row with some big fat woman psychiatrist who was going on about men treating women badly.

'I told her that I was the battered bride in reverse and we needed a Royal Society for the Prevention of Cruelty to Men. Granada TV loved it so much they asked me to do a mini-series, so I did *A Rogue in Brogue, A Bounder in the Boudoir, A Toff in Tartan* – I made them all up as I went along – and everyone thought it was a huge bit of fun, proving, I hope, that when someone does you an injustice, it's always better to turn the other cheek.'

A childhood friend of Camilla Parker Bowles (née Shand), Brod Munro-Wilson read Economics at Cambridge, served in 21 SAS, played polo alongside the Prince of Wales, and masterminded the flotation of The Body Shop, which grew from a £5 million company on flotation to one worth £652 million when it was sold to L'Oreal for cash.

In the City he was known as 'The Brodfather' and achieved the Share of the Year on the London Stock Exchange twice, with The Body Shop and a company called Tadpole Technology, founded by Brod and his colleagues as a start-up on the Science Park in Cambridge.

He rode six winners at Sandown's Grand Military meeting, including the Gold Cup twice. He took part in the Maryland Hunt Cup, the American Grand National, the Velká Pardubická and the Grand National itself.

In fact, there was nobody that more epitomised the true Corinthian spirit throughout the 1980s. He had his own, unique, upright, all arms and legs style. Some said it was reminiscent of a 17th-century cavalry officer, while others remarked it resembled someone trying to put up a deck chair in a gale.

'I like to ride like a gentleman, not a monkey up a stick, which is why I rarely take a tumble. Length of leg, that's what it's all about,' was his rejoinder to such criticism.

And yet it worked. He gained a famous victory in the Foxhunters' Chase at the Cheltenham Festival and was placed three times in the Aintree Fox Hunters' over the Grand National course.

He was brought up in Sussex and, like everyone in his circle, joined the Pony Club, hunted with the Southdown and the Crawley and Horsham, and rode in point-to-points. His first ride under Rules was on a horse called Laroon in the Soapey Sponge Hunters' Chase at Newbury on Schweppes Gold Trophy day in February 1975 – he pulled up. The second was when finishing a narrowly beaten second on Champers Galore in the Corinthian Hunters' Chase at Kempton at fortnight later. The third, again on Champers Galore, was his first winner, in

the Clapper Challenge Cup Hunters' Chase at Plumpton on 4 March, with his
left wrist in a disguised plaster cast, having broken it in a point-to-point two
days earlier, earning him the accolade of 'fearless' from Audax (Lord Oaksey)
in the *Telegraph*.

In 1977 he rode Can Cottage in the Iron Curtain's version of the Grand
National, the Velká Pardubická, in what was then known as Czechoslovakia,
falling three times before calling it a day. The following year he had his first
encounter with Aintree, completing the course aboard Champers Galore in the
Fox Hunters' Chase.

Then in the summer of 1979 he bought two horses from Peter Harris, Beeno
and Coolishall. The latter had finished fourth behind Lucius in the 1978 Grand
National and had fallen four out the next year when trained by Peter Cundell.

Brod won an early season Plumpton novice chase on Beeno and decided to
aim him at the Grand Military Gold Cup. He had even loftier aspirations for
Coolishall, who would be his mount in the 1980 Grand National.

'I'd always said to myself that I'd like to take a year off and live the life of a
professional jockey,' he says. 'I'd been in the army but I was really a City guy, but
even in the early 80s there was such a thing as "burn out". I thought it would be
fun to take a sabbatical year. I was thirty-five years old; I had seventeen horses
in training all over the country. I decided that for a year I'd only go to my office
on a Wednesday. I'd ring people up on very old-fashioned mobile phones the
size of bricks and shout at them "Do this, do that, do the other", mostly while at
second horses with the Quorn.'

He even trained some of the horses himself from a base near Horsham, in
Sussex. During the exceptionally cold winter of 1979/80 he took them down
to Climping, just south of Arundel, to gallop on the beach. His efforts were
rewarded when Beeno and Coolishall landed him a famous double at Sandown's
Grand Military Meeting.

Beeno, the 25-1 outsider of the seven runners, took over at the open ditch
going down the back second time round and stayed on to give his owner-
trainer-rider victory in the coveted Grand Military Gold Cup. Twenty-four
hours later he won the Duke of Gloucester Memorial Trophy Hunter Chase on
Coolishall, beating former Cheltenham Gold Cup winner Ten Up, ridden by
the Duchess of Westminster's nephew, Captain James Hodges.

That year's Duke of Gloucester Trophy was the subject of national attention
due to the presence of the world's most famous amateur rider. HRH the Prince
of Wales, having his first ride in a steeplechase, finished a distant last of four
on Sea Swell.

As for Coolishall and Brod, their next assignment was the Grand National
three weeks later.

The going had been soft on the Thursday and Friday at Aintree but incessant rain on Friday night rendered it heavy by Saturday. That suited Coolishall
perfectly, for he had a very high knee action and loved soft ground. He was set

to carry 10st 6lb but the weight was always going to be a problem for his rider. In the end he got down to 10st 10lb, just 4lb overweight.

'I was very concerned about doing the weight,' says Brod. 'If you stand nearly 6ft 1in, it's a fairly unnatural weight to be. I had this little postage stamp of a saddle – it was really a Flat-race saddle – with aluminium stirrups. I should have put up another pound overweight and had stainless steel stirrups but I was determined to ride as light as I could.'

Rubstic, the previous year's winner, was favourite at 8-1 as the testing conditions saw joint top-weight Man Alive and the quietly fancied Wagner withdrawn on the day of the race. Brod and Coolishall were 40-1 chances and duly took their place alongside 29 others, the smallest field for ten years. Having served in the SAS, with its reputation for derring-do, he might have been expected to take a mere horse race in his stride, but then, the Grand National is more than just a horse race.

'It's such an international arena,' says Brod. 'More people watch the Grand National than any other horse race. The eyes of the world are on you and, certainly when you're going round at the start, you've definitely got butterflies. And then you've got that very long run to the first and you need not to be travelling too fast.'

The tape rose and the tearaway Delmoss went straight to the front down the inside rail, while on the opposite side of the course, Coolishall jumped off and led those on the wide outside. That's how it was over the first two fences. And then it happened.

'It's the one race in the world where you need amazingly strong kit,' he reflects. 'Bugger whether it's a pound or two pounds over. I shouldn't have succumbed to a silly superstition, but this was a favourite saddle. I should never have ridden the National in aluminium Flat-race stirrups. The iron snapped on landing over the third fence and I was catapulted out; in the saddle one second and then I'm on the floor.'

Meanwhile, Delmoss was setting a relentless gallop and led Rubstic back onto the racecourse, with Lavanka, Sandwilan, Kininvie, Prince Rock, Rough And Tumble, Zongalero and Ben Nevis all close up. Rubstic departed at the Chair, his first fall in 68 races, but 22 of the original 30 starters remained jumping the water.

However, the next six fences accounted for thirteen of those, as legless horses fell, refused or pulled up, including Delmoss, who finally departed at Becher's, leaving Ben Nevis and his rider, 32-year-old Baltimore banker Charlie Fenwick, in a clear lead with eight fences between them and Grand National victory.

Rough And Tumble, The Pilgarlic and Royal Stuart were the only others still going as they jumped the third last, though none looked capable of catching Ben Nevis, who stayed on at one pace, sailed over the last fence and went on to score by 20 lengths from Rough And Tumble. The Pilgarlic took third, ten lengths behind Rough And Tumble, with the exhausted Royal Stuart a remote last of four finishers.

Ben Nevis had won a British point-to-point before being purchased by Raymond C Stewart and sent to race in America, where he won five point-to-points and seven chases including two Maryland Hunt Cups over solid post and rail obstacles. He was sent back to Britain in the autumn of 1978 to be trained by Tim Forster in an attempt to win the Grand National. He had been put out of the race by a melee at the Chair in 1979 but now the dream had been realised. Unfortunately, his owner was unable to be present to see the race due to his wife's ill health.

Ben Nevis was the only winner his sire, Casmiri, ever produced. The winner of seven races on the Flat plus three over hurdles, Casmiri was sent to stud in Sussex in 1960 at a fee of £50 8s. He was mated regularly with the stud's resident mare Ben Trumiss, whose only other winner was Ben Nevis's half-brother Gay Truant, who won a point-to-point. From that unlikely mating emerged the winner of the 1980 Grand National.

Charlie Fenwick became the second American amateur to win the Grand National in 16 years following Tommy Smith on Jay Trump in 1965. Although Fenwick had ridden 60 winners in his home country and a couple in Ireland, he had never partnered a winner in Britain and had taken part in only nine races all season.

Says Brod: 'After the race my mother and I walked round the course and we found all the bits of the iron – it was shattered in five different places. It now has pride of place on the mantelpiece in my house in Little Venice in London. It's in a Perspex case, frozen in time, still in the shape of a stirrup but with the pieces assembled in a broken way, rather than joined together.

'Coolishall was a lovely, lop-eared, old-fashioned horse and loved jumping Aintree so much. After he'd got rid of me, he jumped it for fun. It was a really heartbreaking experience, a once in a lifetime chance, because the soft ground following the overnight rain had made the conditions perfect for him.'

Brod hunted Coolishall the following season and returned in hunter chases in 1981. Having won the Grand Military Gold Cup for the second year running, this time on The Drunken Duck, he just failed to emulate the previous year's Sandown double when Coolishall finished a very creditable second to Spartan Missile – who was different class to the type of horse normally associated with military hunter chases – in the Duke of Gloucester Trophy.

Coolishall and Brod came sixth in the Cheltenham Foxhunters' and then returned to Sandown to win the Ubique Challenge Cup at the Royal Artillery Meeting. He was all set to ride him just four days later in the 1981 Grand National but suffered a crunching first fence fall on Highland Drake in the Fox Hunters' on Aintree's opening day.

'I got carried off on a stretcher and they carted me off in the ambulance,' he recounts. 'I was just about to pass out on the way to the Royal Walton Hospital when Bill Smith ran up to the ambulance as it was leaving the course and asked if he could ride Coolishall. I told him he could.'

Despite the ground being faster than ideal, Coolishall finished a respectable eighth under his stand-in rider. He ran in it again in 1982, partnered this time by Ron Barry, but he was past his best by then and failed to get beyond the third fence. He was subsequently found to have broken down.

Brod achieved his biggest success over jumps when winning the 1982 Cheltenham Foxhunters' on The Drunken Duck, getting the better of a protracted duel with Honourable Man to score by a head. He won the 1983 Duke of Gloucester Trophy on The Drunken Duck and finished third on Roman General in that year's Aintree Fox Hunters'. He was third in it again, this time on Talon, in 1984.

He ran both Roman General and The Drunken Duck in the 1984 Grand National but rode neither. 'I'd promised Major Malcolm Wallace the ride on Roman General at a dinner party and I stuck by my word – "My Word is My Bond", that's the old motto of the London Stock Exchange. Malcolm said "For a City man I can't believe anyone would be as honest!" He fell off him at the thirteenth fence.'

The Drunken Duck didn't get much further, Alan Brown pulling him up at halfway when out of contention.

Talon was Brod's big hope for the 1985 Grand National. Professional jockey Anthony Webber was booked months ahead to ride him and the combination made the best of starts when winning the Red Rum Handicap Chase at Carlisle in September 1984. Talon was then sent hunting and Brod finished third on him in the 1985 Cheltenham Foxhunters'. With only ten stone to carry, hopes were high, but Talon over-jumped at the first fence and came down.

Rues Brod: 'When I saw Talon afterwards with Anthony Webber and [trainer] Roddy Armytage in the racecourse stables at Aintree, the horse turned his head towards me with a seemingly apologetic look as if to say "What a silly boy I was; I messed that one up, didn't I?"'

In 1986 he finished third in the Aintree Fox Hunters' for the third time in four years, this time on Poyntz Pass. Later that season he won the Prince of Wales Cup at Fakenham on the former Michael Dickinson-trained W Six Times. W Six Times (in 1987) and Brunton Park (1988) gave him back-to-back successes in Folkestone's United Hunts Open Challenge Cup.

In 1989 he rode Eight Springs to victory in the Queen's Cup Hunters' Chase on Fakenham's Easter Monday card, and the Norfolk venue was also the scene of his final ride over fences, when finishing third on Eight Springs in the Prince of Wales Cup on 28 May 1990. Given Brod's friendship with HRH the Prince of Wales, it was an appropriate race with which to end his career.

'I was two weeks short of my forty-fifth birthday,' he says. 'I'd had a wonderful time; I'd hardly hurt myself, and I thought it was probably time to finish. I'd just started to play polo at that stage too, and I then went on to win the European Championships playing for my team Rocking Horse at Guards Polo Club. The Prince of Wales played with us regularly there.'

Brunton Park gained him a third Grand Military Gold Cup, albeit purely as
an owner, when winning the race in 1991.

Today, Brod Munro-Wilson is chairman of one of Europe's top remote
control digital display companies, HoloVis International. He is still a busy man
but he'll always make a point of attending Sandown's Grand Military Meeting.
'Proper people and proper racing,' he says.

Chances are you'll find him at Aintree too. It's the challenge, you see, the
ultimate test for the true Corinthian.

'But I'll always think that the Grand National of 1980 was the one that got
away,' he reflects. 'But for a broken stirrup iron, a race was lost.'

Date: Saturday 29 March 1980 Going: Heavy Value to Winner: £45,595

Horse	Owner	Trainer	Age / weight	Jockey	SP
1 Ben Nevis	Mr R C Stewart Jnr	Capt T Forster	12-10-12	Mr C Fenwick	40-1
2 Rough And Tumble	Mr L Dormer	F Winter	10-10-11	J Francome	11-1
3 The Pilgarlic	Mrs G Poole	F Rimell	12-10-4	R Hyett	33-1
4 Royal Stuart	Mr & Mrs J Murray Begg	S Mellor	9-10-10	P Blacker	20-1

Distances: 20 lengths, 10 lengths, 25 lengths. Time: 10 mins 17.4 secs. 30 ran

Winner trained at Letcombe Bassett, Oxfordshire

1981

PHILIP BLACKER

You don't know what a horse looks like

Royal Mail and Philip Blacker take the last fence in the 1981 Grand National.

'HANG ON, I'LL be with you in a moment,' calls out Philip Blacker as he makes a minor adjustment to the latest work in progress at his studio on the outskirts of Faringdon.

The statues of Red Rum at Aintree, Persian Punch at Newmarket, Desert Orchid at Kempton and Best Mate at Cheltenham were all crafted by this gifted sculptor, whose artistic skills have received worldwide recognition and acclaim for more than a quarter of a century.

But he's not talking sculpture today. He's talking racing; Aintree in particular, and of the time when he was stable jockey to Stan Mellor and came close to winning the Grand National.

'Ever since I rode a pony I was going to be a jump jockey,' he says. 'It always had the most amazing glamour. Nothing compared to it. I used to hero worship Fred Winter and Terry Biddlecombe and all those guys.'

He started as an amateur rider, winning his first race, aged nineteen, when scraping home by a short head on Aberdonian, owned by his father, Major-General 'Monkey' Blacker, in a Windsor selling chase on 16 November 1968.

His brother, Terence, also rode as an amateur around the same time before turning his attention to other things and heading off to university. He is now a novelist and writes a twice-weekly column for *The Independent*.

Philip turned professional at the start of the 1969/70 season and soon struck up an association with Lord Chelsea's mare Trysting Day, trained by Major Verly Bewicke. During the first three months of the 1971/72 campaign, she ran in ten chases, won seven and was second in the other three.

Lord Chelsea and Major Bewicke also provided him with his first Grand National ride, 100-1 outsider Vichysoise in 1971, a horse he describes as having 'some ability but precious little courage'. Despite his rider's misgivings he ran surprisingly well to finish seventh.

'Sometimes it happens at Aintree, whereby a horse that hasn't got a lot of courage takes to it,' he reflects. 'I think it was the slower pace because he was allowed to take his time. He gave me a good ride that day.

'He was a bit unlucky. I think we'd have nearly won but for the fact that we almost got brought down at the Chair. We were going really well but jumped into the back of something that had dived through it and it stopped us in our tracks. He was never going to win after that.

'We ran him again the following year but he didn't like it at all and put the brakes on after a circuit.'

In 1973 he rode Edward Courage's Spanish Steps, a lively 16-1 chance, but, along with Red Rum, soon found himself chasing the runaway leader, Crisp. He eventually finished fourth.

'Before the race I thought we had a really good chance of winning it but we were struggling the whole way. Crisp was so quick over the obstacles, he was gaining two or three lengths at every jump. It was such a fantastically fast pace, completely unlike any other National I ever rode in, so much faster.

'Crisp was nearly a fence in front, it was just ridiculous. I hadn't given up hope by any means but just keeping him in our sights was a struggle. Red Rum was always going a bit better than me and he started to draw away at about Becher's second time. We had 11-13 to carry, and Red Rum had 10-5, so there was a big difference.'

Philip rode Happy Ranger to finish seventh when Red Rum won his third Grand National in 1977. 'He was a lovely horse but he didn't quite get the trip,' he says. 'He gave me a fantastic ride but he got very tired in the last three-quarters if a mile.'

He took over from the retired Jeremy Glover as stable jockey for Stan Mellor at the start of the 1978/79 season. That coincided with the arrival of Royal Mail from New Zealand.

'He'd won the New Zealand Champion Hurdle and he used to jump so very quick that you never felt he'd left the ground,' says Philip. 'He didn't bend his back at all, he just raised his legs. He never gave you a fantastic feel over the obstacles.'

Royal Mail made his British debut in the Fighting Fifth Hurdle at Newcastle in November 1978, finishing third behind Sea Pigeon and Birds Nest. There-after he stuck to chasing, winning over two miles at Nottingham, falling in the 'King George', and then winning Wincanton's John Bull Chase and the PZ Mower Chase at Thurles before finishing a remote second, beaten 25 lengths by Alverton, in the 1979 Gold Cup.

'Stan and I were of slightly differing opinions about him. I felt that two and a half miles was his best trip, whereas Stan wanted to run him in the Gold Cup. I thought, with that quality of race, it was a bit far for him. He finished second but he was a bit lucky to do so, as Tied Cottage fell at the last fence when leading Alverton.'

It was a fruitful Cheltenham for Philip nonetheless, winning the Triumph Hurdle for Stan on Pollardstown and adding the Stayers' Hurdle on the John Edwards-trained Lighter.

Royal Mail returned to Cheltenham twelve months later for a second Gold Cup bid but fell when holding every chance and fractured the lower part of his jaw.

Philip rode Royal Stuart in that year's Grand National and finished a weary last of four finishers behind Ben Nevis. Meanwhile, Royal Mail was making a remarkable recovery. He'd been kept fit by working in a head collar and, when the jaw mended, he was fitted with a Kineton noseband. Just six weeks after his Cheltenham fall he and Philip were reunited and won the Whitbread Gold Cup.

'I always thought he was a two and a half mile horse but Stan proved he was probably right. Royal Mail's Whitbread was the best ride I ever had on any horse. I never rode a horse that jumped the railway fences down the back so fast and accurately.'

Royal Mail failed to deliver in his first four outings of the 1980/81 campaign but bounced back to something like his old form when second over two and a half miles at Sandown in February. His next race was the Grand National, for which he started a 16-1 chance.

Says Philip: 'There's a well-known theory that two and a half milers do well in the National and I'm convinced it's because, generally speaking, the pace is slower and they get their breath back jumping those big obstacles.

'I had two concerns: one was his stamina; the other was his jumping. I thought that his style might not be suited to the fences because he jumped so flat.

'Usually, when a horse isn't used to those fences, they'll go to the first and pitch on landing, and hopefully they'll learn as they go along throughout the race. But he jumped it so flat he never pitched on landing; he jumped it like an ordinary fence and I never felt the drop at all. After the third or fourth I thought "This is going to be okay".

'I went round the inner to go the shortest way to conserve his stamina. I dropped him in but he was a horse that relaxed so it wasn't difficult, and I was having a lovely ride.

'We jumped the Chair in around twelfth but I got a fantastic run up the inner passing the stands first time, just managed to creep up to the leaders without having to make an effort. We made up a lot of ground there and by the time we got to the Melling Road to start the second circuit he was up to third, purely through hugging the rail.

'Stan also ran Royal Stuart in the race. He and I were almost upsides at one point but then Hywel Davies' leather broke and he fell off going down to Becher's.

'Aldaniti was out in front but kept jumping to the left. He did that all the way round. Bob Champion kept pulling him out to the middle but he'd run down the next fence, left-handed. I was on the inner and we kept getting blinded. The problem was I couldn't pull round him because Aldaniti kept coming out again once he'd jumped the fence, so I had to stay where I was.

'At the second last I went to move up on his outside and he ran down the fence again and we just got blinded at that point. Royal Mail made a really bad mistake; he was lucky to stand up.

'On reflection, I probably over-reacted, in that, if I'd just given him time to pick himself up, we might have made a better shot of it, but when he made the mistake I picked him up and chased him back up so that by the time he jumped the last, we were nearly upsides again, which was a mistake.

'Everything had gone so well up to the second last but the mistake there made a big difference. I do think but for that mistake we could have won, because I had a bit in reserve and that really knocked it out of him.

'It certainly made the difference between finishing third rather than second, because Spartan Missile only beat us by two lengths.

'When Royal Mail came in there was blood dripping from his tummy. He'd jumped so low, it had taken the skin off underneath. It was raw. That was just his style of jumping. He jumped so flat but was really quick, which really made a difference over those fences.

'I was pretty sick after the race because I knew I'd probably missed the one opportunity I was going to have of winning the National, but everyone was thrilled for Bob after all he'd been through.'

Philip had planned to hang up his boots at the end of that season but postponed retirement in order to ride Royal Mail in the 1982 Grand National. They won over three and a quarter miles at Doncaster on the first day of March and were made ante-post favourite. But come the big day it was Bob Davies, not Philip, who was in the saddle.

'It was so stupid of me,' he laments. 'I'd been obsessed about not getting injured before the National. I knew it was my last season and my last chance. Stan said "Don't take any dodgy rides".

'I went up to Aintree on the Thursday and rode a horse called Broomy Bank for John Edwards in the Topham. He ran very badly and finished nearly last. John wasn't very happy about it and implied I hadn't given the horse a great ride and that I was saving myself, which most definitely wasn't the case.

'I was due to ride three of his the next day at Ludlow. I'd spoken to Stan about it and he'd advised me to take the day off, so I'd decided that's what I was going to do. When I told John I wasn't going to Ludlow, he said "That proves my point," so I reluctantly agreed to go.

'I had three rides and the last one unseated me at the last fence. I was concussed and cracked a shoulder blade. I felt so annoyed with myself.

'The thing about Royal Mail was that he did need knowing. You needed to organise him, especially with those big fences, otherwise he jumped too flat, so you had to get him back on his hocks, almost like a show jumper, to get some elevation. Bob Davies was a great jockey but he just didn't know Royal Mail and because he gave him a kick going into Becher's, the horse didn't get high enough and he fell.'

That Ludlow fall brought an ignominious end to Philip's time in the saddle, which had yielded just short of 400 winners. He'd combined his last six years a jockey with his burgeoning career as a sculptor.

As for Royal Mail, he ran in one more Grand National, in 1983, again falling at Becher's when partnered by amateur rider Tim Thomson Jones. He was then retired, aged thirteen, and was given to Philip by his grateful owners, Mr and Mrs Begg, to spend his retirement with him.

'He was the most wonderful horse,' he says. 'Most ex-racehorses can be difficult to handle and highly strung but this horse would stand like a rock. I used him as a model for my works.

'I'm not a great one for saying that horses are hugely intelligent but he had more brain than any horse I ever met. He was so incredibly gentle. My young children would run in and out of his box, and I used to canter round the field on him with my daughter in my lap when she was two or three.

'Sadly, we didn't have all that long together. He died at about eighteen or nineteen so didn't live to a ripe old age. He had a heart attack. We came out one morning and found him dead in the field. He was a smashing horse.'

Philip's interest in sculpture sprang from a conversation with sculptor and racehorse owner Margot Dent during a car journey to Devon and Exeter (now Exeter) races in December 1973.

'I had thought about it before but only in that I'd looked at sculpture and trophies and had this feeling that I'd be able to do it,' he says. 'I don't know why. I didn't even know that you could make a living out of it.'

He first tried his hand at sculpture during a racing freeze-up in January 1975. Among his early pieces were Michael Oliver's chaser Master H and some Grand National bronzes. That summer he accepted an invitation from Margot to visit her studio.

'When I went to see her, she saw my work and said "You don't know what a horse looks like". I replied "I think I do", but she was absolutely right.

'I went to the Royal Veterinary College and sat in on a few lectures on anatomy. It was a fascinating experience. Having a good knowledge of anatomy is important. If you don't have the basics you'll never succeed. Learning to draw was a similar thing. I couldn't really draw but I soon realised that I was going to have to learn.'

Aintree supremo John Hughes offered him the job of designing the 1986 Grand National trophy and the longer-term life-size statue of Red Rum for unveiling in 1988. His task was to create a bronze that summed up the drama and the unique quality of the race.

'At the time, when I'd packed in, I just wanted to capture what it was like to be a jockey and I felt I had a unique standpoint because I'd been a professional and I knew all the little nuances, the way we gripped the reins, how your feet go in the irons. My ambition was to authenticate it. If you look at my early works, the emphasis was very much on how a jockey is holding the reins or the angle of his legs, something that you know is authentic.

'I tend to take a non-anthropomorphic, non-sentimental view about horses' capabilities. I don't endow them with human thoughts. When you're a jockey you can't afford to be sentimental because there are some pretty horrible things that happen in racing. If you're going to be a jockey you've got to accept that you're going to be on a horse that breaks a leg and you're going to be there holding them just before they get destroyed.

'Having been a professional jockey certainly put me in a better position than sculptors who hadn't had that first-hand experience with horses, though not so now because the experience I had racing has faded; it's a long time ago, it's not so immediate. Also, I'm doing a lot of other subjects that are not racing related.'

He reflects on his achievements in two widely differing spheres with a sense of whimsy. 'I'm so glad I've managed to get through life without ever having to get a proper job. Being a jockey was fun, and this is fun, and I'm chuffed to be able to make a living out of it.'

Date: Saturday 4 April 1981   Going: Good   Value to Winner: £51,324

Horse	Owner	Trainer	Age / weight	Jockey	SP
1 Aldaniti	Mr S N J Embiricos	J Gifford	11-10-13	R Champion	10-1
2 Spartan Missile	Mr M J Thorne	Owner	9-11-5	A Webber	8-1fav
3 Royal Mail	Mr & Mrs J Murray Begg	S Mellor	11-11-7	P Blacker	16-1
4 Three To One	Mr J C Manners & Mrs J K M Oliver	J K M Oliver	10-10-3	Mr T G Dun	33-1

Distances: 4 lengths, 2 lengths, neck. Time: 9 mins 47.2 secs. 39 ran

Winner trained at Findon, Sussex

1982

ANTHONY WEBBER
The ride that you'd pick to have

Anthony Webber – finished second on Hard Outlook.

'WE ALWAYS THOUGHT that Hard Outlook would stay; we didn't know whether Grittar would – but he did,' says Anthony Webber, reflecting on what might have been in the 1982 Grand National.

It had been almost ten years since he'd ridden his first winner, Foggerty – named after a character in Spike Milligan's book *Puckoon* – for his father, trainer John Webber, in an amateur riders' novice hurdle at Leicester in October 1972.

It was the home-bred chaser Dream Isle that had got Anthony going. Out of a mare called Honey Isle, on whom his father had won three hurdle races during the early weeks of the 1963/64 season, Dream Isle developed into a Towcester specialist during the mid-1970s, winning six times at the Northamptonshire track.

But Ballyrichard Again was the one that really put him the map, scoring seven times over fences during the 1973/74 campaign, providing one-third of his total wins for that season and enabling him to land the amateur riders' championship, beating Lord Oaksey by one.

'I turned professional the following season and he was my first Grand National ride, in 1975,' he recalls. 'I fell clean off him at the Canal Turn first time round!'

His second Grand National ride came in 1979 on Coolishall, who had finished fourth the previous year when partnered by Martin O'Halloran. 'I didn't have a mount in the National but I was riding one for Major Bewicke in the first race. I got stuck in traffic and had to run for the best part of three-quarters of an hour to the track in order to weigh out.

'When I got there, Peter Cundell [Coolishall's trainer] said to me, "Martin's unwell and can't ride. Can you do the weight?" Probably because I'd had that run, I could do it. The horse went well until falling four out; otherwise he would definitely have been in the first four or five.'

Next was Might Be, trained by his father, in 1981. 'He was a decent handicap chaser who'd won the Leicestershire Silver Fox Chase and deserved to be in the race. He was quietly making a bit of progress when he caught his toe and had what you'd call a "racing fall" five out.'

His mount in 1982 was the Wates family's Hard Outlook, on whom younger brother Paul Webber had finished second in the Kim Muir the year before.

'He was a real example of what you think a Grand National horse should be,' says Anthony. 'He was tough and square, game and genuine; he was a professional long-distance chaser. He knew exactly where he was and he worked it out for himself. He was the ride that you'd pick to have, and he took to it just like that. He was a natural.

'It was one of those races where everything seems to open up for you. Horses were coming down but he just had a clear path all through. Up to and across the Melling Road he could well have won, that was until Dick Saunders pressed the button on Grittar. Grittar was the best on the day emphatically.'

Habitual front-runner Delmoss had led to halfway, then Irish challenger Carrow Boy took it up as they went out onto the second circuit, with Saint Fillans, Grittar, Loving Words, Tragus and Hard Outlook all close up. Saint Fillans landed in front at the nineteenth but made a mistake at Becher's, handing the lead to Grittar, who stayed in front from thereon. As Grittar led the way towards the last two fences, only Hard Outlook had any hope of catching him. And that hope soon disappeared.

Grittar, who had won the Fox Hunters' Chase over the Grand National fences the previous season, passed the post 15 lengths clear of Hard Outlook. A distance behind them came the grey Loving Words, who, having been remounted by Richard Hoare after being brought down four out, made up a vast amount of ground to snatch third by a short head from Delmoss. Loving Words was the first horse to make the National frame after being remounted since Derrinstown had finished last of three finishers in 1951.

Indeed, the scene of carnage at the first fence in 1982 had been almost identical to that of 31 years earlier, for ten horses, including the previous year's winner Aldaniti, either fell or were brought down, the highest casualty list at this obstacle since eleven failed to survive in 1951.

At 7-1, Grittar was the first outright favourite to win since Merryman II in

1960. At 48, Saunders became the oldest winning rider in the race's history and immediately announced his retirement from the saddle.

Bred in Leicestershire and trained under permit by his 67-year-old owner Frank Gilman, Grittar was the first Grand National winner to emanate from that county since Reynoldstown, the dual winner of 1935/36. He was toasted in champagne by locals in his home village of Morcott, Rutland, the following day and even made an appearance in his local pub, the White Horse, before being paraded round Gilman's garden

As for Hard Outlook, he proved difficult to train thereafter and ran only three more times over the next two seasons before being retired.

Anthony's next National mount, Mender in 1983, fell at the fourth, but he enjoyed what he calls 'a brilliant ride' twelve months later when finishing sixth on the Roddy Armytage-trained grey Two Swallows.

His final Grand National ride, Talon, in 1985, was also his shortest. Owned by Brod Munro-Wilson and trained by Roddy Armytage, he'd been third over the fences in the Fox Hunters' the year before, after which the Grand National was the long-term plan.

'The whole thing was masterminded so that he got ten stone,' recalls Anthony. 'Down at the start he was the one that I thought would win. And he was going to win all the way down to the first fence!

'He jumped it sensibly, landed running and just turned over. He put his foot on my chest so I couldn't breathe properly. Four or five of us came down at that first fence. While I was unable to move they were saying "Come on Ant, we need a photograph, get up", so they pulled me off the track and stood me up. Somewhere there exists a picture of us, after which I rather think I collapsed!'

It was another injury that ended his riding career. 'I did my neck in on what was just an ordinary fall at Nottingham and had to have some time off. I came back in January 1986 and had three winners in three days. Ronalds Carole won at Towcester, then I won Warwick's Brooke Bond Oxo National on Knock Hill, and Auntie Dot won her maiden hurdle at Leicester. Things were looking good but then I had a really soft fall on a horse of Peter Bailey's at Doncaster in a four or five runner novice chase. When I got up I realised my sense of balance had gone.

'Something had gone wrong with my neck and I was getting a lot of blood to my head. That was the end. The doctors could see what was happening. They gave me a chance and took X-rays but there was no comeback.'

Career highlights had included victories on The Snipe in the 1978 Massey-Ferguson Gold Cup and Sandown's Mecca Bookmakers Hurdle on Golden Vow. But he was never going to take over the training mantle at the family's Cropredy Lawn stables at Mollington, near Banbury.

'It was always understood that "Bro" [brother Paul] would take over as trainer at Cropredy when he was ready. Dad wanted to hand it to him up and running and "Bro" has done loads with it since.

'Anyway, I was going to be a "back man" after race riding.

'Ronnie Longford, one of the first people to become a horse chiropractor, taught my sister and I about horses' backs. He used to put horses right with skeletal alignment and muscle trouble. It was on account of him getting "Bally-richard" correct that we learned how to do it hands on.'

Anthony and his sister, Teresa (now Elwell) also learned the human side of the job and now have a thriving business.

'Largely,' he says, 'it's people whom we've known for over thirty years. I think it's perhaps because we're all getting towards the end of our careers; we creak a bit more than we used to!'

Date: Saturday 3 April 1982 Going: Good Value to Winner: £52,507

Horse	Owner	Trainer	Age / weight	Jockey	SP
1 Grittar	Mr F H Gilman	Owner	9-11-5	Mr C Saunders	7-1fav
2 Hard Outlook	Lady Wates	A Wates	11-10-1	A Webber	50-1
3 Loving Words	Mr A Netley	J Thorne	9-10-11	R Hoare	16-1
4 Delmoss	Mr J K Goodman	F Walwyn	12-10-3	W Smith	50-1

Distances: 15 lengths, distance, short head. Time: 9 mins 12.6 secs. 39 ran

Winner trained at Morcott, Leicestershire

1983

COLIN MAGNIER
The best thrill of all

Corbiere leads Greasepaint over the final fence.

IN BECOMING THE first woman to train a Grand National winner, Jenny Pitman denied what would have been the third amateur rider to win the race in the space of four years, following the triumphs of Ben Nevis in 1980, ridden by an American banker, and the previous year's winner Grittar, partnered by a 48-year-old member of the Jockey Club.

Corbiere's hard fought victory over the Irish-trained Greasepaint in front of a sun-drenched Aintree crowd also provided his 23-year-old jockey Ben De Haan with victory at his third attempt.

Greasepaint's amateur rider, Colin Magnier, was having his first ride in the race but had far more experience than the word 'amateur' might suggest. He'd already tasted success at the highest level, having won the 1982 Champion Hurdle on For Auction, trained, like Greasepaint, by Michael Cunningham. He had also won the 1975 Galway Hurdle on Sir Douglas Clague's Double Default, trained by his father Clem Magnier, a renowned master of his profession.

'Getting the ride on For Auction was just by accident. His two jockeys, Joe Byrne and Tommy McGivern, were both injured at the time and he [Cunningham] asked me to ride him.'

His first ride on For Auction was in January 1982, when he won Leopardstown's Sweeps Hurdle. They then finished fourth in the Schweppes Gold Trophy at Newbury. The Champion Hurdle was their next assignment, run that year on stamina-sapping heavy ground.

'He wasn't the greatest of jumpers; he was a bit awkward, but for some reason he jumped well for me,' says Colin of For Auction. 'He had to have soft ground to slow the others up a bit. He was very good on the day of the Champion Hurdle. He didn't just plod up the hill, he quickened, and he went away from them. Four of us turned into the straight together and he won seven lengths from Broadsword, Ekbalco and Pollardstown.'

The following season For Auction came within a short-head of a repeat win in the Sweeps Hurdle. But deprived of his favoured heavy ground he could only finish third in the Irish Champion Hurdle and in the Champion Hurdle itself.

The Cunningham-Magnier combo made up for their disappointment by winning that year's Kim Muir Chase with Greasepaint. It provided particular consolation for Colin, as he had been leading the Kim Muir field on Indecision two years earlier when falling at the second last.

He had ridden Greasepaint on his racecourse debut, finishing second in a Naas bumper on the first day of March 1980. The following season he rode him five times over hurdles, winning his maiden at Navan and finishing in the first three on the other four occasions. Then stable jockeys Byrne and McGivern took over.

Sent over fences for the 1981/82 campaign, he made a winning debut at Punchestown, won the Troytown Chase at Navan and finished third in that season's National Hunt Handicap Chase at Cheltenham.

The next season, Greasepaint won at Fairyhouse and Punchestown but finished a disappointing last when favourite for the Harold Clarke Leopardstown Chase. His next target was to be the Kim Muir, which, being an amateur riders' contest, meant Colin would regain the ride.

'I schooled him over fences at Leopardstown before Cheltenham,' he recalls. 'He went round with a heap of others and he pulverised them. Cunningham thought he'd entered him in the wrong race; he should have gone for the Two-Mile Champion Chase. The Kim Muir was the first time I rode him over fences in a race and he won it very easy.'

On the strength of that, Greasepaint, an eight-year-old chestnut gelding by Gala Performance, became a leading contender for the Grand National. Colin would keep the ride, his first over the Aintree fences.

'It was my first ride in the National and I hadn't a clue what to expect,' he admits. 'I knew the horse was good enough to jump round but it's just luck in running. He was a very well balanced horse and just lobbed along. He'd never go off and win a distance for you but he'd give you whatever you were asking him for. He was a lovely natured horse, very agile, always alert, and very cat-like with his jumping. He was a clever old devil; if he was wrong he could quickly change himself.

'Michael Cunningham said I could go any way I wanted to go. I said "The shortest way is the easiest way", so I went down the inside. He was a very straightforward ride; never got into any trouble. I never had any problems with him; jumped like a buck.'

Corbiere was up there from the start, jumping the early fences alongside Delmoss. Delmoss landed a length in front of Corbiere at Valentine's and maintained his advantage as the field came back onto the racecourse, where Hallo Dandy began to improve his position. Delmoss was badly hampered by riderless horses at the thirteenth fence but still led the way over the Chair.

Greasepaint, who had been towards the rear early on, was just starting to creep into the picture.

Recounts Colin: 'They tightened up a good bit from the Melling Road coming back in and I had to pull out wide to get a bit of light at the Chair. I jumped it on the outside then moved back to the inside as we went round again. He flew the Chair; I'd say he must have made two or three lengths at it.

'Going down to Becher's he jumped from outside the wings at everything. He was brilliant. He was just ... on springs.

'He only made one mistake and that was at the smallest fence, the Foinavon, second time. He just never took off, for some reason. He had plenty of daylight; it's just one of those things that happen.

'He pinged the Canal Turn and I must have got six or eight lengths on them there. He looked after me well that day, I have to give it to him.'

Hallo Dandy and Corbiere took Valentine's together in front, with Greasepaint and outsiders Yer Man and Colonel Christy close up, though the latter began to fade soon after.

Turning for home there were four still in with a chance – Corbiere, Greasepaint, Hallo Dandy and Yer Man. Hallo Dandy was the first to falter, leaving it between Corbiere and the two Irish challengers at the second last.

'We met a bad patch of ground on the inside between the second last and the last,' says Colin. 'He got lost in the ground. I probably should have gone to the outside, especially after first time round. I didn't realise it was so holding on the inside, second time. He just lost a couple of lengths.'

Corbiere jumped the last better than Greasepaint, and with Yer Man finally weakening out of contention, the 1983 Grand National lay between the pair. Corbiere was two lengths up and looked to have it won but Greasepaint wasn't done with.

Greasepaint began to eat into the deficit and coming into the last 100 yards it looked as though he was going to get there. Surely Colin must have thought he was going to win the Grand National at his first attempt?

'No, I didn't; never,' he replies. 'I knew I was getting there but I always felt the line would come too soon. You nearly always know in a photo finish whether you're going to get there or not, and I never thought I was going to get there. Another two strides and he'd have gone by him.'

He failed by just three-quarters of a length. Twenty lengths further back, Yer Man was an honourable third, with Hallo Dandy fourth and then a long gap back to the 6-1 favourite Grittar, followed by Peaty Sandy and four other finishers.

Colin had carried 1lb overweight on Greasepaint. Could that have made a difference between victory and narrow defeat?

'No,' he insists. 'He made up ten lengths going round. I don't think it made an ounce of difference. It was just that patch, 30 to 40 yards, between the last two fences, where he lost all balance. As soon as he got the good ground again, he ran on. If the ground had been good he wouldn't have even come off the bridle; he'd have won that easy.'

That was last time he rode Greasepaint. The horse's owner, bookmaker George Todd, sold him shortly afterwards to Michael Smurfit and he was sent to be trained by Dermot Weld.

Ridden by Tommy Carmody, Greasepaint finished second, beaten four lengths by Hallo Dandy, in the 1984 Grand National. He started favourite for the 1985 race, again partnered by Carmody, but could finish only fourth behind Last Suspect.

The following season he produced a heroic effort in defeat in the Galway Plate, finishing third under top-weight of 12 stone and conceding a stone to the winner and 35lb to the runner-up. In a fourth and final bid for Grand National glory in 1986, ridden once more by Carmody, he again completed the course, this time finishing in tenth place.

As for Colin, he never rode in the Grand National again. 'The opportunity just never came up,' he says.

After he retired from riding he trained for a couple of years but was plagued by one virus after another, so he gave it up and, together with his wife Jessica, went into liveries, preparing horses for going into training. They also have a sand and fibre exercise gallop and schooling facilities which are open to point-to-point trainers.

They are based in the village of Skryne, overlooked by the Hill of Tara, in County Meath. Colin's brother Paul trains not far away, while his first cousin, John Magnier, runs the mighty Coolmore operation.

Sitting at the his kitchen table one autumn afternoon, 26 years on from the 1983 Grand National, he is asked whether that ride on Greasepaint was the highlight of his career.

'Oh yes,' he answers straight away. 'It was the best thrill of all.'

Date: Saturday 9 April 1983   Going: Soft   Value to Winner: £52,949

Horse	Owner	Trainer	Age / weight	Jockey	SP
1 Corbiere	Mr B R H Burrough	Mrs J Pitman	8-11-4	B De Haan	13-1
2 Greasepaint	Mrs N Todd	M Cunningham	8-10-7	Mr C Magnier	14-1
3 Yer Man	Mr N Keane	A McNamara	8-10-0	T V O'Connell	80-1
4 Hallo Dandy	Mr Richard Shaw	G W Richards	9-10-1	N Doughty	60-1

Distances: 3/4 length, 20 lengths, 2½ lengths. Time: 9 mins 47.4 secs. 41 ran

Winner trained at Upper Lambourn, Berkshire

1984

VAL JACKSON

Ee my God, it's a tart!

Bush Guide and Valerie Alder jump the last to win the Burnley Handicap Chase at Haydock in December 1983.

VAL JACKSON HARKS back to her days at primary school in the sixties and laughs. 'When the teacher asked the kids what they'd like to be when they grew up, I told her I wanted to be a boy, because I wanted to ride in the Grand National!'

In 1965, she had seen her father, John Alder, do just that, completing the course on his own horse, the almost white Tant Pis. 'I was five but I remember watching it on television like it was last week,' she says. 'The other grey in the race was Loving Record and we've got a water colour print at home of the two of them jumping one of the fences.'

Home for the Alders is Northumberland; north-east hunting country. It has been for generations. Both Val's grandfathers were farmers; her great-grandfathers were butchers. They all rode and there were always horses around. John Alder trained a few under permit, first at Kirkwhelpington, then at Kirkley West Thorn.

Tant Pis had been discovered at the back of a hen house in South Shields. Says Val: 'My grandmother, father's mother, bought him for 150 guineas as a twenty-first birthday present for my mother. He was small and looked like a ladies' horse, so he was bought as a hunter. He turned out to be a bit better than a ladies' hunter.'

In 1962 and ridden by John, Tant Pis opened his account by winning the Morpeth Hunt race, followed by the Haydon Adjacent, and went on to finish second in a Hexham hunter chase.

During the 1962/63 National Hunt season he won three chases, then three more the following season. In February 1965 John rode him to victory in the Wetherby Grand National Trial. Six weeks later the pair lined up as 40-1 outsiders for the Grand National itself, staying on when others had cried enough to come home ninth of the fourteen finishers.

Tant Pis went on to win five more races, the last coming as a fourteen-year-old at Hexham in May 1969. Sadly, later that year he lost his life in a match race with Red Alligator at Newcastle. Recalls Val: 'It was firm ground and they'd watered the take-offs and landings of the fences. He slipped as he took off, lost his hind legs and broke his femur on the guard rail.'

He is still remembered at Hexham by the Tant Pis Handicap Chase.

Amongst the horses to carry the Alders' colours of pale blue, black hoop and armlets with distinction was Lothian Brig, a multiple winning chaser who went on to provide seventeen-year-old Valerie Alder with her first success under Rules in a Nottingham hunter chase in May 1977. There was double reason for celebrating as she had passed her driving test the same day.

More than thirty years later finds her training point-to-pointers at home at Belsay and continuing to ride between the flags and under Rules. In 2008 she owned, trained and rode Robbers Glen to win Stratford's John Corbet Cup, the champion novices' hunter chase, and she was still winning races on him in 2011, living proof that there is life after fifty.

It was in the summer of 1979 that Val first set eyes on Bush Guide. 'Bush Guide belonged to a long-standing family friend who was breaking him in when she suffered a linear fracture of her jaw. The doctor told her that if she had another fall, all her teeth would drop out, so we got him to finish breaking so that he could be sold on.

'We got him in July but it was Christmas Day before we could ride him without being attended by somebody with a lead rein. Nobody would ride him but me. With that amount of effort having been put in, my father bought him. The following year he gave me Bush Guide for my twenty-first birthday.'

In 1982, twenty years after Tant Pis had won the same race, Val Alder rode Bush Guide to land the Morpeth Members' race at Tranwell, her local point-to-point course. In September that year, Bush Guide made his debut under Rules in a Hexham bumper. He made the running, went clear six furlongs out and was untroubled to win by twelve lengths.

That was to be his only run in a bumper. Bypassing the hurdling phase, he was put straight over fences. Partnered throughout by Val, Bush Guide finished a creditable second to Michael Dickinson's Righthand Man before landing three Newcastle novice chases and Sedgefield's Durham National.

In December 1983, Bush Guide made all to win the Ladbroke Trophy over three and three-quarter miles at Newcastle, followed twelve days later by a three and a half mile chase at Haydock. The horse was not yet eight but was clearly an out and out stayer. Those victories were achieved shortly before the 1984 Grand National entries were due to close and the opportunity was too tempting to miss.

She recalls: 'I'd never been to Aintree until I walked the course on the morning. To be honest, I thought the fences looked more scary when I'd seen them on television. When I saw them in real life they looked quite jumpable.

'You're very isolated as a lady jockey. There's not that atmosphere of the weighing room. You're stuck round the corner in a portacabin so it's difficult to get involved in the prelims. Even so, I was really pleased to be there because it was my lifetime ambition just to take part.

'What first hit me and made me realise that this was the Grand National was the noise at the start. It was almost like having to pinch yourself that you were really there. The atmosphere made it so different from any other race. Not just because it was over the big fences. Everyone was in Grand National mood.

'The screaming and the cheering when the tapes went up was quite incredible. Bush Guide liked to front run but they went so quickly over the first few fences, it was damn near impossible. I don't imagine that I've gone any quicker to a first fence in my life than I did that day.

'He was overjumping, landing too steeply. The one he jumped best was Becher's Brook. Coming down to Becher's you could hear the crowd cheering as you approached the fence. Then he got in too deep at the Canal Turn, hit it in front and toppled over. There was nothing else involved; it was just an unfortunate fall that could happen anywhere.

'We were both okay. He obviously realised he'd lost his jockey and there was no point in galloping round after everyone else. He came back towards me and a gentleman caught him. The ambulance man had got me by then and ferried me into the ambulance. The horse was taking chunks out of this poor bloke, so I got out of the ambulance and climbed back on him.

'It's about three-quarters of a mile from the Canal Turn to the stands. I rode back across the course with Peter Scudamore [who'd pulled up Burnt Oak there second time round]. I remember riding past the scouse crowd in the middle. One man looked up and shouted "Ee my God, it's a tart!" Talk about the shock of seeing a woman on a horse in the Grand National. I found that quite entertaining!'

Meanwhile, the stands towards which Val and Scu were heading erupted as Greasepaint and Hallo Dandy, separated by the width of the course, fought out the finish. Neale Doughty, whip in his right hand, was doing all he could to stop Hallo Dandy drifting over to the stands side rails. What had looked a certain victory was suddenly wide open again as Greasepaint drew level a hundred yards out. But his 14lb weight concession told its tale close home and Hallo Dandy ran on to score by four lengths.

Hallo Dandy had started his racing career in the care of Red Rum's trainer Ginger McCain before joining Gordon Richards at Greystoke, near Penrith. His owner, Richard Shaw, had bought the horse shortly before the 1983 Grand National, in which he'd finished fourth.

By the time Bush Guide reappeared in the autumn of 1984, Miss Alder had become Mrs Jackson, having married Peter Jackson in August. Over the next three seasons the horse made the frame several times without winning. He finally scored his first victory for more than four years when winning the Stewart Wight Memorial Trophy at Kelso in January 1988.

'I point-to-pointed him when he was thirteen and he was second every time he ran,' says Val. 'It was one of those seasons with a dry spring and it was always fast ground. The one that kept beating him was an old horse called Mossy Moore, ridden by Sandy Forster, Ken Oliver's granddaughter. We had some ding-dong battles but Mossy Moore was a fast-ground horse, whereas mine wanted softer.'

Bush Guide ran his last race, aged fourteen, when fifth in a Newcastle hunter chase in March 1990. Val recalls: 'After he'd been retired, Bush Guide lived with me until Christmas Day 2000 when he had a stroke. I had to have him put to sleep on Christmas morning.

'I'd put him out in the field as normal, went to ride another one and, as I rode past the field, he'd gone down. I put the other horse back in, ran to him, phoned the vet. It was the circulation to his legs. The vet was almost certain he'd had a blood clot somewhere. He was twenty-four but there was nothing wrong with his heart. We put him to sleep in the field where he lay.

'There was a special significance about it being Christmas Day because that was the day, twenty-one years earlier, that I first rode him without a lead rein. I'll always think about him on Christmas Day.

'He's buried at home, in the front paddock, and I'll be buried next to him. That's what I want, to be buried next to the horse. When he won those two handicap chases at Newcastle and Haydock, there were people interested in buying him for £60,000. But you couldn't buy what Bush Guide gave me. You just couldn't buy it.'

Date: Saturday 31 March 1984 Going: Good Value to Winner: £54,769

Horse	Owner	Trainer	Age / weight	Jockey	SP
1 Hallo Dandy	Mr Richard Shaw	G W Richards	10-10-2	N Doughty	13-1
2 Greasepaint	Mr M J Smurfit	D Weld	9-11-2	T Carmody	9-1fav
3 Corbiere	Mr B R H Burrough	Mrs J Pitman	9-12-0	B De Haan	16-1
4 Lucky Vane	Miss B Swire	G Balding	9-10-13	J Burke	12-1

Distances: 4 lengths, 1½ lengths, 2½ lengths. Time: 9 mins 21.4 secs. 40 ran

Winner trained at Greystoke, Penrith, Cumbria

1985

PETER SCUDAMORE
Two were quicker

Peter Scudamore – eight-time champion jockey

JUMP RACING IS full of ups and downs. The Grand National-winning winning jockeys of 1983 and 1984 were both *hors de combat* when the 1985 renewal came round. Almost as if to exemplify the sport's unforeseen hazards, Corbiere's rider, Ben De Haan, had been kicked by a horse in the unsaddling enclosure at Wolverhampton, while Hallo Dandy's partner, Neale Doughty, was unseated on the flat before even reaching the first hurdle at Worcester.

Peter Scudamore duly came in for the ride on Corbiere and Graham Bradley inherited the mount on Hallo Dandy, giving both jockeys a solid chance of riding their first Grand National winner and adding their names to the list of lucky substitutes like Bob Davies, who had deputised for David Goulding on Lucius, and Pat Taaffe, the stand-in for Terry Biddlecombe aboard Gay Trip.

De Haan had been due to ride Corbiere the day after his accident in a three-and-three-quarter mile marathon chase at Chepstow, his final race before the Grand National. 'Scu' took the mount and won easily. Soon afterwards he was booked by Corbiere's trainer, Jenny Pitman, to ride him at Aintree.

It turned out to be a close call because Scu was in the wars himself on Aintree's opening day, when his Topham Trophy partner, Burnt Oak, fell heavily when leading at the fence before Becher's, breaking the jockey's nose and badly bruising the calf muscle of his left leg.

Pitman was understandably concerned, making it clear that she didn't want a half-fit jockey riding her horse and that Scu would have to prove his fitness by riding on the Friday. Despite a heavily-strapped leg, he was passed fit to ride by the racecourse doctor.

Shouldering top-weight of 11st 10lb, Corbiere led the parade of Grand National runners past the packed stands. With orders to obtain a prominent position down the inside, Scu took his place in the line-up, close to the rail.

Greasepaint, runner-up for the last two years, went off the 13-2 joint-favourite with West Tip, the mount of young Richard Dunwoody, who was having his first ride in the race.

No sooner were they off than the shock news came from the commentator's box that Hallo Dandy had fallen at the very first. No 'substitute's luck', then, for Bradley, but Scu was still there with a chance on Corbiere.

'He was a bit frightened of the ditches,' he recalls. 'At the first ditch he sort of stretched a bit. It's the width of the fences that catch them out second or third time, rather than the height. Having been round there before, they know it hurts their back legs if they drag them through, so they're a bit sensitive. He was a bit hesitant at the first ditch but after that he was brilliant.'

Twenty-seven of the forty starters made it to halfway, where Dudie and Rupertino led West Tip and Corbiere out into the country for the second circuit. Lying in fifth place was the 50-1 outsider Last Suspect, whose trainer, Tim Forster had said of him that he 'hates human beings and other horses', hence his jockey, Hywel Davies, had endeavoured to keep him away from the other runners, charting a course near to the outside rail.

An exhausted Dudie departed three fences later, leaving Rupertino, West Tip and Corbiere in front coming to Becher's for the second time. Scu observed how well Dunwoody was going on West Tip and thought 'I'm not going to beat him.'

But no sooner had the thought crossed his mind, West Tip jumped the fence slightly to the left, almost collided with Rupertino, and any chance of staying on his feet disappeared when a riderless horse hit him from behind.

West Tip's fall left Rupertino and Corbiere in front, pressed by Last Suspect, Greasepaint, Classified and the improving Mr Snugfit. Rupertino's stamina ran out at the fence after Valentine's, leaving Corbiere in front, a lead he still held approaching two out.

'From three out, as we came back onto the racecourse proper, I thought he'd win from that point,' Scu recalls. 'He'd done all the hard work. I'd produced him at the right place in the race and it was whether he'd gallop home from there. Unfortunately, two horses galloped home quicker.'

One of those two was Mr Snugfit, who jumped past Corbiere at the second last and, with Greasepaint under pressure and looking beaten, Phil Tuck, Mr Snugfit's jockey, sensed victory as he led that tiring pair over the final fence. But behind them was Last Suspect, who jumped the last in fourth position, fully ten lengths behind the leader.

Hywel Davies had wasted down to his minimum of 10st 5lb, still 3lb overweight, and was in no mood to compromise with the recalcitrant and misanthropic Last Suspect. On the run-in he drove his mount past Greasepaint and Corbiere, and finally past Mr Snugfit close home to win by a length and a half.

'I suppose the weight beat Corbiere in the end; there were no other excuses,' says Scu. 'He galloped all the way to the line. He'd won a National before and had suffered the consequences of doing so by having to carry top-weight.'

Last Suspect's jockey wore the 'yellow, narrow black band and cap with gold tassel' colours made famous by Arkle, whose owner, Anne, Duchess of Westminster, had vehemently refused to run her champion in the National. Indeed, if she and Tim Forster had had their way, Last Suspect would not have run in it either. It was purely down to Hywel Davies's powers of persuasion that coerced them into letting the horse take his chance.

Last Suspect paid over 120-1 on the Tote, the longest priced National winner since Foinavon, who at one time had also been owned by the Duchess of Westminster.

Last Suspect's dam, Last Link, had won the Irish National for Tom Dreaper in 1963, just at the time when Arkle was beginning to show Dreaper, the Duchess, and the sporting world, that he was no ordinary horse.

By the time of the 1988 Grand National, Scu was on his way to becoming champion jockey for the fourth time and had just won the Champion Hurdle on Celtic Shot. His Grand National mount that year was Strands Of Gold, trained by Martin Pipe.

'He'd just come to us from Jimmy FitzGerald,' he recalls. 'He gave me a great ride throughout the first circuit and on the run down to Becher's, on the inside, jumping boldly. But at Becher's, when I asked him to quicken to jump out over the drop, no stride came and he hit the fence very hard, landed too steeply, and there I was, picking myself up off the floor. It was a gut wrencher at the time.'

He at least gained partial compensation later that year when Strands Of Gold gave him his first victory in the Hennessy Cognac Gold Cup at Newbury.

By 1993 he'd been champion jockey eight times. He had what was to be his final Grand National mount on Captain Dibble, who had given him his second Scottish National victory the previous year.

Scu arrived at Aintree fresh from a triumphant Cheltenham, where he had won the Champion Hurdle on Granville Again, the Sun Alliance Novices' Chase on Young Hustler, and the Coral Cup on Olympian. Could he at last add an Aintree Grand National to his collection of three Welsh and two Scottish Nationals?

The answer, of course, was 'no'. It was the year when nobody won the Grand National; the year when the majority of runners failed to observe the second false start recall flag.

Says Scu: 'I looked over after Becher's and thought "Bloody hell, there's not many left". Then you concentrate, over Valentine's, turning into the home straight and you've almost done a circuit and you're beginning to think about how well you're going and getting a position.

'I got to the Chair and there were two bollards in front of it. I thought "We haven't jumped the Chair so there can't be anybody lying on the other side of it; there can't be anything wrong". Mine knocked the bollards out of the way, still jumped the Chair, and when I landed on the other side I saw everybody flagging us down.

'Those jockeys that went out on the second circuit...I'm sure they knew!'

Just four days later, on Wednesday, 7 April 1993, he surprised the racing world by announcing his retirement. He journeyed to Ascot for his final three rides and, fittingly, won on the last of them, Sweet Duke, trained by his good friend Nigel Twiston-Davies, in the Alpine Meadow Handicap Hurdle.

Had the void Grand National influenced his decision to retire so soon after the debacle?

'Not really,' he answers. 'I was 34 years of age and I thought it was time. It's a young man's game and I just felt I'd had enough. I didn't fancy going round the small meetings on the hard ground any more. Whereas a Flat jockey can pick and choose their rides to an extent, as a jump jockey I didn't feel that was what it was about.'

He joined forces with Twiston-Davies and shared the joy of turning out two Grand National winners, Earth Summit in 1998 and Bindaree in 2002.

Nowadays Scu resides in Scotland. He is still involved with training racehorses, but this time with his partner Lucinda Russell.

He doesn't miss riding races that much. 'Sometimes I look back at my autobiography and I think "I wish I could still go out and do it," and then I see somebody turn over at the last and I thank God I got out in one piece.'

Date: Saturday 30 March 1985 Going: Good to soft Value to Winner: £54,314

Horse	Owner	Trainer	Age / weight	Jockey	SP
1 Last Suspect	Anne, Duchess of Westminster	Capt T A Forster	11-10-5	H Davies	50-1
2 Mr Snugfit	Mr A Greenwood	M W Easterby	8-10-0	P Tuck	12-1
3 Corbiere	Mr B R H Burrough	Mrs J Pitman	10-11-10	P Scudamore	16-1
4 Greasepaint	Mr M J Smurfit	D K Weld	10-10-13	T Carmody	13-2fav

Distances: 1½ lengths, 3 lengths, 7 lengths. Time: 9 mins 42.7 secs. 40 ran

Winner trained at Letcombe Bassett, Oxfordshire

1986

CHRIS GRANT

It's Kelso on Monday

Durham Edition and Chris Grant just fail to peg back Mr Frisk in 1990.

HE NEVER CARED much for the nickname 'Rambo', coined by fellow jockey Steve Smith Eccles. Even so, Chris Grant was regarded as the iron man among his weighing room colleagues.

Widely acknowledged as one of the best of all time on the northern racing scene, he met with triumph and disaster and treated, in the words of Kipling, 'those two impostors just the same'. Renowned for his strength in the saddle during his twenty-year riding career, his style was that of a natural horseman, no frills and no nonsense.

So here's a no nonsense synopsis: Born 'just outside Catterick village' on 14 October 1956, the son of a farm worker. Left school at fifteen and joined Bishop Auckland trainer Denys Smith. First ride on Tanora, over hurdles at Catterick, 11 January 1974, finished fifth. Waited over three years for first winner, Trim Lawns at Hexham, 4 June 1977.

Rode 788 winners, including the Scottish National, Melling Chase, Charlie Hall Chase, two Greenall Whitley Chases and the Supreme Novices' Hurdle. Second in Cheltenham Gold Cup and in three Grand Nationals. Retired 1994, aged 37.

He was always going to be too heavy to ride on the Flat. For a time it looked like he'd be too heavy for jumps as well.

'I had a few rides; never really took off,' he says. 'I was struggling with my weight, thinking about getting out of the game. I was twenty-two and I'd had three winners in four years, about a dozen rides a year. Then one day Denys said I could ride a horse called Laen in a lads' race at Cartmel. It won, then it won again, and then I rode it a third time and it won again. I thought I'd give it one last try and ended up riding seven winners that season from about sixty rides. The next year I finished second in the conditional jockeys' title and by the end of that season I could control my weight.'

He had his first Grand National ride for Denys Smith in 1980 on Flashy Boy. Says Chris: 'He'd been a good horse in his younger days but had a reputation for making mistakes. Denys got him in his later life and I won three races on him. I was a claimer at the time and with the horse having the reputation he had, it did me a lot of good. In the National he fell at the Canal Turn, second circuit. To be fair, looking back, I should have pulled him up. He was a tired horse and it was a tired fall, but I was young and keen, it was my first ride and I was trying to get him round.

'Then I rode The Vintner [in 1981] who refused. My next National ride was on Midnight Love for Denys in 1984. He was a horse with a lot of ability but he was very straight-backed, didn't bend his back legs very well, and Becher's caught him out. He just landed too steep, crumpled up and that was it.'

In 1985 Chris completed the course for the first time, finishing last of the eleven finishers on 100-1 outsider Captain Parkhill for owner-trainer Brian McLean.

He had a lot of outside rides and rode regularly for John Wilson, who was based at Ayr. Chris won Cheltenham's Waterford Crystal Supreme Novices' Hurdle for him on Harry Hastings in 1985.

Among the other inmates in Wilson's Cree Lodge yard around that time was one named Young Driver. He'd won two novice hurdles for Wilson back in the 1981/82 season, then joined Mick O'Toole in Ireland, for whom he finished third in the Ritz Club Chase at the Cheltenham Festival. The horse had suffered from leg and back problems prior to returning to Wilson for the 1985/86 campaign. He ran six times that season without winning before lining up as a 66-1 outsider for the Grand National, with Chris in the saddle.

Says Chris: 'Young Driver had an engine, always had a lot of ability, although he hadn't the best of legs. I went out to hunt the first circuit then get into the race second circuit.

'When we came back across the Melling Road for the last time, I'm in front upsides Steve Smith Eccles on Classified. Ecc's shouting to me, "Go steady. Wait until after the last." As soon as he said that, I knew he was struggling to get home. I also knew my fellow would stay and when Smith Eccles was telling me to hang on until we got over the last, I thought he was wanting to turn it into a sprint. So I've kicked my fellow in the belly and tried to make it a bit more of a staying job.

'However, what I was really doing was giving West Tip a lead, because [Richard] Dunwoody was sat behind the pair of us getting a tow. I heard West Tip coming from the second last and thought of poor old Phil Tuck [on Mr Snugfit] the year before.'

Although Young Driver still led over the last, Dunwoody brought West Tip to challenge nearing the Elbow. Young Driver had nothing left and West Tip stayed on to win by two lengths. Classified battled on for third place, with the previous year's runner-up Mr Snugfit finishing fourth.

In March 1987 Chris came in for a spare ride on Peter Easterby's Cybrandian in the Cheltenham Gold Cup, finishing second to The Thinker, the mount of Ridley Lamb. It was the year of the snowstorm, which delayed the start of the race by 80 minutes. The snow-softened going just suited The Thinker, who outstayed Cybrandian up the hill. The Thinker's trainer, Arthur 'W.A.' Stephenson, had adopted his traditional 'little fish are sweet' policy and preferred to saddle runners at Hexham.

A fortnight after the Gold Cup, Chris rode Stephenson's horse Fortina's Express to finish second to Strath Leader in the Whitbread (Topham) Trophy over the big fences on Liverpool's opening day. Two days later he had his first Grand National ride for Stephenson, completing the course 19th of the 22 finishers on Why Forget. By the start of the next season, Chris was at Crawleas Stable, three miles down the road from Denys Smith's yard, installed as Stephenson's stable jockey.

'Denys Smith and "W.A" were neighbours and big buddies,' says Chris. 'I'd been riding the odd one or two for Arthur for a year or so when [stable jockey] Ridley Lamb couldn't do the weight. Then when Ridley retired, my name got mentioned. Arthur didn't want to fall out with Denys and neither did I because he'd been so good to me. I told Denys that I'd got the chance to go to Arthur's as stable jockey, that he'd got a lot of horses and it was an opportunity I couldn't really refuse. He was very good about it and I always rode for Denys second after Arthur.

'Denys has always been like a second father to me. If I wanted advice over anything I would always ask him. We've always had a great relationship.'

In 1988 Chris rode Stephenson's Durham Edition in the Grand National for the first time. Approaching the penultimate fence, the race lay between four horses, Durham Edition, Rhyme 'N' Reason, Monanore and West Tip. Rhyme 'N' Reason met the fence wrong and, with Monanore and West Tip merely slogging on at one pace, Durham Edition looked to have the race in safe keeping jumping the last.

But Chris's worst fears that he had hit the front too early were realised as, halfway up the run-in, Durham Edition's stamina began to run out. Rhyme 'N' Reason, despite drifting to the right, responded to Brendan Powell's urgings and got up in the last 100 yards to win going away by four lengths and deprive Chris of what had appeared certain victory.

He told reporters afterwards: 'I flew the second last and landed in front sooner than I wanted. I thought I had the race won at the last, and when I got to the Elbow I thought it would help me, but I could see Rhyme 'N' Reason coming again out of the corner of my eye. He didn't do anything wrong but the other horse wore me down.'

Now he reflects: 'Two out, Rhyme 'N' Reason was wandering about all over, so I took it up. I did him a favour basically, because it rejuvenated him and he came back and beat me. Looking back, I should have waited longer.

'The next year I rode him in the National [1989] it was wet. We had two horses in the race, The Thinker and Durham Edition. I had the choice of the two and had to make my decision a bit before the race. I couldn't really leave Durham Edition after the way he ran the year before. As soon as I'd made my decision, the heavens opened. Of course, that suited The Thinker [on whom Simon Sherwood took the ride]. He finished third in the race and I was fifth. My fellow ran a blinder on ground that was too soft for him.

'The next time, in 1990, it was fast ground, which suited Durham Edition. I decided to wait and wait. Mr Frisk was always up there disputing the lead all the way. I had him in my sights and got a tow right to the last, jumped the last and asked him to go on.'

It looked like the Grand National glory that had so far eluded Grant and Stephenson was about to be theirs. But although Durham Edition got to within half a length of Mr Frisk, he could find no more and was still three-quarters adrift at the line.

'I got to his girths but I just couldn't get past him. If I was ever going to win it, that was the year. I felt I did everything right but he just wasn't good enough to get past Mr Frisk. He was one of those horses that carried you, and then when you asked him to quicken there was nothing left, he fizzled out.'

He told reporters: 'He didn't quite get home. It's a sickener to have come so close twice now but equally it's nice to finish second. You cannot dwell on it,' he concluded typically. 'It's Kelso on Monday.'

Reflects Chris: 'That's the way I was. The first two times I was second in the National it was a great buzz. By the third time I'm thinking it's never going to happen. If it was going to happen, it would have happened that day in 1990. I just thought, "Crack on; let's go for the next winner".'

There were plenty of other horses to be cracking on with during that 89/90 season, which turned out to be his best numerically with 94 winners. They included a pair of potential stars in Southern Minstrel and Blazing Walker. Southern Minstrel landed Haydock's Timeform Chase, Ayr's Edinburgh Woollen Mills Future Champions Chase, and was a half-length runner-up to Waterloo Boy in the Arkle Chase. Blazing Walker won five novice chases, then the following season won six races in a row, including the H&T Walker Gold Cup at Ascot and culminating in a ten-length demolition of Katabatic, Waterloo Boy and company in the 1991 Melling Chase at Aintree.

'When he was on song, Blazing Walker was something special,' says Chris. 'The day he won the Melling Chase he was probably the best I'd ever sat on.'

Blazing Walker missed the whole of the next season due to injury and ran only twice the following season, while Southern Minstrel was also injured and, though he did race again, never recovered sufficiently to realise his full potential. The details of their respective injuries remain a mystery to Chris to this day.

'When you worked for Arthur you tended not to get to know too much,' he laughs. 'Arthur wouldn't have you riding out. You went to the races and rode the horses, simple as that. I had to twist his arm to let me ride out, and when I did ride out I didn't ride proper work. He'd put me on a "breaker" or something like that.

'In the summer I used to try and ride out to get fit for the start of the season, but Arthur would say, "Ee, man, you'll be alright; do a bit of runnin' or summat." So I never got to the bottom of what exactly was the problem with Southern Minstrel or Blazing Walker. I wouldn't be able to tell you anything about the injuries of any of the horses in that yard because he kept it all to himself.'

Chris won the Scottish National in 1991 on Stephenson's Killone Abbey, but his ill luck at Aintree continued, particularly in the Topham Trophy. He just failed to make it back from injury in time to ride Villierstown when he won the race in 1989, with Simon Sherwood deputising. Twelve months later, Chris rode Villierstown but finished second. He was then second twice more, beaten a neck both times, in 1992 on Captain Mor and 1993 on Southern Minstrel. He was also second on Southern Minstrel in the 1993 Becher Chase.

Altogether, he finished second eight times in races over the Grand National fences without winning one. Nonetheless, Aintree apart, he and 'W.A.' formed a successful trainer-jockey partnership, lasting six years.

Arthur Stephenson died in December 1992, aged 72. It was the conclusion to a tragic year which had also claimed the life of Chris's first wife, Dawn, after a five-year battle with cancer.

Life went on and the training operation continued. 'Arthur's son, John, didn't really want to take the whole job on himself, so Peter Cheesbrough, who'd been Arthur's assistant, came in and they did it together. Things carried on but on a lot smaller basis because there wasn't the number of horses there.'

Chris stayed on as stable jockey until the end of that 1992/93 season. He retired on a winning note after riding Micky Hammond's Capital Punishment to victory at Perth on 21 April 1994.

'It was never the plan to go training,' he insists. 'I never fancied it, to be honest with you. I got out of racing for a year and it absolutely did my head in, I was missing it so much. I was going round selling food supplements but what I ended up doing was going to a yard where I knew I'd get a ride out or where I'd school something, just to be involved.

'My wife, Sue, rode point-to-pointers. We started getting a few more in so I started training a few pointers with her. Then we took it one step further.'

Chris is now a successful licensed trainer with his stables at Wolviston, near Billingham, and is looking for a horse that will take him somewhere that he didn't quite get – the Aintree winner's enclosure. Sure, he's trained winners at Liverpool but he's yet to win a race over the big fences.

'That's the goal,' he says, 'one day to win a Grand National.'

Date: Saturday 5 April 1986 Going: Good to soft Value to Winner: £57,254.50

Horse	Owner	Trainer	Age / weight	Jockey	SP
1 West Tip	Mr P Luff	M Oliver	9-10-11	R Dunwoody	15-2
2 Young Driver	Mr J B Russell	J S Wilson	9-10-0	C Grant	66-1
3 Classified	Cheveley Park Stud	N Henderson	10-10-3	S Smith Eccles	22-1
4 Mr Snugfit	Mr T P Ramsden	M W Easterby	9-10-7	P Tuck	13-2fav

Distances: 2 lengths, 20 lengths, ½ length. Time: 9 mins 33.0 secs. 40 ran

Winner trained at Droitwich, Worcestershire

1987

CHARLIE MANN
From Becher's to Pardubickás

Charlie Mann aboard Its A Snip at Pardubice.

AT 93, TIME was running out for Jim Joel. Twenty years earlier he had watched his colt Royal Palace win the Epsom Derby, yet his attempts to join that select band who had owned both a Derby and a Grand National winner had foundered on Aintree's turf.

Glorious Twelfth had gone closest, fourth to Sundew in 1957, but none of his subsequent runners had survived the first circuit. On the face of it, there seemed no reason why Maori Venture should fare any better. If the Grand National was run at Lingfield (where he'd won four times), the experts reckoned, he'd have some sort of chance, but surely the 11-year-old's erratic jumping would be found out at Aintree?

As is often the case, the so-called experts were proved wrong, for Maori Venture flew those fences as though they were hurdles, making not the semblance of a mistake and galloping home five lengths clear of his nearest rival, The Tsarevich. The following day, Joel announced Maori Venture's immediate retirement and that it was his intention to leave the horse to winning jockey Steve Knight.

The experts didn't think that 500-1 shot Lucky Rew would get far either. This time they were right – he parted company with his rider at the very first fence. For Charlie Mann it was the quickest end to his four Grand National attempts, all of which had been on horses starting at 100-1 or more.

Dumfries-born Charlie had been raised among horses. 'Father rode in a couple of point-to-points; mother was a show jumper. I was brought up on ponies. We'd win a class and they'd be sold on. Always rode, all my life. In fact, from the age of seven all I wanted to be was a jump jockey.

'I left school when I was fifteen, far too early, went to Newmarket and worked as an apprentice for Peter Poston for £6 a week, and loved it. I had my first ride for Bill Clay and then joined Tony Gillam at Boroughbridge in Yorkshire. I rode my first winner for him, La Valse at Southwell in November 1977.'

A move south to Nicky Henderson's yard in 1979 was Charlie's introduction to Lambourn. He's been there ever since.

'I always wanted to ride in the National,' he says. 'My first time was on a horse called Tenecoon [in 1981], owned and trained by Fred Smith, a greengrocer from Swindon, a lovely old fellow. I think I got as far as the second ditch.'

His second Grand National mount came two years later on Mrs Mita Easton's Williamson. Prominent early, they survived a bad blunder at Becher's before going their separate ways at the Chair.

In 1986 came the most memorable of his four rides, though it is surprising that he remembers it at all. On the morning of the race, Charlie met up with the sporting amateur Gavin Wragg who, for all his enthusiasm, was hardly the most stylish of riders. Wragg had achieved his aim of completing the course, albeit in arrears, on Abervanter in the Fox Hunters' the previous day and was in celebratory mood. Charlie was due to partner the 500-1 no-hoper Doubleua-gain for Clive Holmes.

He recalls: 'Gavin and I got so drunk at the Adelphi Hotel on the morning of the National that we couldn't find the racecourse. I was as pissed as a newt when I rode Doubleuagain but, with some of the horses I rode, you had to be fairly well cut to ride them.'

It was the first time he'd ridden Doubleuagain, yet he refused to let his astro-nomical odds spoil the fun. Jumping boldly, they led or disputed the lead with 200-1 chance Tacroy throughout the first circuit. The free-running Czechoslo-vakian raider, Essex, went with them for the first mile before fading, a broken stirrup leather eventually causing rider Vaclav Chaloupka to pull him up before the Chair. Meanwhile, Doubleuagain led Tacroy over the water and out into the country.

'The only reason I made the running,' insists Charlie, 'was that I was lined up near to the Czech horse who was going berserk at the start and I wanted to get in front of him before the first fence. I was having a lovely ride and then I got knocked over by a loose horse at the first fence on the second circuit when still in front.'

The riderless horse swung in from the left and cannoned into Doubleuagain, just as he was about to take off. Despite being stopped in his tracks, Doubleua-gain cleared the jump but had no chance of standing up. A frustrated Charlie hurled his whip to the ground.

That same obstacle claimed his fourth and final Grand National ride twelve months later, as Lucky Rew, another 500-1 shot, blundered badly and unseated him at the first. At least Charlie saw the funny side of it this time: 'I'd been offered £400 to ride the horse and I hadn't had the money. I wouldn't give the trainer the saddle until I'd been paid. It was getting quite late and we were still fighting over the saddle. Eventually, he produced £360 in cash; I said "Fine" and gave him the saddle.

'I got onto this horse and he was tiny. I took him to look at the first fence and he was actually looking up at it, he was so small. In the race, when he got to the first he used it as a springboard. I got up laughing my head off.'

He hitched a lift back to the stands courtesy of fellow 500-1 outsider, La Bambino, whom Chris Warren had pulled up at the same fence on the second circuit. Another 500-1 shot, the Czech raider Valencio, made it to Valentine's second time round before coming to grief.

On a Saturday evening in May 1988, Charlie suffered a broken neck when his mount, Lightning Wind, was brought down two out in a steeplechase at Warwick.

'It was a clean break, a C2, at the top. I was in a frame for three months and was told that I had to have a year off. When I went to get my licence a year later, they wouldn't give it to me. I'd expected to get it back and I was devastated because I didn't know, or want to do, anything else. I didn't have a clue what to do.'

Maybe it was the participation of the Czech horses in those two Grand Nationals that sowed the first seeds of interest in that country's equivalent, the Velká Pardubická. The iron curtain had been partly raised in the late 1980s with democratic reforms being introduced in the Soviet Union. Czechoslovakia itself demanded change and free elections were held in 1990. It was during these turbulent times that Charlie first went to see the race, accompanied by his Aintree drinking companion, Gavin Wragg.

He recalls: 'I looked at the race and thought then that it wouldn't take a lot of winning with the right horse. So I endeavoured to find one.'

Irreconcilable differences between the Czechs and the Slovaks led to the division of the country and, on New Year's Day 1993, the Czech Republic gained independence. It was in August of that year that Charlie Mann made his own bid for independence by taking out his first trainer's licence. His Upper Lambourn yard housed a dozen horses of varying abilities, though within a year the size of the string had doubled. Among the newcomers, one possessed the necessary credentials for a trip to Eastern Europe.

Charlie takes up the story: 'There was a horse going through Doncaster Sales called Its A Snip, trained by Ted Walsh. He'd bits of form but he'd got round in the La Touche over the Punchestown banks. I got him for 4,000 guineas. He was as slow as a wet weekend but he always got round. He managed to win a couple of chases for us.

'We hadn't had "Snippy" very long when I first rode him in the Pardubická in 1994. He just got beat, finished second. I really did think he'd be a certainty the next year.'

Before that second attempt came an ambitious tilt at the 1995 Grand National, in which he was partnered by John Kavanagh. It was ambitious in that the horse was rated only 86 and was a full four stone out of the handicap.

'He shouldn't have been in the Grand National,' Charlie acknowledges. 'He wasn't anywhere near good enough to run in it but we did it just for a day out for the syndicate who owned him. He was a very slow horse and probably didn't see which way they went. At the twelfth fence a horse fell in front of him, he side-stepped the horse but, unfortunately, the jockey went out the side door.'

There were no such reservations about returning to the Pardubická. A prep race at Newton Abbot a fortnight earlier, with Richard Dunwoody on board, had put him spot on. The plan was that Its A Snip would be Charlie's final ride before hanging up his boots for good. The only fly in the ointment was obtaining a licence to ride him.

'I couldn't get a licence anywhere. I tried in places like Tobago, the United States, anywhere basically. I ended up getting one from Tanzania, or Tasmania, or somewhere like that. It was just a piece of paper and it enabled me to ride.

'I got fined £1,000 by the Jockey Club because I tried to get an Arab horse racing jockey's licence. There was one question on the form that asked if I'd ever been turned down for a licence before. I answered "No" when I should have said "Yes".'

With a jockey's licence having finally been obtained – from whatever dubious source – Charlie was reunited with Its A Snip for the 1995 Velká Pardubická and scored a famous victory. In front at half-way, Its A Snip lost ground soon after but regained the lead before the last fence and (to quote *Chaseform*) 'held on well to give his trainer-jockey Charlie Mann a glorious end to his riding career.'

It was the second British-trained winner of the gruelling four mile two-and-a-half furlong cross-country steeplechase in recent times, following the success of Chris Collins on Stephen's Society in 1973.

Six days later, General Rusty gave Charlie his first big training success on home soil, cruising home under Richard Dunwoody in the Charisma Records Gold Cup at Kempton. The training bandwagon was starting to roll.

An hour or so before Rough Quest landed the 1996 Grand National, Its A Snip won for the final time, a long-distance handicap chase at Hereford. He returned to the Czech Republic that autumn and finished third in the Velká Pardubická, ridden this time by Dunwoody. On his next start he was pulled up lame in the inaugural running of Cheltenham's Sporting Index Cross Country Chase and was promptly retired.

It wasn't the end of Charlie Mann's involvement with the Velká Pardubická, or indeed with the Grand National. But that's for another chapter. His successful, if occasionally controversial, training operation has proved more lucrative – and somewhat less painful – than his riding career, which yielded 149 winners among the broken bones, aches and pains.

'I was a journeyman jockey,' he reflects. 'I'd get 200 to 300 rides a year but, to be quite honest, I used to ride a lot of rubbish.'

When asked which gave him the greater excitement, jumping Becher's Brook or negotiating the Pardubická's fearsome Taxis fence, he replies: 'Oh the Taxis, by far. With "Snippy" you knew you were on a good jumper, whereas the only mounts I got in the Grand National were the ones no-one else would ride!'

Date: Saturday 4 April 1987 Going: Good Value to Winner: £64,710

Horse	Owner	Trainer	Age / weight	Jockey	SP
1 Maori Venture	Mr H J Joel	A Turnell	11-10-13	S C Knight	28-1
2 The Tsarevich	Major I C Straker	N Henderson	11-10-5	J White	20-1
3 Lean Ar Aghaidh	Mrs W Tulloch	S Mellor	10-10-0	G Landau	14-1
4 West Tip	Mr P Luff	M Oliver	10-11-7	R Dunwoody	5-1fav

Distances: 5 lengths, 4 lengths, 4 lengths. Time: 9 mins 19.3 secs. 40 ran

Winner trained at East Hendred, Oxfordshire

1988

CLIVE COX

It was like a bad dream

Clive Cox canters to post on Sacred Path.

RHYME 'N' REASON, picked up off the floor by Brendan Powell after losing his legs on landing at Becher's first time round, staged one of the most remarkable recoveries in Grand National history.

Left in front when Little Polveir unseated Tom Morgan five fences from home, Rhyme 'N' Reason was headed two out by Durham Edition but fought back from five lengths down on the run-in to regain the lead and pull clear to win the 1988 National by four lengths.

Rhyme 'N' Reason's owner, Juliet Reed, told the press afterwards that he had been a birthday present five years earlier from John Moreton, her partner in the Woodhaven Stud, near Newbury. It was only the previous summer that the horse had joined David Elsworth from David Murray Smith, for whom he had won the 1985 Irish Grand National but subsequently lost his form. The change of yard obviously worked wonders, as this was his fifth success of the season.

For Miss Reed, Elsworth and Powell this was a day they would always remember. For Clive Cox, rider of the favourite, Sacred Path, it was one he wanted to forget.

Clive was born in Bristol into a farming family, who duly moved south to a farm near Bridgwater. He began his racing career on the Flat with Peter Cundell.

'My grandfather was the main reason behind it,' he explains. 'He was a garage owner in Bristol and had horses in training shortly after the war with Ken Cundell, Peter's father. That was where the connection and introduction came from, but as a youngster we had ponies and show jumpers at home, plus the odd point-to-pointer.

'When I left school I was just under seven stone, so that directed me into a Flat yard. Nature took its course and I started to gain weight, but I was lucky enough to ride a couple of winners on the Flat. The first one was at Doncaster, the very last race of the 1981 season, the Last Post Handicap on Swift Palm. I beat John Lowe a short head in a driving finish.

'My other winner was at Bath for Ken Cundell. He owned the filly and my grandfather was there to see it, which meant a lot to me.

'When I got heavy I moved down to the West Country and joined Stuart Pattemore, who had twenty to twenty-five horses at the time, but good quality horses. My first ride for him, a horse called Akram, won a handicap hurdle at Exeter. My first ride over fences was also a winner, when I rode a double at Wincanton [on Easter Monday 1984].

'At the time, John Francome was riding a lot for Stuart. I knew John from my days with Peter Cundell, because he used to ride Celtic Ryde for him. It was through John, and Oliver Sherwood's head lad, Chris Clarke, that I ended up going to Oliver's. That was where Sacred Path came into it.'

Owned by Christopher and Maggie Heath, Sacred Path had previously been trained by James Bethell. Clive won on him the first time he rode him in a race, at Warwick on 29 November 1984.

He recalls: 'It was my first ride for Oliver and obviously, I was trying for my life. I jumped the second last hurdle about three lengths clear, picked my stick up and gave him a smack – and dropped my stick. It was probably the best thing that could have happened because he resented too much stick and he carried on and won. After that I was second on him at Nottingham, Newbury and Sandown.

'He went novice chasing the next season. Oliver's brother, Simon, had just turned pro and was riding as first jockey, so he rode him in his first novice chase at Worcester. He unshipped Simon at the second fence, so I got the leg up next time at Nottingham and finished third, just getting beaten for second by Cross Master. Cross Master went on to win the Sun Alliance Chase, so it was a serious run by Sacred Path. Things moved on from there and he became a very good friend.'

Clive won on him at Lingfield, Southwell and Cheltenham that season, and finished third in the following year's Mildmay-Cazalet Chase, but the horse was then sidelined for over a year with a tendon injury. He returned in a blaze of glory on 8 March 1988, winning Warwick's Crudwell Cup with Clive on board, firing them both straight into the Grand National picture.

Was he afraid that he might lose the ride to a bigger-name jockey?

'I think you're always aware of that possibility,' he responds openly, 'especially as a second jockey; you become hardened to it, but it had been reported that I would keep the ride in the National. Also, he only had ten stone, which was a good point in my favour.

'On our way up to Aintree on the Friday night it absolutely poured down. Sacred Path was a renowned mud-lark and handled the soft ground very well, so it was logical that people were looking to him to find the key to the race.'

As the rain continued to fall, so did Sacred Path's odds. After opening at 14-1, a huge public gamble on the day saw his price drop to 17-2. Clive Cox, having his first ride over the course, was on the favourite. And he didn't even know it!

'I knew we were fancied but I didn't realise until afterwards the strength of support. It didn't affect anything in any way, shape or form.

'I was at the course early, rode the horse out on the morning. Everything was pretty tense. Sadly, the build-up lasted a lot longer than the race for me.

'We had a false start; we got to the first fence and then turned round and went back.

'Sacred Path was a beautiful jumper and one of those horses that had the gift of putting himself right at a fence. He met the first on a perfect stride, and he took off, and kept going up. He overjumped and we were past the point of no return in the air, just through jumping it too well. There was no going back.

'It was like a bad dream. You just wanted to wake up and start all over again because the build-up to the whole thing had been so positive. The horse's preparation for the race had been absolutely perfect. Oliver had done a wonderful job with him and, just knowing the horse as I did, I knew he was on song for the day. I watched him go round and jump, riderless, and once he'd sussed out the situation with the drop fences, he was poetry.'

That first fence exit wasn't the only cloud to darken his day.

'While my wife, Tina, who was my fiancée then, was watching the race, somebody bumped into her and said "Mind your bag, love." It wasn't until afterwards that she realised she'd had the contents of her bag stolen during the race. It wasn't a good day.

'The sad thing in all of it was that the horse bit his tongue quite badly when his head went back underneath him at the first. It was just the very tip of his tongue but it bled a lot and, a couple of days afterwards, he did actually lose a bit of his tongue.

'The National took a toll on him and he never won afterwards. Mentally, the fall played a part, undoubtedly. He never had the same zest in his performances.'

Sacred Path ran six races over the next two seasons, pulling up in four of them, before being retired.

'Christopher and Maggie very kindly gave him to me when I retired from riding. He enjoyed many days' hunting and, in his later years, he was a companion for some very high-class yearlings at a stud in Marlborough. He had a good life there and that's where he was buried when he died in 2001. I was pleased to be able to repay his helpfulness to my career.

'Through Oliver being Fred Winter's son-in-law, I was extremely grateful and proud to have ridden winners on the likes of Admiral's Cup for Fred. He was an icon and racing hero way above any, so for me to have been involved in a small way but in a very appreciated way with that team was very lucky.

'I rode a lot of talented horses for Oliver and for Fred Winter, including Plundering, The West Awake and Rebel Song, as well as Sacred Path. I knew what it felt like to be involved with good horses and every year there was a youngster or two coming through the ranks.'

Even so, his riding career ended not long after Sacred Path's.

'I rode just short of a hundred winners, my best year being in 85/86 with thirty-three. I think I realised I'd peaked and, after riding those good horses, I was concentrating on the next step. With regard to injuries, I'd had five or six different wedge fractures – vertebrae, ribs, wrists, collarbones. There's virtually nothing above the waist that escaped.

'Tina and I had a livery yard in Lambourn, where we did a lot of breaking and dealing with young horses that were going into training. That was giving me an income, whereas going to Plumpton to ride something in a novice chase for somebody I didn't ride for much, didn't stack up as being as important as keeping the business going, and that's why I retired when I did.

'We set up training, initially near Wootton Bassett with a business partner, but we agreed to disagree about things, so it only lasted a year. I took the horses with me when I joined Mikie Heaton-Ellis as his assistant at Barbury Castle.'

'Mikie was a great person and a great tutor of life itself. I was privileged to have known him closely. He had very strong morals and views. Hopefully, some of those have rubbed off.'

When Mikie died in 1999, one of the yard's main owners moved his horses elsewhere, ruling out any hope of Clive taking over at Barbury Castle. However, in a triangular game of musical yards, Alan King switched from Jackdaws Castle to Barbury Castle, while Richard Phillips vacated his Beechdown Farm premises in Lambourn to become the new incumbent at Jackdaws Castle, thus facilitating Clive to take over at Beechdown Farm, where his landlord is John Francome.

Says Clive: 'John has always been an absolute star. He's very helpful, full of fun; a first-class man.'

The training has gone from strength to strength. New Seeker put him on the map with victories in the 2003 Britannia Stakes and the Tote International Handicap from opposite sides of the Ascot turf. Since then it's been an upward curve to success at Group race level.

'It's funny how, even after training a Royal Ascot winner, the first thing that sprang to Jonathan Powell's mind when he interviewed me on television after the Tote International was about Sacred Path's first fence fall in the National fifteen years earlier. People remember you for it.

'Thankfully,' he reflects, 'enough time has passed now that I can laugh about it. But at the time, it was all that mattered.'

Date: Saturday 9 April 1988 Going: Good to soft Value to Winner: £68,740.50

Horse	Owner	Trainer	Age / weight	Jockey	SP
1 Rhyme 'N' Reason	Miss Juliet Reed	D Elsworth	9-11-0	B Powell	10-1
2 Durham Edition	Mr Robert Oxley	W A Stephenson	10-10-9	C Grant	20-1
3 Monanore	Full Circle Thoroughbreds	W Harney	11-10-4	T J Taaffe	33-1
4 West Tip	Mr P Luff	M Oliver	11-11-7	R Dunwoody	11-1

Distances: 4 lengths, 15 lengths, 8 lengths. Time: 9 mins 53.5 secs. 40 ran

Winner trained at Whitsbury, Hampshire

1989

RAY GOLDSTEIN
All he can do is fall

Ray Goldstein – King of Plumpton and rider of Hettinger.

'MY DAD USED to like having a bet on the horses and watching it on television,' recounts Ray Goldstein. 'I was thirteen years old; never seen a live horse in my life, but I said to my dad, "I want to be a jockey when I grow up."

'It looked easy, loads of money, loads of glory. Wrong, wrong, wrong!'

Born on the first day of June 1952, Ray lived in Tottenham with his four siblings and parents until he was four, when his mother died of cancer.

'We were put in a children's home for six years until my sister was old enough to look after us,' he says. 'My dad was a working man so he couldn't look after five kids.

'I used to sit next to a fellow at school, two Tottenham wallahs, and we both wanted to be jockeys. I wrote sixty letters to different trainers all over the country. I got four replies and I got a week's trial during the Easter Holiday with Peter Cazalet.

'It was an absolute disaster. I couldn't ride but I rode a pony called Rhapsody with a big string of horses and, of course, he ran away with me. By the time he stopped I looked round for the others and I could see all the horses in the distance walking round Cazalet on a big stretch of grass as he told the riders what to do. I went straight through the middle of them!

'He said I wasn't suitable, which was fine. The feeling was mutual.

'Then me and my mate booked some riding lessons after school at Oakwood, near Cockfosters, on the Piccadilly Line. Eventually he got a job with Alec Kilpatrick. He wrote back saying the stable needed another apprentice and to apply for the job. That was in '67; I stayed there for four years. That was the first in a string of mistakes.

'It was a 100 per cent jumping yard so we never rode fast work. The first time I came off the bridle was when I jumped the last fence alongside Richard Dennard on my second ever ride, my first over fences. I finished third. I should have gone to a mixed yard but I had no racing ties or contacts. I had five rides, four over fences, for him when I was eighteen. I used to look after an old horse called Stickler, a Fontwell specialist. He was my favourite horse.

'From there I went to Mick Masson at Lewes. I was there three years. That was my second mistake. He had a mixed yard, only twenty-odd horses. He had some good two-year-olds and about six of them won, so he knocked a lot of the jumpers out and trained mainly Flat horses.

'Then I went to David Morley at Bury St Edmunds. I was there another three years. Another mistake. When I went there, there were four lads but he didn't really use them. I did the best but it was nowhere near good enough, just five or eight rides a season.'

His first winner was Turk at Southwell on 17 February 1977 for Grimsby permit holder Louis Furman, who had ridden his own horse Binghamstown in the 1950 and 1951 Grand Nationals. By that time Ray was twenty-four.

'I came back to Lewes and joined Giles Beeson. I rode four winners for him that season. Then the Jockey Club decided that once you were over twenty-five you couldn't claim any more. It seemed that every time I got going, something would slap me down again. Then they brought it back so you could claim 4lb. I was with Giles for four years.'

Besides riding for Beeson, he also rode for other local trainers such as Gardie Grissell and John Ffitch-Heyes. Throughout the 1980s he earned the accolade of King of Plumpton. He was leading jockey there for years and roughly one-third of his near 200 career victories were achieved around that tight Sussex circuit.

He made a cracking start to 1989 with a treble at Windsor's New Year meeting. That same month he won a brace of two-and-half-mile chases on the Ffitch-Heyes-trained Hettinger.

Hettinger had won a Plumpton novice chase the previous season, ridden by the trainer's daughter Penny, but had fallen or unseated on his next four starts. Ray had then taken over at Lingfield and won easily.

'He was a fair sort of animal but he used to make the odd bad mistake. In general, if he had plenty of time and you put a fence in front of him, he'd go straight ahead and jump it. But racing was different. It was mainly towards the end of a race, so whether he was under pressure and couldn't sort himself out, or whether the noise from the stands put him off, I don't know. I was placed on him round Cheltenham and Newbury, but then he'd go to Folkestone and turn arse over tip.'

An ambitious attempt on the 1988 Grand National, when ridden by Penny Ffitch-Heyes, had ended at the first fence. Surprisingly, despite being two stone out of the handicap and owning a record of nine fell or unseated riders in twenty chases, he would take his place in the 1989 line-up. And nobody was more surprised than his jockey.

'I didn't even know the horse was running. He'd run at Plumpton over Easter, which was before the National that year. John had said that that was his last race of the season and finished him off. I think him and the owner must have had a boozy weekend because they decided to run him. On the Sunday morning, six days before the race, Sue brought me the papers in bed. The National runners were on the back page and I saw I was jocked up for Hettinger. I got up and went straight to the toilet!

'Then I thought "All he can do is fall", and I'd fallen loads of times before. The only difference was that this time you knew he probably would fall, whereas in other races you didn't think he was going to fall until he actually did. I was getting towards the twilight of my career and I knew I wouldn't get another ride in the National.

'Because it was Hettinger, all that week the press phoned me every day. I had one prat from the *Sport* who was trying to put words in my mouth. He asked "Do you think Hettinger's the unluckiest horse around because he's fallen a lot?" I said "No, he's won races." He said "You've broken a lot of bones; do you think you're the unluckiest jockey?" I said "No, don't you write that."

'Then he rang back and asked if I'd pose in my shorts if he sent a photographer round. I said "I want some money for this" so we agreed on eighty quid. I got the *Sport* when it came out and there was a picture of me falling off and the headline "Unluckiest jockey rides the unluckiest horse." The bastard!

'The owner of Hettinger had paid for me, Sue and the kids to stay at the Adelphi for two nights, which was fantastic. We had a great night on the Friday, sobered up on the Saturday morning and walked the course. It was fate that I only got as far as Becher's then ran out of time, so we turned round and came back.

'All the jockeys asked me where I was going to line up. I said "I'm going up the middle," so everyone moved away to the left or to the right. Mark Richards gave me some good advice. He told me to get my position then as soon as I hit the Melling Road, to pull back, get back off your hocks and pop it, rather than galloping and jumping on your forehand.

'He flew the first and jumped the first five brilliantly. I was thoroughly enjoying myself. We came out to jump the part of Becher's that wasn't so steep and the horse on my outside overdid the coming back in and knocked me over in mid air, and I'm pitching on my way down before I'm over the fence. It was such a shame in that, yes, he did fall but it wasn't his fault.'

Hettinger was one of half a dozen fallers at Becher's, including the favourite Dixton House. Sadly, two of those falls proved fatal. Seeandem broke his neck and was killed instantly while Brown Trix broke a shoulder and was subsequently put down in the racecourse stables.

Little Polveir, running in his fourth Grand National and partnered by Devon cattle farmer Jimmy Frost, having his first ride in the race, took up the running jumping the water and was never headed thereafter, winning by seven lengths from the 1986 victor, West Tip, with 1987 Cheltenham Gold Cup winner The Thinker a close-up third.

A 28-1 shot, Little Polveir was named after a salmon pool on a stretch of the River Dee, and was a second Grand National winner for his trainer Toby Balding.

Recalls Ray: 'I was knocked out by the fall and came round in Walton Hospital. I'd had a whack on the head and felt sore all over but I thought "I don't want to spend the night in hospital," so we concocted a story that I could remember everything that had happened. So they sent us home and said I wasn't to have any alcohol.

'When I got back to the hotel room I ordered two large gin and tonics for Sue and three orange juices for me and the kids, but the waiter arrived with a bottle of champagne from the owner. Half an hour later we were on the dance floor giving it some!

'I was off for three weeks – compulsory when you're knocked out – and I missed winners, but I wouldn't have given that weekend up for anything.'

Known as the 'iron man' for his ability to bounce back from injury, his catalogue of broken bones included a left leg, right arm, vertebrae, ribs, left collarbone four times, right collarbone twice, plus a punctured lung and a fractured skull. But there was to be no coming back from the Market Rasen fall that shattered his right thigh in March 1991.

The last day of February had seen him partner Gardie Grissell's Dalrymple to victory at Lingfield. Two days later he journeyed to Lincolnshire to ride Adbury in a hurdle race for Roger Curtis.

'The fall itself was fine but then another horse came along, tripped over mine and landed on top of me.

'The whole of my body hurt. When they put me on the stretcher my leg flopped over the side. I picked it up and put it back on. I knew then that it was my last ride. I was thirty-eight and you don't come back at thirty-eight. The press kept going on about it and for the next eighteen months I said I'd be back, but I knew I wouldn't.'

Fortunately, he had something to fall back on. For the previous ten years Ray and Sue had been renting a riding school on the outskirts of Lewes. Sue, a qualified instructor, ran it while Ray was riding races. Backed by loans from the Injured Jockeys Fund and owner Jack Joseph, Ray and Sue bought the riding school premises and built it up to where they had seventeen boxes.

'Breaking my leg was the best thing that could have happened,' he reflects. 'It stopped me going on too long. I was enjoying the riding but hating the driving and the politics and I was beginning to think I'd had enough. But what was I going to do? I'd left school at fifteen, wasn't very good with my hands and, having been a freelance jockey, I didn't want to go back into stables and do horses for somebody.

'I was a late starter. I rode my first winner when I was twenty-four, my second when I was twenty-five. I was still doing well; my last three seasons were my best. I knew it was going to finish soon and I didn't want to go on to where people stopped using me because I was getting old, or that I started to lose my bottle and faded out, but I would have found it difficult to say "That's it, I'm finished." Breaking my leg stopped it.'

Sons Jamie and Marc were both riding almost before they could walk and have followed their father's footsteps into the weighing room.

Jamie achieved his biggest success aboard Nigel Twiston-Davies's King's Road in the 2000 Hennessy Cognac Gold Cup, but was deprived by a broken leg from riding Bindaree when that horse galloped home in the 2002 Grand National. He is now a vital cog in Sheena West's training operation at Lewes and forged a successful partnership with hurdler Golan Way.

Date: Saturday 8 April 1989 Going: Heavy Value to Winner: £66,840

Horse	Owner	Trainer	Age / weight	Jockey	SP
1 Little Polveir	Mr Edward Harvey	G Balding	12-10-0	J Frost	28-1
2 West Tip	Mr Peter Luff	M Oliver	12-10-11	R Dunwoody	12-1
3 The Thinker	T P M McDonagh Ltd	W A Stephenson	11-11-10	S Sherwood	10-1
4 Lastofthebrownies	Mrs A M Daly	M F Morris	9-10-0	T Carmody	16-1

Distances: 7 lengths, ½ length, 6 lengths. Time: 10 mins 6.8 secs. 40 ran

Winner trained at Weyhill, Andover, Hampshire

1990

KENNY JOHNSON
Piller's pair

Kenny Johnson, stalwart of the northern weighing room.

BISHOP AUCKLAND TRAINER Arthur (WA) Stephenson celebrated his seventieth birthday by saddling three runners in the 1990 Grand National. Stable jockey Chris Grant stuck with the well fancied Durham Edition, who had finished second to Rhyme 'N' Reason in 1988 and fifth the following year. The other pair, Sir Jest and Nautical Joke, were both 66-1 outsiders owned by Stephenson's main patron, Peter Piller.

Piller's silks of 'yellow, royal blue stripe, armlets and cap' were among the best known in National Hunt racing at the time. His first colours were carried by Sir Jest, the mount of Brian Storey, while the distinguishing white cap was worn by Stephenson's 21-year-old amateur Kenny Johnson, who took the ride on Nautical Joke.

Kenny is the son of Bob Johnson, a wholesale butcher by trade, who trains a string of jumpers at Newburn, on the outskirts of Newcastle-upon-Tyne. Johnson senior had graduated from training 'flappers' and point-to-pointers before setting up under Rules. His son Peter rode winners for Stephenson as an amateur in the mid-1980s and it was through regular drives over to the yard to pick up his elder brother that Kenny's face gradually became known at Crawleas.

He recalls: 'I was nineteen when I joined Mr Stephenson as a working lad. Nautical Joke was one of the first horses I was given to look after. He was awful to begin with, a nightmare. He couldn't jump, kept falling. He had real problems with his nerves, didn't trust anybody. I remember the first day I sat on him down in the front field. He was bucking and kicking all over the place. He used to pull so hard I had to stand up in my irons to stop him.

'Eventually, we just clicked and you didn't even need to put a head collar on him. You'd turn him out in a field and when you called him, he'd come over to you and follow you back to the yard. He trusted me and he'd do anything for me. He was almost human.

'I got my first chance on him in a three-mile handicap chase at Market Rasen towards the end of the 1988/89 season. John Edwards had a good horse in the race but Arthur Stephenson gave me fantastic orders. He told me not to let the favourite get away from me and, if I was still there turning down the back, to take it up. This worked a treat, as it upset the other horse. I kicked clear and we won by a distance. Then we won again at Market Rasen the following week.'

In October 1989, Kenny won the John Eustace Smith Trophy at Newcastle on Nautical Joke before Chris Grant took over to land Newcastle's Peaty Sandy Chase and finish third at Haydock.

'He got a slight touch of a leg after the Haydock race,' continues Kenny, 'so the idea was to rest him and give the Grand National a miss. It wasn't until three or four weeks before the race that the boss gave me an indication that he might run. You couldn't put a lot of fast work into him so it was lots of steady work and I still didn't know for certain if he was going to run.

'About a week before the race "WA" told me to jump one of the yard's hunters over some big post and rails for a potential owner. He kept making me do it, back and forth, back and forth. There was a drop on the landing side and I think this was his way of building me up for the National, to get me used to those type of fences. I've never leaned back so far in my life, not even in the National itself.

'It was after he'd sold the hunter that he told me he'd run Nautical Joke in the National. That was at the five-day stage.'

'He ran a great race. We were behind early but when we jumped Becher's second time, I was about tenth or eleventh and still in with a little bit of hope of getting sixth place. But from the Canal Turn onwards I could feel him weakening on me. He had every right to weaken because he hadn't had a great build up to the race.

'By four out, the last ditch, he was getting weaker and I was trying to hold on to him just to get home. On the first circuit the horses had taken the brush off the fence and left the stakes exposed. My horse caught sight of that and went to jump what was the smallest part of the fence. When he tried to push through the stakes he got dragged back, which stopped him but the momentum carried me on. I almost got back but he ran off and left me lying on the ground.

'I remember to this day, I lost my stick in the fall and, while I was looking for it, a bunch of kids grabbed it and ran off. It was lucky I had hold of my cap and breeches!'

Belying his 66-1 starting price, Sir Jest was bang there in second place at the Canal Turn second time but weakened from three out to finish ninth.

Stephenson's third runner, Durham Edition, once more came close to victory, with Mr Frisk beating him by just three-quarters of a length.

Owned by 82-year-old American Mrs Lois Duffey, Mr Frisk had been left in an eight lengths lead by the departure of American challenger Uncle Merlin at Becher's second time round. Thereafter he was never headed, although the lead had been cut to six lengths by Durham Edition at the second last. By the last fence only two lengths separated them. By the Elbow, Durham Edition was within three-quarters of a length but that was as close as it got.

Given a fine ride by the amateur Marcus Armytage, Mr Frisk was in his element on the fastest ground Aintree had seen in years. The state of the going was reflected by the time of the race, 8 minutes 47.8 seconds, slashing an incredible 14.1 seconds off Red Rum's time in that never-to-be-forgotten 1973 duel with Crisp.

It was a bitter pill for Stephenson and stable jockey Grant, for they had now finished second in three of the last five Grand Nationals.

Kenny was the leading amateur rider in 1990/91 with 24 wins and turned professional the following season.

Whereas the rigours of a gruelling Grand National experience often leave their mark, this was not the case with Nautical Joke, who proved to be the very model of consistency. In the 1991/92 season, Kenny won on him six times, the last of these being, appropriately at Market Rasen, where their racecourse partnership had begun. This was Nautical Joke's final start, for he was by then thirteen and his connections wisely retired him on a winning note.

Kenny's next Grand National ride was Stay On Tracks in the void 1993 running. Despite finishing ninth the previous year, he was giving him a disappointing ride when his race was brought to a halt at halfway.

He had to wait until 2002 for his next opportunity, on Norman Mason's Red Ark, but he failed to get beyond the first fence. By the following year, Richard Guest had taken over the licence and Kenny once again had the leg up on Red Ark. This time he lasted far longer, racing in midfield for the first circuit but losing ground steadily from halfway. He was well in arrears when Kenny pulled him up at Valentine's second time round.

Kenny's career has been one of ups and downs. Bob Johnson had his most successful training season in 2003/04 and his stable jockey son likewise enjoyed a good campaign with 15 winners. But the following season was barely a month old when he sustained multiple injuries in an horrific fall from Red Perk at Uttoxeter, breaking five ribs, his right shoulder, and also puncturing a lung. Remarkably, he was back riding races only four months later.

He was out of action for 16 months between the summer of 2009 and the autumn of 2010 recovering from complicated shoulder surgery, the result of three falls in quick succession that left him with no power in his left arm and

which looked to have ended his career. His comeback winner, on 25-1 shot
Lindseyfield Lodge at Kelso on 16 October 2010, was greeted with cheers all
round from racegoers and fellow jockeys.

'This is fantastic – a great day,' Kenny told the *Racing Post*'s Tom O'Ryan
amid much back-slapping and congratulations. It was certainly better than
another occasion at Kelso years earlier when he was thrown in the paddock
prior to a schooling session, which resulted in a snapped peg at the back of his
neck, necessitating a bone graft to strengthen it.

It was back in August 1988 that Kenny Johnson rode his first winner, on Duke
Of Dollis at Cartmel. More than twenty years later the popular 42-year-old is
now the senior member of the northern weighing room. It's been a long career
during which he has typified the journeyman jockey who forms the backbone
of National Hunt racing, yet time has not diminished his love of the game.

Date: Saturday 7 April 1990 Going: Firm Value to Winner: £70,870.60

Horse	Owner	Trainer	Age / weight	Jockey	SP
1 Mr Frisk	Mrs Harry J Duffey	K C Bailey	11-10-6	Mr M Armytage	16-1
2 Durham Edition	Mr Robert Oxley	W A Stephenson	12-10-9	C Grant	9-1
3 Rinus	Mr A M Proos	G W Richards	9-10-4	N Doughty	13-1
4 Brown Windsor	Mr W Shand Kydd	N Henderson	8-10-10	J White	7-1fav

Distances: ¾ length, 20 lengths, 12 lengths. Time: 8 mins 47.8 secs. 38 ran

Winner trained at Upper Lambourn, Berkshire

1991

DAI TEGG

Fate rules us, not Wisdom

Dai Tegg, jockey turned pub landlord.

'I HOPE YOU'RE not squeamish,' the ward sister warns.

Les Hurley, racecourse photographer, reckons he isn't, but what he sees on that hospital bed still shocks him. For there among the tubes and the wires lies the remains of a jockey; the barely recognisable shadow of a man.

Wasn't this the same body that less than a week before was scrubbing horses round Worcester and Chepstow? That not twelve months ago had completed the course in the Grand National? . . .

Dai Tegg sits in the beer garden of The Horseshoe, one sunny afternoon in high summer 2002. The pub, located on the main street in the Herefordshire market town of Ledbury, is bursting at the seams.

Ledbury was the birthplace of Poet Laureate John Masefield, whose works include 'Cargos' and 'Sea Fever' as well as the great racing poem 'Right Royal', from which this book takes its title. But it is World Cup fever that has gripped the Horseshoe customers, for England have just trounced Denmark 3-0 in a second round match and an exuberant crowd revels in the glory.

Dai's taken a half-hour out from running the bar to recall the highs and lows of his riding career. There were plenty of both along the way.

'I came from a horsey but not a racing family; pony club and show jumping mostly,' says the lad from Porthcawl. 'I was riding flapping races when I was eleven. Four times round for a mile at one track. Scary that was!

'I started with Derek Haydn Jones at Pontypridd. I had my first ride for Bryn Palling, a horse called Carreg-Wennol on the Flat at Warwick in 1984. I got down from nine stone to 7st 6lb to ride at 7st 13lb. Bryn already had one conditional, Colin Evans, and a professional, Tony Griffiths, who were good jumping lads, so the opportunities were never going to be there for me.'

He joined Chepstow-based Milton Bradley and it was for him that he recorded his first winner, 33-1 shot Seasoned Embers at Devon and Exeter on 26 May 1986. He rode out his claim in a season and a half. By then he was second jockey (to Tom Morgan) at John Edwards's 80-horse stable at Ross-on-Wye. Number two at one of the top yards in the country was a good job to have.

In 1989 he had his first ride in the Grand National, 300-1 outsider Rausal for Herefordshire trainer Tom Bailey. This was a horse that needed extreme distances. Dai had already won on him twice that season, a Haydock four-miler and a three-and-a-half-mile slog round Bangor-on-Dee.

'God, he was hard work,' he grimaces. 'You couldn't hit him with the stick, you had to keep driving him from the word go. In the National he didn't do a tap. He went the same gallop all the way, then at the third last a loose horse came across him and I ended up on the other side of the fence. I jumped back on and he wouldn't have blown a candle out. Hywel Davies, who'd fallen on the first circuit, asked me for a lift and jumped on the back. Rausal cantered back with his ears pricked.'

By the spring of 1991 Norman Williamson was John Edwards's first jockey with Dai remaining as number two. They both had rides in that year's Grand National, Norman on Yahoo, Dai on the 100-1 outsider Forest Ranger. Though behind from halfway, Dai did at least have the satisfaction of finishing in front of his better-fancied stable companion as they trailed in fifteenth and sixteenth respectively.

Meanwhile, at the business end, Cheltenham Gold Cup winner Garrison Savannah and Mark Pitman jumped the last fence six lengths clear and with no sign of stopping, the race apparently within their grasp. They looked sure to emulate Golden Miller and Gerry Wilson by winning the Gold Cup and the National in the same year.

But jockey Nigel Hawke's adage that 'you never give up on Seagram' rang true, for approaching the Elbow he was getting noticeably closer. Suddenly, Garrison Savannah's stride was shortening. It was not until the last hundred yards that Seagram hit the front but that was enough for him to surge away and win by five lengths. Poor Mark Pitman experienced the same fate as his father Richard, who had seen victory snatched from his grasp when Red Rum got up close home to beat Crisp eighteen years earlier.

The mare Auntie Dot was a gallant third, with Over The Road a distant fourth, ahead of Bonanza Boy and Durham Edition. Seventeen runners completed the course.

A fortnight before that year's Grand National, Dai had won Newbury's Hoechst Panacur Novices' Hurdle Final on Richard Price's five-year-old mare Flakey Dove. A product of the Price family's famous 'Dove' line, stretching back a quarter of a century to the prolific Red Dove, 'Flakey' looked to have a bright future.

With Dai as her regular partner, she developed into a model of consistency the following season, winning three of her first five races and finishing second in the others.

At Aintree on Grand National day 1992 they landed the opening race, the Cordon Bleu Handicap Hurdle. Says Dai: 'Going to the last I had to take a pull on her because I didn't want to hit the front too soon. We've pinged the last and hit the front just after. I didn't have to get serious with her at all, just one flick.

'When I walked into the paddock to ride Forest Ranger in the Grand National, I was feeling ten feet tall. I'd decided the only way to ride him was down the paint [on the inside rail]. I bounced out of the gate and I was always there.

'As we've gone down to Becher's Brook first time, Richard Dunwoody was to my right on Brown Windsor. His horse decided he didn't want to jump Becher's and tried to run out to the left. I could see him coming across, he was out of control. Richard called out "Teggy" and I had to go long, at Becher's, down the inside. I thought to myself "This is not the place to be." We met in the air and the two of us lost our footing. Richard fell and I stayed up, but if old "Ranger" hadn't come up long for me, it would have been carnage, because Brown Windsor was going out, no doubt about it.

'Forest Ranger was a horse that was always on his fore. He wasn't the easiest sort but I had a great ride off him that year. He got tired and made a bad mistake at the fourth last. That was my fault. I've gone to the fence and they're all coming around me. I saw a long one but he didn't pick up and hit it hard. If he'd come up, he'd have been back in the race. Apart from that he jumped like a stag.'

Forest Ranger kept on to finish twelfth of the twenty-two finishers, while the gigantic Party Politics strode ahead of Romany King to give Carl Llewellyn his first Grand National victory.

Dai looked forward with eager anticipation to the 1992/93 campaign, in particular to renewing his partnership with Flakey Dove. She made a belated start to the season but made up for lost time with three races within eighteen days in February, culminating in victory at Warwick. Despite being beaten at Newbury next time out, the plan was to run her in the Champion Hurdle ten days later.

With eighteen winners thus far, he needed just half a dozen more to beat his seasonal best and there was almost three months left in which to do it. Everything was going well, apart from the occasional spills.

He reflects: 'I'd had a few bad falls in the weeks before. I got regular nosebleeds. One night I bled from the nose, both barrels, for about an hour.

'I drove back from Nottingham one day. Norman Williamson was with me. I never spoke a word to him all the way home. I just wasn't there, I was somewhere in cuckoo land. Norman thought he'd upset me. When we got to the Traveller's Rest in Ross, he opened the car door and said "See you, Teggy", and I said "Yeah, see you, mate". Then he looked at me and said "Teggy, I've just travelled two hours with you and you never said a word to me. You're not right. Go and see a doctor."

'Of course, I didn't.

'A few days later I had a fall at Chepstow and then drove on to Stratford for a ride in the last. My nose started bleeding again at Stratford. I washed my face and saw blood coming out of my ears. Like a prat I just wiped it away and pretended it didn't exist. Totally stupid.'

Soon after came the brain haemorrhage. On a Sunday afternoon, two days before Cheltenham; without warning, total paralysis.

'I was just lying there, couldn't move at all. I could hear what my wife was saying. She had my head in her lap and she was crying. I remember feeling her tears on my face as she cried "Wake up, Dave, wake up."

'By the time the ambulance arrived, the top half had come back to life. I crawled off the bed, got myself to the top of the stairs and let myself roll down. I had to get out of there, it was so hot and I was sweating terrible. I sat by the front door, looking at the floor and saying over and over "I'm going nowhere, I'm going nowhere."

'They put me in the ambulance and off we went. The ambulance man put all these machines on me – they all started going ballistic. He shouts to the driver, "John, go!" Then all the sirens came on and I was promptly sick all over him.

'Two or three weeks after the haemorrhage came the blood clot. They had to go into my brain twice – "flip top", taking the top of my head off to operate.

'It was a new operation. There were two choices. They said that if they performed one operation I'd have a 60-40 chance of not surviving but, if I did survive, I'd be a cabbage. If they performed the other one, I'd have a 70-30 chance of not surviving but, if I did, I'd be okay. My wife and my mother decided to go for the second one. Thank God they made the right decision.

'I remember when I first came round and I wanted to go for a pee. The nurse said "You haven't got to, David, it'll be extracted through the tubes."

'I do remember dying once. My nephew, Craig, was talking to me, holding my hand and chatting away. I remember waking up, looking at him and whispering "Craig, help", then the doctors and nurses came piling in.

'They turned the machines off in the end, because my body was giving up. They needed to see if it would work on its own.

'I was in hospital for three and a half months and my weight went down to five stone. Tubes and wires up every orifice. I jumped on the scales the day I left hospital and I was 6st 2lb. That was three weeks after I came round and I was eating proper food. When I got home I was so weak I couldn't get up the stairs.

'My wife and I split up. I think the pressure got to her and she left just after I came out of hospital. I became a recluse for a while. Imagine waking up one morning, looking in the mirror – you're ugly, your face is a mess, no hair; your wife's just left you. It isn't good, is it?

'Richard Price was a great friend to me, asking me to school horses for him. He didn't really need me but he knew it would get me out of the house.'

During this time there was one crucial spur to keep him going, the peg on which he hung all hope. Price had promised that the ride on Flakey Dove was still his when he came back. She had finished only seventh in the 1993 Champion Hurdle but by the spring of 1994 had developed into a live contender, having won the Haydock Park Champion Hurdle Trial, Cheltenham's Cleeve Hurdle, and Newbury's Berkshire Hurdle, all in the hands of Richard Dunwoody.

'I met a girl named Lee who was a darling to me,' he continues. 'I used to go for runs to try and get fit. Some days I'd go a mile or two miles, no problem at all; other days I'd run forty yards and end up in a hedge. She'd follow me in her car and pick me up. When I told her I was going to try and get my licence back, she begged me not to do it because she'd seen me in all sorts of states.

'Eventually, I went to London to apply for my licence. I went in and saw the doctor, who told me I couldn't ride again. I said "I had no chance from the beginning did I?" He said "No, you didn't."

'I'd had that hope to hang on to. It was all I had. All I had in the world. And he said I couldn't do it.

'I cried. It broke my heart.

'I'd being doing so well. I was just a lad from the valleys of Wales; had nothing all my life. I was just going to have something and I'd worked hard for it. I was that close to getting it. Then it was gone, and … '

The voice trails away. There is silence. It is a full drawn-out minute before conversation resumes.

'It's hard to wake up to that. I still struggle with it now. It was something I was good at. I wasn't the best jockey in the world but I certainly wasn't the worst.'

Flakey Dove won the 1994 Champion Hurdle, ridden by Mark Dwyer.

At the start of 1998, with the help of the Injured Jockeys Fund, Dai and his new wife, Karen, took ownership of the tenancy of The Horseshoe. A painting hung on the wall of the bar, of Flakey Dove and Dai Tegg jumping the last in the 1992 Cordon Bleu Hurdle at Aintree.

Around the edge of the painting were the signatures of Dai's weighing room colleagues – Richard Dunwoody, Peter Scudamore, Carl Llewellyn, Graham Bradley and many more. And there, in the bottom right-hand corner, was the inscription 'Best wishes, Richard Davis'.

In July 1996, Richard Davis died following a fall at Southwell.

'I miss that boy so much … he was a really good friend.'

Again, a pause, and then a whisper: 'That could have been me. I nearly died but I didn't. Obviously it wasn't my time.'

It's called Fate. Masefield told us that.

My vision was Wisdom, or the World as it is,
Fate rules us, not Wisdom, whose ways are not his,
Fate, weaponed with all things, has willed that I fall;
So be it, Fate orders, and we go to the wall.

Date: Saturday 6 April 1991 Going: Good to soft Value to Winner: £90,970.00

Horse	Owner	Trainer	Age / weight	Jockey	SP
1 Seagram	Sir Eric Parker	D Barons	11-10-6	N Hawke	12-1
2 Garrison Savannah	Autofour Engineering	Mrs J Pitman	8-11-1	M Pitman	7-1
3 Auntie Dot	Mrs R Wilson	J Webber	10-10-4	M Dwyer	50-1
4 Over The Road	Mr J R Upson	Owner	10-10-0	R Supple	50-1

Distances: 5 lengths, 8 lengths, 25 lengths. Time: 9 mins 29.9 secs. 40 ran

Winner trained at Kingsbridge, South Devon

1992

BILLY WORTHINGTON
Unsung hero

Billy Worthington, Michael Chapman's long-time stable jockey.

MICHAEL CHAPMAN'S STABLES are situated just 400 yards from Market Rasen's back straight, but the road from Lincolnshire to Berkshire became a regular route when Ascot, in a bid to attract bigger fields, instigated a scheme rewarding trainers with the most runners there. Chapman was among the first to take advantage and came away with bonuses for himself, his owners and the stable staff.

Non Vintage, who won Ascot's Ladbroke Trial Hurdle in November 1995, earned Chapman and his long-standing stable jockey Billy Worthington an all-expenses paid trip to Ireland for the Ladbroke itself. The heavy going at Leopardstown was all against Non Vintage and he did well to finish mid-field but all the connections thoroughly enjoyed themselves. The horse elevated Chapman and Worthington into the big time during that 1995/96 season, finishing third in Newcastle's 'Fighting Fifth', Newbury's Tote Gold Trophy and Cheltenham's County Hurdle, earning upwards of £20,000 in place money alone.

Billy Worthington was born in Coventry in December 1960 and took part in gymkhanas and show jumping as a lad. On leaving school he signed up as an apprentice with John Hill at Barnstaple and had his first ride in public, carrying 6st 10lb, in a selling race at Kempton.

Pat Buckley, rider of 1963 Grand National winner Ayala, was Hill's assistant trainer at the time, but moved to join Nick Vigors at Lambourn. He encouraged

Billy to do likewise and it was there that things started to happen. His first ride for Vigors was also his first winner, Piercing Note at Pontefract on 19 April 1978.

Increasing weight meant that Billy's career on the Flat was destined to be a brief one. 'I was struggling to do 8st 6lb and I used to have to go days without eating even to do that. Eventually, Mr Vigors told me I was wasting my time stopping with him because the only rides I could have would be those carrying nine stone or over, and I'd stand more chance over jumps. So he had a word with Nicky Henderson, who was willing to take me on with a licence to ride over hurdles.'

He was with Henderson for two seasons, then accepted an offer to ride as first jockey for Lord Leigh, who was a permit holder at the time but planned to take out a full licence to train 25 horses. Unfortunately, just two months later, Leigh decided to give up training altogether.

After that, Billy spent three years with Ken Bridgwater at Knowle and then freelanced. It was while riding at Catterick one day in February 1990 that he first made Michael Chapman's acquaintance.

'It was a chance meeting,' Billy recalls. 'He had a horse in the novice chase called Tadbir. It was his first run over fences. The lad who was due to ride had a fall in an earlier race and Mr Chapman went round the weighing room asking different jockeys but nobody would ride it. Eventually he asked me and I agreed. We got round safely and after that I started riding for him regularly.'

Around that time, Chapman bought a horse called Why So Hasty at Doncaster sales, complete with a 1990 Grand National entry. He was all set to give Billy his first Grand National ride when he got cast in his box the night before the race, banged a joint and had to be withdrawn

Two years later, Why So Hasty was finally able to take his chance, running in the pink and white colours of his new owners, Black Horse Racing. As a forlorn 250-1 outsider running from 23lb out of the handicap, he was dismissed by Spotlight of the *Racing Post* simply as 'No-hoper'. However, it still rankles with Billy that the horse's participation was so roundly condemned by people who were not in possession of the facts.

He explains: 'As we were on the way out from the paddock, one of the police horses shied and knocked him into the rope for holding back the people. My horse got tangled up in the rope and became worked up and I had to jump off him. A chap in the crowd had to cut the rope to set the horse free. Up until then he'd been quiet and placid but, as a result of that experience, he sweated up.

'As I came out on the course for the parade, they were saying "This sort of horse gives the race a bad name; he shouldn't be here". But they hadn't seen what had happened and the horse undeservedly got some bad publicity.

'My orders were to get up there, on the inner, have him handy and enjoy myself. I certainly did that. I couldn't have wished for a better ride; he never touched a twig. I was always in the first half-dozen throughout the first circuit, yet he was never mentioned in the commentary. You can see him in almost every shot, with his big white boots on, but not once did the horse get a mention.

'He gave me a fantastic ride round on the inside. Even coming to Becher's I was enjoying myself so much I hadn't noticed it was Becher's. He never even pecked on landing. Unfortunately, he burst a blood vessel jumping the Canal Turn second time round, so I had to pull him up after Valentine's.'

At that point the giant Party Politics, standing over 17 hands high, had just taken the lead off Romany King, with Docklands Express and Stay On Tracks close up. This quartet crossed the Melling Road clear of the weakening Cool Ground. But Stay On Tracks was beaten turning for home and Docklands Express could find no more from the second last fence.

Party Politics, ridden by Carl Llewellyn, jumped the last with an advantage of three or four lengths, and though Romany King whittled away some of that on the run-in, Party Politics held on to score by two-and-a-half lengths. Laura's Beau plugged on to be third, 15 lengths farther away, landing a hefty each-way bet for his owner JP McManus.

The winner had been bought for £80,000 by Cheveley Park Stud's David Thompson, who then gave him to his wife, Patricia, as a present. He also ended a winnerless drought of more than three months for trainer Nick Gaselee.

'To be honest,' says Billy of Why So Hasty, 'he ran better than I thought he would for a long way. It would have been nice to get round. It would have been nice for me and for the horse because he'd had some bad write-ups, saying that horses like him shouldn't be in the National. But he outjumped a lot of horses that day. As you can imagine, the video has been played so often, it's nearly worn away.'

Just three days after experiencing one of the rides of his career, another nearly ended it. Billy was leading the field at Southwell when his mount Dry Gin fell heavily at the third last fence. Rarely can so many body parts have simultaneously been mangled.

'I broke seven ribs, punctured a lung, punctured my spleen, broke my pelvis in three places, broke vertebrae in my neck, dislocated one shoulder and broke the other one. I was in hospital for two months, then I went on holiday to the Grand Canarias for a fortnight to help recuperate. I started doing a bit of running up the mountains.

'I didn't know until afterwards that my wife had been told that, with the pelvis dislodged and broken in three places, I'd never be able to run or ride again. They said that I'd never get the full use back in my arm. Yet three months later I was riding again.'

He rode Why So Hasty four times the following season, finishing third in the Stan Mellor Cup at Nottingham and an unlucky half-length second at Market Rasen. But it was the trainer's amateur rider son, Mark Chapman, who rode Why So Hasty in what was to be his last appearance, at Nottingham on 2 February 1993, as Billy was riding Dry Gin in the same race. The pair finished within a length of each other, though well behind the leaders. Both horses were later given away to local people to spend their retirements as hacks.

In National Hunt racing, few trainer-jockey partnerships endured as long as that of Chapman and Worthington. Billy became leading jockey at Market Rasen and had more rides there than any other. Horses such as course specialists Ei Ei and Cromwell ensured that the wheels kept turning at their home track, while their Bank Holiday forays to Cartmel rarely saw them leaving Cumbria empty handed.

During the 2000/01 campaign Billy notched a personal best eighteen winners, then rode seventeen the following season. After years of failing to reach double figures, things were finally beginning to pick up. Very few jump jockeys were still riding at forty-one. Fewer still rode against their son, as Billy did against young William one day in April 2002 at Market Rasen.

Later that year the Chapman-Worthington combo made their traditional August Bank Holiday trip to Cartmel, being rewarded with their customary winner in novice hurdler Alvaro. It was to be Billy's last.

Five days later, on the final day of August 2002, at his favourite Market Rasen, he suffered a broken neck when fired head first into the ground by a horse named Terdad. He broke the same vertebrae as Superman actor Christopher Reeve. Luckily, the two halves of the damaged vertebrae moved outwards rather than inwards. Had they gone in, it could have meant paralysis from the neck down, or even death.

The initial diagnosis was that he could expect to make a full recovery. He spent three months in a moulded neck brace but the fractures failed to heal properly. Still in great pain but with the help of the Injured Jockeys Fund, he underwent reconstructive surgery at London's Wellington Hospital. The operation, though successful, could not bring back full movement in his neck. Finally, in September 2003, thirteen months after the fall, his neurosurgeon gave him the news he had feared. His 24-year career in the saddle was over.

While accepting that he was fortunate to emerge from his injuries in one piece, Billy was naturally disappointed. 'Things were going well. I was as fit as I'd ever been and had a lot more knowledge than I'd had ten years before.'

At least he still has the memory of that 1992 Grand National and the day he proved the so-called experts wrong on Why So Hasty, the horse they said shouldn't have been in the race.

Date: Saturday 4 April 1992 Going: Good to soft Value to Winner: £99,943.20

Horse	Owner	Trainer	Age / weight	Jockey	SP
1 Party Politics	Mrs D Thompson	N Gaselee	8-10-7	C Llewellyn	14-1
2 Romany King	Mr L J Garrett	G Balding	8-10-3	Richard Guest	16-1
3 Laura's Beau	Mr J P McManus	F Berry	8-10-0	C O'Dwyer	12-1
4 Docklands Express	Mr R H Baines	K C Bailey	9-10-4	P Scudamore	15-2fav

Distances: 2½ lengths, 15 lengths, 8 lengths. Time: 9 mins 6.3 secs. 40 ran

Winner trained at Upper Lambourn, Berkshire

1993

SEAMUS O'NEILL and ANDY ORKNEY
Hurling a brick through your shop window

The grey Howe Street and Sure Metal head out onto the second circuit.

'LAUGHING STOCK OF the world,' roared the headline of Monday's *Sporting Life*. 'National humiliation,' screamed the *Daily Telegraph*. 'World looks on as race is turned into a farce'.

A plethora of similar headlines abounded as Aintree came to terms with the aftermath of a Grand National declared void in farcical circumstances, following a second false start of which three-quarters of the jockeys were oblivious. All the papers were full of it, with 'Shambles', 'Fiasco', 'Blundering officials' and 'Bungling incompetence' being the most commonly-used words or phrases.

As with Devon Loch and Dick Francis 37 years earlier, the names of Esha Ness and John White would forever be remembered for not winning the Grand National.

How could it have happened? Confusion reigned over whom to blame as the media, racing's professionals and racegoers alike all sought a convenient scapegoat. Was it the starter, Keith Brown, or the race recall official, Ken Evans? Was it the jockeys themselves, many of whom had their horses' heads over the starting tape? Was it an indirect result of the delay caused by having to remove protesters from the course?

Journalist and Grand National-winning amateur rider Marcus Armytage, writing in Monday's *Telegraph*, gave a jockey's view of the circumstances that led up to the greatest non-event in the race's history. His mount, Travel Over, had the starting tape knotted round his legs when the second false start occurred.

Without apportioning blame, Armytage cited 'a combination of factors', such as the hanging around through having been down at the start eight minutes early, the further delay with the protesters, an antiquated starting mechanism, and a strong and bitter east wind which, coupled with the roar of the crowd positioned behind the starter's rostrum, blew Brown's instructions away from the jockeys and prevented him being heard when the tapes went up.

All were contributory factors, no doubt, in a shambolic episode that saw 30 of the 39 jockeys, unaware of the confusion going on behind them, steer their mounts over the Melling Road to the first fence and beyond.

Throughout the first circuit the lead alternated between Ginger McCain's 50-1 shot Sure Metal, ridden by Seamus O'Neill, and the grey 66-1 outsider Howe Street, the mount of Andy Orkney. Among the most experienced riders in the race, Seamus was having his last Grand National ride in this, his final season. As for Andy, he'd finished seventh on Old Applejack the year before and was participating for the third time.

Surprisingly for someone born at the Curragh, Seamus O'Neill had no family connection with racing, his father having served as a soldier for 27 years. But growing up in the heart of Ireland's training quarters, an interest quickly developed. He served a five-year apprenticeship with Mick Rogers and had 'about a dozen' rides for him on the Flat.

He rode his first winner on 7 July 1975 aboard Yellow Sam in a novice riders' handicap hurdle at Wexford. Two weeks earlier, that horse had been the subject of an audacious betting coup pulled off by Barney Curley in a hurdle race at Bellewstown, a sting so meticulously planned that it made headlines throughout the racing world.

Shortly after that first success, Seamus came to Britain and joined Tarporley trainer Ray Peacock. He eventually went freelance and remained so throughout his career, his biggest successes coming in the 1984 Sun Alliance Novices' Hurdle on Fealty, and Newcastle's 'Fighting Fifth' on Tom Sharp in 1986.

He had his first Grand National mount in 1988 on Michael Chapman's Preben Fur, who gave him 'a good, safe ride for a circuit' before pulling up at Becher's second time. Two years later he partnered Mick's Star for Jenny Pitman, completing the course nineteenth of the twenty finishers.

His third Grand National ride came in 1991 on New Halen, who had pulled off a 66-1 shock victory for trainer Paul James in the previous year's Mildmay of Flete at Cheltenham.

Says Seamus: 'He got rid of me at the fence after Becher's second time. He stumbled badly at Becher's and a great big piece of fern got stuck in his girth. Then at the next fence he just seemed to drop his hind legs and I've gone out the side door. It wasn't a pretty picture on TV because it was head on and it looked as though I fell off him.'

His final Grand National mount was to be Sure Metal in 1993. Graham McCourt had ridden the horse all season but was scheduled to partner Roc De Prince for Martin Pipe, so Seamus was happy to accept when McCain asked him if he'd like the ride.

It's not much fun riding down to Becher's with no stirrups – 'and with a voice that rose an octave at every fence after that', as Iain Mackenzie so memorably wrote of that 1985 Fox Hunters' Chase.

'It was very unlucky,' recalls Andy Orkney of that ride on Golden Ty. 'I finished second but I was no help to him without stirrups. My iron broke jumping the fence before Becher's. It's the last fence in the world you want to see coming up without pedals.

'Golden Ty was probably the best horse I ever rode. He was my first "proper" winner under Rules and I went on to finish second [to Run and Skip] on him in the Welsh Grand National.'

That initial victory had come in a Nottingham hunter chase in February 1985, just days after his first 'winner', Joca, at Ayr, had been disqualified after failing a dope test.

Later that same year Andy found himself in the jungles of Peru. It was a far cry from the streets of Sheffield, the city of his birth, or tranquil Bedford, where he had spent most of his childhood. Further still from the pleasant academia of university life, studying to be an optician.

'I went to Peru primarily as a venturer through Operation Raleigh,' he explains. 'I was there for three months helping to build a bridge in the jungle. I wasn't recruited for my professional skills as an optician but I bumped into a missionary who had a suitcase full of spectacles. I took them off his hands and was able to distribute them to the natives.'

He joined the ranks of professional jockeys in 1987 but combined his riding career with running an optician's practice at Leyburn, close to the Yorkshire training centre of Middleham. Nor were his foreign adventures curtailed. A trip to the darkest depths of Cameroon in 1989 saw him testing more natives' eyes and handing out glasses.

It was also in 1989 that he came in for his first Grand National ride, aboard 300-1 rank outsider Kersil. 'I was right up there for the first circuit,' he recalls. 'I've got a photograph of Kersil jumping the water alongside West Tip and Little Polveir. He would have got round but the ground was very soft and he got tired, so I pulled him up.'

Howard Johnson's Howe Street gave Andy his biggest success when winning the Tote 7th Race Handicap Chase on the Friday of Aintree 1992. The following day he finished seventh on Johnson's Old Applejack in the Grand National.

In November of that year, Andy won a three-runner chase at Newbury on

Howe Street, beating Richard Dunwoody and Peter Scudamore. That's the kind of thing a journeyman jockey remembers. So he was delighted when Johnson offered him the ride on Howe Street in the 1993 Grand National.

Seamus O'Neill and Andy Orkney: two jockeys among 39, all focussed on the race ahead. So what happened?

Andy: 'Howe Street was a two-miler who pulled quite hard. On the day it was raining heavily and I had no grip at all on the reins. Because he was a two-miler I was trying to get some cover, trying to hold him up, so I was behind horses and didn't see the first false start. We just pulled up and came back.'

Seamus: 'Sure Metal was a front runner over two miles, so Ginger said "Jump him out; don't blind him at anything". I lined up about five from the inner. With the first false start, a few got caught up in the tape on the outside. We saw the chap waving the red flag so we pulled up and came back. They had to tie the tape up again. Everyone was getting revved up and excited by now.

'When we set off the second time, I didn't see the chap with the flag down the course. I was on the inside and when there are horses around you, you don't think of pulling up. I knew I'd be up there because I couldn't hold one side of him and he was in front after 400 yards.'

Andy: 'I had no idea anything was wrong the second time. I was on the inside and it was all happening on the outside.'

Seamus: 'Andy and I spoke to each other early on in the race about going too quick, because we were both on front runners. It was difficult because we were bound to take each other on. If you notice from the video, we were quite wide apart, trying to keep out of each other's way.'

Andy: 'I took it up jumping Becher's Brook. Howe Street was only a little horse, about 15.3, but he was jumping really well.'

Meanwhile, down at the start, the nine jockeys who had not started were deep in conversation. The consensus was that the race would be re-started, but the events that followed would render that impossible.

Andy: 'The first time I realised there was something not quite right was when I saw the bollards in front of the Chair. There had been trouble at the start with some animal rights protesters and I wondered if maybe they'd put the bollards there.'

Seamus: 'As we were going down to the Chair, somebody ran out in front of it with a police cone and started waving his arms. I shouted to Andy but we didn't know if he was an "anti", or somebody who'd been drinking and was messing about; we just didn't know. It put my horse off and he galloped straight through the fence.'

Andy: 'I knew if I didn't jump the Chair, if I went round it, I'd be out of the race. When you're in front in the Grand National you don't tend to miss fences out, so I went between the bollards. Just in the split second beforehand I thought perhaps an animal rights protester had tied himself to the Chair and maybe that's why they'd put the bollards out. I hadn't a clue what was going on.'

Seamus: 'Sure Metal soon recovered; he was back in front at the water and led them out into the country second time. We'd no idea that there was a "no go" because there was nothing really to stop us. I was aware of something just out the corner of my eye, but you're not going to sit up, look and listen, because it could be people cheering you on, so off we went again. You don't want to pull up in a race like that, half thinking is it yes or no.'

As far as Seamus and Andy were concerned, it was still a race. As Sure Metal and Howe Street led them out into the country, behind them a dozen riders were flagged down amid chaotic scenes. John Bradburne, aboard Interim Lib, one of the fourteen who carried on, was to say later 'There were two cones at the Chair and a man wandering around as if he was at a Sunday school picnic.'

Sure Metal and Howe Street were still disputing the lead when both fell independently two fences before Becher's. Neither jockey was hurt.

Seamus: 'I got in very close to the fence, got it wrong and he didn't get his undercarriage out. Whether he'd have lasted out I don't know, but he got round the year after with Ginger's son Donald on. One of the groundsmen pulled up in his car to pick me up. I got in and listened to the commentary on Radio 5. I heard Peter Bromley say it was a void race. I couldn't believe it. That was the first I knew of it.'

Andy: 'Ron Barry was driving round the inside of the course and picked me up. He'd got the radio on and I heard Peter Bromley's commentary. I asked Ron what he meant and he explained that there had been a false start and the recall man had gone.

'I thought at the time that perhaps I was lucky to escape blame. I'd led them over the Chair and maybe if I'd gone round it, maybe the race would have been started again and they'd have had a Grand National. I don't know. Who knows?'

Seamus: 'The only way they could have stopped the race was by diverting the runners off the course. They should have diverted us down the long run-in before the Chair. All they'd have had to do was put the tape out, like they do for the run-in, doll the Chair off and send us down that chute. Instead, they tried to stop it by getting a man to stand in front of the Chair. Why did they need to put a man there when all they had to do was bypass the fence and filter you down the chute? That way, everyone would have known there was something wrong.'

By the last fence there were just seven left. Esha Ness held off the fast-finishing Cahervillahow, followed by Romany King, The Committee, Givus A Buck, On The Other Hand and Laura's Beau. But it was all academic. Within moments the jockeys who had completed were told the race was void. John White fought back the tears.

There were recriminations all round as emotions rose to the surface, chief among them being shock, anger and embarrassment. Down in the ring, race-goers and bookmakers accepted the situation with an air of resignation. By and large, a sense of humour prevailed in most areas, and one bookmaker jokingly made a book on 'Who Would Be Found First', offering 2-1 on Lord Lucan, 2-1 Salman Rushdie and 20-1 Keith Brown!

Seamus announced his retirement before the start of the following season. He hadn't planned to but a broken thumb, incurred in a fall at Ludlow in May, took three months to heal and gave him plenty of time to mull things over.

'I was getting towards the end of my career. I was nearly thirty-nine and I thought it was time to get out. I'd ridden over 300 winners and had plenty of good times. I didn't want to get to the stage where my boots were hung up and I was still in them!'

He spent twelve months as assistant trainer to Bangor-on-Dee permit holder Frank Lloyd, then got a job selling saddlery for a sales company. In 2000 he took up the Jockey Club post of assistant starter, and is now a full-time starter in his own right.

Andy followed soon after Seamus, bowing out aged thirty-two with two unplaced rides at Carlisle on 30 December 1993. He had ridden 99 winners under Rules, plus one in Russia and three in point-to-points.

While continuing to run his optician's practice in Leyburn, he also acted as racecourse steward at Ripon and Catterick and worked as a part-time judge for the Jockey Club.

In addition, he fulfilled an ambition to become a commentator when calling his first race at the Sinnington point-to-point in 1994. He later joined SIS as a racecourse commentator, covering Scotland and the north of England, making his debut at Carlisle in June 2000.

Neither Seamus O'Neill nor Andy Orkney will ever forget that fateful 1993 Grand National, the day when horseracing hurled a brick through its shop window.

Date: Saturday 3 April 1993 Going: Firm Value to Winner: £102,495.20

Horse	Owner	Trainer	Age / weight	Jockey	SP
1 Esha Ness	Mr Patrick Bancroft	Mrs J Pitman	10-10-0	J White	50-1
2 Cahervillahow	Mrs Miles Valentine	M F Morris	9-10-11	C F Swan	25-1
3 Romany King	Mr Urs E Schwarzenbach	G Balding	9-10-7	A Maguire	15-2
4 The Committee	Corcrain Enterprises Ltd	J H Scott	10-10-0	N Williamson	25-1

Distances (estimated) 1½ lengths, 2½ lengths, ¾ length. Time: 9 mins 1.4 secs. 39 ran

Winner trained at Lambourn, Berkshire

Race declared void.

1994

SIMON BURROUGH
Just Slow

Miinnehoma passes the post ahead of Just So.

A LENGTH AND a quarter isn't far, especially after four and a half miles and thirty fences. But it's the difference between winning and losing. After Just So had been touched off by comedian Freddie Starr's Miinnehoma in the 1994 Grand National, his owner-trainer-breeder Henry Cole and jockey Simon Burrough could be forgiven for not wanting front row seats for the winning owner's Croydon stage show.

However, reflecting over a glass in their Taunton local that night, Henry, his wife Veronica, and Simon came to appreciate the significance of their achievement. 'We couldn't be disappointed,' reflects Simon. 'The horse had run a great race. He'd given me the perfect ride. We'd thoroughly enjoyed ourselves and made the most of it.'

The home bred 11-year-old Just So was one of three horses trained under permit by Henry Cole. The racing press tagged him 'Just Slow' and it is true that stamina, rather than speed, was his forte. Bags of it; a seemingly endless supply. A seven-mile race on ground resembling the Somme would probably have seen him at his best.

Just So had been part of Simon Burrough's life for six years, since they both took part in point-to-points in the late 1980s. Born in Axminster, Somerset, Simon was then just another young, unknown amateur in search of rides. He started riding out for a few point-to-point trainers, one of whom was Julie Barrow, who then had Just So in her livery yard.

The first time he rode the horse was at the now defunct venue of Nedge in March 1988. It was not a good start, for Just So ran out. After that, things gradually got better as they gained experience together. They were third on their next start at Williton, then second at Kingston St Mary before winning the Adjacent Hunts Maiden at Holnicote.

After Just So had won twice during the 1989 point-to-point campaign the Coles decided to put him into training under Rules with Taunton-based John Roberts. Ridden by Simon, he won a three-mile novice chase at Chepstow in January 1990, finished fourth to Garrison Savannah in the Wincanton Challenge Cup, then came in twelfth behind Topsham Bay in the National Hunt Chase at Cheltenham.

The next season, Simon's first as a professional, they combined to win a four-mile-two-and-a-half furlong chase at Taunton. It was clear that the eight-year-old was an out and out stayer. 'He was still a big immature horse then,' recalls his jockey, 'but we all agreed that he could be a National horse in a year or two's time.'

Roberts gave up training at the end of that season, hence Just So joined the rapidly emerging Paul Nicholls at Ditcheat. Frustratingly, he finished second on four of his first five outings, including Chepstow's John Hughes Grand National Trial, when beaten seven lengths by Cool Ground, and the Eider Chase at Newcastle, with Cool Ground back in seventh. When Cool Ground won the Cheltenham Gold Cup a month later, spirits rose in the Just So camp.

In his final start before the 1992 Grand National, Just So finished fourth behind Laura's Beau in the Midlands National at Uttoxeter. But the ground at Aintree that year was good to soft, whereas he'd have preferred it softer. In the circumstances he put up a good performance in finishing sixth, as the massive Party Politics galloped to victory from Romany King and Laura's Beau.

'He ran a blinder,' said Simon afterwards. 'They just went a bit fast for me early on, but he jumped brilliantly and finished like a train after jumping the last. At the line there was only a head between him and the fifth horse, Twin Oaks. The ground was too quick for him. With some rain he must have made the frame.'

Henry Cole had two other horses to run the following season, including Just So's half-sister, Dubacilla. Rather than putting them all into training with Nicholls, he elected to take out a permit and do the job himself. Simon kept the ride on Just So, whose best performance came when finishing a neck runner-up to Riverside Boy in the Taunton four-and-a-quarter-mile marathon he'd won two years earlier. But there was consolation for trainer and jockey that day, with the classy Dubacilla winning her second novice chase of the season.

Firm ground left Cole no alternative but to pull Just So out of the 1993 Grand National on the day itself. Given the fiasco of that year's void race, it was a decision he had no cause to regret.

Says Simon: 'As the horse got older, we obviously knew more about him and it wasn't worth running him on good to firm ground. He was a big, genuine horse and at home he just loved his work. He was a dream ride. Having said that, he had a roach back [a hump in his back], so instead of sitting behind the horse, you were always sitting forward. It was quite awkward in that the saddle never fitted properly. It definitely made him harder to ride, particularly over the bigger fences.'

Just So's 1993/94 campaign was again targeted at the Grand National. He had his first two runs of the season within six days in December, finishing fifth at Exeter and third in a Haydock four-miler. He was then a staying-on runner-up to Moorcroft Boy over four miles at Cheltenham's New Year meeting. He won the John Hughes Grand National Trial at Chepstow but his tendency to get behind during a race cost Simon a ten-day ban for misuse of the whip. That ruled him out of Just So's next intended engagement, the Eider Chase, so the horse was re-routed to the Midlands National.

Despite his favoured heavy ground, he finished only seventh. However, his connections were not too disappointed as there were excuses. He lost ground at the start and his blinkers became caked in mud during the race. It was decided to leave them off at Aintree.

Veronica Cole elected to stay home, milk the cows and watch the race on television. Given the weather on the first two days of the meeting, it looked a wise decision. Incessant rain had rendered Thursday's good to soft ground heavy by Friday.

A severe mid-morning hailstorm on Saturday ensured that only the strongest would survive the four-and-a-half-mile marathon. The conditions were perfect for a slogger like Just So and his starting price, backed down from 25-1 to 20's, reflected the fact.

Simon's height and frame meant there was no prospect of making the ten stone allotted by the handicapper. A spartan diet, hours in the sauna and plenty of running saw him weigh out on the day at 10st 3lb.

The sun came out as racing got under way but it was far too late to have an effect on the going. Richard Dunwoody was heard to say afterwards: 'The ground was so testing it made the fences seem about six inches bigger.'

Predictably, Just So did not have the pace to go with them for the first half of the race and was well behind on the first circuit. He was nearly brought down when Romany King fell directly in front of him at the fourth fence. 'He jumped the fence, went a stride and jumped the horse,' recalls Simon. 'He was very clever and did marvellously well to stand up. It was all credit to him for getting back into the race.'

Although the pace was by no means fast, the testing conditions saw to it that more than half the field failed to survive the first circuit. Most of the casualties were outsiders, though the fancied trio of Master Oats, Double Silk and Mr Boston all fell at the thirteenth, while Young Hustler had been unluckily brought down by a loose horse two fences earlier.

Only seventeen of the thirty-six runners were left jumping the water and six of those would drop out on the run down to Becher's. When the recalcitrant Riverside Boy virtually refused to race going back out into the country, Miinnehoma and Richard Dunwoody were left in front. But Simon Burrough and Just So were just warming up.

'Going out onto the second circuit,' he continues, 'it suddenly clicks that you're lying sixth or seventh in the Grand National and the horse is doing his best work now. We've made ground steadily going to Becher's and jumped Valentine's in front. When I went upsides Richard, he said "What the hell are you doing here?"'

Accompanied by the Irish mare Ebony Jane, Just So led them back onto the racecourse, closely followed by Moorcroft Boy and Miinnehoma, this quartet being clear of the chasing Into The Red, with the remaining three runners out of contention. The riderless Young Hustler was an unwelcome distraction for the leaders and he seemed determined to make his presence felt.

Ebony Jane cried enough at the second last, while Just So blundered his way over the fence. Moorcroft Boy went on there and jumped the last in front of Miinnehoma, who immediately quickened to go clear on the flat. Dunwoody was about to win his second Grand National. But then Just So dug deep and unexpectedly found enough to mount another challenge.

'When I got to Miinnehoma's girth on the run-in I thought I was going to win but there's no harder man to beat in a finish than Richard Dunwoody. Just So just needed to pull out that little bit more at the end but he couldn't.'

The time of 10 minutes 18.8 seconds was the slowest since Quare Times triumphed in similar glue-like going 39 years earlier, and Just So had revelled in the conditions.

Says Simon: 'Driving home – and it was a long way back; took us about four hours – we were excited but disappointed. It hadn't yet sunk in that we'd finished second in a Grand National. But when we got home, put the horse away and went out to the pub on the evening, how we celebrated. And we carried on celebrating for the next two or three nights because we'd had a chance that not many people get. We'd come second in the Grand National. We'll never forget it. You can never take that away from us.'

Did the 3lb overweight make the difference between victory and defeat?

'To be honest,' he reflects, 'if he'd carried twelve stone I don't think it would have stopped him. He was that kind of a horse, so big and strong he would have carried any weight. But in racing, "a pound a length" is what they say. I hope it didn't make a difference but you never know. I couldn't do any lighter and the owner stood by me, and I'm very grateful to him for doing so.'

Just So ran four times the following season, finishing well behind at Wincanton, Sandown and Newbury before pulling up in the Greenalls Gold Cup at Haydock, his final start. Meanwhile, his sister Dubacilla, trained now by David Nicholson, excelled in the highest class, finishing second to Master Oats in the 1995 Cheltenham Gold Cup and fourth behind Royal Athlete in that year's Grand National.

Simon continued to ply his trade in Somerset as assistant trainer cum stable jockey to Pat Rodford. Aged 36, he had his final rides at Exeter on 27 January 2003 before taking over the licence at Rodford's yard. His training career got off to a flying start when he saddled Bally Lira to land a shock 40-1 victory at Chepstow the following week, scoring by 25 lengths in the hands of Liam Cummins. He told the *Racing Post*: 'This is the first time for 48 races that I haven't been in the saddle on the mare and after seeing that I suppose I should have retired earlier!'

Later that year Simon moved to a new yard at West Buckland and had his first winner from there when Pamela Anshan took an incident-packed novice chase at Taunton. He continues to train there with a string numbering around a dozen.

The memory of Just So's heroic effort in the 1994 Grand National will stay with him always. No tinge of regret, for as he said, he'd had 'a chance that not many people get.' Hence the celebrations that lasted for days. It puts into context the measurement of what constitutes success and happiness.

Date: Saturday 9 April 1994   Going: Heavy   Value to Winner: £115,606

Horse	Owner	Trainer	Age / weight	Jockey	SP
1 Miinnehoma	Mr Freddie Starr	M C Pipe	11-10-8	R Dunwoody	16-1
2 Just So	Mr H T Cole	Owner	11-10-3	S Burrough	20-1
3 Moorcroft Boy	Mr K G Manley	D Nicholson	9-10-0	A Maguire	5-1fav
4 Ebony Jane	Mr James Lynch	F Flood	9-10-1	L P Cusack	25-1

Distances: 1¼ lengths, 20 lengths, 25 lengths. Time: 10 mins 18.8 secs. 36 ran

Winner trained at Wellington, Somerset

1995

LUKE HARVEY
Leg Lock Luke

Luke Harvey, jockey turned TV presenter.

'IT'S IRONIC WHEN you get famous for that sort of thing,' reflects Luke Harvey. Of the 253 winners he rode, none is more widely recalled than the unlikely triumph of Too Plush in the Nightingale Sings Handicap Chase at Wincanton on 2nd December 1996.

'It was shown as a "What Happened Next?" on A *Question of Sport*,' he says. 'There were only four runners that day, one of which had fallen. I must have been a fence and a half behind the other two. Then the loose horse came across the second last, baulked one, baulked the other, and I sailed home in splendid isolation, waving to the crowd.'

A similar incident happened to him three months later at Windsor. He rode a horse called Quick Quote in her first start over fences. She whipped round at the start, losing all chance, and was at least 25 lengths behind in third place when both the leaders came to grief at the last fence. As *Chaseform* commented: 'Luke Harvey is becoming something of a specialist in these disaster-type races and reckons this is about the fifth time it has happened to him.'

'It happened with my first point-to-point winner, a horse called Shining, at Hackwood Park,' he grins. 'On the last circuit there was a spur off to go up the home straight. There were seven runners and six of them ran out at the horsebox park on the last circuit. I was left a distance clear but when I came to the spur I went the wrong way. By the time I'd pulled up and gone back, two others had caught up with me. So the three of us went to the last fence upsides – and the other two fell off, so I still won by a distance!'

Nicknamed Leg Lock Luke by weighing room colleague Guy Landau, having seen a photo of him jumping the last fence at Plumpton, sitting precariously with legs fully extended and hailing a cab, the jockey-turned-broadcaster reflects on his career in the saddle.

'I was very lucky. Mum's got some of my diaries at home from when I was six or seven, saying I wanted to be a jockey when I grew up. To the day I gave up I'll always be tremendously proud that I managed to achieve and make a living as a professional sportsman, doing what I'd wanted to do from an early age.'

At fourteen he was riding out for local trainer John Roberts at Tiverton. On leaving school at sixteen, he joined Captain Tim Forster as an amateur rider.

'I wrote off to three or four trainers in Lambourn, and the Captain was the only one to reply. I met him in my village when he was down in Devon. He used to come down in the summer to go stag hunting. I was a keen hunting man as well so we hit it off immediately. In Devon, hunting is a way of life and learning to ride was a matter of survival. I got knocked out a couple of times hunting, dragged off underneath trees, that sort of thing. It developed you as a rider, gave you a competitive edge.'

He rode his first winner under Rules for John Roberts on 33-1 outsider Bickleigh Bridge in an amateur riders' hurdle at Taunton in December 1984. His first major triumph came courtesy of Jim Wilson's Taberna Lord in the 1987 Coral Golden Hurdle at Cheltenham.

That same year he had his first Grand National ride, on 500-1 outsider Spartan Orient for Jeff King. 'Jeff King is fairly colourful with his language at the best of times. I was sitting at home one Sunday night, watching the telly, when he phoned up. He said "Do you want to ride a horse for me in the National?" "Yeah". "Fine". That was it; put the phone down.

'Of course, I was a bit apprehensive with it being my first National ride; excited as much as anything. I walked into the paddock and stood there with the owners. They were excited too; it was great just to have a runner in the Grand National. I asked Jeff what he wanted me to do and he said, "Make it down the inside". I laughed, and he said "What are you laughing at?"

'I bounced him out but he was nowhere near quick enough to make the running. The reason he'd told me to go down the inside was because the horse kept jumping left. There was a loose horse in front of me that was jumping really badly, so I pulled off the inside. At the twelfth, mine jumped straight across the fence, hit the running rail and fired me out the side door!'

Luke rode out his claim later that year – and that's when things started to go wrong. 'The minute I'd lost my claim I broke my collarbone. I came back too quickly and broke it again ten days later. In fact, it was so weak I broke it seven times that summer but, being stupid, I kept on coming back. In the end, I had to have a section of it taken out.

'So just when I most needed the rides, everything dried up on me and I was in a pretty low state of affairs. I wasn't getting many rides and the ones I was getting were horrible.'

The tide turned in May 1989 when he won on a horse called Air Broker for Reg Akehurst. Within a week he was offered the job of stable jockey. It was a real culture shock from the training methods employed by Captain Forster.

'The Captain's traditional way of doing things was six weeks on the road, two weeks cantering, then three or four weeks galloping, whereas at Reg's, two weeks after coming in from the field they were galloping. I couldn't believe it. He was unorthodox but the best trainer I ever rode for.

'I won the SGB Chase at Ascot for him on Solidasarock. He'd been allocated 9st 3lb for this £30,000 handicap so he couldn't win it, yet he jumped brilliantly and won. It was the day of his lads' Christmas party and I can remember being literally carried out, still singing, "Solid . . . solid as a rock"!'

He won the 1990 Welsh National for Akehurst on Cool Ground, landing a huge gamble in the process. The horse was thrown in with only ten stone and duly won with his head in his chest. They went on to win the Mildmay-Cazalet Memorial and finished fourth in that season's Gold Cup.

In terms of pure quality, the best horse Luke rode was Andy Turnell's Katabatic. He first partnered him in the 1991 Victor Chandler Chase at Ascot, finishing third, but was off injured when the horse won at Wetherby next time out. Simon McNeill deputised and duly kept the ride when Katabatic won that year's Queen Mother Champion Chase.

It was agreed that the two jockeys would share the rides on Katabatic the following season. It wasn't Luke's turn when he was second in the Queen Mother, but he did win the South Wales Showers Silver Trophy Chase on him at Cheltenham in April, beating Waterloo Boy by eight lengths.

Turnell also trained the useful Country Member, with whom Luke struck up a successful partnership, winning four times during the 1992/93 campaign. Following a six-length victory in Sandown's Agfa Diamond Chase, they went off the strong 5-4 favourites for the Ritz Club National Hunt Handicap Chase, but failed by a short head to peg back Givus A Buck up the Cheltenham hill.

Country Member missed the whole of the next season due to heat in a tendon, but when he returned, the 1995 Grand National became the plan. He had his final preparatory race in the Grand Military Gold Cup, winning nicely in the hands of Major Ollie Ellwood. It was all systems go for Aintree, with Country Member a well-fancied 11-1 chance.

Says Luke: 'To me, riding in the National was everything. If I had the choice of going to Huntingdon on the Wednesday of Cheltenham for three or four that could nearly win, or go to Cheltenham for one run round, I'd go to Huntingdon every time. But if someone said that I could ride a one-eyed donkey round Aintree, I'd do it because I liked it so much. The camaraderie, the excitement, the sense of danger; it's definitely more of a challenge than a race.

'I'll never forget that day. I gave him a canter round the course in the morning. The taxi driver that took me there said he fancied Country Member. I said, "I ride him." It was a lovely feeling.

'I went into the race unusually confident. My final memory before I went out is of Andy Turnell, who is refreshingly honest and the most loyal trainer I ever came across, saying, "If you get over the first three, you'll win."

'There was a lot of pressure on me that day. I'd put a lot of pressure on myself because I thought he could win. There was confidence in the yard and a lot of the daily newspapers had gone for him.

'I cantered him down to the first. I always tried whenever I rode over the big fences to make sure the horse walked into the fence so that he knew that it was solid. I walked up to it and he started to get jittery.

'I can remember it seemed like an age that we were walking round at the start. He was on his toes, he was jig jogging, starting to sweat down his neck. He was quite highly strung. I lined up next to Graham McCourt, who had a dismal record in the race. I think he'd fallen at the first fence three or four times. I looked across and said to him, "Bloody hell, McCourt, it's bad luck lining up next to you."

'The tapes went up and we set off at the most tremendous gallop. I can remember thinking that he was running as if – you know when you're running downhill and you're running too fast for your legs? It was like that.

'Carl Llewellyn had always told me to make sure I got my horse back on his hocks, so, ten strides before the fence, I eased him back and I saw what I thought was a beautiful stride, and he stood off. In mid-air he suddenly thought, "Oh my God, it's something different; I haven't seen one of these before", and he lifted his legs right up so as not to touch the fence. Of course, with the speed we were going, the first thing that hit the ground was his head. Everyone went over the top and I think seven or eight of us fell there.

'I'll be honest, it's quite surreal after the hullabaloo of the crowd, the lads; there's so much going on in your head. Then suddenly you're lying in the grass after thirty-odd horses have gone over you – and there's nothing. There's silence. Absolute silence. I lay face down and just cried. I knew that was my one chance. I was heartbroken.

'Rodney Farrant, who'd fallen on Lusty Light next to me, was laughing because he was alright. He didn't care about it. But the boot was soon on the other foot. We brushed ourselves off and got back to the finishing line to watch the horses come up the run-in. That was the year that Jason Titley won on Royal Athlete. Ironically, it was the horse that Rodney Farrant had turned down! I'd started off crying with grief and finished up crying with laughter. It was the funniest thing I'd ever seen!'

Twelve-year-old Royal Athlete had jumped the last fence with a lead of five lengths and galloped all the way to the line to win by seven from Party Politics, with 100-1 outsider Over The Deel staying on to snatch third, half a length in front of Dubacilla.

Continues Luke: 'Three weeks later I rode Country Member in the Whit-bread. He'd come out of Aintree well but I didn't really fancy him, as it was a bit of an afterthought. I nearly fell off him at the first but everything just clicked after that and if ever there was a horse that's gone faster or jumped the whole line of fences down the back better second time round, I've certainly never seen it. After that it suddenly dawned on me that I was going to win the Whitbread. I'm in front and he's absolutely flying.

'I've jumped the Pond fence, still cruising in front. And then it was as if a horse had just jumped into the race next to me, as Richard Dunwoody came sailing past on Cache Fleur. He beat me easily and I finished second.

'Country Member never ran again. He had a recurrence of a leg injury. But the nice thing was that the head lad's wife had had him in retirement and she adored him.'

It was around the time of Country Member's exploits that The Racing Channel came on air. Recalls Luke: 'I was a guest on The Racing Channel a few times. Not exactly being backward at coming forward, I got on well with the people. For a year and a half, Mark Richards and I were still riding and would quite often do the presenting and interviews while wearing our breeches.

'Then I made a conscious decision. I could either be a broadcaster that could ride, or a jockey that could broadcast. I was thirty-three so I bit the bullet.'

Luke had his last ride on juvenile hurdler Zola for Mick Quinn at Chepstow on 2 October 1999. There was no fairytale ending, for Zola could finish only a distant fourth, but his weighing room colleagues gave him a fitting send-off in the winner's enclosure afterwards, hoisting him onto their shoulders and spraying him with champagne.

He reflects: 'I had no regrets because I achieved everything that I ever wanted to achieve – riding over the big fences, riding in the Cheltenham Gold Cup, riding plenty of winners, riding at the top racecourses and enjoying all the perks of being a jockey. It just suited me, that giggly, schoolboy, laddish culture.'

From The Racing Channel he moved into radio as racing presenter for the BBC's Radio 5 Live. The Racing Channel metamorphosed into various incarnations of At The Races and he is still there, thoroughly enjoying being one of its presenters.

Date: Saturday 8 April 1995   Going: Good   Value to Winner: £118,854

Horse	Owner	Trainer	Age / weight	Jockey	SP
1 Royal Athlete	Mr G & L Johnson	Mrs J Pitman	12-10-6	J Titley	40-1
2 Party Politics	Mrs D Thompson	N Gaselee	11-10-2	M Dwyer	16-1
3 Over The Deel	Mr George Tobitt	J H Johnson	9-10-0	Mr C Bonner	100-1
4 Dubacilla	Mr H T Cole	D Nicholson	9-11-0	D Gallagher	9-1

Distances: 7 lengths, 6 lengths, ½ length. Time: 9 mins 4.0 secs. 35 ran

Winner trained at Upper Lambourn, Berkshire

1996

DAVID BRIDGWATER

At the end of the day, it's only a horse race

Encore Un Peu and David Bridgwater are clear at the last fence.

'EVERYONE HAS A tale to tell about their ride but it's the winning jockey that gets all the plaudits. Sat in the corner of the weighing room afterwards, having been beaten a length and a quarter … you're so near.'

So says David Bridgwater. He makes the statement not with any vestige of envy through having been there himself. It's purely matter of fact. Facts are what you get from 'Bridgy'.

The late Ken Bridgwater's training set up at Knowle, Solihull, was always a family affair, with wife Mary as secretary, eldest son Kenny as assistant trainer and Gary driving the horsebox. When youngest son David entered the world on 5 January 1971, it was odds-on that he would follow the family's racing heritage.

However, it was a different kind of sporting ambition that the youngster harboured at school. To be a footballer was his aim. It would have continued a family tradition, for his great grandfather, Frank Perry, was captain of West Bromwich Albion, and dad Ken was a goalkeeper who passed a trial with Birmingham City. It was the toss of a coin that determined the direction Ken's career would take. It came down on the side of racing.

Though riding almost as soon as he could walk, David did not sit on a racehorse until he was twelve. Despite being run away with the first time he cantered one, he was riding out at fourteen.

He left school at fifteen and became apprenticed to Lester Piggott, who had just embarked on a training career. After two and a half years at Newmarket, increasing weight saw him return to the Midlands to join David Nicholson.

His father's Deadly Going, at Warwick, provided him with his first ride over hurdles in January 1989, but he had to wait another twelve months until Winnie The Witch gave him his first winner, at Leicester on 22 January 1990. Ken Bridgwater had claimed her out of a Leicester selling hurdle for 4,300 guineas. It proved an inspired decision, for in the spring of 1991, partnered by David, she won the County Hurdle at Cheltenham and Haydock's Swinton Insurance Hurdle.

After four years with 'The Duke', David joined Nigel Twiston-Davies at the start of the 1992/93 season. His Great Yorkshire Chase victory on Young Hustler in January 1993 advertised his burgeoning talent to the racing world.

The following season he rode 58 winners, including Cheltenham's Grand Annual on the Bill Clay-trained Snitton Lane. Young Hustler provided him with his first Grand National ride, deputising for injured stable jockey Carl Llewellyn.

'Young Hustler was the toughest horse you'd ever come across,' he says. 'It was good fast ground, perfect for him. He gave me a beautiful ride. We were in the right place at the right time and I was loving every second. When you're in a rhythm it's a magical feeling and I was in that rhythm. He was going really well and I hadn't asked him any questions. Then, when I got to the eleventh, the riderless Ushers Island fell in front of me and brought me down.'

He received a measure of compensation at Ayr seven days later when landing the Scottish Champion Hurdle on Corrouge and the Scottish Grand National on Earth Summit. Later that year he journeyed to Australia, representing Britain in a jump jockeys' tournament in Melbourne, where he won two races and was crowned world champion.

His second Grand National mount, in 1995, was on General Pershing for Gordon Richards, this time substituting for the injured Tony Dobbin. 'He was very free and I couldn't hold him going down to the start. He jumped the first and second fences big and bold, came to the third and took off four strides early. We landed in the ditch and I got fired so far forward it was unbelievable. I was covered in blood, my colours, boots and breeches were ripped to shreds. It looked as though I'd been in the ring with a lion.'

The following season saw David take over as stable jockey to Martin Pipe after the Pond House trainer and Richard Dunwoody had gone their separate ways. What seemed at the time to be the best job in racing propelled David towards the top of the jockeys' table, with only Tony McCoy standing between him and the championship.

Cheltenham's opening day in 1996 brought only misery for the Pipe-Bridgwater combination, when Champion Hurdle contender Mack The Knife and Arkle Chase favourite Draborgie met with fatal injuries. However, the final day

brought a dramatic turn round in fortunes, with Cyborgo winning the Stayers'
Hurdle and Challenger Du Luc landing the Cathcart.

Runner up in the Fulke Walwyn Kim Muir Challenge Cup that year was the
French-bred chestnut Encore Un Peu, a Pipe import of the previous season. It
was a good enough performance to make him a lively each-way contender for
the Grand National in eighteen days' time. One of three Pipe runners in that
year's Aintree marathon, he was to be David's third ride in the race.

'He was nothing out of the ordinary, no Young Hustler,' he says candidly.
'I was told to drop him out for the first mile then quietly creep into it on the
second circuit. As soon as the race started, straightaway I'm in that rhythm, he's
settled, he's jumping, everything's going lovely and I'm just having the dream
ride. Wherever Mr Pipe told me to be, that's where I was. Horses were falling to
the right, falling to the left but never in front of me. It was like going round on
a calm sea, the gaps were opening up for me.

'Going across the Melling Road for the last time and onto the racecourse I'm
absolutely cantering. Young Hustler was upside me and I thought that was the
one I'd got to beat, then once he cracked I thought I was going to win. From that
point, at the second last, it was just quiet, I couldn't hear anything. My thoughts
were a million miles away.

'I jumped the last four lengths clear. I looked behind me and saw "Fitzy"
[Mick Fitzgerald] absolutely pulling a cart on Rough Quest. As soon as I saw
him there the world dropped out my pants. I'm thinking I'm going to win, then
I see Mick behind me, swinging on a horse that's carrying 10st 7lb.

'The only way I thought I could beat him was that when Rough Quest hits
the front, he always hangs left, so if I could keep him on my right and he comes
past, he'll "do" me. If he "does" me sufficiently and I can keep with him so that
he cuts across and makes contact, I'd have him. It almost worked. As soon as he
came past me he came across. A second earlier and I'd have clipped his heels. I
pulled on my reins and switched to the outside. It stopped my momentum but
it didn't stop me from winning the race. I wouldn't have beaten him. He was a
much better horse than mine.

'What was going through my mind from the last to the winning post was my
mom and dad sat at home watching it. I'm thinking they must be going mental.
I was more disappointed for them than me because I knew what it would have
meant to them.

'Immediately after the race everyone wanted to talk to me and Fitzy. I was interviewed by Des Lynam on *Grandstand* and admitted to some pretty good acting!

'There was a stewards' enquiry and everyone was saying "You'll get this".
The stewards asked the usual questions about the race – "in your opinion, Mr
Bridgwater, blah, blah" – I said "Yes, he did cross me; there was slight interfer-
ence but the best horse won the race". Then they asked Fitzy and of course you
couldn't shut him up. I didn't say very much else because everyone could see
what I could see.'

The stewards' enquiry took fifteen minutes to decide that Rough Quest should keep the race. Mick Fitzgerald looked a relieved man. For the horse's Northern Ireland-born trainer Terry Casey, destined to be taken so cruelly by cancer just a few short years later, it was a realisation of a dream.

'It was no surprise that I didn't get it,' says David. 'I've had to snatch up a little bit and had it been a hurdle race at Hereford, I'd probably have got it. But it was the Grand National, Rough Quest was favourite, there was so much money on him, I couldn't win it.

'Looking back on it now and what happened to poor Terry Casey, I'd have gladly given him the race anyway. Life is too short. At the end of the day it's only a horse race. I didn't want to win the National on a stewards' enquiry. I wanted to win like Jason Titley on Royal Athlete the year before, miles clear and waving my whip, knowing I'd won it.'

When the decision had been announced, the winning connections interviewed and the trophies presented, Des Lynam praised the sportsmanship of David Bridgwater. His views were echoed by John Oaksey, whose Friday column in the *Daily Telegraph* was entitled 'Sportsmanship in Defeat'.

'Sportsmanship was the real winner on Grand National day,' he wrote. 'David Bridgwater did not win last week's Martell Grand National but his second on Encore Un Peu should never be forgotten. How many so-called sportsmen these days can accept disappointment and defeat with such grace and cheerful humour?'

Seven days after his Grand National defeat, David rode his 100th winner of the season on Martin Pipe's Balasani at Newton Abbot. He finished that season with a score of 132, second only to Tony McCoy's 175. All looked set fair for another successful campaign in 1996/97 but then came the shock announcement that Pipe and Bridgwater had parted company.

'It was my decision,' insists David. 'To be champion jockey like Peter Scudamore, Richard Dunwoody and Tony McCoy, you have to be a certain type of person. I'm as hungry as the next man for winners and success but you have to be obsessive, so obsessed that it hurts. I was never like that.

'Mr Pipe used to be so intense about the chances of a selling hurdler, whereas I was always "He'll win if he's good enough" and that used to infuriate him because I was so laid back about it. I'm one of those people that, if I don't like something, I don't do it. I didn't enjoy winning any more.

'That season I had a double at the Cheltenham Festival, Cyborgo and Challenger Du Luc. To ride a winner at the Festival should be the pinnacle. I remember how it felt with Winnie The Witch. But to ride two winners for Mr Pipe wasn't like "That was fantastic"; it was "Thank God for that." It was expected and there was no enjoyment about it. When I'd come back from riding a winner at the Festival, it felt like I'd just won a selling hurdle at Hereford.'

Without the backing of the Pipe stable, David's number of winners inevitably fell, though a score of 69 by Grand National day 1997 was still respectable enough. He was due to ride Bishops Hall for Robert Alner in the big race, but a spare ride on Time Won't Wait in the Martell Red Rum Chase changed all that.

'He buried me at the fifth fence and I smashed my right arm at the elbow. I'd got my foot hung up in the iron and I got dragged what seemed like half a mile, though it was only a few yards. While I was being dragged, my arm was under the horse's back legs. It was already broke but while it was underneath, he kicked it and really messed it up.

'From the time I broke my arm I could count on one hand the amount of genuine people that came by to see how I was. It didn't bother me but I noticed it. I suppose every walk of life is like that. When you're up, you've got so many friends and hangers on. But when you're down and need a pat on the back, you get nothing.'

The operation to rebuild the shattered elbow necessitated several metal plates being inserted in the arm. He returned to the saddle in October and rode a few more winners, but another fall at Sandown in January 1998 resulted in an infection, requiring the removal of part of a plate and several pins.

He made one more comeback the following month and rode what was to be his final winner on Graham McCourt's Red Curate at Fontwell on 9 February. Two days later, he damaged the elbow again on novice hurdler General Assembly at Ascot.

'The horse was hanging and cocking his jaw,' he recalls. 'I jarred the elbow landing over the second flight. I was riding with one arm and struggling to pull him up. I had no strength.

'It was uncanny. I'd never once fallen on my arm until the day I broke it. After that, every time I had a fall I'd land on the same arm. When things aren't going right you lose that little bit of confidence. Every time I got beat I kept thinking it was because I couldn't use my arm properly.'

With less than 90 degrees of movement in the elbow and specialists advising that no significant improvement could be expected, he reluctantly accepted that he had to give up. Later that year he set up as a trainer at Hill House in Lambourn, but, almost before he started, the injury jinx that had haunted him since the Aintree fall struck again when he suffered a badly broken right leg while returning from the gallops.

'A horse came past me bucking and out of control and caught me with both barrels. It was like a shotgun going off. I thought he'd struck my horse's shoulder but when I looked down, my foot was spasming in the stirrup iron. It had killed all the muscle in my leg and you need muscle for the bone to heal.

'It was an horrendous time. They took muscles from my back and transplanted them into my leg. While I was in hospital I was in a sort of plastic bubble because I couldn't have cold air. I had to be in a warm environment and I was sweating buckets 24 hours a day.'

The training itself could hardly have made a better start, with his first three runners all winning. Rake Hey started the ball rolling at Kempton on 18

November 1998, then followed up at Hereford two weeks later. Dargo, his first runner on the Flat, romped home at Wolverhampton by a margin clocked at 38 lengths.

In the summer of 2001 David upped sticks and moved his string to Slade Barn stables on the outskirts of the Gloucestershire village of Ford, later relocating to Wyck Hill Farm, near Stow-on-the-Wold.

'Lambourn's a great place to train,' he says, 'but it wasn't really for me. I'm my own person and I like to get on my own tractor and do my own gallops, build my own fences and do my own thing.

'We had a good start to training but I didn't go out and prostitute myself, saying "Look at me, aren't I good?" I don't go out wining and dining. The owners that I have now are good friends and they'll be there through thick and thin. That's the way I like it.'

Date: Saturday 30 March 1996 Going: Good Value to Winner: £142,534

Horse	Owner	Trainer	Age / weight	Jockey	SP
1 Rough Quest	Mr A T A Wates	T Casey	10-10-7	M Fitzgerald	7-1fav
2 Encore Un Peu	Mr Vincent Nally	M C Pipe	9-10-0	D Bridgwater	14-1
3 Superior Finish	Mr Peter McGrane	Mrs J Pitman	10-10-3	R Dunwoody	9-1
4 Sir Peter Lely	John Doyle Construction Ltd	M D Hammond	9-10-0	Mr C Bonner	33-1

Distances: 1¼ lengths, 16 lengths, short head. Time: 9 mins 0.8 secs. 27 ran

Winner trained at Dorking, Surrey.

1997

SEAN CURRAN

A mattress at the Adelphi

Sean Curran on Killeshin with trainer John Manners.

THEY CALLED HIM 'Mad Manners', yet he knew the time of day. Never one to refrain from voicing an opinion on any subject, John Manners was hardly the epitome of an 'establishment' figure. Nor, right up to his death in September 2009, aged 83, was he your typical racehorse trainer.

His madcap training regime left inhabitants of Lambourn and Newmarket open-mouthed but they had to admit that it worked. He won the Aintree Fox Hunters' Chase twice with Killeshin and Cavalero, plus Cheltenham's Foxhunters' Challenge Cup and Newcastle's Eider Chase.

Killeshin had begun his racing life in training with Karl Burke, achieving just a single placing from a dozen starts over hurdles and fences. Manners bought the black gelding at Ascot Sales and when he ran him in hunter chases in 1994 it was a very different story. Following easy victories at Leicester and Fontwell, he beat Brown Windsor in that year's Martell Fox Hunters' Chase at Aintree, ridden by Gary Brown.

Conditional jockey Sean Curran also had good reason to remember that 1994 Aintree Festival. On the opening day he rode 20-1 shot Meditator to win the Barton & Guestier Handicap Hurdle, then on Grand National day he won the Champion Bumper on Nahla. Both horses were trained by Jacqui Doyle, who provided nine of his thirteen winners that season.

Sean was just starting to get noticed and those Aintree winners gave him the chance to display his riding abilities to a wider audience. They were moments to savour – yet emotional and poignant ones too. His father, Matt, had passed away just a couple of months earlier.

Sean reflected on how proud he would have been. 'That was his favourite time, coming to Liverpool. For years I used to come over with him, ever since I was twelve or thirteen. We used to walk round the course every time.'

Matt Curran was no casual observer. He had been a leading jockey in Ireland, riding for the legendary Paddy Mullins and winning the Irish Grand National for him twice, on Vulpine in 1967 and Dim Wit in 1972.

Matt's father, Paddy Curran, had also worked for Mullins, so it was no surprise that Sean should follow them to the Goresbridge, County Kilkenny, stables of one of Ireland's greatest trainers. Sean stayed there for four and a half years, rode on the Flat and over jumps, but had no winners to show for it.

He came to Britain and initially joined Ginger McCain at Southport before moving to Ferdy Murphy, who was then training Geoff Hubbard's horses at Woodbridge in Suffolk. He rode a few winners but it was not until he began his association with Compton trainer Jacqui Doyle that things really started to happen.

Killeshin's partner, Gary Brown, had turned professional at the start of the 1995/96 campaign but had suffered a career-ending fall at Uttoxeter soon after. Sean had got to know him when they rode out together at Jacqui Doyle's and the pair had become good friends. Gary put Sean in for the winning ride on Killeshin in a four-and-a-quarter-mile chase at Taunton in January 1996. He kept the ride for Killeshin's next start, the Eider Chase at Newcastle. Hitting the front between the last two jumps, they won with authority by five lengths.

Killeshin looked a tailor-made Grand National contender but he would have to wait another year, for the weights had been published before he won the Eider and he wasn't rated high enough to get into the race.

The following season, 1996/97, Killeshin appeared not to be running with the enthusiasm of before. He finished third in the Eider, and fourth in Warwick's Crudwell Cup and in the Midlands National. Nonetheless, he would still take his place in the Grand National line-up, with Sean having his first ride in the race.

The events of Saturday 5 April 1997, brought about by an IRA bomb scare, ensured a never to be forgotten weekend. Operation Aintree, the 'biggest evacuation in the history of sport', saw 60,000 people being ushered from the racecourse into the streets of Liverpool.

Millions saw the drama unfold on television. Racegoers mixed with owners, trainers, jockeys, bookmakers, officials, sponsors, politicians, celebrities and the world's media, their cars impounded, not knowing how long it would be before they could return. There were so many heroic and heart-warming tales; the lads who refused to leave their horses, the doors flung open in welcome by local residents, the makeshift accommodation in schools and sports centres.

The jockeys, bereft not just of transport but also of clothes, money and mobile phones, gratefully accepted any hospitality that was going.

Sean Curran was among them and recalls: 'When we were told to leave, everyone thought we'd be back within the hour, so we left everything behind. I was lucky enough to get back in and pick up my car keys, but it made no difference because I couldn't get out of the car park. On the Saturday night we went out and had a few drinks and a bit of craic. I ended up sleeping on a mattress at the Adelphi Hotel. There was no racing on the Sunday and most of us thought the National wouldn't be held that year. Then we heard on Sunday morning that it was being rescheduled late on Monday afternoon.

'By Monday the ground had dried out, which was all against Killeshin. Although he had plenty of speed at home, in a race he liked pootling along and then getting into it at the death, staying on past tired horses. That's the way he ran but John liked all his horses ridden that way; jump off, drop them in at the back and ride them to finish.'

The first ever Monday Grand National, a defiant response by those who steadfastly refused to submit to the tactics of terrorists, was the greatest of triumphs. Ten thousand people turned up to recreate the atmosphere of Saturday's pre-bomb threat carnival. Lord Gyllene's pillar to post victory over Suny Bay, in a race that hardly any other horses got into, was cheered to the echo.

Killeshin and Sean Curran were staying on at the end. 'The ground was miles too fast for him and we got well behind early on. Then he crept into the race and ran on to finish seventh. He jumped great. I think that on his best form he was a genuine National horse, but he needed soft ground.'

Conditions for the 1998 Grand National were most certainly in Killeshin's favour, although his build-up to Aintree offered little encouragement. His best effort had come in the Welsh National, a staying-on fourth to Earth Summit in bottomless ground. Subsequently, however, he was well beaten in all four starts. But heavy going at Aintree brought his limitless stamina into play and, at 25-1, he was a popular each-way tip.

His chances received a further boost when stablemate Cavalero won the Martell Fox Hunters' Chase the day before the National. However, it was his Welsh National conqueror Earth Summit who outstayed them all, finishing eleven lengths ahead of the luckless Suny Bay, the pair being a distance clear of the third horse, Samlee.

'I think I'd have finished third that year,' reflects Sean. 'Crossing the Melling Road to go out for the second circuit, he was only just starting to get into it. Coming to the fourth last, I was almost upsides Richard Dunwoody and Andrew Thornton, who eventually finished third and fourth, when I was knocked off by

Him Of Praise. He refused and I cannoned into the side of him and came off. I got back on and continued to finish last of the six to get round.'

Killeshin was retired after that race, with his successor, Cavalero, being pencilled in for the 1999 National. Hence Sean had a Grand National mount for the third year running.

It was a mount he had looked like missing for most of the season, having been sidelined for six months with a lacerated liver, suffered when a horse kicked him in the back while schooling. He returned in February, just in time to partner Cavalero for the first time in the Greenalls Grand National Trial at Haydock.

'In the National itself, I rode him carrying one of the BBC's "jockeycam" cameras. I didn't really want the camera on my helmet, because it weighed 2lb and that made the difference in deciding which saddle I could use. It meant I had to use a lighter, smaller saddle. Unfortunately, the smaller saddle slipped round during the race and I had to pull him up at the last with a circuit to run. Up to then he was jumping from fence to fence and in a great rhythm.'

In March 2000, Cavalero realised a long-held ambition for Manners by winning the Foxhunters' Challenge Cup at Cheltenham.

When asked to compare the two horses, Sean thinks long and hard. 'Cavalero had never actually proved himself in anything other than hunter chases, whereas Killeshin had won the Eider Chase. Cavalero was able to lay up and travel easier in a race but Killeshin was the better stayer.

'There probably wasn't much between them but I have to say that Killeshin was a favourite of mine.'

Sean retired from riding and took out a trainer's licence in 2006. He enjoyed dual Grand National success in 2008 courtesy of Iris De Balme, saddling him to win the Kent version at Folkestone and, more importantly, the Scottish Grand National at Ayr.

After sending out nearly fifty winners he announced his decision to quit the training ranks at the end of January 2011, saying he felt he'd 'got stale at the job.' He added that he planned to take time out to 'recharge the batteries' and visit friends in Australia and South Africa before assessing where his future lies.

Date: Monday 7 April 1997 Going: Good, Good to firm patches   Value to Winner: £178,146

Horse	Owner	Trainer	Age / weight	Jockey	SP
1 Lord Gyllene	Mr Stanley W Clarke	S Brookshaw	9-10-8	A Dobbin	14-1
2 Suny Bay	Uplands Bloodstock	C P E Brooks	8-10-3	J Osborne	8-1
3 Camelot Knight	Mr Michael Gates	N Twiston-Davies	11-10-0	C Llewellyn	100-1
4 Buckboard Bounce	Mr Robert Ogden	G W Richards	11-10-1	P Carberry	40-1

Distances: 25 lengths, 2 lengths, 1¾ lengths. Time: 9 mins 5.8 secs. 36 ran

Winner trained at Shrewsbury, Shropshire

1998

TOM DASCOMBE
Pipe's outsiders

Pond House and Tom Dascombe head to the Grand National start.

OSCAR WILDE ONCE observed that 'Nothing succeeds like excess'. It was a maxim often adopted by Martin Pipe, a trainer renowned for multiple entries in everything from the humblest of selling hurdles to the most competitive of handicaps. He saddled ten horses in the 2001 Grand National, a quarter of the entire field.

In 1998 a total of five Pipe representatives made the Grand National cut. The enigmatic Challenger Du Luc was by far the best of these and Tony McCoy would have lost little sleep in choosing which one to ride. The remaining quartet, Pond House, Diwali Dancer, Damas and Decyborg, were between 19lb and 32lb out of the handicap and only wild optimists or clueless pin-stickers would have fancied their chances.

Bristol-born Tom Dascombe, the son of an accountant, had spent five years with Pipe. His father and grandfather were enthusiastic Saturday punters and they fuelled the youngster's interest. By the time he left school, his sights were fixed on a life in racing.

'I went to Martin Pipe because he was the best,' says Tom. 'I'd ridden pony club, dressage, eventing and show jumping, but it's amazing how little you know about racing when you actually go into it. I held a conditional jockey's licence for three years and rode about eight winners for him – not a very good strike rate for the amount of rides I had but it was brilliant experience; a very professional yard.'

A Boxing Day 1994 winner on Morstock, a spare ride for Ron Hodges, forged a link that resulted in Tom leaving one Somerset trainer and joining another. He rode out his claim for Hodges and went on to partner some forty winners for him over the next three seasons.

He still had the occasional ride for Pipe, such as on the Thursday before the 1998 Grand National. While most of the big name jockeys were at Aintree, Tom was having a typical day at the office at Taunton, with two rides for Hodges plus one in the last for Pipe, which finished third.

After the race, Tom rang Pipe to explain how the horse had run, only to be greeted with depressing news. 'Martin said "You should have rung a quarter of an hour ago; I've been trying to get hold of you. I was going to give you a ride in the Grand National but it's gone now". I was desperately depressed.

'Then shortly after, Martin rang back to say that the lad he'd booked couldn't take the mount because he hadn't ridden the required fifteen winners. He asked me if I'd like to ride it, to which I replied "Of course I do, I'd love to". He said "You don't even know what the horse is yet". I told him it didn't matter; I didn't care what it was. He said "You can ride Pond House".

Pond House was a genuine outsider and looked up against it. A front runner, he was best on firm ground at two or two-and-a-half miles, whereas this was four-and-a-half miles in desperately heavy going. He hadn't run since winning at Cartmel in August, and in his one previous venture over the Grand National fences the previous spring he had failed to get beyond the first in the John Hughes Chase. They were hardly the best credentials but the horse had qualified for the race and would take his chance.

Not that Pipe's other 100-1 shots had any better prospects. Damas, the mount of Australian Jamie Evans, was two stone out of the handicap and a two-and-a-half miler. Diwali Dancer, with Robert 'Choc' Thornton up, was a novice who had only made his steeplechasing debut in January. Decyborg, partnered by Irish jockey Paul Carberry, was officially rated the least talented runner in the race and appeared hopelessly out of his depth.

Tom hadn't ridden Pond House in a race, though he'd got to know him at Pond House itself, the name of Pipe's training establishment.

'The horse had ten stone and that's usually a bit of a struggle for me,' he admits, 'but from the moment I knew I was riding him, the weight just fell off, no problem. I stopped eating on Friday morning, had a sauna on the night and again on Saturday at the racecourse. Normally, by the time of the race I'd be in a terrible mood and fed up, especially riding a complete no-hoper, but because it was the National, this was different.

'I remember sitting in the sauna two and a half hours before the race. Some of the jockeys were saying to me "God, I wouldn't like to be riding that." Others said "Not only would I not want to ride it; I don't want to be anywhere near you. You've no chance of getting round."

'Martin saw me an hour and a half before the race to make sure I knew exactly what I was doing. His instructions were "Ride him as you like. Look after the horse, look after yourself and enjoy yourself – and whatever you do, keep out of the way of Challenger Du Luc".

Whether that was a warning to keep clear in case he brought Challenger Du Luc down, or vice versa, is not clear, but it was something Tom didn't have to worry about for long, as Pipe's main hope crashed out of the race at the very first fence. Diwali Dancer was one of four others who got no further.

Tom recalls: 'I knew this was the biggest ride of my life and I was determined to enjoy it, so I jumped him out, knowing that he'd have the pace to go with them. I thought he'd probably be better off in front where he could see the fences, rather than stuck behind a wall of horses. He jumped the first well and I started taking each fence as it came.

'Although I'd walked the course, I was concentrating so much on what I was doing that I didn't even know it was Becher's until I'd jumped it. At the time I couldn't remember a thing, I was just concentrating on the next fence. But looking back now, he jumped fantastically, stood off for every fence. He wouldn't have gone four and a half miles like that but he could certainly do two.

'He jumped the last with a circuit to go [the fourteenth] and I felt him go lame behind, so I pulled him up immediately. He was taken straight to the equine hospital in Liverpool where he stayed for quite a while. He was retired there and then and had a happy retirement out in the paddocks.

'He ran a great race for a mile and a half or two miles. Until I pulled him up I was one hundred percent happy with him and he felt like he'd keep galloping all day.

'I knew I'd never get the chance to ride in the Grand National again. Martin's instructions were "Enjoy yourself", which is exactly what I did.'

The second half of the race developed into a duel between Earth Summit, the mount of Carl Llewellyn, and the previous year's runner-up Suny Bay, with Earth Summit out-slogging the lionhearted Suny Bay in the most gruelling of Aintree mud marathons for many a year. Only six horses finished, one of them having been remounted.

Tom subsequently moved to Lambourn as assistant to trainer Ralph Beckett. The two had met when Beckett spent a year as assistant to Pipe and they became great friends. He continued riding but with mounts hard to come by, called an end to his eleven years as a 95-winner jump jockey after finishing last on Sex Bomb in a Fontwell novice hurdle on 7 October 2001.

He immediately left for Kentucky to work for a bloodstock agency in Louisville. From there he moved down to Florida, breaking in yearlings for the breeze up sales. He returned to Britain in 2002 and resumed his post of assistant trainer to Ralph Beckett.

When Beckett sent two horses over to Dubai later that year, Tom went with them. There he met up with top South African trainer Mike de Kock and joined his operation in April 2003, just days after stable star Victory Moon had won the UAE Derby at Nad Al Sheba. Tom accompanied Victory Moon to England that summer. The horse was campaigned at the very highest level in the Queen Anne, the Eclipse and the 'King George'.

In February 2005 he took on the post of assistant trainer to John Jenkins at Royston, before setting up on his own at Lambourn and forging a successful career.

In the summer of 2009 came the news that he was teaming up with foot-balling legend Michael Owen and Betfair founder Andrew Black to train at the purpose-built Manor House Stables, near Malpas in Cheshire. He sent out his first winner from the new yard when Mondovi, owned jointly by footballers Kieron Dyer and Craig Bellamy, won at Wolverhampton on 25 September.

As for Martin Pipe's Grand National class of 1998, only one of his quintet made it beyond halfway, the unconsidered 200-1 shot Decyborg. He was one of just nine remaining when being pulled up four from home.

Maybe Decyborg's better than expected display had something to do with the jockey, for Paul Carberry certainly knew how to give a horse a ride. Twelve months later he would prove just how good he could be when riding one with a fighting chance. That horse was Bobbyjo.

Date: Saturday 4 April 1998 Going: Heavy Value to Winner: £212,569

Horse	Owner	Trainer	Age / weight	Jockey	SP
1 Earth Summit	The Summit Partnership	N Twiston-Davies	10-10-5	C Llewellyn	7-1fav
2 Suny Bay	Uplands Bloodstock	C P E Brooks	9-12-0	G Bradley	11-1
3 Samlee	White Lion Partnership	P J Hobbs	9-10-1	R Dunwoody	8-1
4 St Mellion Fairway	St Mellion Estates Ltd	P R Webber	9-10-1	A Thornton	20-1

Distances: 11 lengths, distance, 1¼ lengths. Time: 10 mins 51.4 secs. 37 ran

Winner trained at Naunton, Cheltenham, Gloucestershire

1999

LORCAN WYER
*The biggest f***ing kick ever*

Blue Charm and Lorcan Wyer lead the 1999 Grand National field.

'IT WAS VERY hard to walk away from a horse of Barton's calibre,' says Lorcan Wyer of his decision to quit the saddle, 'but I'd had such a good relationship with Peter and Tim Easterby and I didn't want to spoil it. I'd seen it in other yards where maybe a guy goes on a year too long, leading some owners to express a preference for another rider.

'I'd ridden one short of 600 winners all told, including a couple of Cheltenham Festival winners. With the exception of Barton it wasn't going to get much better.'

And in addition to all those winners there was that never to be forgotten ride on Blue Charm in the 1999 Grand National.

Lorcan was born and raised in County Dublin, the son of a furniture manufacturer. 'We had a few stables at the back of the house,' he says, 'and a local trainer called Frank Oakes asked if he could rent the boxes as an overflow yard. I started riding out for him before school and at weekends and I had my first ride in public for him. It was a baptism of fire, on the beach at Laytown. I can't tell you a great deal about it except that my legs nearly buckled with exhaustion after the race.

'My first winner was at Navan in July 1984, a smashing horse trained by Michael O'Brien called Champion Prince. He was difficult to train but a very talented horse on his day. Mick did a great job in getting him right that day and he never came off the bridle. It was a complete steering job. He went on to win two or three races in quick succession and got me going.'

Britain's first sighting of Mr L Wyer came at Chepstow in March 1986, the Saturday before Cheltenham, when he brought the Homer Scott-trained Canute Express with a well-timed run to land the BBC-televised Racing Post Hurdle. Just four days later he rode Scott's well-backed Omerta to a comfortable victory in the four-mile National Hunt Chase.

His arrival on a permanent basis came through what he describes as 'a mixture of circumstances', with Grand National day 1986 having something to do with it.

'I was asked by Colonel Dick Warden, who was a patron of Peter Easterby's, to ride a horse called Jobroke for him in the amateurs' hurdle at Aintree. I won on him and then won on Canute Express again for Homer Scott. So a double on Grand National day was extra special.

'The great Jonjo O'Neill got very ill and Peter Easterby asked me to go over. I didn't need to be asked twice and I joined Peter in August 1986. The Easterbys were brilliant people to ride for, I couldn't speak highly enough of them. I had a really good relationship with them over the years.'

The Tim Easterby-trained Barton was undoubtedly the best horse he rode during his career and his highly acclaimed triumph in the 1999 Royal & SunAlliance Novices' Hurdle was Lorcan's only other Cheltenham Festival winner, coming thirteen years after Omerta. However, his long association with father and son Easterby boasts a thick catalogue of success.

Several of the Easterby-Wyer combo's big race victories were gained at Aintree, courtesy of horses such as Young Benz, Nohalmdun, and the 1996 Martell Cup winner Scotton Banks. Barton followed up his Cheltenham Festival triumph by winning Aintree's Martell Mersey Novices' Hurdle.

Although his early attempts in the Grand National can be filed in the drawer marked 'best forgotten', the veteran Kildimo, trained by Sue Smith, provided Lorcan with success over the big fences when winning the 1992 Becher Chase.

But there was one day at Aintree went it all went wrong, on Saturday, 23 November 1996. Shrugging off the disappointment of having turned a somersault on Simply Dashing, the 5-2 on 'banker' in the opening novices' chase, he weighed out to ride Thornton Gate in the six-runner Children in Need Handicap Hurdle. He was a horse that Lorcan knew well and trusted.

'It was a pretty innocuous fall,' he recalls. 'Thornton Gate stepped at the second hurdle going down the back. I remember lying on the ground thinking "That wasn't too bad" and was just about to pick myself up when, unfortunately, another horse following stood on the left side of my face. Talk about your face being in the wrong place at the wrong time. I knew immediately all wasn't well.

'Both cheekbones, both eye-sockets, split palate top and bottom, plus a fractured pelvis and broken collarbone which were the least of my worries. Luckily, if you're ever going to get your face kicked in, Liverpool is the place to go because they've got the most wonderful staff in Walton Hospital. It's amazing when I think back to what they did for me.

'They cut me open from ear to ear across the top of my head, pulled the skin down and basically rebuilt my face. It was an eight and a half hour operation. Then they wheeled me out and said to my wife "We've put him back together pretty well. We've even managed to restore the gap between his teeth". She replied "He never had a gap between his teeth". They said "Wait there" and wheeled me back in for another half-hour's surgery.

'Initially, after an operation like that you feel good for a while, but after I signed myself out of hospital and went home I just hit a bit of a lull and coming back riding was the last thing on my mind. They tell me it's kind of a natural reaction.'

He was back at Aintree the following spring, completing the course for the first time on General Wolfe in the 'Monday National', albeit a distant sixteenth of seventeen finishers behind Lord Gyllene. His 1998 mount, Scotton Banks, ran well enough until they parted company four from home.

Then in 1999 Lorcan came in for a Grand National ride he could tell his grandchildren about in years to come. The horse was Blue Charm, trained by Sue Bradburne up in Cupar, Fife. Her amateur rider son Mark was set to partner him but was ruled out by a broken collarbone, sustained when Rough Quest had fallen in the Martell Fox Hunters' Chase two days earlier.

Says Lorcan: 'I felt sorry for Mark because it was going to be his first ride in the National. I'd ridden for Sue and Johnny Bradburne and I'd ridden with Johnny when he was going round. He was a great feller and a talented enough amateur but we professionals used to bollock him for getting in our way. It was always good banter with him.

'I was delighted to get the ride because, at that late hour, you don't really expect to get on anything. I'd watched Blue Charm run round Haydock and I always thought he made great use of himself. He could dance in front of a fence; a supple little horse, brave and tough. Even though he was over a stone out of the handicap he'd certainly be a good ride, but I never thought he'd be up to running as well as he did.

'A lot depends on how a horse takes to the atmosphere because it's very intense. I remember he had two people leading him up in the paddock and his eyes were popping out of his head. He was white with sweat and I was thinking to myself "Christ, I've really done it now. This is the end of L Wyer".

'In the parade he was getting wound up. You really don't want a horse too wound up because you want your horse to spit it out and relax on the run to the first. But he was keen and buzzed and I thought "He's not going to be paying much attention to the first fence". I don't mind saying that I was a little bit apprehensive because I didn't want my race to end at the first, but the signs were there that it might.

'We set off in the race and I thought I might as well get his name mentioned and give the owners a bit of a thrill over the first two fences and then make my exit at the big ditch, the third.

'I think "rhythm" is the best word to describe it. We just clicked. Lovely rhythm, met the first fence brilliantly and just popped away. The horse was thinking for himself but at the same time enjoying it. That's just the perfect mixture, you couldn't ask for more.

'I'm thinking "This can't be happening". I'm coming to the second last with a circuit to run, jumping away like a gazelle, having a chat with a few of the lads around me, Norman Williamson, Andrew Thornton, and we just seem to be going our gallop. We jumped the Chair and I thought he'd drop away. Even though I'm really enjoying it, I'm still thinking "This doesn't happen to me. I don't get a ride like this in the National".

'We went out to the second circuit and I said to myself "This is unbelievable". Then I got a little bit too cocky going down to the first ditch. I thought I saw a stride but I was a little bit long and he saw another stride and put down on me. It was the one and only mistake he made, nodded on landing. That was his way of saying "You just sit there and hang on tight and I'll take care of the jumping department". That was my lesson learned and I never asked him again.

'I went down the middle at Becher's second time; I didn't want the drop to catch him out. It was just a dream, it was like slow motion. When your horse is clicking and jumping and operating, there's no better thrill.

'Going down to the third last I still didn't want to go for him. Just try and nurse him because he'd given his all, he'd run so enthusiastically for me. I wasn't being cocky, I was trying to be kind to him.

'I took half a pull going to the second last, took half a pull again going to the last, just to save a bit because it's such a long way home from the last. Save, save, save. Still thought I might win at the last because he hadn't emptied on me yet, but then two strides after it I knew Paul [Carberry] had gone. From there, my lad was going up and down on one spot.'

Bobbyjo and Paul Carberry were gone beyond recall, drawing further clear with every stride. Lorcan was now riding for second place.

'The closer the line came, the more I was aware of Richard Dunwoody [on Call It A Day] coming at me. My horse held on for second. Another three strides and we'd have lost it. I wanted to congratulate Paul but he'd disappeared amid a crowd of people.

'On the way in, people were saying "Bad luck, Lorcan". I said "What do you mean, bad luck? I've had the biggest fucking kick ever. There's nothing to be sorry about". I felt so happy and proud. The Bradburnes were speechless, nearly in tears.

'It would have been a tragedy if the little horse had lost second place because he'd run the most wonderful race. How sad it was when the news came during that summer that Blue Charm had passed away out at grass. That was the real tragedy.'

Lorcan's aspirations for the 1999/2000 campaign received a setback when injury ruled out Barton for the season. By the time the horse returned the following year, Lorcan had announced his retirement. Towards the end of his career he had been a regular contributor to The Racing Channel, his outgoing personality being well suited to appearing in front of the cameras. Many people presumed that this was the direction he would take when quitting the saddle but a vacancy arose for a racing official with the Irish Turf Club and Lorcan jumped at the chance.

'I was delighted to join an organisation like the Turf Club. I'd enjoyed my work with The Racing Channel and gained a lot from that, but I felt I owed it to my family to avail them of long term security.

'A racing official with the Turf Club is expected to wear five different hats – starter, stewards' secretary, clerk of the scales, clerk of the course and judge. You have to be flexible and every week brings a lot of variety and new challenges.'

When he's overseeing runners in the paddock and at the start, does he ever yearn to jump back up on one of them?

'Not very often,' he laughs. 'It's best leaving in the frame of mind that "Yeah, maybe I'd like to have one more go", rather than "God, I never want to see another horse in my life". I think I left just at the right time. I certainly have no regrets at all.'

Date: Saturday 10 April 1999   Going: Good   Value to Winner: £242,600

Horse	Owner	Trainer	Age / weight	Jockey	SP
1 Bobbyjo	Mr R Burke	T Carberry	9-10-0	P Carberry	10-1
2 Blue Charm	Mrs M Lindsay	Mrs S C Bradburne	9-10-0	L Wyer	25-1
3 Call It A Day	Mrs J Lane	D Nicholson	9-10-2	R Dunwoody	7-1
4 Addington Boy	Mrs B Jamieson	F Murphy	11-10-7	A Maguire	10-1

Distances: 10 lengths, neck, 7 lengths. Time: 9 mins 14.0 secs. 32 ran

Winner trained at Ballybin, Ashbourne, County Meath, Ireland

2000

ROBERT BELLAMY
Bells hasn't got long!

Robert Bellamy jumps a schooling fence on Trinitro.

LITTLE OVER AN hour after Steve Knight had returned in triumph to Aintree's unsaddling enclosure after winning the 1987 Grand National on Maori Venture, an unknown amateur found himself being escorted into that same hallowed arena. Jenny Pitman's hurdler Molojec had just given him his first success under National Hunt Rules. What a time and place to do it; Aintree on jumping's biggest day of the year.

'It was all a bit of a shock coming back in between two mounted policemen to such a vast crowd,' Robert Bellamy admits. It was certainly a larger stage than his local point-to-point course at Garnons, where he had ridden Spritestown Lass to victory on his first ride in public.

Robert hails from 'Scudamore country'; Kings Caple, near Ross-on-Wye, where his family own a 300-acre arable and soft fruit farm. He trod the traditional countryman's path into racing, starting out with ponies and graduating via the pony club to eventing and the point-to-point circuit, riding a total of seven winners from 'about a hundred' rides between the flags.

On leaving school he spent a year learning the family business, which focuses on strawberry farming, before working at a livery yard for twelve months. A brief spell with James Bethell at Didcot was followed by a one-year farm management course at the Royal Agricultural College at Cirencester, a sensible contingency in case a life in racing failed to materialise. His first job came about at the start of the 1986/87 season when Peter Scudamore put him in touch with Martin Pipe, resulting in an eighteen-month stint as his pupil-assistant-cum-amateur rider. Two weeks after that Aintree success on Molojec, Robert scored on Pipe's Golden Raider at Market Rasen, finishing the campaign with two winners from 57 rides.

Rather than spending that summer picking strawberries, he opted for six weeks in America, working for trainers Pat Byrne at Atlantic City, New Jersey, and Michael Dickinson in Maryland. He then returned to Pipe as amateur rider for the start of the 1987/88 season. A double at Bangor-on-Dee just before Christmas fired thoughts of turning professional. Further incentive came courtesy of Memberson on New Year's Day at Cheltenham, in a remarkable climax to the four-mile ASW Chase. Turning for home, Memberson was tailed off and in a seemingly hopeless position but he developed equine wings from two out to collar Knock Hill halfway up the run-in and rob him of what appeared to be certain victory.

Having taken the plunge and become a conditional, Robert joined David Nicholson's yard in February 1988. Things were going well approaching the end of the season, with six winners from 101 rides, but the 102nd was a disaster. It came at Warwick on a Saturday evening in May. Riding Royal Effigy, he fell when leading two out, bringing down Charlie Mann, whose mount, Lightning Wind, rolled on Robert, smashing his right thigh in seven places. Complications with pinning the injury hindered his recovery and the jockey's spirits were at their lowest ebb.

The road back to fitness was long and painful. It was February 1989 before he resumed race riding. Gradually, the winners started to come, but at Stratford in the spring of 1991 came another bone crunching fall, in which he compressed three vertebrae in his neck. This time he was out for six months.

His belated start to the 1991/92 campaign meant that he missed riding out his claim by two winners, losing it on his twenty-fifth birthday in January. It was nonetheless a season that brought some notable milestones, beginning with a first Grand National mount on Paul James's New Halen.

He recalls: 'We parted company at the nineteenth, the third fence second time round. There was a loose horse in the ditch, running up and down. Poor old New Halen had to try and jump that and the fence; he ended up just breasting it and didn't even come over, shot me into orbit. I actually jumped the fence well but he didn't come with me!'

That month of April 1992 was to get even better for Robert. Four days after the National, he rode the fiftieth winner of his career on Petty Bridge at Ludlow. The following week he partnered the same horse to victory in the George Duller Handicap Hurdle at Cheltenham. Then came what he describes as 'one of the highlights of my career' in the Whitbread Gold Cup at Sandown. Riding Martin Pipe's The Leggett, he led all the way to the last fence before being overhauled on the run-in by Topsham Bay and Arctic Call.

He achieved another ambition in May 1993 when scoring on Michael Scudamore's Bird Of Spirit at Hereford. He explains: 'Michael trained two miles down the road from my parents. From the age of fourteen I used to cycle down and ride out for him. He was a terrific help to me and the one thing I wanted to do was to ride him a winner. To do it at Michael's local track was fantastic.'

Robert rode for Paul Webber during the 1995/96 season, partnering that popular grey Flying Instructor to his first three victories. He subsequently freelanced and supplemented his income by guesting on The Racing Channel, putting into practice the media training he undertook courtesy of JETS, the Jockeys' Employment Training Scheme.

He also did his share of travelling, notably around Scandinavia, and in September 1999 won the Norwegian Grand National on Trinitro. The race was run over two and three-quarter miles in hock-deep going, with live hedges and a couple of wooden rails among the obstacles to the negotiated, in addition to the traditional birch fences. In beating Philip Hobbs's Ashwell Boy by a length, Trinitro earned a handicap rating for the Grand National itself.

Trinitro had been purchased for 4,000 guineas out of Newmarket trainer Conrad Allen's stable as an unraced three-year-old. He was now trained by former Norwegian champion jockey Rune Haugen on a private estate above the port city of Drammen, an hour's drive from Oslo. With Trinitro having qualified to run in the 2000 Grand National, Haugen persuaded the horse's owner, Liv Myskja, to go for the race. Robert Bellamy would keep the ride.

As no racing takes place during the Norwegian winter, it was decided to send Trinitro straight to Aintree without the benefit of a preparatory run. The week before he left, the BBC's Peter Scudamore arrived with a film crew in tow and filmed Robert cantering the horse in the snow. It looked all very picturesque and made for a good story.

Racing is regarded as a minority sport in Norway and it is many years since Norwegian television last screened the Grand National. Hence, there was comparatively little local interest with regard to Trinitro's participation in the world's most famous steeplechase. But in Britain the publicity associated with the horse provided a welcome boost for Robert, who was struggling for rides and had only one winner to his name all season. He was keen to remind trainers that he was still around.

Journalist Rodney Masters also visited the horse's connections to pen an article for the Racing Post. His concluding paragraph was all too prophetic: 'Trinitro has never fallen, and all concerned with the horse agree the worst result will be a first-fence exit. A natural front-runner, he can take a fierce hold. Many of that inclination jump the first too well, and at a velocity which causes them to somersault on landing.'

Says Robert: 'The horse had never seen anything like Aintree. He was used to seeing a crowd of 600 people and there were only four other runners in the Norwegian Grand National. In the paddock he was white with sweat. When we went out to parade in front of the stands, the commentator announced "And now we have the Norwegian challenger, Trinitro". Of course, the crowd all roared. That was it for the horse, he blew his brains.

'He ran away with me to post. It was as much as I could do to pull him up when we went to look at the first fence. When we had our girths checked at the start he was pawing at the ground, just like a stallion. Warren Marston looked over and shouted to the others "Bells hasn't got long!"

'It was quick ground and I thought the horse wouldn't be good enough to even lay up. I thought "I'll be fine as long as I can hunt round at the back and do a circuit. I'll probably get given the key to the city of Oslo and be acclaimed a national hero there."

'By the time we got to the Melling Road I was in front, going flat to the boards. I tried to take a pull to get him back on his hocks about ten strides before the first, just to have some hope of getting over it. He didn't take a blind bit of notice, just kept galloping and never left the ground.

'I was lucky in that Trinitro was in front. He catapulted me to the ground and slid along behind me. The field fanned out and left me in a little triangle and I didn't get a kick of any sort as the other thirty-nine went by me.

'Warren Marston jumped the second, looked at the loose horse upsides and called out "I told you boys, he's gone!"

'To earn an extra few quid I had one of the jockeycam cameras on my head. The jockeys in the weighing room thought it was the funniest thing when they saw me with a camera on my head because, whenever I rode a puller and couldn't stop it, my head used to nod until the horse stopped pulling. You could just imagine the picture – you weren't going to see a damn thing. And as we went at the first, it didn't last long.'

That year's race brought another family triumph as Papillon repelled the challenge of Mely Moss for a second consecutive Irish victory. The winner was trained by Ted Walsh and ridden by his twenty-year-old son Ruby, following in the footsteps of Tommy and Paul Carberry, the father and son combination that had succeeded with Bobbyjo twelve months earlier.

In beating Mely Moss by a length and a quarter, Papillion landed a huge public gamble, having been backed down from 33-1 to 10-1 on the day. The runner-up, who had finished second in the previous year's Fox Hunters' over the National fences, was returning from a 346-day absence, following leg problems and a viral infection.

Robert's Racing Channel experience led to him being asked to provide paddock interviews at various racecourses. At Hereford on Easter Monday, two weeks after Trinitro's first fence exit at Aintree, he not only doubled his score for the season by scoring on novice hurdler Long Room Lady but also interviewed winning connections after each race over the public address system.

A fortnight or so later he had a bad fall at Uttoxeter, puncturing a lung and fracturing ribs. While recuperating he enquired whether one or two other courses might allow him to do the interviews. Towcester, Worcester and Newton Abbot quickly snapped him up.

That Easter Monday victory on Long Room Lady turned out to be his last. He retired at the end of the following season, aged 34 and with 115 winners to his name, finishing third on his final ride, Barnane Walk at Wincanton.

But when he left the confines of the weighing room he didn't go far, merely to the room next door, officiating as Warwick's Clerk of the Course. He also adopted the role of Jonjo O'Neill's representative when the Jackdaws Castle trainer was elsewhere. Nowadays he is Clerk of the Course at Towcester.

Robert harbours fond memories of his years in the saddle. He'll never forget the day in December 1991 when he 'went through the card at Uttoxeter'. Well actually, he won the opening novices' hurdle on Barton Bank...and then the rest of the meeting was abandoned due to a waterlogged course!

Date: Saturday 8 April 2000 Going: Good, Good to firm patches   Value to Winner: £290,000

Horse	Owner	Trainer	Age / weight	Jockey	SP
1 Papillon	Mrs J Maxwell Moran	T M Walsh	9-10-12	R Walsh	10-1
2 Mely Moss	Mr Darren C Mercer	C R Egerton	9-10-1	N Williamson	25-1
3 Niki Dee	Mr George Dilger	P Beaumont	10-10-13	R Supple	25-1
4 Brave Highlander	Mr SNJ Embiricos	J T Gifford	12-10-0	P Hide	40-1

Distances: 1¼ lengths, 12 lengths, 7 lengths. Time: 9 mins 9.7 secs. 40 ran

Winner trained at Kill, County Kildare, Ireland

2001

TOM DOYLE

The stand-in's stand-in

Tom DDyle is sent flying by Esprit De Cotte's refusal at the eleventh fence.

'SAD, REALLY. I mean, it's no life at all, a stand-in's stand-in.' The observation comes from a theatre critic named Moon in Tom Stoppard's one-act play, *The Real Inspector Hound*. Tom Doyle would beg to differ.

There's a lot to be said for mobile phones, but jockey Paul Flynn's was switched off that 2001 Grand National afternoon when Nicky Henderson was desperately trying to contact him. He was seeking a replacement rider for his runner Esprit De Cotte. Having ridden in the opening race, Mick Fitzgerald had made a late decision to give up his Grand National mount as he had not fully recovered from the effects of a heavy first fence fall from Bacchanal the previous day.

Flynn was around somewhere but nobody quite knew where. Announcements were broadcast over the public address, more abortive calls made to his mobile, all with no response. The clock was ticking away. However long Henderson's tether may have been, he was nearing the end of it.

Sitting in the weighing room, minding his own business, was conditional jockey Tom Doyle. The 3lb claimer had journeyed to Aintree solely to partner a 40-1 outsider in the bumper, the last race on the card.

His prospects of riding in his first Grand National had seemingly ended the day before when Richard Lee's Samuel Wilderspin had missed the cut by one.

It's a frustrating thing, being number 41 when the maximum field is 40 but as Lee saw the rain continue to fall, with 17mm in 24 hours rendering the course barely raceable, he reflected that Samuel Wilderspin's elimination had been a blessing in disguise.

Tom was destined from an early age to become involved with racing in one form or another. His father, George Doyle, was a bloodstock agent and there were always racehorses to be found around the family's home at Inistioge, County Kilkenny. When Tom was twelve he began working weekends and school holidays for Aidan O'Brien, who was then just starting out on what would be a meteoric rise up the training ladder.

When school days were over, Tom joined O'Brien full time then moved on to trainer Eamon Sheehy and rode six winners as an amateur. After a year there he made the journey to England in search of greater opportunities and joined Lambourn-based Roger Curtis. The link with Curtis had been forged via Tom's father, who had sold him horses over the years. Coupled with the opportunities provided by Curtis, there were plenty of other Lambourn trainers for whom he could ride out.

Having lost his 7lb claim when winning on the Curtis-trained Ourownfellow at Plumpton on the eve of the 2000 Cheltenham Festival, he then finished runner up on Noel Chance's Inch Rose in that year's National Hunt Challenge Cup Chase.

While still an amateur he began riding for Richard Lee, finishing second on Samuel Wilderspin in a valuable amateurs' chase at Cheltenham in November 2000. He turned professional soon after and rode Samuel Wilderspin to a hard fought half-length victory over Banker Count at Wetherby in February.

With Samuel Wilderspin just failing to make the 2001 Grand National field, Tom had dismissed all thought of a ride in the race. But when all efforts to locate Flynn proved fruitless, he was among the first to offer his services.

'Luckily,' says Tom, 'I was one of the few jockeys left there able to do ten stone. It was maybe half an hour before the race when Mr Henderson confirmed I'd got the ride. I didn't have time to think about it and get nervous, which was probably the best way to have your first ride in the National. I just had to get on with things, change into my gear, get my saddle and weigh out as quickly as I could.

'I hadn't ridden the course before, although I'd walked it, just for the sake of walking round and seeing what it was like. I'd never sat on Esprit De Cotte but I spoke to Mick Fitzgerald who knew the horse. I also spoke with some of the other jockeys about riding round there, but Mick was the biggest help because he'd not only been round, he'd won it.

'I went down the middle to inner. I wanted to give him a little bit of light. He really enjoyed it early on, he was keen and loving it. He jumped great.'

The rain-sodden conditions had seen fifteen of the forty runners fall or unseat by the time the field reached the Canal Turn. It was there that the riderless

Paddy's Return veered violently across the obstacle and, in a scene reminiscent of the Easter Hero pile-up of 1928, wiped out ten more.

'I was luckily just a length or two in front of all the trouble,' Tom continues, 'but I did get bumped and knocked around a bit. At the time I didn't know about all the mayhem that had gone on behind. I'd seen one or two go down out the corner of my eye but not half the field.

'After that my horse stopped enjoying it quite so much. He wasn't interested in the next two fences. Then at the big ditch, the eleventh, he's gone to refuse and I've gone over his head. He was about to come up and then he's put back down and stopped halfway, left himself sitting in the middle of it. We parted company and I've gone flying over the fence without him. I pulled the horse out of the fence and hacked him back.

'He gave me a super spin until the eleventh, but then we had different ideas.'

Just a handful survived beyond the halfway point and the number was reduced further when the riderless Edmond impeded three of them at the nineteenth fence. Carl Llewellyn's efforts to regain his lost reins and stay on Beau came to an end at the next, leaving Smarty and Red Marauder with the race between them.

It was Richard Guest who brought Red Marauder home an exhausted winner, a distance clear of Smarty. Both Blowing Wind and Papillon were remounted to trail in third and fourth respectively to end what was another dramatic chapter in Aintree's rich history.

Uncomfortable to watch? Certainly. Should the race have taken place at all, given the appalling conditions? Opinions differed wildly.

Tom Doyle is sure of one thing: his first Grand National ride was an unforgettable experience, even if it did take a while to register. 'I don't think it hit me that I was riding in the Grand National until after the race,' he reflects. 'Because there was such a rush and it happened so quickly, it took a long time to actually sink in. It was great to get the ride, a huge thrill for me. It's every jockey's dream to ride in the Grand National.

'The following year when I rode in the race, it seemed like I'd never ridden in it before. It was more like my first time the second time.'

Paul Flynn's loss had been Tom Doyle's gain. Just seven days later at Newton Abbot came further illustration of their respective fortunes. Whereas Tom rode a Channel 4 televised double on Richard Lee's Master Of Illusion and Cage Aux Folles, Flynn suffered two falls, breaking his wrist in the second of them.

Tom landed the Crandon Park Stud-sponsored Mares' 'National Hunt' Novices' Hurdle Final at Newbury on 25-1 shot Monger Lane in March 2002. Two weeks later he partnered the fancied Samuel Wilderspin in the Grand National, but the partnership ended at the fourth fence. Says Tom: 'He got too high and landed out on his nose; just landed too steep and knuckled over more so than fell. He was unlucky.'

He later became stable jockey to Paul Webber, the association ending in 2007 when Tom decided to continue his riding career in Ireland.

So the advice for jockeys seeking a last-minute Grand National ride is to keep the mobile phone switched on. Handy things, mobiles, particularly for a stand-in's stand-in.

Date: Saturday 7 April 2001   Going: Heavy   Value to Winner: £310,000

Horse	Owner	Trainer	Age / weight	Jockey	SP
1 Red Marauder	Mr N B Mason	Owner	11-10-11	Richard Guest	33-1
2 Smarty	Mrs T Brown	M Pitman	8-10-0	T J Murphy	16-1
3 Blowing Wind	Mr P A Deal	M C Pipe	8-10-9	A P McCoy	16-1
4 Papillon	Mrs J Maxwell Moran	T M Walsh	10-11-5	R Walsh	14-1

Distances: Distance, Distance, Distance. Time: 11 mins 0.1 secs. 40 ran

Winner trained at Crook, County Durham

2002

NOEL FEHILY
Celibate

Noel Fehily on Celibate, pictured at Lambourn's Good Friday open day.

IN WINNING ON Bindaree Jim Culloty became only the sixth rider to complete the Cheltenham Gold Cup and Grand National double in the same year, a feat last achieved by John Burke in 1976.

It was a chance ride for Culloty, substituting for the luckless Jamie Goldstein who had broken a leg at Ludlow three days earlier. Thus Goldstein joined the likes of David Goulding, Andrew Adams and Tom Jenks, each deprived of Grand National glory through injury. History has a habit of repeating itself.

Winning trainer Nigel Twiston-Davies had endured a wretched season that had left him on the verge of relinquishing his licence. Just five days before the National he saddled a winner at Hereford's Easter Monday fixture, his first for weeks. Two more winners came the next day. He appeared to have turned the corner – and not a moment too soon.

Ironically, it was the most fancied of Twiston-Davies' three runners, Beau, who almost cost his stable-mate victory. Having unseated Carl Llewellyn at the fourteenth fence, Beau stalked Bindaree virtually from the moment he took up the running at Becher's second time round. At the final fence Beau almost collided with Bindaree, handing the advantage to Richard Johnson on the blinkered grey What's Up Boys. However, Culloty gathered Bindaree together and, as What's Up Boys drifted right at the Elbow, he switched him to the inside rail and regained the initiative from his rival to score by a length and three-quarters.

Finishing in third place was the 8-1 favourite Blowing Wind, the mount of Tony McCoy, followed by Kingsmark and Supreme Charm. Behind them in sixth came Celibate, a 66-1 outsider ridden by Noel Fehily.

Celibate's gutsy performance vindicated the opinion of his trainer, Charlie Mann. 'I don't think he got the credit he deserved,' he says. 'Before the race, everyone said he shouldn't be there. Yet he'd made all to win the Desert Orchid Chase first time out at two miles five, beating some decent horses such as Cenkos. He deserved to take his place and he proved me right by running the race of his life. I knew he'd jump round because I'd never seen a horse jump like him.'

Noel Fehily agrees: 'Everyone was saying he wouldn't stay but I always thought he would. He'd run around Ascot over three miles and got it well so I was quietly confident. He wasn't really fancied but he put up a super performance that day.

'He was always a very bold jumper. In the National he gave the first one a rub, went down on his nose – there were a lot of fallers at that first fence – but after that he didn't put a foot wrong the whole way round.'

Celibate chased the leaders to just beyond halfway but then began to get tired. Says Noel: 'On the second circuit I was more or less riding him to get round safely. I didn't really think I could win from there. I think that ended up being the right thing to do, to accept it early on rather than forcing him to go the pace, because I probably wouldn't have got home. In the end I've run past a few tired horses.'

Adds Charlie: 'It was great running him because the previous year we had the favourite, Moral Support, and there was a lot of pressure on, whereas with Celibate it was great because nobody thought he should be there and we'd no pressure.'

Moral Support had been sent off the 10-1 co-favourite along with Edmond and Inis Cara in 2001. Not that Noel had felt much pressure on what was his first Grand National ride. 'To be honest, it didn't bother me. I don't think he was made favourite until near the off so I didn't really know anything about it. He was fourth or fifth in the betting but, with all the rain, he was heavily backed.

'He was little more than a novice that year. He won four on the bounce then was second in the Welsh National then was third up at Haydock after that. When he went to Aintree, if he was ever going to win, that was just his time because it pissed down with rain. He loved really soft ground; it gave him a chance to travel.

'We didn't know what he'd be like over those fences but, once he got over the first three, I was really getting into a rhythm with him and he was starting to travel with me.

'Coming to the Canal Turn I was somewhere about mid-div. I didn't really see what happened at the time but I know it was a loose horse [Paddy's Return] coming across the fence. A pile of horses stopped in front of me and I'd no choice but to more or less pull up. With the horses and the fence I just couldn't get through so I had to stop.'

Moral Support was one of ten horses, a quarter of the field, put out of the race at the Canal Turn that year. It was a disappointing end to his first Grand National ride.

Noel had started out on his racing career, like many a fledgling Irish jockey, by riding in pony racing and point-to-points around his native West Cork. 'They do a lot of point-to-pointing round there,' he says, 'and my parents have always had a couple of point-to-pointers. I rode one winner under Rules in Ireland, a hunter chase at Clonmel, plus about seventy point-to-point winners.

'I spent a bit of time at David Nicholson's one summer, then I went back home for another year or two. Then I got an offer of going as an amateur to Charlie Mann so I decided to take it. My first winner here was Ivy Boy in a maiden chase at Plumpton in November 1998.'

Having won the 1995 running of the Velká Pardubická on Its A Snip, Charlie Mann knew more than most about what was required to win the Czech Republic's gruelling test of stamina and jumping. Its A Snip was rated a lowly 86, whereas Celibate was rated 138. Following the horse's sixth place finish in that 2002 Grand National, Charlie was convinced that he was tailor-made for the race.

Noel takes up the story: 'After the National that year we went over for the Pardubická. We had him well schooled before. We'd been to Tweseldown's event course; we'd been to a few places with him.

'You're allowed to school over the hedges and the Irish banks on the Thursday morning before the race. He was an intelligent horse; he just took to it straight-away. I think he was the biggest certainty ever to win that race. He would have been absolutely ideal for it, but he didn't get to run.

'It was raining all morning and we were debating would we or wouldn't we run. Then, in the race before – and we still hadn't pulled him out at that stage – three horses fell going through the ploughs and one of them broke a leg. After that we decided we wouldn't risk him.'

Not long after that, Celibate sustained a suspensory injury at home. 'It was probably the only time he had an injury,' says Noel. 'It happened after a routine piece of work. He got a bit of heat in his leg.'

He reappeared, aged thirteen, at Kempton Park in February 2004. Noel was again on board and recalls: 'On the first circuit he was really flying. He jumped better than ever and I was having a great spin off him. But then the second circuit, when we started to race, the old enthusiasm wasn't quite what it used to be. He was a little stiff after the race as well. I think that made our mind up for us.'

Celibate was retired after that Kempton run and Charlie Mann announced that the horse would have a home for the rest of his life at his Lambourn stables.

His fourteen wins over jumps had included the Desert Orchid Chase, Newbury's Game Spirit Chase and the Grade 1 BMW Chase at Punchestown. He owed his joint-owners, Bob Michaelson and Andy Tolhurst, absolutely nothing.

Date: Saturday 6 April 2002   Going: Good   Value to Winner: £290,000

Horse	Owner	Trainer	Age / weight	Jockey	SP
1 Bindaree	Mr H R Mould	N Twiston-Davies	8-10-4	J Culloty	20-1
2 What's Up Boys	R J B Partners	P J Hobbs	8-11-6	R Johnson	10-1
3 Blowing Wind	Mr P A Deal	M C Pipe	9-10-6	A P McCoy	8-1fav
4 Kingsmark	Sir Robert Ogden	M Todhunter	9-11-9	R Walsh	16-1

Distances: 1¾ lengths, 27 lengths, 9 lengths. Time: 9 mins 8.6 secs. 40 ran

Winner trained at Naunton, Cheltenham, Gloucestershire

2003

OLLIE McPHAIL
Crazy Horse's National runner

Ollie McPhail, now lead education officer for BHEST.

OLLIE McPHAIL'S SECOND encounter with the Grand National course was very nearly his last. You can still see the scar and feel the hole in the top of his head. They are the legacies of two operations he underwent to repair his broken face.

Born in Stockton-on-Tees but raised in Winchester, it was while studying business and finance at college that he began riding in point-to-points on a horse his parents had bought him.

The month of March 1997 had been a banner one for young Ollie. He finished third on Kim Bailey's Lucky Dollar in the Fulke Walwyn Kim Muir Chase on his first ride at the Cheltenham Festival. Two weeks later he rode his first winner under Rules when Jim Goldie's Bright Destiny won an amateur riders' handicap chase at Hexham.

In November that year, he had his first experience of the Grand National fences in a one-off running of the Sefton Amateur Handicap Chase, over two and three-quarter miles. Riding The Carrot Man, he completed the course, albeit a distant last of five finishers.

His racing career began in earnest when joining David Nicholson's Jackdaws Castle establishment. By the time Aintree 1998 arrived, the young amateur's career was starting to take off. With seventeen winners to his name already that season, more and more trainers were keen to put him up, but the ride on 40-1 shot Blue Cheek in the Martell Fox Hunters' Chase was one he could have done without.

Richard Burton was unseated from Lord Relic at the first fence. Julian Pritchard parted company with Viridian at the next. Ollie found himself going to the Chair accompanied by the two riderless horses, one on either side. He remembers taking off and both loose horses colliding with him in mid air. When he hit the floor it was the flying hooves that did the damage.

'My cheekbone was fractured where I got kicked. They sent me home from Fazakerley hospital after three days because I had to wait for the swelling to go down before they could do the main operation. They cut the top half of my head open from ear to ear, pulled my face down, took a piece of bone from the top of my skull and put it under my right eye to repair the damage. The eye had dropped about a centimetre where the bone was destroyed. I stayed in hospital for about two weeks after the operation and I had double vision for a while.'

It was six months before Ollie could return to the saddle, by which time he'd relinquished his amateur status to ride as a conditional. He did not have to wait long for his next mount over the National fences, coming in for a spare ride on Howard Johnson's Strong Hicks in the Becher Chase at Aintree's November meeting.

'He was giving me a good ride until we crossed the Melling Road but then he bolted with me going down to what would be the first fence in the National. He was getting longer and lower at his fences and he finally fell at the fifth down that line, the one before Becher's. He was clear when he fell, though I wasn't intending to be that far in front.'

His next Aintree mount, however, was the epitome of safe conveyances – Camelot Knight in the 2000 Grand National. The fourteen-year-old veteran certainly knew his way round, having finished third to Lord Gyllene in 1997 and twice been fourth in the Becher Chase. Now he was having his last race before retirement.

Says Ollie: 'Tom Jenks was going to ride him but he was offered the ride on one for Venetia Williams. It was only three days before the National that I knew I'd be riding him. The old horse had been round before and he gave me a fantastic ride, didn't put a foot wrong. I was outpaced early on and had to push him along. I half got back in the race with a circuit to go and then he just plodded round and finished fifteenth.'

His second Grand National ride was on 200-1 outsider Mantle's Prince in 2003. Trainer Alan Juckes and his father Rod had bought the horse specifically to run in the race, safe in the knowledge that he was sufficiently high in the handicap to guarantee getting in.

Former Liverpool, Wolves and England soccer star Emlyn Hughes, nick-named 'Crazy Horse' during his playing career, had enjoyed a long association with the Juckes family, who trained at Abberley in Worcestershire. Hughes was the horse's co-owner along with members of the local Cleobury Mortimer Golf Club.

Mantle's Prince had been a useful horse in Ireland, winning races on the Flat, over hurdles and two chases, but he was relatively inexperienced over fences. 'Alan had made a couple of Aintree-type fences at home and he'd schooled over them,' says Ollie. 'I was pretty confident going into the race that he'd be okay.

'Obviously, I didn't know how the horse would jump the fences – you never do until you get there – but he was a clever horse with a lot of ability and he'd won decent novice chases in Ireland, so it wasn't as if he couldn't jump. They're not the same fences they used to be years ago so, if you've got a safe jumper over regulation fences, you've got half a chance.

'My instructions were "Don't be out the back, have him in the race and see what happens". They weren't under any illusion that he was going to win the race; they just wanted to see him run well and get as far as he could. And he did that.

'He ran a blinder to be fair to him. He was always up in the van, in seventh or eighth, jumping really well, yet on television he never got a mention.

'He got a bit tired going over Becher's second time, then at Valentine's he just left his back legs behind, skewed on landing and unshipped me. With normal fences you can get away with that but you can't round Aintree. He only had another five fences left to jump. That was the first mistake he'd made, he hadn't put a foot wrong.

'When I came back, the owners were ecstatic to have had a horse run so well for so long in the National.'

Even more ecstatic were the connections of the winner, Monty's Pass, who turned the closing stages of the race into a procession, romping home by twelve lengths under jockey Barry Geraghty to land a huge Grand National gamble. Supreme Glory stayed on in the closing stages to deprive Ginger McCain's Amberleigh House of second place, with Gunner Welburn in fourth.

Winning owner Mike Futter, who fronted the five-strong Dee Racing Syndicate, estimated that he had won close to £1 million and that, combined with his four co-owners, they had scooped well into seven figures. He also revealed that he had advised all his clientele at his eleven bingo halls scattered north and south of the Irish border to back the horse.

Monty's Pass, who had been runner-up in the 2002 Topham, thus became the third Irish-trained winner in five years. Jimmy Mangan, who trained a dozen horses on his 150-acre farm at Conna in deepest County Cork, had his roots just as deeply planted in the worlds of farming-cum-dealing and point-to-pointing and combined the training operation with raising cattle, as well as keeping a few broodmares.

As for Mantle's Prince, Ollie rode him again in the 2004 Grand National but pulled him up when tailed off at halfway.

The horse did finally manage to win a race for Emlyn Hughes's Cleobury Golfers – a selling hurdle at Huntingdon in May 2005. There was no bid for him at the subsequent auction.

Ollie called time on his riding career at Cheltenham on 26 January 2008 after partnering 100-1 outsider He's Mine Too for David Bridgwater in a juvenile hurdle. He'd ridden a total of 128 winners. Cheltenham was perhaps an appropriate place to finish, for it was there that, in December 2002, he'd enjoyed a rare moment in the limelight with a 'made all' victory on 33-1 outsider Paxford Jack in the inaugural running of the Doncaster Bloodstock Sales Future Champions Novices' Chase.

Since the spring of 2006 he'd combined race riding with a part-time role for BHEST – the British Horseracing Education and Standards Trust. After bidding farewell to the weighing room he began a full-time job as regional education officer, helping to run BHEST's Racing to School programme in the southern half of the country. In 2010 he was promoted to lead education officer. He has lots of stories to tell the children about what it's like being a jockey, and of course, to ride in the world's greatest steeplechase.

Date: Saturday 5 April 2003   Going: Good   Value to Winner: £348,000

Horse	Owner	Trainer	Age / weight	Jockey	SP
1 Monty's Pass	Dee Racing Syndicate	J J Mangan	10-10-7	B J Geraghty	16-1
2 Supreme Glory	Mr C Moorsom & Mr J Dyson	P G Murphy	10-10-2	L Aspell	40-1
3 Amberleigh House	Halewood International Ltd	D McCain	11-10-4	G Lee	33-1
4 Gunner Welburn	Mr W A Ritson & Mr D H Hall	A M Balding	11-10-2	B Fenton	16-1

Distances: 12 lengths, 2 lengths, 14 lengths. Time: 9 mins 21.7 secs. 40 ran

Winner trained at Conna, Mallow, County Cork, Ireland

2004

MARK BRADBURNE
We're not there for the glory but . . .

Lord Atterbury takes the last fence behind Clan Royal.

IT WAS THE year that twelve-year-old Amberleigh House, despite having looked too far back jumping the third last to play a part in the finish, remorselessly clawed his way into the race to overhaul the wayward Clan Royal, who had appeared to have it in safe keeping at the last fence but then wandered left towards the Chair.

For Ginger McCain – forever linked with Aintree as the man who trained Red Rum – it was a record-equalling fourth Grand National triumph. Jockey Graham Lee, not even born when Red Rum won his first two Nationals, told reporters afterwards that it had climaxed an unbelievable season. 'It can't get any better than this,' he said.

It did. Two weeks later, Lee led throughout to win the Scottish Grand National on the front-running Grey Abbey, thus becoming the first jockey since Brian Fletcher thirty years earlier to win both the Aintree and Scottish Nationals in the same year.

Back in third place at Aintree that year was the hunter chaser Lord Atterbury, ridden by Mark Bradburne, having his third ride in the race. It should have been his fourth.

In 1999 he'd missed out on runner-up Blue Charm, trained by his mother, Sue, having been injured in a fall from Rough Quest in the Fox Hunters' two days earlier.

'We came to the second ditch, the third fence on the National course, and we failed to take off at it,' he recalls. 'I hit the ground hard and dislocated my collar-bone. We did everything we could but Graham Bradley had the same injury and said there was no chance, so the owner decided to put up Lorcan Wyer.

'We always knew he'd run well but I was surprised how well he jumped and took to it. He was a better horse round Aintree. I rode him when he won twice over the Mildmay fences.'

His father, John, had ridden Interim Lib in the 1993 void Grand National. 'He was one of those that carried on,' grins Mark. 'He saw the man with the bowler hat and red flag wandering across and thought he was an "anti". Then he fell off at the Canal Turn, thinking he would have won!'

Like his father, Mark began as an amateur in Scottish point-to-points. He had his first ride at Friars Haugh and his first winner at the Fife's meeting at Balcormo Mains on a horse called Needwood Nomad. His first winner under Rules was at Kelso on the opening day of March 1996, aboard Off The Bru, on whom John Bradburne had finished third in the 1992 Scottish National.

The Henry Daly-trained Relaxation provided Mark with his first Cheltenham Festival success when winning the four-mile National Hunt Chase in 2000. He turned professional the following season.

His first Grand National ride was on Mister One for Colin Tizzard in the mud-bath conditions of 2001 but they went their separate ways at Valentine's first time round.

'He nearly fell at the Foinavon,' says Mark. 'We just got away with the Canal Turn, which is where the pile-up happened. We had our back feet taken away from us and we landed awkwardly. Then we went to Valentine's and I've sat back a bit too far, with wet, slippery reins. He didn't make a mistake. Just one of those desperately disappointing things, because it was his year; he loved the soft ground.'

In 2002 he rode the Ian Balding-trained Logician but was brought down at the first fence.

Lord Atterbury had made his debut under Rules in 2003, winning a Leicester maiden hunter chase for trainer David Pipe and following up with victory in Aintree's novice hunter chase on Grand National day. He then won a four mile one furlong hunter chase at Cheltenham on the last day of April, when carrying David Johnson's blue and green colours for the first time.

In January 2004 he continued his winning run in a Barbury Castle point-to-point but then hit training problems and wasn't seen out until the Cheltenham Fox Hunters' two months later, where he weakened quickly on the final circuit and was pulled up. Nonetheless, the Grand National was to be his next race.

Now officially trained by Martin Pipe rather than son David, Lord Atterbury was one of seven Grand National runners that year for the master of Pond House, and Mark was booked to ride him.

'My agent, who also did Rodi Greene at the time, got me the ride. My sister's boyfriend [now husband] Harry Fowler used to ride him in hunter chases and point-to-points, and then David Johnson bought him. They decided I'd suit the horse. I was only booked on the Thursday, two days before the race. I'd never seen him until I walked into the paddock. They didn't tell me an awful lot. They just said "Go out there, be handy but don't rush him, and see what he's like".

'He jumped the first circuit lovely and the second circuit awful.'

Of the seven-strong Pipe contingent, only two made it beyond the sixth fence. The stable's first string, 10-1 favourite Jurancon II, ridden by Tony McCoy, fell at the fourth, and four of them departed at Becher's.

The remaining pair, novice chaser Puntal and Lord Atterbury, lay second and third respectively at halfway, behind the Irish-trained second favourite Hedge-hunter, the mount of David Casey, who led the 22 survivors onto the second circuit.

Puntal unseated his rider three fences later and it was Hedgehunter who led Lord Atterbury and Clan Royal over Becher's.

Lord Atterbury made three consecutive mistakes at the Canal Turn, Valen-tine's and the 26th fence, where Clan Royal also blundered, causing his rider to drop his whip.

At the third last, Hedgehunter, Clan Royal and Lord Atterbury were well clear of Amberleigh House and the rest and the race looked to lie between them. But turning for home, Hedgehunter suddenly looked a spent force. Clan Royal took over approaching two out, where Lord Atterbury still looked to be going well. But appearances can be deceptive, as his rider testifies.

'I was legless. I was sat there just holding on to see if he'd got anything left for the end; trying to get a second wind, or a fourth wind by that time.

'He kept going and, I have to say, jumping the last, for about four strides when I saw Liam Cooper going towards the Chair on Clan Royal, I thought "this is my one chance. If I keep my line straight and he barges me out of the way, I might just get the race that way."

'You always read the stories about not picking up your stick up till the Elbow, which I didn't, but when I gave him a kick he found nothing more. And then Graham Lee came past on Amberleigh House in the last 75 yards.

'After the race he got the wobbles. He didn't collapse but he was struggling and we had to give him oxygen. I had to jump off him so I never got to walk down to the old unsaddling enclosure. I missed out on that, which was a shame, but the horse's welfare obviously came first.

'Although you never like finishing second or third in any race, to be third in the National is the one occasion when you don't mind. I had to walk with the horse because, by that time, we were late getting in.

'We're not there for the glory, but on days like that it is good fun with all the people cheering.

'He was a good, honest, genuine horse and I was quite happy to ride him again the next year. The problem was, the next year he realised that he didn't have to get very high over them, and decided not to get very high at the first!

He went round loose and broadsided one of the support vehicles and injured a stifle. He spent many months in Liverpool's veterinary hospital.'

Henry Daly's Palarshan had given Mark his second Cheltenham Festival victory in the 2003 Grand Annual. The following year he enjoyed Grade 1 success when Hand Inn Hand won the Ascot Chase.

He's come close in other major races, finishing second, beaten a neck, in the 2001 Hennessy Gold Cup on Behrajan; second on Possol in the 2009 Racing Post Chase; and second, again beaten a neck, on Briery Fox in what used to be known as the Whitbread Gold Cup.

'If I'd just had a bit of luck in those races, I could have had a Hennessy, a Whitbread, a Racing Post, or a National to my name,' he reflects. 'Sometimes that's just how your luck goes. You look back and rue those few missed opportunities. I'm not bitter – yet!

'But that ride on Lord Atterbury would certainly be one of the highlights of my career. I had a wonderful time round there.

'He's still around, in retirement with a point-to-point trainer, whose girlfriend used to work for my mother. It's a small world, isn't it!'

Date: Saturday 3 April 2004   Going: Good   Value to Winner: £348,000

Horse	Owner	Trainer	Age / weight	Jockey	SP
1 Amberleigh House	Halewood International Ltd	D McCain	12-10-10	G Lee	16-1
2 Clan Royal	Mr J P McManus	J J O'Neill	9-10-5	L Cooper	10-1cofav
3 Lord Atterbury	Mr D A Johnson	M C Pipe	8-10-1	M Bradburne	40-1
4 Monty's Pass	Dee Racing Syndicate	J J Mangan	11-11-10	B J Geraghty	20-1

Distances: 3 lengths, 2 lengths, 29 lengths. Time: 9 mins 20.3 secs. 39 ran

Winner trained at Cholmondeley, Cheshire.

2005

BRIAN HARDING
One Man made the difference

One Man and Brian Harding return to the winner's enclosure after winning the 1998 Queen Mother Champion Chase.

'I WAS VERY lucky I was with Gordon Richards,' reflects Brian Harding. 'If I'd been working for a smaller trainer, well ... a year away from racing is a long time.'

Born on on 26 September 1972, the son of a dairy farmer and point-to-point trainer in Castletownroche, County Cork – the same village as Jonjo O'Neill – Brian had followed the traditional aspirant's route into the sport via pony clubs and pony racing. Apprenticed to Kevin Prendergast, he rode five winners on the Flat and had a couple of unsuccessful attempts over hurdles.

Rising weight led to Prendergast arranging for him to join Richards, for whom he rode his first winner over jumps at Kelso on Palm House in October 1992. His career took off during the 1995/96 campaign, in which he rode thirty winners and lost his claim. But soon after, his world came tumbling down.

'The season after I lost my claim I got a fall off a horse at Newcastle and fractured my skull. I also suffered tremors, which they classified as a fit, and was signed off for a year. I worked as a lad; I could ride out but wasn't allowed to race ride. When I came back in '97, the boss looked after me brilliant.'

On the opening day of the 1998 Cheltenham Festival, Brian was in the more mundane surroundings of Sedgefield. It was a typical day at the office – three rides, a third, a fourth and an unseated rider from which he emerged unscathed. Not so lucky was Tony Dobbin, who broke a thumb in a crashing fall from Direct Route at Cheltenham and was unable to ride for the remainder of the meeting. He'd been due to partner One Man in the following day's Queen Mother Champion Chase.

One Man had started favourite and joint-second favourite for the previous two Gold Cups but had palpably failed to stay. Dropping him back in distance to two miles was seen as a bold move – he'd only ever raced at that trip once, when well beaten in his first run over hurdles at Hexham in October 1992 – but nonetheless, Richards would not have been short on offers from top jockeys eager to take Dobbin's place. Whatever pressure there may have been to put up a big name rider, he elected to stay loyal to his stable jockey's understudy, Brian Harding.

'To be honest,' Brian recalls, 'I don't know whether there was pressure on him or not because it all happened that quick. But he was always very loyal to me and I don't think there was ever any doubt I'd ride him. I'd schooled One Man at home and rode him in work but I'd never ridden him in a race before.'

Pressure on himself, perhaps?

'Yes and no. Yes, obviously you're in a big race like the Queen Mother. No, because he'd been to Cheltenham for the last couple of years and it had ended in disappointment, so it wasn't as if you were going to ride a horse that had won there three times before. Because he'd disappointed at Cheltenham, there wasn't so much pressure on. Everything was a bonus really. The boss was great and told me to just go out and enjoy myself.'

Enjoy himself he certainly did, to the full. One Man proved a revelation over two miles and had the race in the bag before the second last fence, coming home four lengths clear of Or Royal. It was a pivotal point in Brian's career.

But after the elation of Cheltenham came the despair of Aintree just sixteen days later. Bowling along, three lengths in front in the Mumm Melling Chase, One Man misjudged the ninth fence and took a heavy, fatal fall. As news of the popular grey's death came through, a sombre mood enveloped not just Aintree but the whole of British racing.

'From the best day I ever had to the worst day I ever had. Horses fall with you all the time but One Man was obviously very, very upsetting. The boss hadn't been well enough to make Cheltenham, but he was actually at Aintree. I didn't see him after the race but I went and saw him that night. He said, "Son, don't worry. We'll just go and get another one".

'It would have upset him more than anybody. He used to ride him out and do whatever else with him.'

For a man dying with cancer, the death of One Man was a cruel and savage blow. Gordon Richards died less than six months later.

Nicky Richards, Gordon's son, took over the licence at Greystoke and provided Brian with his first Grand National ride on Feels Like Gold in 1999. Allotted a mere 7st 12lb in the long handicap but obliged to carry 10 stone on the day, Feels Like Gold was 30lb 'wrong' and started at 50-1. Nevertheless, he ran a terrific race, being up with the leaders from the start and still in with a chance two out before weakening to finish fifth.

'He was a lovely horse round Aintree,' says Brian. 'Crossing the Melling Road for the last time, he was up there but only just. Fifth was probably as good as he was. The next year he got round again but, aged twelve, wasn't quite the same horse. I rode him again the year after that, when Paddy's Return stopped me dead at the Canal Turn.'

In his first eight rides over the Aintree fences Brian completed the course six times, including twice finishing third in the Becher Chase.

He failed to get beyond the first on Ferdy Murphy's 200-1 outsider Luzcadou in the 2004 Grand National, but better times were just around the corner.

On Easter Monday, Granit d'Estruval, trained by Murphy and owned by Walter Gott, a retired poultry producer, scored a 33-1 surprise victory in the Irish Grand National at Fairyhouse, giving 31-year-old Brian Harding his first win over fences in Ireland.

'Walter Gott had had horses with Gordon Richards and I'd won the Mumm Mildmay Novices' Chase for him on Addington Boy, so I was asked to ride his horse in the Irish National. On form you wouldn't really have fancied him on what he'd shown recently. Sedgefield was on the same day so I wasn't over sure about it but I spoke with [agent] Richard Hale who said I should give it a crack. I had a great ride off him. They're big fences at Fairyhouse but he jumped brilliant and won well. It was a nice surprise.'

In the 2005 Grand National, Brian rode Jonjo O'Neill's 66-1 shot Simply Gifted and finished third, narrowly missing second in a photo with Royal Auclair. Fourteen lengths ahead of them was Hedgehunter, who had still been in contention when falling at the final fence twelve months earlier.

Many observers expressed reservations over Simply Gifted never having won a race beyond two-and-a-half miles and feared that he wouldn't stay the trip. Additionally, he had suffered in the past with his breathing and also had leg problems. But Brian was untroubled by such doubts, settling the horse in midfield and gradually working his way into the race during the second circuit.

'I hunted away for the first circuit. It was his first time round Aintree and I wanted to get him in a rhythm and enjoying the place. That's the way I try to do it. Get a circuit in a reasonable position and then, going away from the stands, you can maybe start thinking about riding a race, creeping away.

'We moved up from Valentine's without him taking anything out of himself. I gave him a couple of backhanders after the third last – it was at that stage I started thinking whether he was going to go forwards or backwards, because I just felt I was at the stage where I'm starting to come off the bridle. And to be fair to him, he kept going.

'Over the last couple the gun was to his head. He was having to jump them and he did. He came up long two out and went in pursuit of Hedgehunter approaching the last. Ruby [Walsh] was still travelling so well and I never thought I'd win, but to be in the frame, it was great.

'He ran an absolute blinder. It surprised me how well he stayed on. They used to say that a two-and-a-half mile horse was ideal, but he stayed really well. He jumped great; did everything brilliant. The only thing more I could have asked was if he was two places closer.'

Trevor Hemmings, Hedgehunter's multimillionaire owner, who also owned Blackpool Tower, had dreamed of winning the Grand National ever since he worked as a builder for holiday king Fred Pontin, who had won the race in 1971 with Specify.

Trained by Willie Mullins at Bagenalstown in County Carlow, Hedgehunter provided a second Grand National victory for Ruby Walsh, who was standing in for the injured David Casey.

Since then, Brian has maintained his fine Aintree completion record by getting round in three of the next four Grand Nationals on horses trained by Ginger and Donald McCain, firstly on Inca Trail in 2006, and then twice on Idle Talk in 2008 and 2009.

'To be honest,' he reflects, 'I very much take Aintree as I find it. The first circuit I try to get into a nice rhythm, which I think is very important. Basically, go where you get to see as much as you can see. The last couple of years I went down the inner on Idle Talk and had a great run round. A lot of people say down the middle is good, but it's wherever you get the most room. I've been lucky to have a few good rides round there.'

Among the most popular residents of the northern weighing room, Brian has won two awards at the Lesters: in 1998 the Jump Ride of the Year for winning the Queen Mother Champion Chase on One Man; and in 2008 he received the Jump Jockey Special Recognition Award.

One of them applauds a long and distinguished career. The other recalls the best horse he ever rode; but it's more than just the equine One Man; it's about the other One Man – the One Man who gave his jockey the chance to re-establish himself after a year on the sidelines...Gordon Richards. That One Man made the difference.

The significance of that is not lost on the man from Castletownroche.

Date: Saturday 9 April 2005 Going: Good to soft Value to Winner: £406,000

Horse	Owner	Trainer	Age / weight	Jockey	SP
1 Hedgehunter	Mr Trevor Hemmings	W P Mullins	9-11-1	R Walsh	7-1
2 Royal Auclair	Mr Clive D Smith	P Nicholls	8-11-10	C Williams	40-1
3 Simply Gifted	Mr S Hammond	J J O'Neill	10-10-6	B Harding	66-1
4 It Takes Time	Mr D A Johnson	M C Pipe	11-10-11	T J Murphy	18-1

Distances: 14 lengths, head, 4 lengths. Time: 9 mins 20.8 secs. 40 ran

Winner trained at Bagenalstown, County Carlow, Ireland.

2006

LEIGHTON ASPELL
The Leighton Aspell Fan Club

Ballycassidy and Leighton Aspell lead over Becher's.

NOT MANY JOCKEYS have their own appreciation society. Leighton Aspell does.

Formed in 2001, the Leighton Aspell Fan Club has its roots in the Marine View Hotel in Worthing, Sussex. Every Friday night a group of friends would meet there and select a horse to back for Saturday's racing, the only criteria being that Leighton Aspell, who was a friend of one of them, had to be the jockey.

The Racing Channel, forerunner of At The Races and Racing UK, was then running a naps table for the presenters and for the public. Although it was during the heart of the Flat season, the friends stuck with Aspell-ridden horses over jumps. Their nominated rider had a summer to remember, riding 20-1 and 33-1 winners and, with the naps table being based on SP, they won easily. That allowed them to enter the presenters' table, for which they called themselves the Leighton Aspell Fan Club, and the run of profitable winners continued.

Their success, coupled with regular mentions on TV, led to an increasing amount of emails and phone calls from people curious to know what the 'club' was all about. There was no such club at the time but, because of its popularity, the Leighton Aspell Fan Club was duly formed. Within six months it had over 100 members from all corners of Britain.

The emphasis is on fun, with members receiving a monthly magazine containing news, views and competitions, plus of course, a report on all Leighton's rides. Any profits that accrue are donated to the Injured Jockeys' Fund.

In February 2006 they provided an opportunity for members to meet at Fontwell Park when sponsoring the Leighton Aspell Handicap Chase, in which their jockey narrowly failed to provide the perfect result, finishing second on 14-year-old veteran Smart Guy, who was retired immediately after the race.

The fan club's adopted figurehead was born just outside Kilcullen, County Kildare, in 1976. His father rode as an amateur in Ireland and held a permit to train his own horses. Leighton had a dozen or so rides 'just to dip my toe into the water' before crossing the Irish Sea and joining Reg Hollinshead's renowned apprentice academy in January 1993. He had his first ride in March and two months later partnered his first winner when making all on Prime Painter for Roger Fisher at Hamilton.

'Whenever there was an apprentice race, Reg would always have two or three riding in it,' he remembers. 'It was a really great place to work. I had about 100 rides, mostly apprentice races, and rode ten winners on the Flat until I got too big and too heavy.'

'I joined Josh and Nick Gifford in August 1994 and was there until Josh retired. I rode out my claim with him. Although it was towards the end of his career, he still had Bradbury Star and Deep Sensation, plus Brief Gale, who won the Sun Alliance Chase, and Brave Highlander, who was close up in three Grand Nationals. There were a lot of well-trained, well-schooled horses; it was a great grounding.'

He cites novice hurdler Rouble as 'potentially the best' he rode. He won Fontwell's National Spirit on him before the horse tragically broke a leg when slipping up in the Royal & SunAlliance Hurdle at Cheltenham in 2002.

'I rode Josh's last winner, Skycab, at Sandown,' he recalls. 'I also rode him for Nick in the 2004 National but we fell at Becher's.'

Twelve months earlier he'd had his first Grand National ride, finishing second aboard the Pat Murphy-trained Supreme Glory at 40-1.

'He was a late starter and went straight over fences. He was second to Good Lord Murphy on his first run at Towcester, and then surprised us all by beating him and some other good novices at Warwick. He finished fourth in the four-mile National Hunt Chase at the Cheltenham Festival.

'The following season he won the four-mile Devon National at Exeter. He ran well to be third in a big £50,000 chase at Warwick, finished fourth in the De Vere Gold Cup at Haydock and was third in the Scottish National.'

In December 2001 Supreme Glory and Leighton romped to victory in the Welsh National, but hopes of Aintree glory that season were dashed when following his next run at Newbury he was sidelined for ten months with a tendon injury. His first two comeback races were disappointing but he then ran well in the Red Square Vodka Gold Cup at Haydock, five weeks before the 2003 Grand National.

'He wasn't very quick but he was a fantastic jumper and that just kept me on the leaders' shirt-tails in the National. I was never that far back. If you watch the replay, second time at Becher's I was about seventh or eighth and having a really good time, and then from the Canal Turn they accelerated and I lost my posi.

'The horses that had accelerated from the Canal Turn began to tire on the long run between three out and two out and I started to catch them. He was a very fit horse who really stayed. I think the fact that I didn't bustle him throughout the first mile or two allowed him to finish so strongly. The bird had flown as regards the winner [Monty's Pass] but we were a good second. Amberleigh House and Gunner Welburn, who'd been in front, were really tired from the last to the line and we outstayed them.

'If the ground had been softer it would have slowed the race down, but because the ground was good the race was run a notch faster. The real stayers were outpaced and couldn't hold a good position in the first half of the race.'

In 2005 Leighton came in for a Grand National 'spare' on Take The Stand for Peter Bowen. 'I couldn't believe it,' he says, 'after he'd just finished second to Best Mate in the Gold Cup. He was a bit hit and miss jumping-wise but I thought he might just take to it. He was giving me a good ride but, unfortunately, at the Chair we just didn't get it right and I came off. Somehow he managed to stay upright, then he ran loose and caused the carnage at Becher's, taking out McCoy on Clan Royal.'

It was another of Bowen's horses, Ballycassidy, who was Leighton's Grand National mount in 2006. His seven wins as a novice chaser in 2003/04 had included the valuable Summer Plate at Market Rasen, but he'd drawn a blank the following season and won only two minor contests (one over hurdles) in the summer of 2005, prior to finishing third in the Summer Plate. Afterwards he was given some tough assignments, including in the 'Hennessy', 'King George', Racing Post Chase and, in his final start before the National, the Cheltenham Gold Cup, performing adequately each time but without threatening to play a part in the finish.

'He wasn't very big but he really took to Aintree,' says Leighton. 'He'd been out of form and Peter told me that because he was small he tended to get intimidated around horses. With forty runners what were my chances of finding daylight?

'Luckily, the ground was softish so they didn't go very fast and I was able to hold a good position. He was good at his fences without being spectacular.'

Taking the lead at Valentine's first time round, Ballycassidy was joined by Puntal (Barry Geraghty) at the Chair and the pair headed out onto the second circuit well ahead of the rest. Puntal began to drop back from the nineteenth, leaving Ballycassidy clear on the run down to Becher's.

'Barry Geraghty was beside me on Puntal for a while. We were chatting away and jumping well. Then he faded away and I was left on my own. It was a bizarre feeling but a super thrill. I was wearing one of those cameras in my helmet that day. I've got a brilliant video of clear daylight in the second half of the Grand National.

'I was surprised how clear the horse was. In hindsight, going down to Becher's I should have put the anchor on a little bit just to save some petrol. He weakened over Foinavon and the Canal, and coming to Valentine's he really was getting tired. He took a crashing fall there. Luckily we both got up okay.'

Ballycassidy's fall left the three market leaders in front: Hedgehunter, Clan Royal and Numbersixvalverde, the trio being just ahead of Risk Accessor, Inca Trail and the improving Nil Desperandum.

All six of them were battling for the lead crossing the Melling Road, with Hedgehunter looking to be going the best of all. Risk Accessor and Inca Trail had dropped away by the second last fence and it was Numbersixvalverde and Hedgehunter who jumped the last together, just in front of Clan Royal. However, the concession of 18lb proved too much for the 2005 winner and it was Numbersixvalverde, named after the house owner Bernard Carroll had in Quinta da Lago in Portugal, who drew clear on the run-in to score by six lengths. It was trainer Martin Brassil's first Grand National runner and a first ride in the race for 20-year-old Niall 'Slippers' Madden. Clan Royal, having dropped back to fourth on the run-in, rallied to regain third place from Nil Desperandum on the line.

'How close would Ballycassidy have gone if he'd stayed on his feet? It's really hard to say,' Leighton reflects. 'Because he was a small horse he had to make so much effort over the bigger fences. He'd been in front a long time, but Peter's really do try, so who knows what would have happened, but he just felt as if he was running out of petrol.

'A testament to Peter's training is that Ballycassidy came out three weeks later, at Perth, and won. I remember saying to people that morning "This horse cannot have recovered from the exertion of Aintree", yet he goes out and wins well. It was a great feat. His horses are so fit that they recover quickly.'

Leighton rode Billyvoddan for Henry Daly in the 2007 Grand National. They pulled up at the nineteenth. Just three months later, when still at the peak of his career and with over 400 winners to his name, including a second Welsh National on L'Aventure for Paul Nicholls, he shocked his loyal fans by announcing his retirement from the saddle at the relatively young age of 31, stating that he was 'losing his competitive edge'.

'Probably for around a year before that the travelling seemed to be peeing me off. I'd got to the stage where I wasn't enjoying it. Life's too short if you're not enjoying it, so I thought "Right, that chapter's closed."

'I managed to get a job as pupil assistant at John Dunlop's Castle Stables and I wanted to build on that. For the first twelve months I thoroughly enjoyed it. I had to keep a close eye on racing through my job but I had no intention of going back riding.

'I was still schooling for Nick and Josh and local point-to-point people. All

of a sudden I felt refreshed and wanted to have another go. I missed the camaraderie of the weighing room. Again, life's too short. I was only 32; I was pretty
fit. I spoke with some trainers and they were all positive and I thought maybe
I'd get five years out of it and then perhaps start training, or do something else.
So I bit the bullet and reapplied for my licence.'

In April 2009 he made his comeback at a lowly Easter Bank Holiday meeting
at Plumpton. 'Although I was riding schooling on a daily basis, race riding is
very different. It's the whole feeling of racing again at that speed and trying to
assess the pace.

'It was the speed that surprised me in my first ride back. I thought 'These
horses can't maintain this pace', but they did. You have to appreciate how fit
horses are now. In this day and age they're fitter than ever, and you have to
match that.'

At Fakenham three weeks later, Lucy Wadham's Saafend Rocket provided
him with his first winner since his comeback. More soon followed.

'I'm grateful to Mr Dunlop,' he says. 'I worked at a great place with a great
man and learned a lot. I enjoyed it, and see myself training one day.

'To take a horse from scratch, get it mentally and physically in good shape,
whatever level they are, it takes a bit of doing and I think I'd really enjoy the
challenge. But meanwhile, I want to ride for as long as I'm wanted and am able
to.'

His fan club is delighted.

Date: Saturday 8 April 2006 Going: Good to soft Value to Winner: £399,140

Horse	Owner	Trainer	Age / weight	Jockey	SP
1 Numbersixvalverde	Mr O B P Carroll	M Brassil	10-10-8	N P Madden	11-1
2 Hedgehunter	Mr Trevor Hemmings	W P Mullins	10-11-12	R Walsh	5-1jtfav
3 Clan Royal	Mr J P McManus	J J O'Neill	11-10-10	A P McCoy	5-1jtfav
4 Nil Desperandum	Mr M L Shone	Ms F M Crowley	9-10-7	T P Treacy	33-1

Distances: 6 lengths, 1¼ lengths, short head. Time: 9 mins 41.0 secs. 40 ran

Winner trained at Dunmurray, Co Kildare, Ireland.

2007

ROBERT and SAM WALEY-COHEN
An act of love

Sam Waley-Cohen on Liberthine.

THE WALLS OF the Waley-Cohens' house at Upton Viva stud, near Banbury, are bedecked with framed photographs of horses in action. Most carry the family's famous brown and orange colours, many over Aintree's big green fences, others at Cheltenham, plus a selection from France. All have tales to tell.

There's one of Makounji winning the Prix de Longchamp at Auteuil in March 1998. She was to become one of the stud's foundation mares and has played her part well.

'Makounji was the first mare we bought,' says Robert Waley-Cohen, who founded the stud in 2001 along with his eldest son Marcus. 'We were only going to have room for a small number – our target was eight – so we set out with the principle that we should only breed from horses that had been successful in their own right.'

The first crop, foaled in 2002, produced a filly called Shatabdi, winner of a Grade 2 hurdle and also successful on the Flat and over fences. The second crop produced Roulez Cool, by Classic Cliche out of Makounji, who won a listed steeplechase in France as a four-year-old before returning to his country of birth and winning the 2010 renewal of Stratford's Champion Hunters' Chase, more familiarly known as the Horse and Hound Cup.

Robert worked for Christie's auctioneers for 12 years and later founded Alliance HealthCare Services in the USA and then in 1989 Alliance Medical, the leading European provider of services to hospitals – everything from scanning patients to supplying freestanding imaging centres to running an entire radiology department.

His grandfather, Sir Robert Waley-Cohen, was a leading British industrialist and director of Shell, while his father, Sir Bernard, 1st Baronet, was a businessman who became Lord Mayor of London. When Sir Bernard died the baronetcy passed to Robert's elder brother Stephen, who is chairman of the Royal Academy of Dramatic Art (RADA) and runs several West End theatres.

In addition to his involvement with the stud, Robert trains a small string under permit plus several point-to-pointers. He is also a member of the Jockey Club, chairman of Cheltenham, director of the Horsemen's Group and of Racing Enterprises Ltd, and chairman of the Point-to-Point Authority, the TBA's National Hunt Committee and the Warwickshire Hunt Point-to-Point.

'We had a sort of double life, spending time in London and weekends on Exmoor,' he recalls of his early years. 'As a child, holidays were always great fun on Exmoor. We lived in the middle of a moor and there was absolutely nothing to do except sheep farm, ride and hunt.

'My father, when he was at Cambridge, discovered the joys of Newmarket and spent more time there than he should have done. His grandfather, my great-grandfather, was a man named Beddington. He had a house in Newmarket and my colours are a version of his: orange, chocolate sleeves, which were carried to victory by Magic in the 1910 Goodwood Cup, beating the heavily odds-on favourite Bayardo by a neck.

'When I came to register my colours I chose chocolate with orange sleeves and cap. They said they didn't recognise "chocolate" as a colour so I opted for brown, and they said I couldn't have a plain cap so I settled for a quartered one. I've still got "orange, chocolate sleeves" registered as my second colours.'

He enjoyed three rides over Liverpool's big fences in the Fox Hunters' Chase. 'I was the classic enthusiastic amateur who probably shouldn't have been there at all,' he reflects of those Aintree experiences. 'I managed to complete twice, the first time in 1977 on a gallant horse called Barouche, who had finished fourth in the Foxhunters' at Cheltenham, which was then a four-mile race, and we then went to Liverpool and finished fourth behind Nicky Henderson on Happy Warrior, with "Boots" Madden in second and Peter Greenall in third.'

As an owner, he encountered both joy and frustration at Aintree with Wont Be Gone Long, who won the John Hughes Memorial Trophy (as the Topham was then known) in 1990 under Richard Dunwoody, smashing the track record by 3.5 seconds. But three years later he was one of nine horses to remain at the start in the void Grand National, when the starting tape failed to rise and became wrapped around jockey Richard Dunwoody's neck.

Robert's son Sam has risen rapidly to become a top-class amateur rider with a penchant for Aintree's big fences. He'd first made their acquaintance when finishing ninth in the 2003 Fox Hunters' on his father's 66-1 outsider Down.

A former City-based commodities trader, Sam now runs his own company, Portman Healthcare, buying private dental practices and revitalising them into efficiently running operations.

Apart from race riding, he has tackled a wide variety of sporting pursuits since entering the world in April 1982, including rugby, boxing, bungee jumping, white-water rafting, mountain-climbing and skydiving. He also holds a pilot's licence. But they're all a mere bagatelle compared to the thrill of riding at Aintree.

'To go round the National fences, the moment you jump it's like jumping out of a plane every time,' he enthuses. 'It's probably as close as you can come to flying without sprouting a set of wings.'

The eve of the Cheltenham Festival is rarely a good time to be riding a horse having its first run over fences, and such was the case in March 2004 when a mare named Liberthine made her debut on a British racecourse.

'I bought Liberthine in 2002,' says Robert. 'She was by Chamberlin, who was from the same sire line as Cadoudal, the most successful French stallion. Liberthine ran in France for me as a three-year-old and won a Listed hurdle there. She then chipped a bone in her knee and had her four-year-old year off. I sent her to Nicky Henderson and it took him quite a long time to get her ready.

'I'd identified the perfect race for her debut, a two-and-a-half mile novice chase at Stratford on the Monday of Cheltenham week. She had the maximum allowances – for a mare and for a five-year-old – and it couldn't have been more perfect. Nicky rang me on the Sunday morning, just before declarations closed, and said "I just have one reservation: Cheltenham starts on Tuesday, all my jockeys have been injured; they are just coming back and I don't really want to put any of them on a mare in her first novice chase on the Monday of Cheltenham week."

'At the time, Sam and I were in the lorry on our way to a point-to-point. I said to Sam "Do you want to ride her?" and he said "Yes", so I told Nicky that Sam would ride and claim his seven. The weight was horribly low and Sam had a hungry 24 hours followed by a nasty time sweating in an extremely unpleasant sauna, partly because it was small, partly because it was full of other jockeys all trying to do the same.'

Thus, Henderson's stable jockey Mick Fitzgerald played safe and went to Plumpton for a couple of rides over hurdles, leaving Sam to take the ride at Stratford on his father's French import. Despite fiddling the last, Liberthine won by eight lengths.

Recalls Sam: I don't think I'd ever seen her before and hadn't got very much experience at that stage. It was a huge step from point-to-pointing and a few hunter chases. It was possibly my first ride against professionals, or very close to it. Luckily, Liberthine was incredibly straightforward, as easy a horse to ride as you could ever hope for, one-paced but jumped brilliantly and completely honest.'

Twelve months later they were at Cheltenham itself with Liberthine carrying a mere 10st 1lb, including her young amateur rider's 7lb claim, in the Mildmay of Flete Handicap Chase. It was Sam's final year at Edinburgh University and the politics student had skipped a tutorial to ride the 25-1 outsider.

At halfway they were last and seemingly going nowhere but, with a combination of courage and coolness that defied his inexperience, the young rider waited, waited some more and brought Liberthine through in the closing stages to win by seven lengths from Banker Count to provide one of the most emotional moments ever seen at Cheltenham. No Festival winner could ever be described as 'ordinary' but this victory revealed a story of extraordinary poignancy.

Just nine months earlier, the Waley-Cohen family had been devastated when Sam's younger brother Thomas had lost his ten-year long battle against a rare form of bone cancer at the age of 20. The victory of Liberthine was dedicated to his memory.

Says Robert: 'It was very emotional. Liberthine's win was the first really bright thing that had happened to us for a long time. Afterwards we came home and watched the race over and over again and continued drinking tea and champagne alternately.'

Since then, the family's charity work, with their brown and orange colours used in wrist bands, has raised well over £1.5 million and witnessed the opening of a 24-bed general surgical ward at Oxford Children's Hospital, named in remembrance of Thomas.

Three weeks after Liberthine's Cheltenham triumph, she and Sam trailed in a well-beaten fourteenth in the Topham Chase at Aintree. But the family had scored another high profile success there the previous day when Katarino, a horse boasting his own extraordinary tale, won the Fox Hunters' Chase over the Grand National fences.

Katarino had won the Triumph Hurdle for Robert in 1999 and had followed that by winning Punchestown's Champion Four Year Old Hurdle. Since then he'd been beset by a combination of breathing and leg problems, including an injury incurred when unseating Mick Fitzgerald at the Chair in the 2003 Grand National.

Katarino was duly retired and Robert's daughter Jessica won a dressage competition on him and took him show jumping and eventing before Robert had him back in 2005 with the intention of using him as a lead horse on the gallops. But Katarino was going so well that Robert decided to enter him in a point-to-point at Didmarton, which, ridden by Sam, he won in a hack canter. He won equally easily at Paxford next time out and followed that by winning the Fox Hunters' Chase at Aintree.

Katarino won the Fox Hunters' again in 2006, and just 24 hours later Sam partnered Liberthine to win the Topham Chase, thus making him the first rider ever to win both supporting races over the big fences.

That took Sam's tally to three wins and two completions from five rides over the National course, yet he was ineligible to compete in the Grand National itself due to a rule introduced in 1999 prohibiting any rider taking part who had not ridden 15 winners over jumps. Indeed, it was for that very reason that Liberthine had run in the 2006 Topham and not the National, with Robert insisting that 'she doesn't go anywhere without her jockey.'

The rules were subsequently amended to allow an element of discretion, with those who had ridden ten winners being considered on their merits. Sam won on home-bred Shatabdi at Plumpton in February 2007 to give him his tenth winner and was duly given special dispensation to ride in the Grand National, meaning he would bid to become the first successful amateur since Marcus Armytage won on Mr Frisk in 1990.

Sadly, Katarino was sidelined by an injury picked up when winning a point-to-point at Brocklesby Park in Lincolnshire and so missed the chance of a Fox Hunters' hat-trick.

Liberthine had three preparatory races, finishing an encouraging fourth over three miles at Cheltenham, followed by a spin over hurdles at Newbury, but then put in a lacklustre effort in the Fulke Walwyn/Kim Muir at Cheltenham.

Says Sam: 'She lobbed round in the Kim Muir to not much effect and we were very disappointed, although in hindsight it was a tribute to Nicky's training abilities, the way he can get a horse to peak at the right time.

'I went down to Nicky's to school her over his Aintree fences, which he'd built up to full size, four or five strides apart, so they took a bit of jumping, and it was like somebody had put a jet engine in her since I'd ridden her in the Kim Muir. She saw the fences, pricked her ears and absolutely flew them. After that, it became more and more exciting, more and more real.'

Libertine and Sam lined up as 40-1 shots on the big day, but a false start and repeated attempts to dispatch the 40 runners tested the nerves of both the starter and participants.

'She got a bit wound up at the start and so I was talking to her, trying to keep her calm and relaxed,' says Sam. 'I had a plan who I wanted to line up with. First time was perfect; second time, perfect; but third time I was lined up alongside two horses I'd not wanted to be anywhere near.

'In her first race over the Aintree fences I'd tried to get her into a rhythm early on and let her find her own time but she'd never really got into the race, so this time I was intending to give her a slap down the shoulder and really ride her into it, so when we slightly missed the start I almost thought the race was gone then and there, so I was quite aggressive down to the first.

'She was immediately jumping brilliantly; she had a perfect National technique – quite flat but with masses of scope, and I could keep asking her to pick up. I don't think I've ever had a round of jumping like she gave me that day in the National.

'The whole way round she was doing a bit too much and I was trying to get her to back off, but when a horse is in a rhythm like that, you don't dare break it. If you try to get them to pop, you'll probably fall, so you have to play the hand you're dealt.'

They moved into second place at the start of the second circuit but found themselves left in front when leader Bewleys Berry came down at Becher's. This was far from ideal for a horse that usually came from off the pace.

'There's quite a lot of shouting going down to Becher's,' says Sam. 'By that stage there are probably only about fifteen left in the race. But when you land there's almost a collective sigh of relief as those that have landed safely are away. I remember when Bewleys Berry fell there was a moment of real silence – you're as far away from the stands as you can be and there's just nothing…I'll always remember that serenity and silence; and then it's "concentrate".'

At Valentine's, where Mercy Rimell-owned Simon fell when going well, Irish challenger Slim Pickings took over from Liberthine. The pair led the field back towards the racecourse, with Philson Run, Thisthatandtother and Silver Birch all close up, ahead of the running-on McKelvey. But when they turned for home to approach the second last fence, Sam realised that Liberthine's stamina was beginning to run out.

'In her previous races I'd always tried to get her to change legs coming round the last bend, because she always found more when she did that. This time, when I tried to get her to change, she didn't, and I knew she was flagging and that she'd given all she had left.'

Slim Pickings led over the penultimate fence, two lengths ahead of Silver Birch. Both horses were still going well but Silver Birch jumped the last better than his rival and landed in the lead.

Approaching the Elbow, Silver Birch drew a couple of lengths clear, the only danger now looking to come from the fast-finishing McKelvey. Silver Birch's jockey, Robbie Power, was desperately looking for the winning post but he had kept just enough in reserve to hold off McKelvey by three-quarters of a length, with Slim Pickings just a length and a quarter away third. Philson Run was 15 lengths further back in fourth. Liberthine and Sam Waley-Cohen finished a gallant fifth.

'For a second I thought she might plug on because she always finished her races well,' recalls Sam, 'but when she landed over the last, the tank was empty and she was running on fumes to try and get home. She was so honest there was never a question of me beating her up because I knew that she'd given me absolutely everything that she had.'

Silver Birch had previously been trained by Paul Nicholls, for whom he had won the Becher Chase and Welsh National in 2004. He was then sidelined for over a year but returned to run in the 2006 Grand National, falling at the Chair.

Michael Donohoe of BBA Ireland had subsequently purchased him for 20,000 guineas at Doncaster Sales on behalf of Brian Walsh, owner of the Rheindross Stud at Kilcock, County Kildare, who was seeking 'a fun horse for cross country racing'.

Silver Birch became the sixth Irish-trained winner in the past nine years. His trainer, 29-year-old Gordon Elliott, had only been training for two years and, remarkably, had never trained a winner in his home country. In fact, the Grand National was only his fourth success since taking out a licence.

Three years later, sitting at a garden table at the family home, Sam reflects on the race and wonders if there is anything he might have done differently.

'In hindsight, if I had a chance to ride it again, I would undoubtedly play my hand a bit differently. I would definitely look to be more conservative and play a more cautious, waiting race. I think there are places on the National course where you can get a breather into a horse, which, until you've ridden it, you don't necessarily appreciate. One of the challenges when you haven't ridden that distance is you don't quite know what the pace is.

'Having said that, she had nearly the perfect round; she saw every fence, didn't get hampered; I think she made one tiny mistake. We got left in front a little bit early and she didn't quite get home but she had as good a chance at it as she could have had.'

Liberthine was retired immediately after the race – for a second time. Says Robert: 'I'd actually retired her after she'd won the Topham and tried to get her in foal but she didn't take. When we finally retired her it was probably for the best, but I've always had slight second thoughts and wondered whether we did right or wrong. She's now got a very nice 2008 Hernando filly. She had a stillborn Presenting colt in 2009, a Polyglot filly in 2010 and she's gone back to Presenting this year.'

As for Katarino, he returned to Aintree in 2008 to bid for a third Fox Hunters' Chase. He'd reached the advanced age of thirteen by then but had run only five times – and won all five – in the previous four years. He still held every chance jumping the last but could not match Christy Beamish on the long run-in and finished a gallant second.

Sam rode outsider Blu Teen in the 2009 Fox Hunters and once again completed to maintain his record of never having failed to finish. But that seven-time sequence came to an end two days later when he rode Ollie Magern in the Grand National and fell at the second fence.

In January 2011 the Waley-Cohens achieved their biggest success so far when Long Run won the King George VI Chase, rearranged from Boxing Day, thwarting Kauto Star's bid for a fifth consecutive King George victory in the process.

However, for Sam the dream that burns brightest is to win the Grand National wearing the family's brown and orange colours.

'It's an amazing race, a true test of horse and jockey,' he says. 'It's also a test of character.

'Trying to win it is an act of love in its own right. It's irrational and frustrating and all of those things that racing is. It's the embodiment of racing; every element is distilled into the National – the luck, the courage, the chance, the good fortune, everything. It's the ultimate one to win. A race like that, it's just … it's just a lot of fun.'

Date: Saturday 14 April 2007 Going: Good Value to Winner: £399,140

Horse	Owner	Trainer	Age / weight	Jockey	SP
1 Silver Birch	Mr Brian Walsh	G Elliott	10-10-6	R M Power	33-1
2 McKelvey	Mr N Elliott	P Bowen	8-10-4	T J O'Brien	12-1
3 Slim Pickings	Doubtful Five Syndicate	T J Taaffe	8-10-8	B J Geraghty	33-1
4 Philson Run	Gale Force One	N Williams	11-10-5	D Jacob	100-1

Distances: ¾ length, 1¼ lengths, 15 lengths. Time: 9 mins 13.6 secs. 40 ran

Winner trained at Kilmessan, Co Meath, Ireland.

2008

TOM O'BRIEN
McKelvey

McKelvey, runner-up in the 2007 Grand National.

FORTY-THREE YEARS EARLIER the BBC had chosen two horses, Jay Trump and Freddie, and focused on their respective build-ups to the 1965 Grand National. It worked to perfection, with the pair battling out the finish and Jay Trump prevailing by three-quarters of a length.

In 2008 BBC1's *The One Show* featured the preparation of McKelvey for that year's Grand National. This time, however, the outcome was very different.

McKelvey had finished runner up to Silver Birch in 2007. His jockey then and in 2008 was Tom O'Brien, nephew of Aidan O'Brien, for whom his father has worked for more than ten years, doing a bit of everything 'from driving the horses to driving Aidan,' according to Tom.

During his schooldays Tom spent weekends and holidays with Aidan at Ballydoyle. A girl that worked there was previously with Philip Hobbs at Minehead and she gave him a ring asking if Tom could come over for a weekend. He did, he asked if there was a job going, there was and, he insists: 'I've loved it ever since.'

He'd had just two point-to-point rides in Ireland, on a 'terrible horse' and finished last both times. But his first under Rules, on Mrs Philip at Taunton on 11 November 2004, fared much better, finishing second to stable companion Red Society.

Tom's first winner came five weeks later on The Names Bond for Andy Turnell in an amateur riders' hurdle at Warwick. He was leading amateur the following season with 22 winners, then turned conditional for the 2006/07 campaign and rode 107 winners to finish third in the table behind Tony McCoy and Richard Johnson.

Among the trainers he regularly rode for was Peter Bowen, with whom he enjoyed plenty of success. Bowen's stables, located near Haverfordwest, in Pembrokeshire, housed around 50 horses including McKelvey, who had won the 2006 English Summer National over four miles and half a furlong at Uttoxeter when partnered by McCoy. He subsequently finished a staying-on sixth under Peter Buchanan in that year's Becher Chase over Aintree's unique fences. With proven stamina and jumping ability, the 2007 Grand National was to be his aim.

Three weeks before the Grand National, Tom rode McKelvey in a race for the first time, winning the three-mile Tommy Shone Handicap Hurdle, named in memory of the jockey who had ridden in five Nationals and held a clear lead on Angel Hill when falling at the Canal Turn second time round in 1950. It was McKelvey's first start since the Becher Chase and it looked to have put him spot on for his return to Aintree.

Tom was given no specific instructions, although with Karen Bowen (Peter's wife) being a fan of Richard Dunwoody, she told him to watch recordings of the years Dunwoody had ridden in it.

He hoped to get a feel for the Grand National course the day before the big race by riding Bowen's Iron Man in the Topham Trophy, but the experience didn't last long for he was unseated at the very first fence. He had to be content with walking the course instead. That aside, there were no special preparations.

'Don't get me wrong,' he says, 'I was excited to have such a good ride in the race, but it's just another day, except that you're jumping bigger fences and you've got to go further.

'To be honest, I missed the start. I just wanted to get over the first couple. And then I picked up Ruby [Walsh, on Hedgehunter] right in front of me. When I saw him I thought I couldn't be going too bad, so I followed him everywhere.

'He jumped brilliant. He didn't make a mistake the whole way round. It was my first National and I really enjoyed it. You need a good jumper to have fun; it's no fun if you're going to turn over.'

Given a patient ride for the first half of the race, McKelvey gradually got closer to the leaders throughout the second circuit and by the time they crossed the Melling Road he was lying sixth behind Slim Pickings, Liberthine, Philson Run, Thisthatandtother and Silver Birch. As they turned for home with two left to jump, Tom gave his mount one backhander just to wake him up. They jumped the last in third place behind Silver Birch and Slim Pickings.

'He picked up a little bit, but not enough, unfortunately,' he reflects. 'I always thought I'd struggle to get there. He picked up again when he got to the Elbow but then he started hanging to his right.'

McKelvey finished strongest of all but failed by just three-quarters of a length to peg back Silver Birch, leaving Tom to reflect on what might have been.

'Maybe I should have been more confident,' he says, 'but at the time I never thought I'd get there and I was surprised how close I got.

'When I pulled up, he pulled up lame; he'd done a tendon. The vet attended to him there and then and he wasn't allowed back into the winner's circle.'

McKelvey was found to have suffered a serious tendon injury and the initial diagnosis was that he would never race again, yet through a combination of patience and meticulous attention to details he was nursed back to fitness.

Bowen spent three nights sleeping in McKelvey's stable to nurse him through the worst moments before the horse embarked on a long programme of rehabilitation, including daily swimming sessions. By the end of that summer Bowen stated he was happy that McKelvey had made a full recovery. Not that he was in any hurry to run him, for McKelvey's campaign revolved solely round the 2008 Grand National.

To add more pressure to his comeback, *The One Show* had identified McKelvey as their Grand National horse to follow and monitored his progress and recovery from injury in the weeks leading up the race, even to the point of putting a night vision 'stable cam' in his box, giving access to the horse 24 hours a day as well as being available on the channel's website. Millions of viewers around the country took McKelvey into their hearts.

He returned to action in March in two three-mile handicap hurdle races, at Doncaster and Newcastle, but was well beaten on both occasions. These were, however, mere pipe openers for the main event and Bowen expressed himself 'absolutely delighted' with his progress.

McKelvey was duly sent off a 28-1 chance for the 2008 Grand National, some of that support no doubt emanating from *The One Show*'s viewers. But although he was still in the race at halfway there was to be no fairytale ending and McKelvey and Tom parted company two fences before Becher's.

It was at Becher's, where Mr Pointment just led from Chelsea Harbour, that Tony McCoy's thirteenth attempt to win the Grand National ended with the fall of Butler's Cabin. Chelsea Harbour took over at the Canal Turn and was still in front approaching the third last but was overtaken there, first by Snowy Morning and then by Bewleys Berry.

As Chelsea Harbour faded out of contention, Bewleys Berry led the field towards the second last, with Snowy Morning, 7-1 joint-favourite Comply Or Die, and last year's third Slim Pickings all in close contention and the grey King Johns Castle hot on their heels.

Bewleys Berry's stamina gave out soon after and between the last two fences it lay between just three. Comply Or Die hit the front with Snowy Morning on his inner and King Johns Castle on the outside. Snowy Morning clouted the last hard, leaving King Johns Castle as the only serious challenger. But Timmy Murphy still had something in reserve on the blinkered Comply Or

Die and, having reached the Elbow with a three-length advantage over King Johns Castle, he stayed on and extended it to four at the line. Snowy Morning plugged on for third, these being well clear of Slim Pickings, Bewleys Berry and the other joint-favourite, Cloudy Lane.

McKelvey, meanwhile, having unseated his jockey at the twentieth fence, jumped the next riderless but then appeared to attempt to clear the running rails adjacent to the inside of the course. He collided with the railings and collapsed. Bowen rushed to his side but McKelvey had fractured his back. He was put down on the advice of on-site vets, who had been on the spot within minutes of his accident. It was a tragic end for the horse whose build-up had been followed by millions.

'He gave me nowhere near the same feel during the race,' says Tom of McKelvey's performance. 'There was no spark at all, not like the previous year.

'He made a bad mistake. He didn't actually fall but he gave himself a terrible bang. Then they say he galloped into a rail but personally I think he did the injury when he made the mistake because he left his backend in the fence and, obviously, halfway up they're solid. I think he injured himself there.'

Having been given such a high profile on *The One Show* in the weeks leading up to the race, the incident inevitably gave rise to heated debate about the safety of the Grand National. On the Monday after the race, the programme opened with a discussion about McKelvey's death. Co-presenter Adrian Chiles revealed that they had received about 500 emails, two-thirds of which were 'extremely sympathetic' and a third were 'rather angry'. The gist of the latter group was, said Chiles: 'What do you expect? You enter a horse in one of the world's most dangerous steeplechases. Horses die there.'

A spokesman for the animal rights group Animal Aid said: 'It's the most gruelling, lethal race in the world. I hope the BBC shows the public that an event it sponsors, and millions of people bet on, leads to the deaths of horses. As an animal lover, it is a very distressing race to watch. I think it should be stopped. The obstacles are intentionally difficult.'

He added that McKelvey had been at particular risk as he could not have possibly recovered sufficiently from the tendon injury he had sustained when finishing second to Silver Birch the year before. This conveniently ignored the fact that the injury which led to McKelvey being destroyed was completely unrelated to the tendon injury incurred twelve months earlier.

It was widely accepted that his death was a tragic accident and came about through no fault of anyone connected to him or the racecourse. The RSPCA said the race had been made safer, with improvements including a reduction in the numbers of runners and modified fences, as well as enforcing stricter entry requirements for both horses and riders.

Perhaps the most balanced article among a plethora of media correspondence was Lydia Hislop's 'Straight Talk' column in *The Times* on 9 April. Referring to the 'rare gulp of oxygen' that horse racing had received from mainstream television with *The One Show* shadowing McKelvey's preparation, she felt it was no wonder that the sport's wider reaction to his death 'was to fear the wrong gas had been administered. But did it wholly backfire?'

She considered it encouraging that the positive emails to *The One Show* had outnumbered the negative by two to one, and noted that the British Horseracing Authority had received just one negative reaction on the subject, that being from Animal Aid, which included a comparison of racing to bear-baiting.

Hislop also noted with alarm that one national Sunday newspaper had been happy to quote the Animal Aid spokesman, repeating his erroneous claim that McKelvey 'could not have possibly recovered' from last year's injury, thus implying it contributed to his death, whereas the two were entirely unconnected.

'These minutiae are important,' she wrote, 'because they let slip an underlying indifference to fact in favour of a predetermined agenda. Such generalisation, error and supposition contrast sharply with *The One Show*'s genuine engagement with and unparalleled access to the professional preparation and care that a racehorse receives.

'McKelvey's legacy may prove a greater understanding of the realities of racing. It would be a substantial epitaph.'

Date: Saturday 5 April 2008 Going: Good Value to Winner: £450,640

Horse	Owner	Trainer	Age / weight	Jockey	SP
1 Comply Or Die	Mr D A Johnson	D E Pipe	9-10-9	T Murphy	7-1jtfav
2 King Johns Castle	Mr J P McManus	A L T Moore	9-10-11	P Carberry	20-1
3 Snowy Morning	Quayside Syndicate	W P Mullins	8-11-1	D J Casey	16-1
4 Slim Pickings	Doubtful Five Syndicate	T J Taaffe	9-11-2	B J Geraghty	10-1

Distances: 4 lengths, 1½ lengths, 16 lengths. Time: 9 min s 16.6 secs. 40 ran

Winner trained at Nicholashayne, Devon.

2009

PAUL MOLONEY
There was a long one there

State Of Play and Paul Moloney parade before the 2009 Grand National.

MON MOME BECAME the first 100-1 winner of the Grand National since Foinavon 42 years earlier when romping home by twelve lengths in the hands of Liam Treadwell, riding in the race for the first time.

But unlike Foinavon's bizarre victory, achieved through him being the only horse to avoid a massive pile-up at the fence that would thereafter carry his name, there was no such fluke about this 100-1 shot, who drew clear on the run-in to beat the previous year's winner, Comply Or Die, followed by My Will and State Of Play.

State Of Play's rider Paul Moloney's first three Grand National rides had all been on 100-1 outsiders. The first was Iris Bleu for Martin Pipe in 2002. It didn't last long, falling at the fifth fence.

In 2004 he rode Terry Ramsden's grey Royal Atalza, who gave him 'a brilliant ride' for a long way but simply didn't get the trip and was pulled up three out.

His third Grand National mount, the Charles Egerton-trained Graphic Approach in 2007, was in rear when falling at Becher's second time round.

Then in 2008 Paul rode David Pipe's Vodka Bleu, a lively 20-1 shot. 'He didn't take to it and chickened out a bit after a couple of fences,' he says. 'He was jamming the brakes on and ballooning his fences, giving them way too much. I was on a hiding to nothing and I pulled up early on the second circuit.'

Four rides, no completions. Not much luck for the jockey who'd established himself in Ireland before journeying to Britain in 2003.

He was born in Tipperary, ten minutes from Ballydoyle but from a farming background. Neighbour Ursula Ryan trained about twenty dual purpose horses and ran a small breeding operation with a few stallions and mares.

'The horses used to pass our house,' remembers Paul. 'I suppose I followed racing from the age of six or seven, and there was only one thing I wanted to be in life and that was a jockey. I'm living the dream!

'When I was small I started doing a lot of hunting and show jumping and hunter trials. Ursula Ryan sent me over to Jim Bolger's in my summer holidays when I was just going on fourteen, and she said "If you still want to be a jockey after three months down there, you really do want to be a jockey!"

'She was right. It was a great experience to go there, and after the three months I knew that was what I wanted to do in life, though my weight meant I was obviously going to be too heavy for the Flat.'

When Ryan stopped training, Paul learned his trade with a couple of local trainers. It was one of them, Danny O'Connell, who provided him with his first point-to-point success, a mare called Murphy's Lady at Quin, County Clare.

He then spent two years with Michael Hourigan, where he enjoyed considerable success and was champion novice point-to-point rider. Hourigan also supplied his first winner under Rules, Vain Princess at Clonmel.

His next move was to Christy Roche at the Curragh. He was based with him for just over five years, during which time he was champion amateur and rode many decent winners.

'My last year in Ireland wasn't a great season for me,' he acknowledges. 'I'd only ridden 22 or 23 winners and I felt I was stuck in a little bit of a rut. A good friend of mine was based in England and he'd been plaguing me for a year or more to come over and give it a go, because there was so much more racing, more opportunities, so I took the bull by the horns and made the move.

'I freelanced, worked hard and tried to get in with a few people. In my first season in England, I rode 28 winners and I was lucky enough to ride for Ian Williams, who supplied half of them.

'I was offered a job up north with Ferdy Murphy after my first season here, but I wasn't absolutely sure about putting all my eggs in one basket as I had quite a few contacts down south, so I decided not to go.

'The following season I got injured and was out for three months of the winter campaign, November, December and January. When I got going again after my injury, I went back doing what I'd been doing, freelancing for various different trainers, including Evan Williams. We had a winner or two and things went on from there.'

Among the recent arrivals at the Williams yard in the summer of 2005 was one called State Of Play, who had been campaigned over hurdles by Paul

Webber the previous season. Paul Moloney schooled him over fences before he ran for his new trainer.

'I'd be telling you lies if I told you then what he was going to achieve, but he was a likeable horse, and I remember thinking "I wouldn't mind getting the chance to ride him".

'I won a novice chase on him first time out at Chepstow. We then went to Plumpton and won again, and we ended the season winning a big handicap at Aintree. We annihilated the field.

'I owe "Ev" a lot and I owe State Of Play a lot. That Aintree win was just what my career needed. Then the following season we went and bagged the Hennessy Gold Cup on only his fifth run over fences.'

State Of Play's 2006 Hennessy triumph, in which he beat Juveigneur by four lengths, was gained on the softest ground he had yet encountered. Winning such a prestigious race played an important part in getting Paul noticed.

'He's a very flexible horse, better with cut,' he says. 'He'd go on good, soft or heavy; he just wouldn't want good to firm ground.

'He's the type of horse that gives you so much when he runs. He was so impressive at Aintree, on the back of not having run for over three months; and then he went to the Hennessy on the back of not having run since Aintree and, again, was so impressive.'

State Of Play did not run again until the 2007 Cheltenham Gold Cup, in which he finished sixth, beaten little over a length for fourth place.

In his first race of the 2007/08 campaign, Wetherby's Charlie Hall Chase, he just failed to peg back all the way leader Ollie Magern, but thereafter his form tailed off. The following season he again reappeared in the Charlie Hall and this time got up in the last 75 yards to beat Ollie Magern by a length.

He returned to Wetherby for its Boxing Day feature, the Rowland Meyrick Chase, but was never travelling well and could only finish fourth. That was his last run before the 2009 Grand National, for which he was set to carry 11st 2lb and was a popular 14-1 chance.

'I can remember being at Aintree that Grand National morning and saying to Ev, "I don't want to be behind one horse going to the first." I wanted to be in the first six or seven jumping the first, but with nobody in front of me, so that I'd got a clear view, because I'd never forgive myself if I got brought down early in the race.

'Ev's instructions were to get a good position, be handy, inner to middle.

'There were a couple of false starts – it was nobody's fault, a lot of lads were getting very anxious, and the starter did a brilliant job – but it didn't do my horse any favours.

'I didn't want to get a bad start. I felt that getting a good start in the race and getting the position I wanted was going to be so important. I was getting a bit worried when we had the second false start. I was fizzing him right up to get out in the first six or seven and get my position where I wanted to be.

'It was a warm enough day and there was a lot of sweating up, and so forth. It was taking its toll on my feller and it didn't do the other horses any good either.

'I got the good start I was hoping for, and for the first circuit of the race I was in cruise control.

'That's one thing I felt about State Of Play; early in the race I was able to restrain him back, because I felt we were just going a common canter. His jumping was like something you'd dream about. He was so good, brilliant on his feet. I was seeing strides ten strides from every fence. I could see exactly where I was going to take off. It was amazing.

'I can remember going to the first on the second circuit and meeting it spot on. I was really confident, it was going so well. I didn't want to be asking him to stand back from fences because you've got to try and reserve as much energy as you can, and down over those first few second time I was thinking "Just pop, son, we don't have to be looking for long ones till later."

'But then, at the one after the ditch, two fences before Becher's, I remember just sitting on him and I was meeting it on a little bit tight of a stride. He might have barely rubbed it in front but he pitched down on his head. Nine out of ten horses would have definitely toppled over. He's knuckled, and then he's knuckled again, and I can remember thinking "Please stay on your feet". On another day he could easily have pitched me over his head, or I could have fallen out the side door.

'He got in a bit deep to the next one, the fence before Becher's. Then one or two, including Silver Birch, fell in front of me at Becher's. State Of Play jumped over Denis O'Regan, who had fallen on Black Apalachi; I might have just barely clipped him. I avoided Silver Birch but I lost five, six lengths.

'The mistakes before Becher's had shuffled me back, so then I had to go to Plan B because I'd lost the position I wanted to be. When we swung around the Canal Turn I was middle-outer, but then I gave him a chance to find his feet and get back into the race, and he flew Valentine's for me.

'Going across the Melling Road I was back where I wanted to be, but the one thing I remembered saying to Ev when we were stood at the Chair that morning, was that if I was turning in with a chance, there was only one way I was going, and that's middle-outer, second last and last, because it puts you spot on with the running rail on the run-in.

'As I turned in, I was exactly where I wanted to be. Despite the two mistakes and nearly getting brought down at Becher's, I was back in it.'

He wasn't the only one. Indeed, nobody could remember so many horses being in with some sort of chance turning for home in the Grand National. There must have been a dozen still in contention, but Paul Moloney wasn't concerned about numbers.

'All the way to the last I was thinking … the thing about State Of Play, in the Charlie Hall, it was winging the last that won me the race. I knew he needed to do it again here.

'I remember, ten strides going to the last fence in the National, I was confident I was going to win the race but we'd got to wing it. There was a long one there, and the horse didn't let me down. I genuinely thought, mid-air and when we landed, we were going to win.

'But then, ten strides after the last, there was just no pick up. I was just one pace from there home. My Will got back in front of me, Comply Or Die's gone past me, and the winner's sprouted wings.

'When we went round the Elbow I was treading water and I wasn't confident I was still going to finish in the first four. Luckily, he kept going, but he was a tired horse.

'He was a little bit distressed in the winner's enclosure afterwards, but so were Comply Or Die and My Will. There were a few leg-weary horses after the race and I think that was probably because of the false starts. For me, the winning and the losing of the race was the start.'

Mon Mome's trainer, Venetia Williams, had ridden in the 1988 National but it had ended with her being knocked unconscious when falling at Becher's. This was much better.

As for the bookmakers, they could not conceal their glee at the 100-1 success of Mon Mome. Not even three well fancied contenders making the frame could spoil their celebrations.

And for the once a year punters it was confirmation of their long-held view that the Grand National really is a lottery and, despite what the experts say, anything can win it.

Postscript: In the 2010 Grand National, Paul Moloney and State Of Play improved on their fourth of a year earlier by finishing third behind Don't Push It and Black Apalachi. Moloney told reporters afterwards: 'It was a serious run from a serious horse who has been very good to me. He might win next year, please God.'

And therein lies the essence, the thread that runs through the tales of those jockeys who have tried to win the world's greatest steeplechase: it's the existence of chance.

Date: Saturday 4 April 2009 Going: Good to soft Value to Winner: £506,970

Horse	Owner	Trainer	Age / weight	Jockey	SP
1 Mon Mome	Mrs Vida Bingham	Miss V Williams	9-11-0	L Treadwell	100-1
2 Comply Or Die	Mr D A Johnson	D E Pipe	10-11-6	T J Murphy	14-1
3 My Will	The Stewart Family	P F Nicholls	9-11-4	R Walsh	8-1
4 State Of Play	Mr & Mrs W Rucker	E Williams	9-11-2	P Moloney	14-1

Distances: 12 lengths, 1¼ lengths, 4½ lengths. Time: 9 mins 32.9 secs. 40 ran

Winner trained at Kings Caple, Herefordshire.

2010

AP McCOY
The existence of chance

The realisation of a dream: AP McCoy passes the post on Don't Push It.

'THE EXISTENCE OF chance is everything and nothing while the greatest achievement is the living of life.'

I first read these words on the cover of an LP called *All of Us*, by Nirvana. Not the infamous American rock band formed by singer/guitarist Kurt Cobain, but an earlier group of the same name whose sole chart success was 'Rainbow Chaser', which reached number 34 in May 1968.

For multiple champion jockey Anthony Peter McCoy, on the verge of attaining his fifteenth successive title, the existence of chance was everything as far as the Grand National was concerned. In fourteen attempts he'd been third three times, while on another three occasions his race had ended at Becher's second time round. But in 2010 AP finally achieved his dream courtesy of a horse named Don't Push It.

The winning owner, Limerick-born JP McManus had had 33 runners in the race prior to 2010. He was once a bookmaker but nowadays has a business portfolio that embraces high finance, international stock exchanges and leisure ventures.

The JP McManus Charitable Foundation Limited, which he formed in 2000, has raised many millions for worthy causes both in Ireland and abroad, while the renowned JP McManus Invitational Pro-Am golf tournament is another huge fund-raiser for Limerick charities.

His distinctive green-and gold-hooped colours, which are those of the South Liberties GAA Club, a Limerick hurling team, are the best-known in jump racing and have been carried by a multitude of top-class performers including triple Champion Hurdle winner Istabraq. His massive string of horses is dispersed among several trainers, most notably with former champion jockey Jonjo O'Neill at the Jackdaws Castle facility which McManus also owns.

Champion in both 1977/78 and 1979/80, the highlight of Jonjo's riding days was undoubtedly his partnership with Dawn Run, the only horse to have won both the Champion Hurdle and the Cheltenham Gold Cup. He also won the Gold Cup on Alverton and guided Sea Pigeon to the first of his two Champion Hurdle victories plus a famous Ebor Handicap triumph on the Flat.

But Jonjo never once completed the Grand National course in seven attempts as a jockey and had saddled 15 unsuccessful runners in the race since turning to training. Clan Royal had finished second and third for the McManus-O'Neill combo and Jonjo had also trained third-placed Simply Gifted in 2005.

AP's first five Grand National rides had all failed to complete before he finished a distant third of four finishers on Blowing Wind in 2001, after his mount had been badly impeded by a loose horse and forced to refuse at the nineteenth fence. It was another riderless horse, Take The Stand, who carried out Clan Royal when leading at Becher's in 2005; and he'd fallen at the same fence on Butler's Cabin when going well in 2008.

'Clan Royal was certainly going very well,' recalls AP, 'and because of the horse he was – even though he'd been very keen – he would have always kept going.

'Taking that into account, Hedgehunter was a very, very good winner and it would be hard to say that any horse would have beaten Hedgehunter on that day.

'Butler's Cabin was going well but, like so many horses do in the Grand National, he knuckled over. There were no hard luck stories with Butler's Cabin. It was his own doing that he didn't win, whereas with Clan Royal, it wasn't his fault.

'Blowing Wind was probably the one that was the most unlucky, I thought. He got carried out by a loose horse, but that's what makes the Grand National the race it is and that's why you need so many things to go right and so much luck to win it.'

It had been a tough call over which of the Jonjo O'Neill-trained pair he would ride in 2010: Can't Buy Time, a 20-1 shot, or Don't Push It, who was available at 50-1.

Don't Push It and Can't Buy Time; virtually opposing philosophies. As the Racing Post's front-page headline asked: 'Can't or Don't?'

With a week left before the race, AP was in no rush to make his choice but observed 'I'd say it's 51-49 that I will ride Can't Buy Time.' However, he eventually opted for Don't Push It, leaving Jonjo's conditional jockey Richie McLernon to ride the other one.

'It was Jonjo's decision ultimately,' says AP. 'It was only really a close decision after Don't Push It ran so bad at Cheltenham [on his previous start, when pulled up in the Pertemps Final over hurdles] when we thought he'd run well. Before that I was always going to ride Don't Push It but he ran so badly that it was hard to believe, so I had to have a rethink, but Jonjo knows his horses better than anyone and he was adamant and he put me on the right one.'

That decision was reflected in the betting market; the day before the race Don't Push It's odds had halved to 25-1 while Can't Buy Time's had drifted out to 33-1.

Still available at 20-1 on the morning of the race, a wholesale public gamble forced Don't Push It's price down to half those odds, meaning that victory for the champion jockey could cost Britain's bookmakers around £10 million.

The field had gone barely a mile when Can't Buy Time crashed out at the Canal Turn first time round. Meanwhile, Don't Push It, reputedly a nervous type who spent much of his time in a field with a couple of sheep for company, had taken a liking to Aintree's unique fences and was travelling well.

'I felt after we had travelled a mile or so that this horse could win the National. He's a very natural jumper and a horse that has always had an unbelievable amount of ability. He really enjoyed himself early on and he was always going to have a chance of winning.'

Having made headway to track the leaders just after halfway, AP brought him through into second place with two to jump, just behind Black Apalachi, the mount of Denis O'Regan.

Until then, Black Apalachi, who had unseated O'Regan when leading at Becher's second time the previous year, had looked to have the measure of his rivals but Don't Push It drew level at the final fence and McCoy drove him clear on the run-in to score by five lengths. State Of Play stayed on to finish third, ahead of joint-favourite Big Fella Thanks and the always prominent Hello Bud, who gave his 17-year-old amateur rider Sam Twiston-Davies a dream first Grand National ride.

'I thought turning for home we would definitely win as long as he stayed,' AP reflected afterwards. 'You are always worried about going too early, but every time I pulled him out and gave him a little bit of light, he picked up. He did run pretty well over three-mile-three in November with a big weight and I had it in the back of my mind that he would stay.'

The memory of the moment immediately after he'd passed the winning post is vivid, albeit still difficult to put into words. 'Lots of emotions – delight, relief... it's very hard to describe, it was a very surreal feeling; the elation of having won the Grand National.

'The first two people to congratulate me were Martin Pipe and Ted Walsh. That meant a lot to me because they're obviously two people that I've a huge respect for, having been lucky to ride for Martin for as long as I did, and I've known Ted Walsh since I was a kid.'

AP admitted immediately after the race to 'being a bit of a wuss' but the level of emotion did not really surprise him. 'It's a race over which emotions run high in everyone. From a public perspective it's the biggest horserace in the world and it's just such a hard race to win. You can never enjoy it too much. If you don't get that elation, that feeling of emotion from winning the Grand National, you're probably not doing the right job.'

It meant far more to him than any other of his 3,000-plus winners; more than being voted BBC Sports Personality of the Year for 2010. It has also given him greater public recognition outside the sport – though that, he insists, is something for others to judge.

'That's not for me to say. I do what I do because I love doing it, and whatever anyone thinks of me is up to them. I just try and do everything to the best of my ability.

'It's important to me that I've finally won it. It means that I've more or less achieved everything I wanted to achieve in racing. If I hadn't won the Grand National I wouldn't be able to say that, but having won it I can't think there's many other things that I would like to have done that I haven't done in racing.'

Both JP McManus and Jonjo O'Neill had at one time beaten cancer, a far tougher battle than any ever fought over the fields and fences of Aintree. For them, to put matters in perspective, the greatest achievement is indeed the living of life.

And whereas this book has been about those people and horses that didn't – or haven't so far – won the Grand National, for some there is still that thing called chance.

Just ask AP McCoy. The existence of chance is everything.

Date: Saturday 10 April 201- Going: Good Value to Winner: £521,052.50

Horse	Owner	Trainer	Age / weight	Jockey	SP
1 Don't Push It	Mr John P McManus	Jonjo O'Neill	10-11-5	A P McCoy	10-1jtfav
2 Black Apalachi	Mr G Burke	D T Hughes	11-11-6	D O'Regan	14-1
3 State Of Play	Mr & Mrs William Rucker	E Williams	10-10-11	P Moloney	16-1
4 Big Fella Thanks	Mrs M Findlay & P K Barber	P F Nicholls	8-10-12	B Geraghty	10-1jtfav

Distances: 5 lengths, 20 lengths, 3 lengths. Time: 9 mins 4.50 secs. 40 ran

Winner trained at Cheltenham, Gloucestershire.

BIBLIOGRAPHY

Bird, Alex and Terry Manners: *The Life and Secrets of a Professional Punter* (1985)

Blacker, Philip: *The Making of Red Rum* (1988)

Buckingham, John: *Tales from the Weighing Room* (1987)

Buglass, Dan: *Ken Oliver – The Benign Bishop* (1994)

Champion, Bob and Jonathan Powell: *Champion's Story* (1981)

Davies, Paul: *The Aintree Festival 1976-98* (1998)

Davies, Paul: *The Grand National 1839-1998* (1999)

Fitzgeorge-Parker, Tim: *Steeplechase Jockeys – The Great Ones* (1971)

Francis, Dick: *The Sport of Queens* (1974)

Francome, John: *Born Lucky* (1985)

Graham, Clive and Bill Curling: *The Grand National* (1972)

Green, Reg: *A Race Apart – The History of the Grand National* (1988)

Hammond, Chas: *Jump Jockeys 1830-1950* (2003)

Herbert, Ivor: *The Queen Mother's Horses* (1967)

Hide, Edward and Mike Cattermole: *Nothing to Hide* (1989)

Mackenzie, Iain and Terry Selby: *Hunter Chasers and Point-to-Pointers* (various years)

Masefield, John: *Right Royal* (1920)

Mortimer, Roger, Richard Onslow and Peter Willett: *Biographical Encyclopaedia of British Flat Racing* (1978)

Oaksey, John: *Oaksey on Racing* (1991)

Payne, Nigel and Dominic Hart: *Everyone Must Leave – The Day They Stopped the National* (1998)

Pearn, Tony: *The Secrets of Successful Steeplechasing* (1972)

Pinfold, John: *Gallant Sport. The Authentic History of Liverpool Races and the Grand National* (1999)

Pinfold, John: *An Aintree Dynasty* (2006)

Pinfold, John and Kamila Pecherová: *The Velká Pardubická and the Grand National* (2010)

Rimell, Mercy: *Reflections on Racing* (1990)

Smith, Vian: *A Horse Called Freddie* (1967)

Tanner, Michael: *My Friend Spanish Steps* (1982)

Tanner, Michael: *The King George VI Steeplechase* (1984)

Welcome, John: *The Cheltenham Gold Cup* (1973)

NEWSPAPERS AND PERIODICALS (VARIOUS YEARS)
Horse and Hound
Horseman's Year

Irish Horse
Raceform/Chaseform Form Book
Racing Post
Racing Review
Sporting Chronicle
Sporting Life
Stud and Stable

PHOTOGRAPHY

Many of the photographs contained in this book are from the subjects' own collections or from the *Racing Post*. While every effort has been made to trace the other copyright holders, this has not been possible in every case. The publishers will be pleased to rectify any omissions in future printings.

The author and publisher are grateful to the following for providing illustrations and permission to reproduce their copyright photographs:

A.C. Cooper: Coolishall (1980)
Bespix: Charles Dickens (1957)
Ed Byrne: Corbiere (1983)
Gerry and Mark Cranham: Royal Mail (1981), Pond House (1998) and Blue
    Charm (1999)
Bernard Parkin: Spanish Steps (1975), Sure Metal and Howe Street (1993)
Mary Pitt: Kenny Johnson (1990), Billy Worthington (1992) and Ollie
    McPhail (2003)
Provincial Press: Roy Edwards (1970)
George Selwyn: Ormonde Tudor (1976)
Turf Pictures: Jeff King (1969) and Ken White (1974)
Universal Press Agency: Buck Jones (1972)
Václav Volf: Its A Snip (1987)
Matthew Webb: Ballycassidy (2006)

INDEX